LOYALTY PROGRAMS

PROGRAMS

THE COMPLETE GUIDE

Visit Loyalty & Reward Co

LOYALTY PROGRAMS

THE COMPLETE GUIDE

PHILIP SHELPER

CO-CREATED BY
STACEY LYONS, SCOTT HARRISON, RYAN DE BOER, MAX SAVRANSKY

WITH CONTRIBUTIONS BY
LINCOLN HUNTER, MICHAEL SMITH

FOREWORD BY
THOMAS F. O'TOOLE

TABLE OF CONTENTS

PRAISE FROM GLOBAL EXPERTS

"Loyalty Programs: The Complete Guide is an extremely valuable resource for loyalty and marketing professionals. In fact, I found it so helpful that Eagle Eye now buys a copy for every new member of our sales team to give them a comprehensive understanding of the global loyalty landscape. I particularly enjoy the case studies which really bring the concepts to life. Highly recommended."

TIM MASON, CEO OF EAGLE EYE AND FORMER
TESCO CMO AND FOUNDER OF CLUBCARD

"An outstanding guide, not only to the mechanics and economics of loyalty programs, but to the behavioural thinking behind loyalty strategy. Having been involved in the loyalty industry for many years, I found it a fascinating source of historical context, a great overview of the industry today, and a practical roadmap to the key drivers of customer value across a range of loyalty program types. A must-have for anyone in the industry."

NEIL THOMPSON, FORMER CEO, VELOCITY FREQUENT FLYER

"Loyalty Programs: The Complete Guide is one of the most thorough resources for loyalty and loyalty programs. It's practical, pragmatic and comprehensively covers all aspects of loyalty from history to psychology through to program design and operating models including commercials. There is something for every loyalty professional in this book – from emerging loyalty marketers through to senior stakeholders and decision makers. We work with Phil regularly – we value his knowledge and expertise. This book is a well-used resource in our organization."

LIZZY RYLEY, CEO, LOYALTY NZ

"The content within Loyalty Programs: The Complete Guide is so rich that even as a seasoned loyalty program operator, I was able to find a ton of valuable insights to apply directly to my own loyalty program. My only wish is that I had a resource like this when I first began my journey! In the loyalty space, we are constantly learning – and this book is one of the best resources I've found!"

ANNE SCHULTHEIS,
DIRECTOR OF LOYALTY AT DUTCH BROS COFFEE

"An industry first, yet much needed resource. Loyalty strategies are complex and can be a daunting endeavor. This comprehensive guide is a must read for all loyalty marketers and any company selling to loyalty marketers. In fact, we give a copy of the guide to all of our employees. It is required reading."

ERIN RAESE,
SVP - REVENUE, ANNEX CLOUD

"Comprehensive and empowering! This book brings together the knowledge of a renowned team, led by Phil Shelper, to provide a complete guide on loyalty programs. After reading this book, you'll feel like you've earned a master's degree in loyalty programs. Whenever someone asks me for a recommendation to learn about loyalty programs, I always point them to Loyalty Programs: The Complete Guide."

ZSUZSA KECSMAR - CHIEF STRATEGY OFFICER,
CO-FOUNDER AT ANTAVO LOYALTY CLOUD

"I've purchased over a dozen copies of the first edition for employees or clients as this book is the most comprehensive and easy to read compendium on the topic of loyalty ever written. Loyalty programs can create magical results for companies, but they require expert design to be effective. Loyalty Programs: The Complete Guide *covers all the science and operational best practice needed by loyalty marketing professionals to ensure the solutions they implement will maximize ROI."*

CHARLES EHREDT,
CEO AND CO-FOUNDER, CURRENCY ALLIANCE

"This is a true gem! Philip Shelper and experts from Loyalty & Reward Co created the perfect guide that is sure helps you understand the essentials of building and managing loyalty programs. Highly recommended to every marketer who wants to enter and excel in the loyalty space!"

KARL BZIK,
CO-FOUNDER AT OPEN LOYALTY

"This book is the perfect resource for those new to the industry or creating a loyalty program from scratch and ensure all bases are covered. It's also a great refresher and source of inspiration on how to take your loyalty program to the next level."

MIRANDA BLISS,
HEAD OF LOYALTY AND RETENTION, ADORE BEAUTY

"Shelper's book is the first resource we point our customers to when they're considering an investment in customer loyalty – and it's required reading for anyone joining Talon.One. From loyalty design frameworks to monetisation and commercial modelling, the book is a must-have desk reference for those working in or thinking about loyalty programs."

CHRISTOPH GERBER,
CO-FOUNDER AND CEO AT TALON.ONE

"Loyalty done right can be a transformative solution for a business. This guide has been my personal reference point for inspiration and is an essential contribution to the practice of customer-centric marketing."

DAVID SLAVICK,
CO-FOUNDER AND PARTNER, ASCENDANT LOYALTY MARKETING

"This is an insightful and comprehensive guide to understanding the world of customer loyalty programs. The book provides a detailed overview of the history of loyalty programs, their evolution, and their role in modern marketing. What I appreciate most is the practical approach to the topic. Real-world examples and best practices of successful loyalty programs are shared. Philip and his team have created an excellent resource for businesses looking to create or improve their loyalty programs, making it a valuable tool for any marketer or business owner looking to boost customer loyalty and engagement."

EMILY ONG CLMP′™, HEAD OF LOYALTY, RAZER

First published in 2020 by Loyalty & Reward Co Pty Ltd

© Loyalty & Reward Co Pty Ltd, 2020

Second edition published 2023

The moral rights of the author have been asserted.

National Library of Australia Cataloguing in-Publication entry:

Creator: Shelper, Philip, author.

Co-creators: Lyons, Stacey; Savransky, Max; Harrison, Scott; De Boer, Ryan

Contributors: Hunter, Lincoln; Smith, Michael

Title: Loyalty Programs: The Complete Guide (2nd edition)/Philip Shelper.

ISBN: 978-0-6452115-4-2 (hardback)

ISBN: 978-0-6452115-3-5 (paperback)

ISBN: 978-0-6452115-5-9 (ebook)

Subjects: loyalty programs, member engagement, lifecycle management, reward programs

Cover design by Scott Harrison.

Editorial services by Stacey Lyons.

Diagrams by Scott Harrison.

Photography by Kate Ireland.

Disclaimer

For the Shelpers and the Irelands.

HOW TO USE THIS BOOK

Business books are not always designed to read from cover to cover. While I would encourage anyone obsessed by loyalty programs to read every word in this book, it can also be used to deep dive into specific topics for research purposes.

I received lots of feedback on the 1st Edition from loyalty professionals who said they have a copy on their desk and refer to it every day to support their strategy development and build their knowledge in specific areas. The team at Loyalty & Reward Co and I do this ourselves.

The book is divided into two parts:

- Part One covers loyalty program theory

- Part Two covers loyalty program execution

The chapters in each section are clearly defined to enable you as a reader to quickly find what you are looking for and jump right in.

The additional reading listed at the end of each chapter is always recommended. When researching, it is a good idea to go directly to the source. I especially recommend this for loyalty psychology and academic research.

If you get really stuck and cannot find what you need, reach out to us at Loyalty & Reward Co. We design, implement and operate the world's best loyalty programs for a living. We would love to help however we can.

FOREWORD

Thomas F. O'Toole

Associate Dean of Executive Programs and Clinical Professor of Marketing

Kellogg School of Management

Northwestern University

In 2017, I developed an MBA course for the Kellogg School of Management at Northwestern University titled "Customer Loyalty" about a strategic approach to customer loyalty, customer value growth and, particularly, the design and use of loyalty programs. While doing so, I searched for a good book to use as a text on the subject. From the outset of the course, and through the next several years, I alternated between books written by practitioners and others written by academics, and didn't find either satisfying. The books by practitioners typically didn't have the depth of content, conceptual frameworks and methodologies required for a sound explanation of the subject. The books by academics, while providing strong intellectual rigor, comprehensive models and detailed methodologies, typically caused me, a former practitioner, to ask, "Has this person ever actually done this in the real world?" After a few years, I gave up my search for a comprehensive text, and shifted to assembling and updating a collection of articles, papers, excerpts and other references to use for the course annually.

Then, as I prepared to teach the course again in 2021-2022, I tried again to find a good text, browsing on Google and Amazon to see if there were any new books out that could be worthwhile. I came across Loyalty Programs: The Complete Guide (1st edition) by Philip Shelper and his colleagues and was interested enough to purchase it. When it arrived and I read it, I immediately could tell that it had been written by experienced practitioners who had actually designed, developed and executed loyalty programs for a broad range of businesses. The authors not only had a deep understanding of loyalty programs but provided an expository discussion of definitions, objectives, metrics, approaches, extensions and considerations. In short, my reaction was, "The people who wrote this book clearly have done this, thought about it and know what they're talking about." And, with that, I'd finally found a book on loyalty programs for my course.

It's a small world and, as it turned out, a student in my class that quarter knew Philip Shelper back in Australia. He told Philip that I was using his book for my course at Kellogg. (Thanks, Keith.) Thus, I unexpectedly was contacted by Philip and got to know him and Loyalty & Reward Co, and have enjoyed talking with him about their loyalty program consulting for clients in a range of industries around the world.

Now, reading this second edition of the book, a phrase jumped out at me. It described loyalty programs as "the 21st century's most important field of marketing". Loyalty programs are certainly a mainstay of marketing that's growing in importance, but the "most important field of marketing" struck me as a bit of an overstatement. Then, I thought about it further, and realized that the statement crystallized an observation that has been emerging for me in the last couple years. Loyalty programs have evolved beyond conventional "earn and redeem" mechanisms into a central element and enabler of today's business models, data use and marketing practices. In other words, loyalty programs have become marketing systems for differentiated customer value growth at the individual customer level.

As a growing range of businesses shift to a customer centric business strategy, development of a loyalty program typically follows logically, to enable and accomplish customer differentiation, targeted customer investments and customer lifetime value growth. A customer centric business approach, to differentiate customers and grow CLV, leads a growing range of businesses to personalization. Loyalty programs are typically the enabler that connects a customer centric business approach to and, most importantly, provides essential data for personalization.

The use of predictive analytics is imperative for the practice of marketing today. Loyalty programs are a foundational source of customer data used to inform predictive analytics.

So, perhaps loyalty programs really are "the 21st century's most important field of marketing". Thinking about emergent developments in business models around the world today bears out this observation further.

Business today is omnichannel. Loyalty programs are a key element of creating a personalized omnichannel customer experience that grows customer value.

Retailers are going through unprecedented disruption and innovation in their business models, customer experience and methods of customer engagement. Loyalty programs are playing a central role in revitalizing retail businesses and advancing the future growth of retail and retailers' customer relationships.

Payment systems are at the forefront of business advances around the world today. Payment systems and loyalty programs have been tightly integrated for many years and are becoming more so. Read about current developments in payment systems and inevitably, before long, one comes to the key role of loyalty programs.

Business ecosystems are developing rapidly today in payment systems and a growing range of other categories around the world. Loyalty programs, and their extension into partnerships, alliances and coalitions, were the progenitors of business ecosystems and are central to many emerging customer ecosystems.

The use of AI, including now, generative AI, is the leading edge of marketing today. The applications of AI to loyalty programs offer a myriad of opportunities that are just starting to be realized.

And, the adoption of loyalty programs and the marketing practices that they enable is no longer confined primarily to conventionally well-established categories of retail, travel, financial services and other familiar businesses. There is robust interest among progressive organizations in emerging fields, such as health care and energy, in utilizing loyalty programs and the customer differentiation and value growth that they enable.

All of this, and more, explains why enterprises in a growing range of businesses around the world are now focused intently on, and investing in, launching or relaunching their loyalty programs to grow the value of their customers.

This second edition of Loyalty Programs: The Complete Guide provides a broad and unmatched introduction to, and explanation of, foundations and practicalities of loyalty programs as core structures and systems for businesses today.

Thomas F. O'Toole

PREFACE

This 2nd Edition of *Loyalty Programs: The Complete Guide* provides updated case studies, additional chapters, and deeper insight into the 21st century's most important field of marketing.

I was inspired to write the 1st Edition after receiving multiple enquiries from young loyalty professionals seeking a book that would tell them everything they needed to know about the loyalty industry. Realising such a book did not exist, I was determined to fill the gap as a way to both give back to the industry and influence companies worldwide to improve the quality of their loyalty programs.

The Loyalty & Reward Co team and I wrote the 1st Edition during the first Covid-19 pandemic lockdown starting March 2020 when the world stopped for a few months and we were banned from leaving our houses. Without the pandemic, *Loyalty Programs: The Complete Guide* may never have been born.

The pandemic lockdown and subsequent economic shocks proved the enormous value loyalty programs provide to companies and consumers alike. A number of major airlines survived the extended lockdown periods by either selling large amounts of points or miles to partners or using their deferred liability to secure desperately needed loans. Companies that had well-established loyalty programs (with an engaged member base, good communications processes, and stored value in member accounts) were better able to navigate the economic turmoil caused by forced retail store closures. With a forced boost in online shopping, consumers became accustomed to the benefits of personalised digital experiences, something which loyalty programs have specialised in for many years. Post-pandemic, members are joining or rejoining supermarket and other retail programs in record numbers to access the value on offer as a means to reduce their cost-of-living expenses.

The book has been useful in many ways; connecting with industry professionals, gaining new clients, as a textbook for our loyalty professionals education course, and for educating our own staff.

The 2nd Edition includes a great deal of additional content. One major change is a complete rewrite of Chapter 4, which now covers Loyalty & Reward Co's Essential Eight™ (the eight essential principles of best-practice loyalty programs). Previously this content was retained exclusively for Loyalty & Reward Co clients, however in the interests of providing additional insight and support for the loyalty industry, I have chosen to share it. Another major change is a complete rewrite of the commercial modelling chapter (Chapter 16: Commercial Benefits and Considerations).

I hope this 2nd Edition provides useful insights to loyalty program designers and operators globally. If it supports the task of improving loyalty programs and driving deeper member engagement, while helping younger loyalty professionals to further their careers, I will feel a profound sense of satisfaction.

My extreme thanks go to the people who helped to construct this book:

- Co-authors Stacey Lyons, Scott Harrison, Ryan De Boer and Max Savransky of Loyalty & Reward Co for their incredible passion.

- Contributors Lincoln Hunter and Michael Smith for their amazing generosity.

- The rest of the Loyalty & Reward Co team (truly the finest group of loyalty program designers and operators on the planet) who spent countless hours researching and updating the many case studies in the book; Georgette Mikhael, Amy Gavagnin, David Schneider, Kate Pay, Federico Rosas Couret, Riley Geraghty, Eli Maynard, Susan Walsh, Hunter Murray, Vinnie Ward and Cameron Barr.

- My wife Kate and my kids Erik and Curtis who give me way more time than I deserve to chase my obsession for everything loyalty.

I would also like to thank Keith Tan for introducing me to Thomas O'Toole.

As always, I love to receive positive and constructive feedback to support continual improvement of this book, so please reach out via LinkedIn with your ideas that you feel should be considered for the 3rd Edition.

Philip Shelper

ABOUT THE AUTHORS

Philip Shelper

Phil is CEO and Founder at leading loyalty consultancy, Loyalty & Reward Co. He has extensive experience within the loyalty industry as a designer, speaker, educator and researcher. In addition to designing loyalty programs for over 100 brands globally, he previously held loyalty roles at Qantas Frequent Flyer and Vodafone.

Phil is a member of several hundred loyalty programs, and an obsessive researcher of loyalty psychology and loyalty history, all of which he uses to understand the essential dynamics of what makes a successful loyalty program.

Connect with Phil: www.linkedin.com/in/philipshelper

Stacey Lyons

Stacey is Loyalty Director at Loyalty & Reward Co. Stacey has extensive experience in loyalty, digital marketing and eCommerce with roles at ModelCo, MyHouse and Boost Juice.

For the past five years, Stacey has worked with over forty Loyalty & Reward Co clients to design and implement loyalty programs, apply loyalty psychology and develop strategies which support client loyalty programs including member lifecycle management, data capture, reporting and analytics and social media strategies.

Connect with Stacey: www.linkedin.com/in/staceylyons

Scott Harrison

Scott is a Senior Strategy Consultant at Loyalty & Reward Co. Scott is a customer experience and digital marketing specialist, with extensive experience across financial services, hospitality, retail and technology.

For over three years, Scott has worked with over twenty-five Loyalty & Reward Co clients to design and implement loyalty programs with a strong user-centric and data-driven approach, specialising in loyalty program design and strategy, complex lifecycle marketing journeys and customer experience design.

Connect with Scott: www.linkedin.com/in/scott-c-harrison

Ryan De Boer

Ryan is CFO at Loyalty & Reward Co. As CFO, Ryan leads the commercial and financial modelling aspects of client engagements as well as overseeing Loyalty & Reward Co's broader financial objectives and governance practices.

Ryan brings a wealth of loyalty expertise to all client engagements, drawing on over 15 years' experience in the loyalty industry working with some of the largest programs across Australia and New Zealand including Qantas Frequent Flyer, Woolworths, MYER, NAB and Air New Zealand.

Connect with Ryan: https://www.linkedin.com/in/ryan-deboer

Max Savransky

Max is the ex-COO at Loyalty & Reward Co.

During his time at Loyalty & Reward Co, Max consulted on over forty projects for major brands including McDonald's, Schneider Electric, CBA, Australian Venue Co, Loyalty NZ (Flybuys), Origin Energy and NRMA.

Max lead the implementation and operations business functions, specialising in all aspects of loyalty program design, the usage of data within loyalty programs, loyalty technology, project delivery and ongoing operational program management.

Connect with Max: www.linkedin.com/in/maxsavransky

ABOUT THE CONTRIBUTORS

Lincoln Hunter

Lincoln is widely recognised in Australia as a leading provider of legal services in the loyalty space and specialises in helping clients get the best out of their customers (in a compliant way) and contracting with or for large coalition loyalty programs.

Lincoln has been practising law since 1994 and advising in the loyalty, data and digital space since 2004. He is also the Founder and Principal of Loyalty Legal, where he has been practicing since 2013, and very much enjoys the legal issues and the business issues that come with operating a modern day loyalty program.

linkedin.com/in/lincoln-hunter-loyalty-legal

Michael Smith

For the last decade, Michael has been working with loyalty programs to help them manage and prevent fraud.

Prior to co-founding the Loyalty Security Association (LSA), Michael worked for the British Airways Frequent Flyer Program.

In addition to the LSA, Michael is a Board Advisor for Ai Events | Airline Information which operates the leading airline/travel loyalty, co-brand and payments and fraud events.

https://www.linkedin.com/in/Chief-Guide-AND-Connector

ABOUT LOYALTY & REWARD CO

Loyalty & Reward Co is a leading loyalty consulting firm that designs the world's best loyalty programs for the world's best brands.

Over the past decade our dedicated team of loyalty experts have delivered real success stories for over 100 companies globally, across every major industry.

Our data-driven and customer-focused loyalty programs generate incremental acquisition, spend, retention and advocacy, adding meaningful value to clients and their members.

Our obsession for loyalty is what defines us. At Loyalty & Reward Co, we constantly engage with and study loyalty programs, loyalty psychology, technology and industry trends. We continually challenge ourselves to deliver and demonstrate value in everything we do.

We help our clients succeed by providing end-to-end services and expert insights across six key areas:

    ✓   Design: We design the world's best loyalty programs

    ✓   Implement: We implement the final program design

    ✓   Operate: We operate and optimise loyalty programs for success

    ✓   Audit: We audit and improve existing loyalty programs

✓ Innovate: We are loyalty innovators, ahead of new trends

✓ Educate: We educate the world's loyalty professionals

For more information or to engage our services, visit www.loyaltyrewardco.com

Connect with Loyalty & Reward Co:

Website: www.loyaltyrewardco.com

Email: hello@loyaltyrewardco.com

LinkedIn: www.linkedin.com/company/loyalty-&-reward-co

INDUSTRY AND SHORTENED TERMS

Term	Description
Affiliate revenue	A marketing revenue model by which commission is earned when a company promotes another company's e-commerce offering, leading to a trackable transaction.
Attitudinal commitment	Repeat purchase behaviour driven by an emotional connection.
Behavioural commitment	Repeated purchase behaviour driven by habitual consumption.
Billings	Coalition loyalty programs generate billings when a partner company pays for a member to earn points.
Bitcoin	A type of digital currency designed to act as a form of payment outside the control of any one person, group or entity.
Bot	A software application that runs automated tasks over the internet.
Breakage	Currency (e.g., points) issued which expires due to different rules. This may be because the member has not engaged in account activity, or because the currency has not been redeemed within a specified time period.

Churn	Customers that have ceased using a company's products or services.
Coalition	Where a loyalty program operator develops partnerships with third-party companies (a 'coalition' of partners) to participate in the program by promoting loyalty currency earn to their customers.
Cookie	Text files with small pieces of data used to identify an individual computer and keep track of browsing visits and activity.
Customer centric	A business approach which places the customer as the central focus of all company operations.
Data brokers	Data brokers collect extensive personal data about billions of individuals from all around the world, which they may package up and sell to loyalty programs to help build out and standardise their member profiles.
Deferred liability account	An account which holds the deferred revenue to cover the cost of points that have been issued but not yet redeemed.
Digital EQ	The ability to anticipate and recognise customer sentiment and deliver a digitally enabled response which optimises the customer experience in real time, serving to build a deeper emotional connection.
Efficient rewards	Rewards which are inexpensive for a company to provide compared to the perceived value by the member.
First-party data	Data which is collected via customer interactions which the company owns.
Halo effect	Occurs when positive first impressions positively influence future judgments or ratings of unrelated factors.

Mere-exposure effect	Where people tend to develop a preference for things they are familiar with.
Metaverse	An emerging 3D enabled digital space that uses virtual reality, augmented reality, and other advanced technologies that allow users to have lifelike experiences online.
Mileage run/ status run	Where a loyalty program member engaged in additional transaction activity (i.e., unplanned flights) with the sole purpose of earning status credits.
Pareto Principle	An observation which asserts that 80 per cent of outcomes result from 20 per cent of all causes (e.g., 80 per cent of company revenue is generated by 20 per cent of members).
Scarcity	The state of being in short supply.
Share of wallet	The percentage of total dollar spend a customer regularly devotes to a particular brand.
Smart contracts	Programs stored on a blockchain that run when predetermined conditions are met.
Staking	Where users lock a specific amount and type of cryptocurrency in a wallet to support the operations of blockchain network or platform, in return for rewards.
Zero-party data	Data that is owned by the consumer that they intentionally and proactively share with a brand that they trust.
2FA	Two factor authentication
AI	Artificial intelligence
API	Application programming interface
B2B	Business-to-business
B2C	Business-to-consumer
BOPIS	Buy online, pick up in-store

CDP	Customer data platform
CRM	Customer relationship management
CX	Customer experience
DAO	Decentralised autonomous organisation
DLT	Distributed ledger technology
DM	Direct message
EBITDA	Earnings before interest, taxes, depreciation and amortisation
EBITDAR	Earnings before interest, taxes, depreciation and amortisation, and rent/restructuring
eDM	Electronic direct mail
FOMO	Fear of missing out
GAAP	Generally accepted accounting principles
GDP	Gross domestic product
GDPR	General data protection regulation
IFRS13	Defines fair value, sets out a framework for measuring fair value, and requires disclosures about fair value measurements
IP address	Internet protocol address
KYC	Know your customer
MLM	Member lifecycle management
NBA	Next best action
NFT	Non-fungible token
OCR	Optical character recognition
P&L	Profit and loss
PII	Personally Identifiable Information
PIN	Personal identification number
POS	Point of sale
QR code	Quick response code
QSR	Quick service restaurant
RFID	Radio frequency identification

ROI	Return on investment
RFM	Recency frequency monetary value
SDK	Software development kit
SKU	Stock keeping unit
SME's	Small-to-medium enterprises
SMS	Short message service
UX	User experience

LOYALTY PROGRAMS

'77 per cent of brands could simply disappear and no-one would care'

- Havas Media Group[1]

IT IS BECOMING increasingly important for brands to build a meaningful emotional bond with customers to generate genuine customer loyalty. Generating sustained, meaningful engagement with members requires a deep understanding of consumer behaviour and expectations to effectively respond to their needs at each stage of their journey.

Loyalty programs are structured programs which reward and recognise registered members for repeat transactions. A well-designed loyalty program can work to successfully drive engagement between a brand and members, building deeper emotional connections which manifest in increased acquisition, spend, retention and advocacy.

With the death of cookies, the rise of walled garden data strategies and tightening privacy regulations, loyalty programs have become *the* most important marketing discipline on the planet. The companies that will win over the next decade will use their best-practice loyalty programs to capture member data, interrogate it to generate critical insights, develop reporting that key stakeholders across the business can access to influence strategic decisions-making,

---

1   Havas Group, 2019, 'Meaningful Brands', https://www.meaningful-brands.com/en, accessed 3 July 2020.

and build sophisticated omnichannel personalisation strategies to deliver relevant communications, offers and experiences at each touchpoint.

The overarching goal of this book is to provide the definitive guide for loyalty program theory and practice. Real world case studies from existing loyalty programs globally are used to illustrate the concepts detailed throughout.

Each chapter answers important questions which loyalty professionals can draw on to strategically design, execute, operate and optimise best-practice loyalty programs.

Loyalty Programs: The Complete Guide has been organised into two parts and 20 chapters which cover all facets of loyalty programs:

Part 1: Loyalty theory and fundamentals

- **Chapter 1:** defines what a loyalty program is, and is not, the many benefits and challenges of loyalty programs for consumers, loyalty program operators and merchant partners, as well as consumer expectations from a loyalty program.

- **Chapter 2:** provides a historical review of loyalty programs, detailing the evolution of loyalty program designs, currencies and rewards over time.

- **Chapter 3:** reviews a large body of academic research which both proves and disproves the claim that loyalty programs work to effectively generate genuine customer loyalty.

- **Chapter 4:** outlines Loyalty & Reward Co's Essential Eight principles for best practice loyalty program design and execution which will boost a program's chances of success.

- **Chapter 5:** reviews the extensive body of consumer psychology research which can be directly applied to loyalty program design in an effort to drive desired behavioural changes among consumers.

- **Chapter 6:** defines the loyalty-specific biases and heuristics which influence consumer decision making processes and how loyalty programs can be designed to appeal to them.

- **Chapter 7:** outlines the critical importance of desirable rewards in the overall success of a loyalty program, and the types of rewards or reward aggregators available. The types of rewards which are best suited to influencing specific behaviours in different circumstances are also detailed.

- **Chapter 8:** presents a range of loyalty program and member engagement conceptual design frameworks. Each framework, and variations of each model are detailed, together with the associated benefits and challenges. Combining multiple frameworks into a hybrid design is also discussed.

- **Chapter 9:** defines gamification and games, and outlines the way each can be used within loyalty programs to motivate specific behaviours and drive deeper member engagement.

- **Chapter 10:** details how Business-to-Business (B2B) loyalty programs can deliver significant results to companies. The characteristics of a B2B loyalty program are defined, with the differences between B2B and B2C programs distinguished.

Part 2: Loyalty program enablement

- **Chapter 11:** covers the role technology plays in the execution of a loyalty program, capabilities of a best-practice loyalty platform, emerging trends and technological innovation in the loyalty industry.

- **Chapter 12:** defines blockchain and Web3 and explores the ways loyalty programs can adopt this technology to create novel and impactful member experiences.

- **Chapter 13:** discusses the value of member data and provides insights into how loyalty programs collect and store member data, as well as consumer awareness about the data being collected and traded.

- **Chapter 14:** details how companies should treat data collected by their loyalty program and the many ways data analysts can structure and interrogate loyalty program data.

- **Chapter 15:** details the approach to member communications across each different stage of the member lifecycle and how data can be used to drive personalisation across member communications, offers and experiences.

- **Chapter 16:** outlines the commercial benefits and considerations associated with designing and implementing a loyalty program including the ways loyalty programs can create value, the costs involved and building a business case.

- **Chapter 17:** details a general introduction to legal considerations for loyalty programs globally. With different jurisdictions regulating the loyalty industry in various ways, local legal guidance is critical to ensure appropriate compliance.

- **Chapter 18:** presents loyalty-specific security and fraud risks which can affect loyalty programs, with details on how risks should best be mitigated and/or remediated.

- **Chapter 19:** determines the teams, roles and responsibilities involved in operating a loyalty program including all business functions impacted by a loyalty program. Options for insourcing or outsourcing are outlined, with the benefits and challenges associated with outsourcing some, or all, of the loyalty program operations.

- **Conclusion:** considers what the future of loyalty may hold for consumers, loyalty program operators and loyalty solution providers.

PART 1
LOYALTY THEORY & FUNDAMENTALS

Part 1 covers loyalty theory and fundamentals. It provides the essential foundational knowledge required to understand how loyalty programs work and how they can be strategically designed to incentivise and reinforce desirable member behaviours.

Part 1 answers the *why* behind a company choosing to implement a loyalty program

CHAPTER 1

LOYALTY PROGRAM BENEFITS AND CHALLENGES

'You don't earn loyalty in a day. You earn loyalty day-by-day.'

- Jeffrey Gitomer

Focus areas

This chapter will address the following questions:

- What is a loyalty program?
- What is the ambition of a company in operating a loyalty program?
- What are the benefits and challenges of loyalty programs for consumers, program operators and third-party partners?
- How are consumer expectations of loyalty programs changing?

LOYALTY PROGRAMS ARE extremely prevalent globally. They are available to consumers across almost every industry, with new programs being launched, or existing programs being relaunched, on a regular basis. Loyalty programs are also increasingly provided to companies as part of business-to-business (B2B) loyalty strategies.

According to research, more than 90 per cent of companies have some sort of loyalty program[2] with 81% of consumers reporting they are loyal to one or more brands[3]. On average, each American is active in 16.7 loyalty programs,[4] Canadians belong to an average 13.4 programs[5], Australians an average of 4.3 programs[6] and South-East Asians an average of 3.5 programs.[7] One article reports Austrians are members of an astonishing average of 14 programs.[8]

To begin the journey into understanding loyalty programs, it is important to define what a loyalty program is. Here are some simple definitions:

- **Loyalty program:** A structured program which rewards and recognises registered members for repeat transactions.

- **Membership program:** A structured program which provides registered members with access to benefits not available to non-members.

- **Customer engagement program:** A strategic campaign structure which attempts to stimulate consumers to engage more with a brand or company without the customer needing to register to access benefits.

While these are adequate, Loyalty & Reward Co's preferred definition for a loyalty program is a *desirable member behaviour stimulation program*. If a company is clear on the types of behaviours they would like their members to exhibit across the customer journey (from awareness to advocacy), they can

---

2   Accenture, cited in fabric blog, 2022, 'Customer Loyalty Programs Guide: Building Loyalty in 2023, https://fabric.inc/blog/product/customer-loyalty-programs#:~:text=According%20to%20Accenture%2C%20over%2090,lifetime%20value%20of%20each%20individual, accessed 18 July 2023.

3   Loyalty Science Lab at Old Dominion University, 2023, 'The Future of Loyalty Report', accessed 18 July 2023.

4   Bond Brand Loyalty, 2021, 'The Loyalty Report,' US edition.

5   Bond Brand Loyalty, 2021, 'The Loyalty Report,' Canadian edition.

6   The Point of Loyalty, 'For Love or Money 2022'.

7   Vivid Engagement, 2020, 'Loyalty Asia Report; 2020 ASEAN Insights'.

8   Ehredt, C., 'Innovators Break The Mould, At The 2020 Loyalty Magazine Awards', Currency Alliance, https://www.linkedin.com/pulse/innovators-break-mould-2020-loyalty-magazine-awards-charles-ehredt/, accessed 18 June 2020.

design their loyalty program to focus on stimulating and reinforcing those behaviours.

Where consumer behaviour is involved, the opportunity exists to apply consumer psychology. As will be seen in Chapters 5 and 6, psychology is widely applied in loyalty program design and execution.

Loyalty programs and membership programs are the primary focus for this book, although the subject may occasionally extend to customer engagement programs. Engagement itself is discussed extensively, being a primary driver of loyalty. Loyalty programs are about more than just points, miles, tiers, discounts and rewards. They involve ideas, processes, interactions and technologies working together to drive meaningful member engagement which strengthens relationships, fosters commitment and generates loyalty *as an outcome.*

For a consumer, the primary intention in engaging with a loyalty program is to access rewards. Arias-Carrion and Poppel (2007)[9] stated that rewards are experienced as 'making things better' and are therefore liked, desired and pursued. Consumption of rewards produces pleasure. At a base level this pleasure can 'initiate learning processes that consolidate liking the rewarding goal, learning cues that predict its availability and actions that permit its consumption.' Pleasure can also work to assign value, which helps consumers determine what level of effort to put towards obtaining the reward.

There are a range of academic studies which measure the effectiveness of loyalty programs. Nevertheless, most industry experts agree on the ambition of a loyalty program; to drive deeper engagement between members and a company or brand, manifesting in incremental acquisition, spend, retention, and advocacy.

A recent study by Loyalty Science Lab and Old Dominion University (2023)[10] asked consumers globally how loyalty programs affect their purchase behaviours. 68 per cent of respondents said they influence 'where to buy from',

---

9   Arias-Carrión, O. & Pöppel, E., 2007, 'Dopamine, learning, and reward-seeking behavior', Acta neurobiologiae experimentalis, Vol 67, pp481-8.

10   Loyalty Science Lab at Old Dominion University, 2023, 'The Future of Loyalty Report', accessed 18 July 2023.

72 per cent said they influence them to 'buy more', 76 per cent said they influence them to 'stay longer' and 75 per cent said they influence them to 'feel more favourable'. This aligns directly with the ambitions of loyalty program operators.

Consumer benefits and challenges

From a consumer perspective, the benefits a loyalty program can provide, include:

- **Value:** members may be rewarded with desirable tangible or non-tangible benefits.

- **Exclusivity:** members may be provided with access to exclusive benefits that non-members do not receive.

- **Recognition:** members may be shown appreciation through the delivery of surprise gifts or rewards.

- **Relevancy:** members may receive tailored communications, offers and experiences specific to their individual preferences, increasing their usefulness and appeal.

Core challenges consumers face when engaging with loyalty programs can include:

- **Value:** the rewards provided by the program may not be perceived as adequate, compelling or accessible.

- **Program saturation:** consumers may be overwhelmed by the sheer volume of loyalty programs being promoted to them, with most consumer companies offering a program to their customers.

- **Marketing assault:** many loyalty programs send large volumes of marketing materials to members via email, SMS, push notification, banner advertising and mail. For some members, the volume of marketing received may be perceived as excessive, while the content may not be relevant.

- **Data capture and control:** a loyalty program may capture personal data in ways the member is not aware of, or does not approve of, and use it for purposes the member may not deem appropriate. The member may also feel they have a lack of control over how their data is captured and used by the program.

Company benefits and challenges

For a program operator, the potential benefits are numerous:

- **Grow and protect share of wallet:** a loyalty program can grow the recency, frequency and value of member transactions by making the engagement process more rewarding. It can also reduce member churn by developing meaningful relationships and introducing barriers to exit.

- **Better understand members:** a program can play a useful role in better understanding members as individuals and tailoring communications, offers, products and services to meet their needs more accurately.

- **Drive advocacy:** a program can successfully turn members into promoters by delighting and rewarding them above their expectations.

- **Build a marketing database:** a program can be an effective way for a company to build a member database and collect zero- and first-party data. In the age of digital marketing, this is one of the most valuable assets a company can possess, as it increases the effectiveness of marketing while reducing advertising costs.

Core challenges program operators face when executing loyalty programs can include:

- **Expense:** designing, implementing and running a loyalty program can be expensive. Companies generally need to hire expertise to design, implement and operate a program. The may also need to buy, build or lease the required technology systems and solutions. Additional expenses can include marketing, training, legal, analytical analysis, accounting and customer service. There is also the cost of rewards.

- **Ability to deliver meaningful value:** the key driver of engagement with most loyalty programs is value. Members will join a program because they believe they will access value, and they will continue to engage because they perceive they are accessing value. Some companies do not generate sufficient margin to be able to deliver enough value directly to the majority of the member base to ensure their engagement is maintained.

- **Disengagement:** maintaining consistent member engagement can be challenging. Many loyalty programs have significant numbers of members on their database who no longer engage with the program at all.

- **Competition:** the loyalty industry is incredibly competitive and growing more so every year. Loyalty program operators need to continually innovate and evolve to ensure they remain attractive and relevant to their members, especially when compared to competitor programs.

Customer retention is a key driver for many companies in introducing a loyalty program. In a study of over 14 industries, Riechheld (1996)[11] reported that a 5 per cent increase in customer retention can generate a profit increase from between 25 per cent and 95 per cent.

With such a wide range of benefits, it is not surprising that loyalty programs have expanded into most industries and most countries globally. However, many companies struggle to navigate the range of challenges and, as a result, operate at a suboptimal level for both the members and the company. Loyalty consultancies, such as Loyalty & Reward Co, can be used to conduct health check audits of existing programs and recommend strategic enhancements to improve program effectiveness.

---

11   Reichheld, F., 1996, 'The Loyalty Effect: The Hidden Force Behind Growth, Profits, and Lasting Value', Harvard Business School Press, Boston.

Proprietary vs Coalition loyalty programs

A loyalty program structure may be proprietary or coalition.

Proprietary loyalty programs are exclusive to a single brand or business, meaning customers can only earn and redeem rewards with that specific company. An example would be a retail program where members earn points or account credit which they can redeem on future transactions with the same brand.

Proprietary loyalty programs are designed to enhance brand loyalty by offering unique benefits and rewards that can only be enjoyed by the customers of that particular company. They allow companies to create a loyalty program tailored to their specific needs, goals, and member base, giving them more control over the rewards structure, promotions, and other aspects of the program. They enable companies to have a direct relationship with their members, which can support more personalised marketing and better understanding of member preferences and behaviours.

While they offer more control, they also come with the responsibility of managing all aspects of the loyalty program, including costs, marketing, technology, and member support. Some members may not spend enough with the brand to earn a desirable reward, which can lead to disengagement.

Coalition programs involve partnerships between multiple brands (a 'coalition' of partners), allowing members to earn across a wide range of participating companies. An example is a frequent flyer program where members can earn points or miles for flying, but also for shopping with multiple brands, and for using a loyalty program-linked credit card.

Partner companies provide the coalition program operators' branded points/miles to their customers as a reward for transacting with them. The coalition partners pay the coalition program operator an agreed amount for the points/miles conferred on members, and in return the coalition program operator may promote the third-party partner to their member base.

Members can sometimes redeem their rewards at any of the participating partners, giving them more options and flexibility in how they use their earned benefits. Coalition programs help companies expand their customer base by attracting members who are loyal to other participating brands. This can lead to increased cross-selling and up-selling opportunities. Partners can enjoy lower running costs as the coalition program operator will pay for all marketing, customer support, and technology infrastructure. As members can earn across multiple brands, the likelihood they will accumulate sufficient value to access a reward is greater than with a proprietary loyalty program.

Coalition programs are more complex to manage due to the involvement of multiple brands and the need for effective coordination and communication among partners. With large coalition programs, partners (especially smaller partners) may not receive the level of marketing support they require to generate the benefits they seek.

A coalition program may be controlled by a single operator (as per most frequent flyer and hotel programs) or it may run more independently (e.g., global loyalty coalition player Payback).

In many countries, the loyalty industry is dominated by coalition programs. They are often run by large airlines, hotels, banks and supermarkets, and have the potential to generate massive revenues for their parent companies. Proprietary loyalty programs typically do not have the same potential to generate new revenue streams, but there are still opportunities. Chapter 16 explores the different commercial models for proprietary and coalition loyalty programs.

Evolving consumer expectations

The modern digital age has made it more challenging for loyalty program operators (and companies in general) to deliver to consumer expectations. Netflix, Amazon, Uber, Spotify and other companies have redefined what it means to be a service business through the seamless delivery of ultra-convenience, personalisation and value. Sawhney[12] argues that these companies have developed a new customer manifesto:

---

12   Sawhney, M., 'Applications of AI in Marketing and Customer Experience Management', Course 5, https://www.course5i.com/blogs/

- Know me (who I am, what I like)

- Respond quickly (preferably real-time)

- Be where I want to be (I will choose the channel to engage, not you)

- Tell me what you stand for (your values, mission)

- Speak to my pains and passions (create meaning for me, do not just sell your product)

- Give me value for my privacy (what are you giving me in exchange for my data), and

- Reward me for loyalty (rewards, convenience, etc.)

Sawhney further argues that the only way to keep consumers engaged is to understand the customer journey, and respond to customer expectations and meet their needs at each stage of the journey, a central theme throughout this book.

Key insights

- Loyalty programs are structured programs which reward registered members for repeat purchases.

- The ambition of a company in operating a loyalty program is to drive deeper engagement between members and a company or brand, manifesting in incremental acquisition, spend, retention, brand affinity and advocacy.

- Consumers and companies can enjoy a range of benefits with loyalty programs, but also face many challenges. Program operators should consider these carefully when designing and operating a program to maximise their chances of success.

- Netflix, Amazon, Uber, Spotify and other companies have raised

applications-of-ai-in-marketing-and-customer-experience-management/, accessed 23 May 2020.

consumer expectations of service standards and have made it more challenging for loyalty program operators (and companies in general) to satisfy member needs. Consumers expect a program to know them, respond quickly, communicate through their preferred channel, create meaning for them, provide valuable rewards and ultra-convenience.

Suggested reading

- Arias-Carrión, Oscar & Pöppel, Ernst, 2007, Dopamine, learning, and reward-seeking behaviour', Acta neurobiologiae experimentalis, *Vol* 67, pp481-8.

- Sawhney, M., 'Applications of AI in Marketing and Customer Experience Management', Course 5, https://www.course5i.com/blogs/applications-of-ai-in-marketing-and-customer-experience-management/

CHAPTER 2

THE HISTORY OF LOYALTY PROGRAMS

'No Money! And You Need Tea Towels, Bath Towels, Sheets and Pillow Cases? Here's a SECRET! There's MAGIC in GROUP TOKENS. They grow rapidly and CHANGE QUICKLY into "Dri-glo" Bath Towels.'

- Group Tokens advertisement,
Merchants Trade Expansion Group Ltd (date unknown).

Focus areas

This chapter will address the following questions:

- When did loyalty programs first appear?

- What are the different types of loyalty currencies which have been used throughout history?

- When did coalition loyalty programs first appear?

- How have loyalty programs changed over time?

- How have loyalty programs stayed the same over time?

LOYALTY PROGRAMS HAVE been around for hundreds of years, with approaches becoming more sophisticated over time. This chapter chronologically details the evolution of currency-based loyalty programs used over time.

Beer and Bread Tokens (Ancient Egypt)

In *Ancient Egypt: Anatomy of A Civilisation*[13] Professor Barry Kemp argues that ancient Egyptians practiced a type of reward program similar to modern frequent flyer programs, including the presence of status tiers and the ability to redeem on a wider variety of rewards.

For much of the pharaoh's thousands of years of rule, they did not have money. It simply was not invented yet. Instead, citizens, conscripted workers and slaves alike were all awarded commodity '*tokens*' (similar to loyalty points or miles) for their work and temple time. The most common were beer and bread tokens. The tokens were physical things, made from wood, then plastered over and painted and shaped like a jug of beer or a loaf of bread.

The more senior people in the hierarchy were rewarded with the same tokens but received bonuses. The Rhind Mathematical Papyrus details examples and mathematical equations regarding how higher positions, such as the skipper, crew leader and doorkeeper, received double bread tokens compared to the rest of the crew. This could be construed as a variant of the status tier bonus, where higher tier members earn bonus points for transactions to reward them for their greater loyalty.

The tokens could also be exchanged for things other than bread and beer. Those high up enough to earn surplus tokens could redeem them on other goods and services, in the same way that frequent flyer members with lots of points can redeem them on flights and on non-flight rewards such as iPads, KitchenAid mixers and Gucci handbags.

While some of the characteristics are quite similar to a modern loyalty program, is this really a loyalty program? Some might argue it is simply a societal exchange system developed in the absence of fiat currency. Others might contend that is exactly what a modern loyalty program design is; a non-fiat exchange system utilising tokenised currencies.

---

13   Kemp, B. J., 2005, 'Ancient Egypt: Anatomy of a Civilization, 2nd Edition'.

Copper Tokens (c. 1700 – 1800s)

The first modern loyalty program, according to a New York Times article by Nagle (1973),[14] commenced in 1793, when a Sudbury, New Hampshire merchant began rewarding customers with '*copper tokens*'. The tokens could be accumulated and used for future purchases, thereby generating repeat visits, the core behavioural objective of loyalty program design. The idea was quickly replicated by other retailers and carried into the 18th century.

Is there evidence to support this claim? While copper loyalty tokens from Sudbury dating back to 1793 could not be found, Loyalty & Reward Co research did identify other merchant-branded copper, brass and aluminium tokens created in the US in the 1800s. For example, the New York Times article by Nagle refers to a brass token created by Robinson and Ballou Grocers, dated 1863, which can be found online for sale by various coin dealers worldwide for as little as US$50.

This would appear to provide support for the existence of merchant loyalty tokens, however further investigation reveals these coins to be more accurately referred to as 'Civil War' tokens, which may not be related to loyalty programs at all.

During the 1861-64 US Civil War, high inflation sparked a frenzy of hoarding, with the focus on gold, silver and copper coins. With few coins left in circulation, merchants began to suffer as small denomination coins were the most commonly tendered at that point in time. To alleviate the situation, merchants began minting their own tokens to fill the void.[15] These were typically one cent in value, made of copper or brass, and were similar in size to government issued coinage.

This was not the first time such an approach has been taken by merchants. Between 1832-1844, 'Hard Times' tokens were created when the United States

---

14   Nagle, J., 1971, 'Trading Stamps: A Long History', New York Times, https://www.nytimes.com/1971/12/26/archives/trading-stamps-a-long-history-premiums-said-to-date-back-in-us-to.html, accessed 22 April 2020.

15   Fuld, G. & Fuld, M., 1975, 'U.S. Civil War Store Cards', Quarterman Publishing, Inc.

went through an economic depression over the fate of the Second Bank of the United States and the powers of the Federal Treasury.

The climax of that period was the 'Panic of 1837', brought on by President Andrew Jackson's requirement that banks and receivers of public money only accept gold or silver in payment for public lands as a way to reduce speculation. As a result, gold and silver were hoarded and loans were called in, generating a run on the banks. An insight from an article by the American Numismatic Association (Mudd, 2015) [16] states, 'The immediate reason for the issuance of the tokens was the ongoing shortage of small change in the United States – a situation that had existed ever since the Colonial period despite the best efforts of the United States Mint'.

This provides an important clue for the investigation of the famed Sudbury merchant from 1793. It appears that coinage shortages also existed at that time right across the US.. A Quarterly Journal of Economics article (Barnard, 1917)[17] references merchants minting their own coins of brass and tin as early as 1701 after the Massachusetts mint was closed in 1697. Further examples are cited from Virginia as early as 1714, with many more coins created between 1773-74. In Connecticut, copper mine owner John Higley created the first recorded copper tokens between 1737-39, while Chalmers, a goldsmith of Annapolis, Maryland issued tokens in at least three denominations (shillings, sixpence, and threepence) just after the American Revolution in 1783. Barnard states that so many other merchants created silver and copper coins that laws were passed by Pennsylvania, Connecticut and New Jersey prohibiting the circulation of coins not expressly authorised.

Thus, the historical record appears to show the primary driving force for the creation by merchants of branded copper (and other metal) tokens was to address a severe shortage of coinage which was inhibiting commerce.

Did a Sudbury, New Hampshire merchant invent the world's first loyalty

---

16 Mudd, D., 2015, 'Hard Times Tokens', American Numismatic Association, https://www.money.org/ana-blog/TalesHardTimesTokens, accessed 22 April 2020.

17 Barnard, B. W., 1917, 'The Use of Private Tokens for Money in the United States', The Quarterly Journal of Economics, Vol 31, No. 4, pp600-634.

program when they began rewarding customers with copper tokens in 1793? It is possible that such a merchant created branded copper tokens, however there is no evidence to support the claim made in the New York Times article (and repeated extensively across numerous books and websites) that they created the tokens in order to reward loyal customers. In fact, the likelihood is they were created to address a local coin shortage, and this was later misinterpreted as an early form of loyalty program currency.

Irrespective, the Coinage Act of 1864 enacted by Congress made the minting and usage of non-government issued coins illegal, ending this era forever.

Trade Marks (1850s)

Based on the available evidence, the true godfather of the modern loyalty program would appear to be B.T. Babbitt.

Born in 1809, Benjamin Talbot Babbitt found his fortune in New York City in his early 1830s by designing an original and cheaper process to make *saleratus*, a key base ingredient of baking powder. He soon expanded his product range to include yeast, baking powder and soap powder. He became the first to sell individually wrapped bars of soap, with 'Babbitt's Best Soap' becoming a household name across the US.[18]

To boost repeat sales, in the 1850s[19] B.T. Babbitt, Inc. launched a new (and truly revolutionary) promotional program, where they invited customers to cut-out and collect the '*trade marks*' from product packaging of Best Soap and 1776 Soap Powder. The trade marks could initially be redeemed for coloured lithographs by mailing them to the company. Soon after, the rewards range was expanded into a more comprehensive offering, which was promoted in the company's 'Mailing List of Premiums'.

As an example of the rewards on offer, The 1905 *Mailing List of Premiums* offers a wide range of choices, including a harmonica, felt pencil case or box of

---

18 Ingam, J.N., 1983, 'Biographical dictionary of American business leaders', Greenwood Press.

19 National Commission on Food Marketing, 1966, 'Organization and competition in food retailing', Technical study No.7, p41.

school crayons for 25 trade marks; a buckhorn handle pocket knife (2 blades), sterling silver thimble or pair of Uncle Sam suspenders for 50 trade marks; all the way up to a lady's locket chain (14k gold filled), lady's gold ring (12 pearls) or lady's handbag for 225 trade marks.[20] These are not just practical, utilitarian products, but truly aspirational items which would have captivated the member base in a way which history had never seen before.

B.T. Babbitt also introduced the option for customers to visit their premium stores located in major cities across the US, as well as Canada, Porto Rico and Scotland, to redeem trade marks for 'a large number of household articles, dolls, toys, etc.'.

---

20   B.T. Babbitt, Incorporated, 1905, 'Mailing List of Premiums'.

As a new approach to marketing, the company positioned the program as a profit-sharing plan, potentially taking inspiration from dividends paid on shares, or rebates for volume sales. The 1912 *B.T. Babbitt's Profit Sharing List*[21] states 'B.T. Babbitt was the originator of premiums… the firm has continued since that time to give its customers in the form of premiums a very material share of the profits of its immense business.'.

The Profit Share Plan also cautions, 'When you buy all B.T. Babbitt's Products, consisting of Soaps, Cleanser, '1776' Soap Powder, and Pure Lye or Potash, you are entitled to a return in the form of a premium. If you do not save the trade marks from any of the Babbitt articles you are losing just so much. These trade marks are worth fully one-half cent each to you if redeemed from our premiums.'

Checks (c. 1860s)

In the 1860s, the Great Atlantic & Pacific Tea Co. (which was set to become the largest retailer in the world under the A&P brand between 1920 into the 1960s[22]) launched a comparable program to reward their customers for purchasing a selection of their products. When transacting, customers would receive a red coupon known as a '*check*', detailing the amount it was worth and the terms. One 1890 example states, 'This Check (good for the amount as engraved for presents of Glass ware, China, etc.) is redeemable at any of our 200 Stores. Provided it is Stamped with the Address of the Store that issued it. Managers will be particular and allow no Checks to be given out before they are stamped. This Check is of no value except Stamped as per the foregoing. ALL CHECKS MUST BE PUNCHED AFTER REDEMPTION. PUNCHED CHECKS ARE OF NO VALUE.'[23]

---

21   B.T. Babbitt, Incorporated, 1912, 'B.T. Babbitt's Profit Sharing List'.

22   Levinson, M., 2012, 'Don't Grieve for the Great A&P', Harvard Business Review.

23   The Great Atlantic And Pacific Tea Co, 1890, '1890 Great Atlantic & Pacific Tea Co. Coupon Premium - Handstamp of Big Bleecker'.

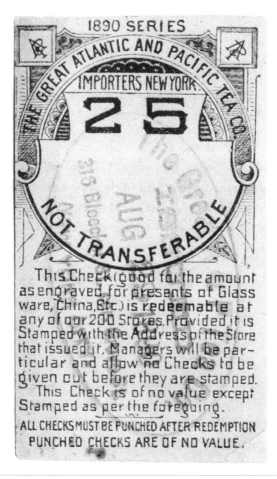

Checks could be accumulated and redeemed in stores for a range of consumer goods. This was incredibly popular with customers, and it provided a strategic competitive advantage over smaller merchants who could not afford, and did not have the space, to provide such a sizeable reward range.

It also posed some challenges. According to Levinson,[24] 'the premiums not only were costly, but also took up shelf space that could have displayed merchandise for sale. Many stores of the period looked more like gift shops than groceries'.

---

24 Levison, M., 2011, 'The Great A&P and the Struggle for Small Business in America,' Hill & Wang, 2011.

To address this issue, in the early 1900s the company published The Great Atlantic & Pacific Tea Co. Catalogue. This promoted a range of day-to-day homeware products including saucepans, teapots, knives, ironing boards, sugar tins, wash bowls, spoons, bread trays and more.[25] Once enough checks had been saved, members could send them to a central office and receive the reward by return freight,[26] reducing the need for each store to range the full rewards range.

A few years later, The Great Atlantic & Pacific Tea Co transferred their loyalty program operations to Sperry & Hutchinson, a stamp program covered later in this chapter.

Tickets (1872)

The Grand Union Tea Company was formed in 1872 in Pennsylvania and followed the lead of the Great Atlantic & Pacific Tea Co with their loyalty program design. The owners chose to sidestep retailers and sell their product directly to consumers, starting with door-to-door sales. They rewarded customers with 'tickets' which could be collected and redeemed for a wide selection of products from the company's Catalog of Premiums.[27] The 1903 version of the Catalog of Premiums lists the full product range and prices (coffee, tea, spices, extracts, baking powder soap and sundries), as well as 17 pages of rewards. These include an Oak Roman Chair (100 tickets), lace curtains (120 tickets a pair), Ormolu clock (300 tickets) and dinner set Berlin 1903 (440 tickets). Customers could earn one ticket by buying a pound of coffee at 20 cents, two tickets for premium tea at 40 cents and one ticket for a packet of cloves at 10 cents. The catalogue proudly proclaims, 'We advertise by giving presents with our goods, thus SHARING WITH OUR CUSTOMERS the profits of our business. Remember, you pay less for our goods of same quality than at other stores, and get presents in addition.'

---

25 The Great Atlantic & Pacific Tea Co, 'Great Atlantic & Pacific Tea Co Catalogue,' 1908.

26 Levison, M., 'The Great A&P and the Struggle for Small Business in America,' Hill & Wang.

27 Grand Union Tea Company, 1903, 'Catalogue Of Premiums'.

The 1971 New York Times article by Nagle included an interview with William H. Preis, senior vice president of the Grand Union Tea Company. Preis joined the company in 1933. By the time of the interview, the company had transitioned their tickets program to a coalition-based stamps program run by Stop & Save Trading Corporation. Customers could earn Triple-S Blue Stamps which cost the company 1 ¼ per cent of sales. Preis indicated they had been providing the stamps program for 16 years.[28]

Certificates and Coupons (1890)

This period may have potentially been a boom time for the newly designed loyalty marketing function, with companies big and small adopting the approach. One example from 1890 is a '*People's Trading Coupon*' from Hunsicker & Warmkessell Photographers, based in Allentown, Philadelphia. The coupon is a sophisticated punch card which, when completed, provides the member with

28 Nagle, J., 1971, 'Trading Stamps: A Long History', New York Times, https://www.nytimes.com/1971/12/26/archives/trading-stamps-a-long-history-premiums-said-to-date-back-in-us-to.html, accessed 22 April 2020.

'one dozen of our best $4 Cabinet Photographs'. The member is reminded to 'Tell your friends to get a ticket.'[29]

Another example is The United Cigars Store Co., founded in 1901 and sporting over 3,000 retail outlets at its peak in 1926.[30] They ran a successful 'certificates and coupons' rewards program (where five coupons were equal to one certificate). United built a coalition of partners by making deals with companies including Wrigleys, Swifts, Danish Pride, National, Barkers, Votan and Tootsie, all of which put United coupons within their product packaging. Certificates and coupons were redeemable by mail or at 250 redemption centres around the country. Rewards included a men's gold-filled watch or six place settings of Rogers silver plate flatware (900 coupons), room-size oriental style rug (4,000 coupons), a Remington automatic shotgun (5,000 coupons and a four-wheel Studebaker carriage (25,000 coupons).

29   Hunsicker & Warmkessel, 1890, 'People's Trading Coupon', Allentown, PA.

30   United Cigar Stores, IMASCO, http://www.imascoltd.com/united-cigar-stores/, Accessed 7 April 2020.

The United Cigars Store Co 1924 *Premium Catalog*[31] features a selection of well over one thousand reward items, including clothing, umbrellas, smoking accessories, razors, cutlery, leather goods, toiletries, jewellery, clocks, watches, kitchenware, headphones, cameras, sporting goods, toys, games and silverware.

Stamps (1891)

In the 1890s, companies began using physical '*stamps*' to reward loyal customers. Customers could earn stamps when making purchases and were encouraged to stick them into collecting books. The books could then be exchanged for a wide range of rewards.

The first company to introduce stamps was Schuster's Department Store in Milwaukee in 1891. Customers earned one stamp for every US10c spent. A filled book of 500 stamps was worth US$1 to redeem on rewards (a 2 per cent return on spend). By WWII, it appears the program had expanded into a

31   United Cigar Stores Company of America, 1924, 'Premium Catalog'.

small coalition, with a stamp book dating from that era promoting 'Valuable Schuster Stamps Are Now Also Given By Many Food Markets.'[32]

In 1896, The Sperry & Hutchinson Company embraced the coalition loyalty program as their central business model. Rather than a company issuing their own loyalty currency, Sperry & Hutchinson created the entire loyalty program apparatus as a service. New England retailers were provided with S&H Green Stamps, books, and catalogues to provide to their customers, and customers could redeem the books directly with Sperry & Hutchinson.

While other companies replicated their model (Gold Bond, Gift House, Top Value and King Korn amongst some of their competitors[33]), Sperry & Hutchinson remained the biggest globally. At one point, they claimed they were distributing three times as many Green Stamps as the US Postal Service was distributing postal stamps.

---

32 Dahlsad, D., 2013, 'Inherited Values', http://www.inherited-values. com/2013/09/meet-me-down-by-schusters-vintage-department-store-memories-collectibles/, accessed 4 May 2020.

33 Lonto, J. R., 2013, 'The Trading Stamp Story,' StudioZ-7 Publishing, http://www.studioz7.com/stamps.html, accessed 4 May 2020.

Every year, Sperry & Hutchinson would release a print version of their catalogue *Ideabook Of Distinguished Merchandise*. The 1966 *70th Anniversary Edition Ideabook Of Distinguished Merchandise*,[34] provides insight into the scale and complexity of their operations when at the height of their popularity. In addition to being able to order rewards via post, members could visit a vast network of redemption centres, with the entire product range priced in books of stamps. The 185-page catalogue contains over 2,000 products across 59 categories, a similar sized range to some modern frequent flyer program online stores. In the copy possessed by Loyalty & Reward Co, a young lady has worked her way through the toys' pages, circling the items she desired and writing out the number of books she needed to claim everything on her list. It provides a sense of the process so many households around the world would have followed in deciding which rewards they wanted to aim for, with much discussion and debate ensuing.

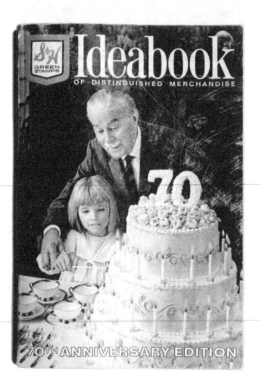

34 Sperry & Hutchinson Company, 1966, 'Ideabook Of Distinguished Merchandise 70th Anniversary Edition', S&H Green Stamps.

The (pre-computer and internet) logistics for claiming a S&H Green Stamps reward were extensive; the member needed to fill books with stamps, choose the reward products, fill out a separate order form for each reward, then send the books and order forms (plus applicable sales taxes) via first class mail to their nearest distribution centre. Alternatively, the member could visit one of hundreds of retail outlets and spend the stamp books directly. The overheads of running such a massive operation would have been enormous.

The demand for stamps went through several phases during the 1900s. According to the US National Commission on Food Marketing,[35] by 1914 around 7 per cent of retail trade involved the awarding of stamps. This reduced to 2 per cent during World War 1. The Great Atlantic & Pacific Tea Co dropped S&H Green Stamps altogether during the war, which would have been a major blow to Sperry & Hutchinson, as they lost the largest grocery chain in the country. Stamp earning stabilised at 2 to 3 per cent of retail trade during the 1920s but fell substantially during the Great Depression and all the way through World War 2.

Post-war, interest in stamps increased substantially. Thirty million US dollars' worth of industry stamps sales were recorded in 1950 in the US, and this grew to US$754 million by 1963, accounting for 16 per cent of total retail trade, and a whopping 47 per cent of grocery trade. Research from the period by Benson and Benson Consumer Studies indicated 83 per cent of all families in the US were saving stamps.[36]

In the US alone there were an estimated 250 to 500 stamp companies operating at the peak of the 'the golden age of stamps'.[37]

Stamps also expanded globally. In the UK, Green Shield and Co-Op Stamps were two popular programs, while in Australia, Green Coupon, Aussie Blue and Group Tokens operated in a competitive market. Other countries also

---

35   National Commission on Food Marketing, 1966, 'Organization and competition in food retailing', Technical study No.7.

36   Ibid.

37   Ibid.

adopted stamps en-masse, including Sweden, Germany, Poland, Switzerland, Canada, Austria, Germany and many more.

Of notable interest is two case studies documented by the US National Commission on Food Marketing which measured whether stamps were successful in helping companies grow revenue.[38] The first related to a business which introduced stamps in a market which did not previously have stamps. The second related to a business which introduced stamps in a market where stamps were already used extensively by their main competitors. While the circumstances for the two studies were different, in both instances within two years gross margins increased by an amount exceeding the cost of the stamps, demonstrating the programs were a success.

Betty Crocker Coupons (1921)

Stamps were not the only major loyalty currency during this period. In 1921, The Washburn Crosby Company, a flour-milling company and largest predecessor of General Mills, Inc., invented fictional character Betty Crocker to personalise responses to consumer inquiries generated by a promotion for Gold Medal flour.[39] In 1931, the company included a coupon for a silverplated spoon within Wheaties cereal boxes and bags of Gold Medal flour.[40] The promotion was so successful, the company followed up the next year with a coupon program which allowed customers to access a complete set of flatware. Starting from 1937, the 'Betty Crocker Coupons' were printed on the outside of the box, enabling customers to see how many they could earn with the purchase. In 1962, the Betty Crocker Coupon Catalog was released, an annual publication 'Featuring over 400 items tested and checked for quality in the Betty Crocker kitchens of the world.'[41]

---

38 Ibid.

39 Betty Crocker, 2017, 'The story of Betty Crocker', https://www.bettycrocker. com/menus-holidays-parties/mhplibrary/parties-and-get-togethers/vintage-betty/the-story-of-betty-crocker, accessed 2 May 2020.

40 McKinney, M., 2006, 'Betty Crocker closing the book on its catalog sales', Minneapolis Star Tribune, https://www.chron.com/life/article/Betty-Crocker-closing-the-book-on-its-catalog-1506961.php, accessed 2 May 2020.

41 Betty Crocker, 1968, 'Betty Crocker Coupon Catalog', No 6.

A study of the history of Betty Crocker Coupons introduces the concept of emotional engagement generated by a loyalty program. Mark Bergen, marketing department chair at the University of Minnesota's Carlson School of Management, said the Betty Crocker program was remarkable for two characteristics – its longevity and the depth of emotion it inspired among its devotees. It became more than a coupon redemption program, Bergen said, by working its way into the fabric of family life.[42]

42 Wilcoxen, W., 2006, 'Betty Crocker retires her catalog', MPR News, https://www.mprnews.org/story/2006/11/28/bettycrocker, accessed 2 May 2020.

*

The mid-1960s marked the beginning of the slow demise of stamps. Some supermarkets dropped stamps and found success by focusing their brand positioning on lowest prices to differentiate against competitors. This approach soon spread to other retail and discount stores.

In the 1970s, a series of recessions and the world oil shock created hardship for most stamp coalition operators, as retail partners sought any way to cut costs. Large-scale rejection of stamps by retailers led to a sudden drop in revenue, and combined with the large cost overheads, ongoing operations became incredibly challenging.

To understand the size of such savings made by supermarkets, in 1977 Tesco in the UK ditched Green Shield Stamps, saving the company an estimated £20m a year[43] (the equivalent of £120m today), which they reinvested in cutting costs.

Miles and Points (1980s)

In 1981, American Airlines launched the world's first currency based frequent flyer program using a new currency ('miles') which corresponded to how many miles a member had flown.[44] Members could earn miles at a set value for free flights allowing them to easily identify what they could redeem their miles for. Brought on by increasing competition with the deregulation of the US airline industry in 1978, the American Airlines AAdvantage program was soon followed by similar schemes from United Airlines, TWA and Delta Airlines.[45]

In 1982, American Airlines upped the ante by introducing a Gold tier to recognise their most loyal members. The same year they launched earn partnerships with Hertz, Holland American Line and British Airways, forming the basis of the first modern coalition program.

---

43   Mason, T., 2019, 'Omnichannel Retail,' Kogan Page.

44   Everett, M. R., 1995, 'Diffusion of Innovations', The Free Press, 4th Edition.

45   De Boer, E. R., 2018, 'Strategy in Airline Loyalty: Frequent Flyer Programs,' Palgrave Macmillan.

Over the next five years, a boom in miles and points-based loyalty programs ensued, including new programs from Holiday Inn (the first hotel program), Japan Airlines, Marriott, Alaska Airlines, Aeroplan, Korean Air, Pan Am, Diners Club, Northwest Airlines, Continental Airlines (which, in conjunction with the Bank of Main Midland, launched the world's first co-branded credit card program), Hilton, Hyatt, National Car Rental, Holiday Inn, Southwest Airlines (which introduced '*points*' rather than '*miles*' for the first time) and Qantas.

As happened with American Airlines, soon after the launch of these large programs, hotel and car rental companies began partnering with the airlines and started offering miles and points as a strategy to grow their share of the lucrative business traveller and high-value leisure traveller markets.

With the rapid expansion of the frequent flyer and hotel coalition models and their new currencies, banks and retailers soon replicated their approach. Points and miles loyalty programs quickly became the dominant loyalty program currency globally, ending the ninety-year reign of stamps.

General Mills tried to revitalise the Betty Crocker program by changing coupons to points in 1989.[46] The program was eventually retired in 2006, with Bergen of the Carlson School arguing the decline in engagement was due to shopping pattern changes.[47] Households had given up the habit of saving for a future purchase and started buying on credit, while the idea of cutting out box top coupons and sending them in the mail became old-fashioned in the age of plastic membership cards and ever-evolving reward ranges.

Sperry & Hutchinson also tried to reinvent themselves in 1989, launching a plastic member card which could be swiped at cash registers to earn points. This evolved into S&H Greenpoints in 1999, an attempt to weave the 104-year-old company into the dotcom boom. By 2000, they had attracted 88 participating retailers, including OfficeMax.com, Borders.com and LandsEnd.

---

46 McKinney, M., 2006, 'Betty Crocker closing the book on its catalog sales,' Minneapolis Star Tribune, https://www.chron.com/life/article/Betty-Crocker-closing-the-book-on-its-catalog-1506961.php, accessed 2 May 2020.

47 Wilcoxen, W., 2006, 'Betty Crocker retires her catalog', MPR News, https://www.mprnews.org/story/2006/11/28/bettycrocker, accessed 2 May 2020.

com.[48] In 2006, the company was purchased by Pay By Touch for over US$100 million in cash and stock.[49] Their demise should be listed alongside such companies as Kodak, such was the scale of their operation and influence on retail marketing globally, not to mention their penetration of households.

Increasing competition, combined with the birth of the digital age, led to a loyalty program innovation boom from the 1990s onwards. Coalition programs launched online reward stores with thousands of consumer products and gift cards, expanded into insurance products, branded credit cards, financial services, food and wine clubs, massive partner networks and digital marketing agencies. In addition, they developed specialised capabilities in data capture, usage and monetisation, all of which will be explored in later chapters.

Cryptocurrencies and Tokenised Assets

From 2017, several start-ups launched new coalition programs rewarding members with tradeable '*cryptocurrencies*', such as Bitcoin, Ethereum and branded crypto tokens. The novel variation with cryptocurrencies as a loyalty currency was that the value could increase or decrease based on speculative trading behaviour. The approach taken by start-ups was to establish a coalition program to drive demand for the cryptocurrency, which would subsequently increase in value, benefiting existing members. Most programs failed to deliver the sustained demand necessary to protect the market price of their cryptocurrencies, which instead decreased in value aligning with market sentiment. Programs offering Bitcoin have achieved market traction and continue to build global engagement.

Other programs have evolved to reward members with '*tokenised assets*'. Examples include BrickX (reward members with real estate), Almond (reward members with carbon offsets/tree planting), and Bits of Stock (reward members

---

48   Slatalla, M., 2000, 'Clicks, Not Licks, as Green Stamps Go Digital', New York Times, https://www.nytimes.com/2000/03/09/technology/online-shopper-clicks-not-licks-as-green-stamps-go-digital.html, accessed 1 May 2020.

49   The Wise Marketer, 2006, 'Pay By Touch snaps up S&H Solutions & Greenpoints', https://thewisemarketer.com/headlines/pay-by-touch-snaps-up-sh-solutions-greenpoints-2/, accessed 2 June 2020.

with partner company shares). Shares and real estate allow the member to earn dividends on their tokens (a hark back to B.T. Babbitts). Carbon credits can be offset against tree plantings or even traded. Ostensibly any physical asset can be tokenised, opening up an exciting new future in the evolution of loyalty currencies.

*

From a loyalty program design perspective, the most fascinating aspect of the historical review is that the core design of a currency-based loyalty program has remained consistent throughout time. The currencies have changed constantly (trade marks, checks, tickets, coupons, certificates, stamps, miles, points, cryptocurrencies, tokenised assets and many other variations have all been used), but the fundamental program design has not changed. All the companies included in the historical research followed the exact same approach; providing a tokenised currency to a customer when they spent and allowing the customer to redeem the accumulated currency for a desirable reward.

Currency-based loyalty programs are a consumer-engagement model which has stood the test of time. And this is just one type of loyalty program design. As will be seen in Chapter 8, there are many other types of successful loyalty program designs which do not involve loyalty currencies but are also highly effective.

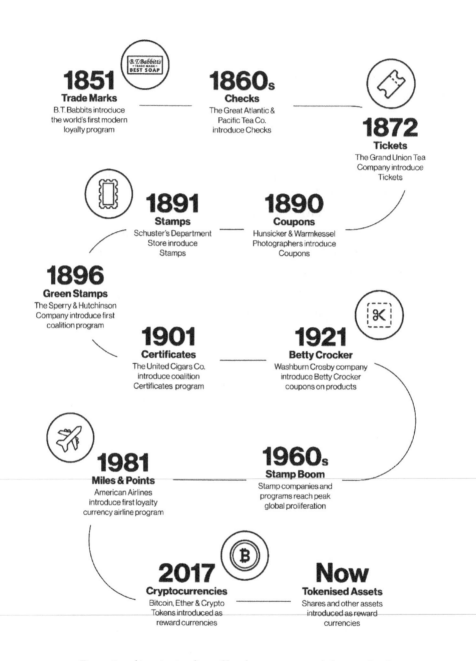

Figure 1: a historic timeline of loyalty programs and the new loyalty currencies utilised within them (copyright Loyalty & Reward Co).

Go to **loyaltyrewardco.com/the-true-history-of-loyalty-programs/** *to view additional photographs of historic rewards catalogues referenced throughout this chapter.*

Key insights

- A model remarkably similar to modern loyalty programs was utilised in Ancient Egypt, but the first modern loyalty program appeared in New York City in the 1850s, created by B.T. Babbitt, the inventor of the individual bar of soap.

- Trade marks, checks, tickets, coupons, certificates, stamps, miles and points have all been used as loyalty currencies over time, as well as tokenised assets such as cryptocurrencies, real estate and shares.

- The first major coalition loyalty program appeared in 1896 when The Sperry & Hutchinson Company launched their S&H Green Stamps program in New England.

- Over time, loyalty programs have become more prevalent, have grown more sophisticated in the capture and usage of member data, and more complex in their design (such as the introduction of status tiers).

- From their inception, the core design of a loyalty program has remained consistent; companies provide a loyalty currency to a customer when they spend, and the customer can redeem the accumulated currency for a desirable reward. In addition, there are many other types of loyalty program design frameworks which do not involve loyalty currencies at all.

Suggested reading

- Barnard, B. W, 1917, 'The Use of Private Tokens for Money in the United States', The Quarterly Journal of Economics, Vol 31, No. 4, pp600-634.

- Lonto, J. R. 2013, 'The Trading Stamp Story', StudioZ-7 Publishing, http://www.studioz7.com/stamps.html.

- National Commission on Food Marketing, 1966, 'Organization and competition in food retailing', Technical study No.7.

- De Boer, E.R, 2018, 'Strategy in Airline Loyalty: Frequent Flyer Programs', Palgrave Macmillan.

CHAPTER 3

DO LOYALTY PROGRAMS GENERATE LOYALTY?

'A study made from 1954 through 1960 by Progressive Grocer indicates that during the early years of the introduction of trading stamps by supermarkets, the supermarkets giving stamps did achieve greater sales gains than those which did not give stamps... Since 1955, however, the surveys made by Progressive Grocer indicate on the average no greater gains by those supermarkets giving stamps than by those supermarkets not giving stamps.'

- National Commission on Food Marketing,
USA, 1966.[50]

Focus areas

This chapter will address the following questions:

- What academic research is there to indicate that loyalty programs actually work to generate incremental acquisition, spend, retention, brand affinity and advocacy?

- What academic research is there to indicate that loyalty programs do not work?

---

50   National Commission on Food Marketing, 1966, 'Organization and competition in food retailing', Technical study No.7.

As DETAILED IN Chapter 2, the 1966 US National Commission on Food Marketing report[51] included two case studies which documented where retailers had introduced stamp programs; one into a stamp-free market and one into a saturated market. Within two years, both retailers recorded gross margin increases by an amount exceeding the cost of the stamps, demonstrating the programs were a success. This may be the first published financial study which attempted to test the effectiveness of loyalty programs.

Is this consistent with other loyalty programs over time, and across different industries and geographies? Are loyalty programs always a success? Do loyalty programs actually work to deliver incremental acquisition, spend, retention, brand affinity and advocacy?

The academic and market research is vast and often contradictory. After reviewing the body of research, the main conclusion which can be drawn is that loyalty programs do work, and they do not work.

Evidence that loyalty programs work

Research which indicates loyalty programs generally do work includes a study by Wirtz and Oo Lwin (2007).[52] They investigated credit card reward programs and demonstrated that the more attractive the loyalty program was perceived to be by members, the greater the perception of rewards gained from participation, which in turn was effective in driving share of wallet. This is particularly relevant for a commoditised product such as credit cards, where customers often lack psychological attachment to any particular credit card company. Offering an attractive loyalty program can have the effect of motivating a member to continue buying or using a particular product, service or brand, otherwise known as behavioural commitment.

In an extensive, three-year study of retail programs, Meyer-Waarden

51   Ibid.

52   Wirtz, J., Mattila, A. S., & Oo Lwin, M., 2007, 'How effective are loyalty reward programs in driving share of wallet?', Journal of Service Research, Vol 9, Issue 4, pp327 -334.

(2008)[53] found the impact of loyalty program membership on customer purchase behaviour was significant. They showed that members and non-members demonstrated significantly different purchase behaviours, irrespective of other factors. Member spending behaviour, in terms of total and average shopping baskets, share of purchases, purchase frequency and inter-purchase time, was significantly higher than that of non-members.

Is this due to correlation or causation? In other words, did members increase loyal behaviour because of the program, or were they already more loyal and as a result more pre-disposed to join the program?

Leenheer et al (2007)[54] conducted a study of Dutch households engaging in seven different grocery loyalty programs. They found a small, positive, yet significant effect of loyalty program membership on share-of-wallet, and concluded that creating loyalty program membership was a crucial step to enhance share-of-wallet.

Lederman (2007) reported significant effects of frequent flyer programs on market share in the US.[55] Her study showed that enhancements to an airline's frequent flyer program in the form of improved partner earn and redemption opportunities could be directly associated with an increase in the airline's market share. The effects were demonstrated to be larger on routes that departed from airports at which the airline was more dominant (hubs), which led her to draw the conclusion that frequent flyer programs can serve to reinforce an airlines' market power.

---

53   Meyer-Waarden, L., 2008, 'The influence of loyalty programme membership on customer purchase behaviour', European Journal of Marketing, Vol 42, Iss 1/2, pp87-114.

54   Leenheer, J., van Heerde, H. J., Bijmolt, T. H. A., & Smidts, A., 2007, 'Do loyalty programs really enhance behavioral loyalty? An empirical analysis accounting for self-selecting members', International Journal of Research in Marketing, Vol 42, Iss 1, pp31–47.

55   Lederman, M.,2007, 'Do Enhancements to Loyalty Programs Affect Demand? The Impact of International Frequent Flyer Partnerships on Domestic Airline Demand', The RAND Journal of Economics, Vol, 38, Iss, 4, pp1134-1158.

Cairns and Galbraith (1990) [56] went as far as to argue that frequent flyer programs are so effective, they impede competition. Firstly, 'that frequent flyer schemes may generate switching costs for travellers' through the awarding of status tiers which confer benefits on the member which they would lose if they moved their business to another airline'. Secondly, 'the main strategic barriers to entry in air transport markets are the dominant airport presence by an airline, which might limit access to airport facilities, and the frequent-flyer programs, which are sunk costs that an entrant has to pay to compete with an incumbent. From the point of view of a potential entrant, frequent flyer programs reduce the expected demand on a certain route and therefore may impede a profitable service on that route'.

Lederman, and Cairns and Galbraith's, conclusions are supported by a real-world example which demonstrates just how effective loyalty programs can be. The Norwegian government perceived the frequent flyer program of the incumbent airline, SAS, to be so successful that they banned the earning of loyalty points on domestic routes for a period. In 1994, the government fully-deregulated the airline market to stimulate market competition against the incumbent SAS. The first new entrant, Colour Air, launched in 1998 but failed after just 13 months. According to a note provided by the competition authorities in Norway to the OECD on airline competition, 'an important reason for this was a lack of an attractive frequent flyer program that could compete with SAS' EuroBonus program'.[57] When a new competitor entered the market in 2002, the Norwegian competition authority banned earning points on the SAS frequent flyer program for all domestic routes for a five year period. This was extended indefinitely after the competition authority found it reasonable to assume that a reintroduction of loyalty programs in the Norwegian domestic airline sector would lead to business travellers choosing the airline with the most attractive program. They argued that business travel-

---

56   Cairns, R. & Galbraith, J., 1990, 'Artificial Compatibility, Barriers to Entry, and Frequent-Flyer Programs', Canadian Journal of Economics, Vol 23, Iss 1/2, pp807-816.

57   OECD, 2014, 'Airline Competition - Note by Norway,' Directorate For Financial And Enterprise Affairs - Competition Committee, http://www.oecd.org/officialdocuments/publicdisplaydocumentpdf/?cote=DAF/COMP/WD(2014)59&docLanguage=En, accessed 12 July 2020.

lers constitute the majority of those paying full price for tickets which could have significant consequences for an airline with the least attractive program. The ban was formally lifted in 2013 after it was considered that competition on domestic routes was significantly robust which resulted in lowered overall ticket prices for travellers. A bounce back could be seen on domestic airline seats sold by SAS after the ban was lifted.[58]

Duque (2017)[59] argued that loyalty programs lure consumers with different types of rewards, some of which can make exit costly. He stated, 'delayed rewards, such as points or miles, can trigger a lock-in problem. Once a consumer has started accumulating points with a provider, switching to a different provider implies losing the endowed progress to redeem the first provider's reward'. The loyalty psychology behind the endowed progress effect is discussed further in Chapter 5.

Reichheld (1996) found that loyalty programs can decrease the degree of sensitivity members have towards competing offers or prices,[60] which can prompt them to pay higher average prices for goods they usually purchase, buy them in higher quantity, or choose better quality products and more expensive brands. In a similar study, Nako (1997),[61] and Bolton et al. (2000),[62] argued that a loyalty program can serve to distract members' minds away from price and other negative evaluations of the company. By spending with a specific retailer more often and more frequently, the member may be confronted with

---

58   CAPA Centre For Aviation, 2016, 'SAS, Norwegian and Finnair. The Nordic three continue to carve out separate niches', https://centreforaviation.com/analysis/reports/sas-norwegian-and-finnair-the-nordic-three-continue-to-carve-out-separate-niches-267005, accessed 5 May 2020.

59   Duque, O. V., 2017, 'The Costs of Loyalty. On Loyalty Rewards and Consumer Welfare,' Economic Analysis of Law Review, Vol 8, No. 2, pp411-450.

60   Reichheld, F., 1996, 'The Loyalty Effect: The Hidden Force Behind Growth, Profits and Lasting Value', Harvard Business School Press.

61   Nako, S., 1997, 'Frequent flyer programs and business travellers: an empirical investigation', Logistics and Transportation Review, Vol 28, pp395–410.

62   Bolton, R., Kannan, P.K., & Bramlett, M., 2000, 'Implications of loyalty program membership and service experiences for customer retention and value', Journal of the Academy of Marketing Science, Vol 20, pp95-108.

competitors' prices less often. Due to being deprived of a comparison, loyalty program members may become less sensitive to higher prices, boosting company revenue and margins.

This was supported by McCaughey and Behrens (2011) who studied actual frequent flyer member flight behaviour in The Netherlands and found that members were willing to pay a price premium of up to six per cent, which could be directly attributable to their frequent flyer program participation.[63]

Basso et al (2009) also supported the idea that loyalty programs may reduce price competition, however, this was in the context of employers paying for employee flights. They presented a model which portrayed frequent flyer programs as efforts to exploit the agency relationship between employers (who pay for tickets) and employees (who book travel).[64] They argued that frequent flyer programs 'bribe' employees to book flights at higher prices in exchange for points (and other perks), with the airline program taking advantage of the fact that employees selecting an airline (or hotel, or car rental agency) will not necessarily have the right incentives to find the lowest possible price when the employer is paying the bill. Of interest, their model also indicated that, in a competitive environment, frequent flyer programs can lead to higher prices incurred by employers and lower profits for airlines, with the employees enjoying the benefits of increased value, meaning the program may not work the way the airline intended.

Chaudhuri et al (2019)[65] conducted an exhaustive review of 322 publicly traded firms that introduced a loyalty program between 2000 and 2015. They found that introducing a loyalty program could increase sales and gross profits within the first year, and these positive effects were sustained long term. They

63   McCaughey, N., & Behrens, C., 2011, 'Paying for Status? - The effect of frequent flyer program member status on airfare choice', Monash University Department of Economics.

64   Basso, L. J., Clements, M. T., & Ross, T.W., 2009, 'Moral Hazard and Customer Loyalty Programs,' American Economic Journal: Microeconomics, pp101-123.

65   Chaudhuri, M., Voorhees, C. M. & Beck, J. M., 2019, 'The effects of loyalty program introduction and design on short- and long-term sales and gross profits', Journal of the Academy of Marketing Science, Vol 47, pp640–658.

also found that programs offering status tiers or earning mechanisms could provide firms with significant increases in sales and gross profits. However, they identified one drawback; the effects on gross profits typically did not become significant until the second quarter after the loyalty program was introduced, and their overall impact on performance lagged substantially behind sales.

Liu (2007)[66] conducted a longitudinal data study of the loyalty program of an undisclosed convenience store franchise. The study demonstrated that members who were heavy buyers prior to joining a loyalty program were most likely to claim their qualified rewards, but the program did not prompt them to change their purchase behaviour. In contrast, members who were initially low or moderate buyers gradually purchased more and became more loyal to the company. In addition, the loyalty program broadened the light buyers' relationship with the company into other business areas.

A global retail loyalty sentiment report conducted by Nielsen (2006)[67] concluded that, 'Done well, loyalty programs can help drive more frequent visits and heavier purchasing. More than seven in 10 global respondents (72 per cent) agree that, all other factors equal, they will buy from a retailer with a loyalty program over one without'. The survey also found that '67 per cent (of respondents) agree that they shop more frequently and spend more at retailers with loyalty programs'.

Many other research studies have also concluded that loyalty programs work, demonstrating that:

- There are positive and significant relationships between loyalty programs, customer satisfaction and customer loyalty (Zakaria et al, 2014).[68]

---

66 Liu, Y., 2007, 'The Long-Term Impact of Loyalty Programs on Consumer Purchase Behavior and Loyalty', Journal of Marketing, 71 (4), 19-35.

67 Nielsen, 2016, 'Global Retail Loyalty Sentiment Report', https://www.nielsen.com/wp-content/uploads/sites/3/2019/04/nielsen-global-retail-loyalty-sentiment-report.pdf, accessed 27 July 2020.

68 Zakaria, I., Ab Rahman, B., Othman, A. K., Yunus, N. A. M., Dzulkipli, M. R. & Osman, M. A. F., 2014, 'The Relationship between Loyalty Program, Customer Satisfaction and Customer Loyalty in Retail Industry: A Case Study', Procedia

- Loyalty programs enhance customers' psychological bonding with service providers (Mattila, 2006).[69]

- Loyalty programs can cause consumers to engage in recursive purchases, which may lead to the development of habitual consumption, further increasing consumer purchases (Wood & Neal, 2009).[70]

- Loyalty programs are effective in increasing customers' perceptions of switching costs and thereby reducing churn (Bendapudi and Berry, 1997).[71]

Evidence that loyalty programs do not work

Research which indicates that loyalty programs typically do not (always) work includes a study by Skogland and Siguaw (2008).[72] They found that business travellers, who constitute a chief target of most hotel loyalty programs, were inclined to switch from one hotel to another even when they had been satisfied with their most recent stays. Furthermore, the results indicated that a strong relationship exists between involvement and loyalty, with the study suggesting that hoteliers should redirect the money spent on loyalty programs to applications that involve the guest emotionally connecting with the hotel, such as better employee training.

Vorhees et al (2015)[73] studied an unnamed major airline's loyalty program

- Social and Behavioral Sciences, Vol 129, pp23-30.

69   Mattila, A. S, 2006, 'How affective commitment boosts guest loyalty (and promotes frequent-guest programs)', Cornell Hotel and Restaurant Administration Quarterly, Vol 47, Iss 2, pp174 -181.

70   Wood, W., & Neal, D. T., 2007, 'A new look at habits and the habit-goal interface', Psychological Review, Vol 114, Iss 4, pp843–863.

71   Bendapudi, Neeli and Berry Leonard L., 1997, 'Customer Receptivity to Relationship Marketing,' Journal of Retailing, Vol 73, Iss 1, pp15-37.

72   Skogland, I., & Siguaw, J. A., 2004, 'Are you satisfied customers loyal? Cornell Hotel and Restaurant Administration Quarterly', Vol 45, Iss 3, pp221 -234.

73   Voorhees, C. M., White, R. C., McCall, M., & Randhawa, P., 2015, 'Fool's gold? Assessing the impact of the value of airline loyalty programs on brand equity perceptions and share of wallet', Cornell Hospitality Quarterly, Vol 56, Iss 2,

and concluded that the effect on share of wallet was significantly stronger for price-seeking customers who are prone to brand switching, but that the loyalty program had no direct effect on share of wallet for brand-loyal customers.

Sharp and Sharp (1997)[74] in a study of coalition loyalty program *Flybuys* , identified 'no across the board impact of *Flybuys* on loyalty patterns'. Specifically, for the coalition partners, they did find a 'trend towards excess loyalty for *Flybuys* brands, though for most it is disappointingly small'.

Ferguson and Hlavinka (2007)[75] analysed data from a 2006 loyalty census by COLLOQUY which identified that while there were 1.3 billion loyalty memberships in the US (12 programs per average household), active participation was just 39.5 per cent. They argued that low participation rates by millions of customer files in a database did not signify a successful loyalty strategy, noting that 'fat membership roles may look good in a press release, but active loyalty program members are the only members who count'. The active participation rate was characterised by COLLOQUY experts as 'dismal'.

Dowling and Uncles (1997)[76] conducted research which concluded that, in the majority of cases, all a customer loyalty program will do is cost a company money to provide more benefits to customers, but it is unlikely to significantly increase the relative proportion of loyal customers and company profitability.

Meyer-Warden and Benavent (2006) found that when all companies in an industry have loyalty programs,[77] the market is characterised by an absence of change of the competitive situation.

---

pp202–212.

74 Sharp, B. & Sharp, A., 1997, 'Loyalty Programs and their Impact on Repeat-purchase Loyalty Patterns', International Journal of Research in Marketing, Vol 14, No. 5, pp473-486.

75 Ferguson, R., & Hlavinka, K., 2007, 'The colloquy loyalty marketing census: Sizing up the US loyalty marketing industry, Journal of Consumer Marketing, Vol 24, pp313–321.

76 Dowling, G. R., & Uncles, M., 1997, 'Do customer loyalty programs really work?', Sloan Management Review, Vol 38, pp71–82.

77 Meyer-Warden, L., & Benavent, C., 2006, 'The Impact of Loyalty Programmes on Repeat Purchase Behaviour', Journal of Marketing Management, Vol 22, pp

A McKinsey study (2014)[78] of 55 publicly traded North American and European companies, showed that overall, companies which spend more on loyalty, or have more visible loyalty programs, grow at about the same rate, or slightly slower, than those that do not (4.4 vs 5.5 per cent per year since 2002). Specific to certain industries, McKinsey identified negative growth impact on airlines, car rentals and food retail, while a focus on loyalty had a positive impact on hotel growth. In terms of overall profitability, companies surveyed that had higher loyalty spend also had EBITDA margins that were about 10 per cent lower than companies in the same sectors that spent less on loyalty.

Caminal and Claici (2006) argued that rather than reinforcing firms' market power and negatively affecting consumer welfare, loyalty programs are 'business stealing' devices that tend to enhance competition by generating lower average transaction prices and higher consumer surplus.[79] They argued against Ledermann's position that the introduction or an enhancement of a frequent flyer program raises the airline's market share by enhancing the airline's market power. Their counterargument was that the use of frequent flyer programs may actually signal fiercer competition among airlines.

A 2015 Roy Morgan study of the Australian supermarket industry found little exclusive loyalty to supermarket brands.[80] When asked how many different major supermarkets they shopped at over the previous four weeks, 37 per cent of grocery-buyers reported shopping at two, 28 per cent said three and 7 per cent said they shopped at all four. Of the respondents who reported shopping typically at Woolworths (the market leader), just 25 per cent shopped exclusively there. For Coles (the main competitor), the comparative number

61-88.

78   Nadeau M-C., & Singer, M., 2014, 'Making loyalty pay: Six lessons from the innovators', McKinsey, https://www.mckinsey.com/business-functions/marketing-and-sales/our-insights/making-loyalty-pay-six-lessons-from-the-innovators, accessed 12 June 2020.

79   Caminal, R. & Claici, A., 2007, 'Are loyalty-rewarding pricing schemes anti-competitive?', International Journal of Industrial Organization, Vol 25, pp657-674.

80   Roy Morgan, 2015, 'Supermarket loyalty: what's that?', http://www.roymorgan.com/findings/6442-supermarket-loyalty-whats-that-201509072312, accessed 20 April 2019.

was 24 per cent. This is despite both companies having robust and highly patronised loyalty programs.

A similar study in the US by Zhang et al (2017)[81] showed that 83 per cent of shoppers visited between four and nine grocery stores over the course of a year, with less than 1 per cent remaining loyal to just one store. More than half shopped at an average of five to seven different stores, and 6 per cent shopped at ten or more.

*

With such a vast and contradictory body of research, what conclusions can be drawn? There appears to be substantial evidence to suggest that loyalty programs can indeed work to generate incremental acquisition, spend, retention, brand affinity and advocacy. There also appears to be evidence that loyalty programs do not always work to deliver the anticipated objectives.

The next chapter will utilise a separate set of questions to further interrogate the available research materials. Accepting there is sufficient evidence to suggest loyalty programs *can* work, under what circumstances *do* they work? And what are the essential design principles loyalty program designers should consider to increase a program's chances of success?

> **Key insights**
>
> - Academic and market research about loyalty programs is vast and often contradictory.
>
> - There is substantial evidence to suggest that loyalty programs can work to generate incremental acquisition, spend, retention, brand affinity and advocacy. Further studies indicate that loyalty programs can reduce price competition where members become less sensitive to higher prices, boosting revenue and margins whilst reducing churn.

---

81   Zhang, Q.,Gangwar, M. & Seetharaman, P., 2017, 'Polygamous Store Loyalties: An Empirical Investigation', Journal of Retailing, Vol 93, Iss 4, pp477-492.

- There is also evidence that loyalty programs do not always work to deliver the anticipated objectives. Research studies have shown that members are inclined to switch brands regardless of the existence of a loyalty program. Some studies also show that loyalty programs may cost a company money without positively impacting company growth.

Suggested reading

- Meyer-Waarden, L., 2008, 'The influence of loyalty programme membership on customer purchase behaviour', European Journal of Marketing, Vol 42, Iss 1/2, pp87-114.

- Lederman, M.,2007, 'Do Enhancements to Loyalty Programs Affect Demand? The Impact of International Frequent Flyer Partnerships on Domestic Airline Demand', The RAND Journal of Economics, Vol, 38, Iss, 4, pp1134-1158.

- OECD, 2014, 'Airline Competition - Note by Norway', Directorate For Financial And Enterprise Affairs - Competition Committee, http://www.oecd.org/officialdocuments/publicdisplaydocumentp df/?cote=DAF/COMP/WD(2014)59&docLanguage=En

- Liu, Y. 2007, "The Long-Term Impact of Loyalty Programs on Consumer Purchase Behavior and Loyalty," Journal of Marketing, 71 (4), 19-35.

- Skogland, I., & Siguaw, J. A., 2004, 'Are your satisfied customers loyal? Cornell Hotel and Restaurant Administration Quarterly', Vol 45, Iss 3, pp221 -234.

- Voorhees, C. M., White, R. C., McCall, M., & Randhawa, P., 2015, 'Fool's gold? Assessing the impact of the value of airline loyalty programs on brand equity perceptions and share of wallet', Cornell Hospitality Quarterly, Vol 56, Iss 2, pp202–212.

CHAPTER 4

LOYALTY & REWARD CO'S ESSENTIAL EIGHT™

'Simplicity is the ultimate sophistication'

- Leonardo da Vinci

Focus areas

This chapter will address the following questions:

- Accepting loyalty programs *can* work, under what circumstances *do* they work?

- What design principles should loyalty program designers and operators embrace to increase a program's chances of success?

THE OVERARCHING DESIGN objective of a loyalty program is to generate member engagement. By definition, this means to 'establish a meaningful contact or connection with' and 'occupy or attract someone's interest or attention'.[82]

Vivek et al (2014)[83] reported that the positive consequences of generating

---

82   Oxford Dictionary, https://www.oxfordlearnersdictionaries.com/definition/american_english/engage, accessed 12 June 2020.

83   Shiri D. Vivek, Sharon E. Beatty & Robert M. Morgan, 2012, 'Customer Engagement: Exploring Customer Relationships Beyond Purchase', Journal of Marketing Theory and Practice, Vol 20, Iss 2, pp122-146.

customer engagement include increases in value, trust, affective commitment, word of mouth, loyalty and brand community involvement.

It is therefore important to identify the essential principles of a best-practice loyalty program which will ensure it remains consistently engaging.

Combining insights from loyalty academic research, consumer psychology, and the industry experience of the Loyalty & Reward Co team (including joining and studying hundreds of loyalty programs globally), eight essential loyalty principles have been identified.

Loyalty & Reward Co's Essential Eight™ are Simple, Valuable, Stimulating, Emotional, Complementary, Differentiating, Cost-effective and Evolving.

Principle 1: Simple

In the current age, customer experience (CX) plays a vital role in whether a customer will decide to keep doing business with a brand. A 2017 Gartner survey[84] found that by 2019, 81 per cent of marketers responsible for CX said they expected their company to be competing mostly or completely on the basis of CX. As mentioned in Chapter 1, companies like Netflix, Amazon, Uber and Spotify have CX as the central focus of their strategic product and service evolution, alongside Google, Microsoft, Samsung and other heavyweights.

In a survey of 15,750 consumers across nine countries, Siegel & Gale (2018)[85] found that 55 per cent of respondents were willing to pay more for simpler experiences, while 64 per cent of respondents were more likely to recommend a brand because it provided simpler experiences and communications.

---

84   Gartner Research, 2017, 'Customer Experience in Marketing Survey 2017'.

85   Siegal & Gale, 2018, 'The World's Simplest Brands; 2018-2019,' https://simplicityindex.com/2018/region/global/, accessed 8 May 2020.

Their research over eight years identified that 'simplicity inspires deeper trust and strengthens loyalty' and that 'simplicity drives financial gain for brands willing to embrace it'.

Bombaij and Dekimpe (2020)[86] found in their extensive study of European grocery brands that those retailers utilising a basic loyalty program which provided direct and immediate rewards enjoyed a benefit, however this positive effect disappeared in instances where the brand was operating a more complex progressive-reward system. They attributed this to the negative effect of complexity found in loyalty program adoption identified by Demoulin and Zidda (2009).[87]

A best-practice loyalty program is simple to join, simple to understand and simple to engage with.

Simple to join

With a near-saturation amount of loyalty programs offered within most industries, member acquisition strategies should be focused on making it as simple as possible for a customer to join. This is because any perceived barrier-to-entry is likely to have a negative impact on member base growth.

KPMG's The Truth About Loyalty Report (2019)[88] indicated that 69 per cent of Millennials agree that most programs are too difficult to join and/or earn rewards, indicating program operators need to try harder to simplify the registration process, which may include providing multiple channel options for members to join.

One design challenge is that the join process is a crucial step to capture

---

86   Bombaij, N., & Dekimpe, M., 2020. 'When do loyalty programs work? The moderating role of design, retailer-strategy, and country characteristics'. International Journal of Research in Marketing, 37(1), 175-195.

87   Demoulin, N.T.M., and, Zidda, P., 2009, 'Drivers of customers' adoption and adoption timing of a new loyalty card in the grocery retail market', Journal of Retailing, Vol 85, Iss 3, pp391-405.

88   KPMG, 2019, 'The Truth About Loyalty Report,' https://assets.kpmg/content/dam/kpmg/xx/pdf/2019/11/customer-loyalty-report.pdf, accessed 10 June 2019.

member personal data. That data, such as the member's name, email address, mobile phone number, date of birth and gender, can be critical in tailoring the member's experience to stimulate early engagement with the program, but it also presents a risk. The customer may not wish to share such personal information, or they may feel apathetic about filling in a form.

Best-practice approaches utilise balance. This means having the marketing discipline to request the minimal amount of information required to operate the program. While it is tempting to ask for more, companies should identify what information is actually needed (e.g., does the program really need the member's mailing address?) and what can be accessed post registration (e.g., transaction data which can be used to identify the member's preferred products). It can also be useful to clarify to the member why the information is being requested (e.g., 'your date of birth will allow us to send you a birthday gift'). Information should only be captured if it can be used to enhance the member's experience as a pathway to driving deeper engagement.

Providing multiple options for members to join a program can be useful, as it increases the likelihood the member has the option to join via a channel convenient to them. This could be in-store, online, via app or over the phone.

Two-step join processes can be challenging, such as programs which provide a membership card in-store and require the member to complete their registration online. Industry insight suggests completion rates can be low for many of these programs (due to the member forgetting, being apathetic or losing their card), and the company has no opportunity to contact them to provide a reminder. A better approach involves the member submitting their email address or mobile number in store to commence the registration process. They can then be reminded or incentivised via email or text message to complete the registration process online if they do not.

Increasingly, companies are structuring loyalty programs around smartphones, with the member required to download an app to join the program. This has its advantages; by the end of 2020, 78 per cent of the world's population were smartphone users[89], with apps providing the ability to deliver a

---

89 Statistica, 'Smartphones - statistics & facts', https://www.statista.com/

rich and convenient member experience. It also has its challenges; the average consumer in the US, South Korea, Japan and Australia has over 100 apps on their smartphone[90], making it increasingly difficult to convince new members to download yet another app as an essential step to joining their program.

Vans Family

Customers of Vans, the 1966 skateboarding company which evolved into the world's largest youth culture brand, can join Vans Family loyalty program simply by providing their email address in store when they transact. New members are then sent an email requesting that they complete the registration process online at www.vans.com[91]

Once the member has provided their email address in store, they are considered a Vans Family Member and they can start earning points for product purchases at Vans Stores (even without completing their registration) and online at www.vans.com.

For complete access to all available benefits, the member must complete their registration, providing an incentive for them to finish the process.

Simple to understand

As a loyalty program increases in complexity, program operators may be challenged to keep it simple enough to make sense to members. A coffee drinker joining a coffee card program can understand very quickly how the program works; buy a coffee, earn a stamp; buy 10 coffees, get a free coffee. By contrast, some coalition loyalty programs are incredibly complex; members can earn points at different earn rates across hundreds of partners, and redeem points

---

topics/840/smartphones/#topicOverview, accessed 24 April 2023.

90   App Annie, 'The state of mobile 2020,' https://www.appannie.com/en/go/state-of-mobile-2020/, accessed 10 June 2020.

91   Vans Family, Terms and Conditions, https://www.vans.com/family/terms-conditions.html, access 20 June 2020.

on travel, gift cards, consumer goods, retail outlets, experiences, charity donations and more.

While a program should be simple to join, understand and engage with, that does not mean it cannot be complex in design. Success requires the operator educating new members about the most essential elements as part of the join and onboarding process.

Post-join, advanced data analytics can play a critical role in maintaining simplicity; identifying the earn and redemption options a specific member is most likely to be interested in, and using personalised marketing communications to persuade them to engage more broadly.

Southwest Airlines Rapid Rewards

Rapid Rewards[92] members can earn points from hundreds of different earn partners, presenting a challenge to the program when trying to explain how it works in simple terms to new and existing members.

To make it more understandable, Southwest Airlines have divided their earn partners into five major, easily digestible categories (credit cards, travel, shop and dine, home and lifestyle, and specialty), and have designed icons for each category. This makes it simpler for members to research where they can earn points.

When members receive their monthly statement or visit the website to view their recent rewards activity, the major category icon for which they earned the points is presented as a line item in the report with the number of points earned calculated and totalled.

Members can easily filter and explore categories where they have earned points and where they are missing out, encouraging them to self-educate on ways to access more value from the program.

---

92   Southwest Airlines, Rapid Rewards, https://www.southwest.com/html/rapidrewards/partners/credit-cards/southwest-airlines-rapid-rewards-cards/index.html, accessed 26 June 2020.

Simple to engage with

Stauss et al (2005)[93] conducted research on frustrations associated with loyalty programs which identified a number of issues where engagement was not simple, including qualification barriers (where the reward is tied to conditions that are difficult or impossible to fulfil), inaccessibility (where members fulfil the conditions, but are unable to access the reward or program benefit) and redemption costs (the rewards can only be accessed by investing additional material or mental costs).

Best-practice execution involves ensuring the member experience across all touchpoints and life-stages is as simple and frictionless as possible, making the earning and accessing of value an effortless process. It is also important that it aligns to the preferred engagement styles of the target segment. For many companies, this may require utilising independent external consultants who can impartially audit the experience.

Albertson's Rewards

The US supermarket Albertson's simplified their rewards program so that members earn points for transacting across Albertson chains and partners without having to scan their Club Card. Instead, members earn automatically when purchasing through the app or website. They can also identify in-store simply by quoting their phone number.

Members earn 100 points translating into 1 'reward'. Members can accumulate rewards and redeem for a small selection of free everyday grocery items (including eggs (2 rewards), cheese (2 rewards), 24pk water (2 rewards), milk (3 rewards), salad kit (3 rewards) or rotisserie chicken (5 rewards), or they can accumulate rewards and redeem for a discount off the bill (1 reward = $1 off).

These small but consistent rewards resonate strongly with

---

93   Stauss, B., Schmidt, M., & Schoeler, A, 2005, 'Customer frustration in loyalty programs', International Journal of Service Industry Management, Vol 16, Iss 3, pp229–252.

customers, who perceive they are receiving regular bonuses which can be redeemed without much effort (making a simple choice whether to redeem now or on another visit). This makes it remarkably simple to engage with the program.

Principle 2: Valuable

Valuable is arguably the most important principle of Loyalty & Reward Co's Essential Eight™. A member will join a program because of the promise of value. And the member will continue to engage with the program if they perceive they are accessing value.

Value can mean different things to different members. Primarily, it will relate to some type of financial benefit (discounts, free products or services, bonus products, etc), but it may also involve access (to member lounges or exclusive events), priority service (boarding first or being served first via exclusive queues), surprise and delight gifts, price protection (cashback if a purchased price reduced in price within a specific timeframe) or education courses (particularly in B2B programs).

Many loyalty programs exist where a large percentage of the member base have partially or fully disengaged because members no longer perceive there is meaningful value to be gained. The member unsubscribes from marketing, the plastic card is thrown in the (recycling) bin, the app is deleted. A disengaged member is a poor outcome for a brand, even worse than a non-member. With non-members, there is a chance they can be encouraged to join, but a disengaged member is very difficult to win back.

The academic research refers extensively to the delivery of value as an essential principle.

Henderson et al (2011)[94] indicated that in order to form a habit, behaviour must be repeated, and the behaviour must be rewarding enough to sustain the supporting intention.

Stauss et al (2005) identified that the inability to access value, via rewards, was a key source of multiple frustrations which leads to program disengagement (or avoidance).

Nunes and Drèze (2006)[95] argued that a successful loyalty program ensures that members feel they are progressing towards a reward outcome (in this case, a reward). The program should also provide members with access to rewards they would not generally splurge on with their own money to stimulate excitement about the program and generate pleasant associations with the brand.

Wansink (2003)[96] identified best-practice as including the continual refinement of benefits to make them relevant for members.

Value is also important in developing customer 'stickiness'. This is where customers maintain their relationship with a company in a competitive environment because of the perception they are accessing a consistently better value transaction. Duque (2017) [97] argued that loyalty program rewards can make exit costly, where switching to a different program implies losing the endowed progress to redeem the first provider's reward.

An example of a switching cost is where a member of a hotel program in a high tier (e.g., Platinum or Diamond), considers switching their affiliation to a different hotel chain, but is reluctant to do so because they will lose access to the executive lounge, complimentary room upgrades, bonus points and other perks.

---

94   Henderson, C. M., Beck J. T. & Palmatier, R. W, 2011, 'Review of the theoretical underpinnings of loyalty programs', Journal of Consumer Psychology, Vol 21, pp256–276.

95   Nunes, J. C. and Drèze, X., 2006, 'Your Loyalty Program Is Betraying You,' Harvard Business Review, https://hbr.org/2006/04/your-loyalty-program-is-betraying-you, accessed 2 Feb 2020.

96   Wansink, B., 2003, 'Developing a cost-effective brand loyalty program', Journal of Advertising Research, Vol 43, Iss 3, pp301-309.

97   Duque, O. V., 2017, 'The Costs of Loyalty. On Loyalty Rewards and Consumer Welfare,' Economic Analysis of Law Review, Vol 8, No 2, pp411-450.

AMC Stubs

AMC Stubs is a program with options for every movie fan.[98] All members earn points when they spend which accumulate towards US$5 rewards vouchers, in addition to ongoing free large popcorn refills, giving all members a sense of value and momentum.

Members can join at three levels; Insider (free), Premiere (US$15 per annum) and A-List (US$19.95-$23.95 per month depending on location), where the relationship between members and AMC products is expanded at every level.

A-List members can enjoy three free movies each week across any format (including IMAX® and Dolby Cinema), free online reservations, 10 per cent back on food and drink purchases (in the form of points), free size upgrades and refills on popcorn and drinks, and priority lanes at the box office and concessions.

Premiere members enjoy all the same perks except for the three free movies per week.

According to Business Insider, in 2019 AMC Stubs had signed up more than 50m moviegoers in the US, penetrating 20m households, a testament to the attractive value provided. This included 800,000 A-List subscribers.

To validate the critical importance of Valuable as a best-practice principle, it is worth considering the reaction of highly engaged members when value is taken from the program.

Dunkin' Donuts Dunkin' Rewards

In October 2022, Dunkin Donuts announced a revamp and name change for its loyalty program DD Perks.

'When we set out to improve DD Perks, we asked our members what they wanted to see in a new program. They told us three

---

98   AMC Theatres, AMC Stubs, https://www.amctheatres.com/amcstubs, accessed 15 July 2020.

things: flexibility, variety, and recognition,' said Scott Murphy, head of the beverage-snack category and president at Dunkin'. 'And we did just that – we solved the three biggest constraints to bring a new and improved customer experience to Dunkin' fans.'[99]

Unfortunately for Dunkin' Donuts, member seized on a more important principle; value. Soon after the relaunch of the program, social media was flooded with complaints by members who had crunched the number to determine significant value erosion.

According to a Rolling Stone article, on member identified that '(before) you would spend $40 and automatically receive a coupon that could be redeemed for a drink of any size available on the menu, minus luxury additions like whip cream or cold foam. With Dunkin' Rewards... you have to spend $70 for a free espresso or cold brew, and a whopping $90 to earn a signature latte.'[100]

The uproar about the program changes was picked up by media around the globe, causing significant brand damage to Dunkin' Donuts and likely the loss of many loyal members.

99   Dunkin Donuts press release,)ctoner 2022, "A NEW WAY TO RUN WITH DUNKIN'®: DUNKIN' REWARDS™ ROLLS OUT NATIONWIDE" https://news.dunkindonuts.com/news/dunkin-rewards accessed 6 July 2023

100 Klee, M, October 2022, "Dunkin' Coffee Drinkers Are in Revolt After Changes to Rewards Program", https://www.rollingstone.com/culture/culture-news/dunkin-coffee-drinkers-revolt-rewards-program-1234608420/ accessed 6 July 2023

Principle 3: Stimulating

It is not enough to simply launch a program and expect members will engage with it. Best-practice execution requires investment in making the program stimulating, thereby encouraging discovery and developing an enthusiasm for regular engagement.

In truth, there are far too many mundane loyalty programs in the world.

There are numerous approaches which can make a program more stimulating.

Nunes and Drèze (2006) highlighted that providing members with a sense they are progressing towards an outcome (a sense of momentum) is critical. Their research on the endowed progress effect (explored in Chapter 5) identified that members provided with artificial advancement toward a goal will exhibit greater persistence toward reaching the goal. It is important to communicate the progress to the member, which can be successfully achieved via progress trackers. Such a visual tool shows members how they are advancing towards their next reward by displaying points/miles/stamps accumulated and the amount required to get to a specific reward on a linear pathway.

Nunes and Drèze also emphasised providing members with aspirational rewards they would not generally splurge on with their own money can stimulate excitement about the program and generate pleasant associations with the brand.

The goal gradient effect[101] (explored in Chapter 5), which states the tendency to approach a goal increases with proximity to the goal, is also relevant

---

101 Hull, C., 1934, 'The rats' speed of locomotion gradient in approach to food', Journal of Comparative Psychology, Vol 17, pp393-422.

here. Loyalty program members can be stimulated to engage more with a brand as they get closer to unlocking a reward via targeted campaigns which support them to reach their goal more quickly.

McCall et al (2010) recommended capturing data on members that can be used to better meet their needs. While this may seem obvious, few companies do it well. Best-practice loyalty programs construct and send individualised communications to members across a variety of channels, then track responses and evolve future communications to optimise engagement potential. This may be via artificial intelligence (AI) or machine-learning platforms; their ability to automatically send individualised communications to members across a variety of channels makes them highly effective, as they deliver relevance at the optimal time, a key stimulation strategy.

Gamification (the application of game mechanics in a non-game context) can be used in very sophisticated ways in loyalty programs. Applied intelligently, gamifying a program can support the stimulation of a wide range of desirable member behaviours, including sharing of personal data (to support analytical modelling and hyper-personalised communications), advocacy and referrals (to grow the member base and promote tactical offers), and incremental visits and spend.

Many app-based programs are utilising digital games to stimulate engagement by offering prizes for competing stages or winning levels. Games can be used to boost promotions, align with product launches or brand initiatives, educate customers and drive referrals. Games can be simple, like spinning, shaking, scratching, guessing or sharing to win a prize. More advanced games can have members playing for hours.

Games and gamification approaches are discussed in Chapter 9.

Timing can be of critical importance when stimulating members to act, react or engage in certain ways. Working out when members need to be stimulated and strategically injecting a stimulation tactic is an optimal approach to influencing behaviour.

Other approaches for stimulating member engagement will be explored through the remaining chapters.

Progress Trackers

Subway, TacoBell, Krispy Kreme, Dunkin Donuts/ McDonalds and Dairy Queen are global quick service restaurant (QSR) brands that operate loyalty programs featuring quality progress trackers within their apps to clearly communicate to members their momentum towards unlocking a reward.

The Dunkin Donuts Dunkin' Rewards program[102] use different colours and sections within the same tab to distinguish between Offers (blue), Loyalty bonus points offers (pink) and Loyalty vouchers (orange). Every $1 spent contributes to progressing towards the next loyalty voucher. Endowed progress is clearly communicated to increase member motivation to reach the next reward.

Burger King Whopper Detour Campaign

Running in December 2019, Burger King's Whopper Detour Campaign targeted members who had downloaded the Burger King app with an offer to buy a Whopper for 1 cent whenever they were within 600 feet of a McDonald's store.

Geofencing technology within the app would trigger an automated push notification to app users when they were within 600 feet of their biggest competitor. Once the offer was activated, members had to redeem it within one hour, with the app also providing directions to their nearest Burger King restaurant.

The campaign drove 1.5 million app downloads (becoming #1 in the US) and 500,000 Whopper redemptions, with mobile sales tripling during the promotion, and continuing at double the rate after the campaign. Campaign return on investment (ROI) was recorded at 37:1 as a result of stimulating members to change their behaviour with the right offer at the right time through the right channel.[103]

---

102 Dunkin Donuts, https://www.dunkindonuts.com/en/dunkinrewards, accessed 14 June 2023.

103 Schmitt, G., Contagious, 'The strategy behind Burger King's Whopper Detour campaign', https://www.contagious.com/news-and-views/

Principle 4: Emotional

Developing an emotional connection between a customer and a brand generates many positive outcomes; a willingness to pay more, stronger commitment, word of mouth promotion, and true loyalty[104].

Loyal members that have formed emotional connections with a brand will continue to purchase over a long period of time and across various product lines, and are more resistant to discounts and promotions from competitors[105].

Academic research highlights the importance of developing emotional connections as part of an effective loyalty program.

Henderson et al (2011) argued that, among other things, loyalty program induced change to consumer behaviour typically results from conferring status to consumers (which generates favourable comparisons with others) and developing relationships (which results in more favourable treatment by consumers). This manifests into two important emotions which support the development of loyalty; feelings of exclusivity and belonging.

A loyalty program which provides members with a feeling of exclusivity and belonging stands to play a central role in members adopting the brand (sub consciously or otherwise) as an element of their own self-definition.

Tajfel (1978) [106] proposed social identity theory, whereby a person's sense

burger-king-whopper-detour-strategy-cannes-interview, accessed 14 June 2023.

104 Veloutsou, C., 2015, 'Brand evaluation, satisfaction and trust as predictors of brand loyalty: the mediator-moderator effect of brand relationships', Journal of Consumer Marketing, Vol 32, Iss 6, pp405-421.

105 KPMG, 2019, 'The Truth About Loyalty Report,' https://assets.kpmg/content/dam/kpmg/xx/pdf/2019/11/customer-loyalty-report.pdf, accessed 12 June 2020.

106 Tajfel, H. & Turner, J. C., 1978, 'An Integrative Theory of Intergroup Conflict', The social psychology of intergroup relations, pp33-47.

of who they are is based on their membership of different groups. He determined that groups give individuals a sense of social identity and a sense of belonging to the social world. This can extend to membership of loyalty programs. Social identity theory is explored further in Chapter 5.

Söderlund (2019)[107] ran an experiment to determine if labelling customers as 'member' versus 'non-member' in the context of a company's loyalty program can influence the customers' evaluations of the brand. He found that evoking member status resulted in a higher level of sense of belonging and higher customer satisfaction. He also confirmed that the customer association with being a member was directly linked to a sense of belonging and satisfaction.

Brands can build emotional connections via the development of communities. A study by Zheng et al (2015)[108] found that social networking tools (such as Facebook Fan Pages) have enormous potential for enhancing brand loyalty by encouraging engagement behaviours amongst communities.

Communities do not need to be online. Harley Davidson turned their business around in the 1980's by focusing on building a brand community of ardent consumers organised around the lifestyle, activities, and ethos of the brand.[109] This included the development of a company-community relationship strategy through the Harley Owners Group (H.O.G.) membership club, where community-building activities were treated not just as marketing expenses but as company-wide investments in the success of the business model.

McCall et al's (2010)[110] guiding principles for designing an effective pro-

107 Söderlund, M., 2019, 'Can the label 'member' in a loyalty program context boost customer satisfaction?', The International Review of Retail, Distribution and Consumer Research, Vol 29, Iss 3, pp340-35.

108 Zheng, Xiabing & Cheung, Christy & Lee, Matthew & Liang, Liang, 2015), 'Building brand loyalty through user engagement in online brand communities in social networking sites', Information Technology & People, Vol 28, pp90-106.

109 Fournier, S. and Lee, L., 2009, 'Getting Brand Communities Right,' Harvard Business Review, Vol 87, Iss 4, pp105-111.

110 McCall, M., Voorhees, C., Calantone, R., 2010, 'Building Customer Loyalty: Ten Principles for Designing an Effective. Customer Reward Program', Cornell Hospitality Report, Vol 10, No 9.

gram feature the development of emotional engagement at the top of their list. 'Loyalty is more than repeat purchases, and programs must evolve to foster a deeper emotional connection between the customer and firms'.

Brands can also build emotional engagement with a member via surprise and delight campaigns. Berman[111] reported significantly higher levels of loyalty from delighted versus satisfied customers. 'Other potential positive consequences of delight include lower costs due to increased word-of-mouth promotion, lower selling and advertising costs, lower customer acquisition costs, higher revenues due to higher initial and repeat sales, and long-term strategic advantages due to increased brand equity and increased ability to withstand new entrants.' The psychology of surprise and delight is covered in Chapter 5.

Naked Wines

Naked Wines[112] have built their brand around the delivery of unique and personalised experiences at scale. The central tenet of Naked Wines proposition is the Angel member. Angels help a network of smaller, talented winemakers to make wines by providing them with guaranteed sales via a distribution channel that delivers a reasonable margin. Angels support the winemakers by depositing as little as $40 per month into their Naked Wines account towards their next order. The money can be spent on any wine whenever the Angel wants. In return, Angels save at least 25 per cent on each order.

Naked Wines encourage their Angels to download their app, which automatically loads the member's order history. This makes it easy and engaging for Angels to rate and review the wines they have tasted and makes them feel part of an exclusive community. After submitting reviews, Angels often receive personal responses from each of the winemakers, thanking them for their feedback.

---

111 Berman, B., 2005, 'How to delight your customers,' California Management Review, Vol 48, Iss 1, pp129-151.
112 Naked Wines, https://www.nakedwines.com.au/, accessed 26 June 2020.

On their birthday, members can receive an email from Naked Wines with a link to a video of one of their favourite winemakers singing Happy Birthday. Generally, this is accompanied by a free bottle of their most highly rated wine as a present. This personalised package works to generate emotional connections with the Naked Wines brand and the winemakers, further fostering loyalty and a willingness to continue to spend with them.

Jeep Badge Of Honor

Launched in 2013, the Jeep Badge Of Honor program[113] is based around its brand-sponsored mobile app for Jeep owners. The program awards physical badges to members who complete off-road trails across the United States. Members use the app to find new trails, track where they've been, upload photos of their adventure, or interact with tens of thousands of their Jeep community friends.

Jeep owners publicly display their 'Badges of Honor' on their cars as a symbol of pride. This is a key program design element which has heavily contributed to the success of the ever-increasing Jeep micro-community.

While the badges are the program's primary benefit, they are not the only thing members can earn. Members can also earn points by posting photos of their trail experiences to the app, and commenting on pictures others have posted.

Those who check in for a trail receive 200 points, while posting a photo is worth 20 points and each comment earns 10 points.

As members accumulate points they also progress through the ranks, another fun way to show off within the Jeep off-roading community.

This program is successful because it is simple, it uses gamified collectible badges as rewards which carry trophy value, it creates a

---

113 Jeep, https://www.jeep.com/badge-of-honor.html, accessed 11 May 2023.

sense of exclusivity and belonging with its tiering structure (label-ling members as trail Commanders, Pro's or Experts), and it is based around community participation, all of which work to drive deep emotional connections with members.[114]

Principle 5: Complementary

For a loyalty program to be meaningful to customers, it needs to be contextu-ally relevant. This can be achieved by designing it to be complementary to the brand positioning.

Wansink (2003) [115] indicated that rewards should directly build loyalty in the consumer by supporting the proposition of the brand.

Nunes and Drèze (2006)[116] reported that effective brands utilise their loy-alty programs to introduce members to new products. An example is a grocery home delivery company which provides members with free product samples and complementary recipes, thereby reinforcing the brand's personality.

Stauss et al (2005)[117] identified 'defocusing' as a key source of member frus-tration, whereby there is a perception that the company has wrongly focused its priorities on the loyalty program instead of on the core service offering. Providing members with poor service while simultaneously rewarding them

114 Lyons, S., 2021, Jeep Badge Of Honour master the micro-community, Loyalty & Reward Co, https://loyaltyrewardco.com/jeep-badge-of-honor-master-the-micro-community/, accessed 11 May 2023.

115 Wansink, B., 2003, 'Developing a cost-effective brand loyalty program', Journal of Advertising Research, Vol 43, Iss 3, pp301-309.

116 Nunes, J. C. and Drèze, X., 2006, 'Your Loyalty Program Is Betraying You,' Harvard Business Review, https://hbr.org/2006/04/your-loyalty-program-is-betray-ing-you, accessed 2 Feb 2020.

117 Stauss, B., Schmidt, M., & Schoeler, A., 2005, 'Customer frustration in loyalty pro-grams', International Journal of Service Industry Management, Vol 16, Iss 3, pp229–252.

with loyalty benefits (with messages that reinforce how much they are valued) can be perceived as contradictory, not complementary. One opportunity for loyalty program operators within a company is to establish themselves as the voice of the customer, building a feedback loop which shines a spotlight on sub-standard areas, and conveys a clear message to stakeholders that fixing the identified problem will serve to grow member loyalty (or at least reduce churn).

Multiple market research studies conducted by Loyalty & Reward Co across a range of industries has consistently ascertained a need by members for contextual fit. This includes members reporting that they would be less likely to remember program benefits if there was a perceived lack of correlation with the brand, and analytical evidence to support this insight.

MECCA Beauty Loop

MECCA Beauty Loop[118] is an example of a loyalty program which successfully complements the brand. Beauty Loop provides members with sample-filled boxes of beauty products four times a year. The higher the status tier, the better the quality of samples provided in the box. Beauty Loop members collect their Beauty Loop boxes instore or when placing an order online, ensuring members visit at least four times a year, providing MECCA with the opportunity to educate and upsell to members.

Higher tier members can access complimentary makeup applications for when they have a big social event or a date night, plus a free birthday gift each year and surprise periodic bonus gifts which are all cosmetics related and all complimentary.

The commercial model is effective for MECCA; the beauty brands supply the samples for free as a way of reaching highly engaged target customers.

Although the beauty products stocked by MECCA can mostly be bought directly through the individual brands, from large

---

118 MECCA, Beauty Loop, https://www.mecca.com.au/beauty-loop.html, accessed 26 June 2020.

department stores or other boutique beauty stores, the Beauty Loop boxes keep members purchasing from MECCA, even though MECCA are known not to offer discounts.

The regular rewarding of the member base with samples complements MECCA's promotional advertising, encourages members to spend on new products, and stimulates a reciprocating response from members in the form of loyalty to the brand.

Principle 6: Differentiating

An observable loyalty program phenomenon is the tendency for competing companies in the same industry to mimic each other's design approaches, so they all end up with very similar programs. Consider the similarities amongst loyalty programs within the airline, hotel, car rental, cinema, cosmetics and fashion retail industries.

McCall et al (2010)[119] postulated that the actual components and structure of most loyalty programs appear to be driven more by what the competition is offering rather than demonstrated effectiveness.

Capizzi et al (2003)[120] discussed a focus group study conducted by COLLOQUY in the hotel loyalty industry which identified that once branding and logos were removed from the rewards catalogues, members could not tell the difference between the different programs.

119 McCall, M., Voorhees, C., Calantone, R., 2010, 'Building Customer Loyalty: Ten Principles for Designing an Effective Customer Reward Program', Cornell Hospitality Report, Vol 10, No 9.

120 Capizzi, M., Ferguson, R. & Cuthbertson, R., 2003, 'Loyalty trends for the 21st century', Journal of Targeting, Measurement and Analysis for Marketing, Vol 12, pp199–212.

Berman (2006)[121], warned of the pitfall of market saturation. 'In many mature markets such as hotel, airline, and credit card programs, competing firms offer loyalty programs with similar membership provisions, purchase requirements, and benefits. In instances where a firm is first to introduce a loyalty program, the gains may be short run since competitors are typically able to quickly introduce a similar or perhaps even better program.'

Berman used United Airlines as an example, who in 1981 launched a competing program just weeks after American Airlines launched the first frequent flyer program, a caution against the commoditisation of a loyalty currency.

Nunes and Drèze (2006)[122] warned against creating a new commodity, which can generate a risk of being 'drawn into the equivalent of a price war, with tit-for-tat competitive moves basically yielding parity and lower profitability all around'. They provided the example of United Airlines, who launched an aggressive campaign against Northwest Airlines by targeting certain customers with double miles offers. Northwest quickly matched the offer for a limited period. United then extended the offer further, which according to Nunes and Drèze simply encouraged price shopping.

McCall et al (2010)[123] recommended developing points of differentiation in order to position the program against the competition. They also acknowledged that program differentiation may be the single biggest challenge facing loyalty program managers as there are only so many ways to differentiate a program, hence the need for expert loyalty consultants to support program design.

Ha (2007)[124] found that a loyalty program that is distinctive relative to

121 Berman, B., 2006, 'Developing an effective customer loyalty program', California Management Review, Vol 49, Iss 1, p123.

122 Nunes, J. C. and Drèze, X., 2006, 'Your Loyalty Program Is Betraying You,' Harvard Business Review, https://hbr.org/2006/04/your-loyalty-program-is-betraying-you, accessed 2 Feb 2020.

123 McCall, M., Voorhees, C., Calantone, R. 2010, 'Building Customer Loyalty: Ten Principles for Designing an Effective Customer Reward Program', Cornell Hospitality Report, Vol 10, No 9.

124 Ha, S. 2007, 'How customer loyalty programs can influence relational marketing outcomes: Using customer-retailer identification to build relationships,' The

other programs can lead the member to produce more favourable responses to the brand. Ha hypothesised that when the success and/or distinctiveness of the group is apparent, people are more likely to associate themselves with the group as a means to distinguish themselves from others and bolster their self-esteem in social contexts. Their study showed that a distinctive customer loyalty program can make the members of the program value their membership more than other less distinctive programs.

A differentiated loyalty program can positively contribute to the value equation in a way that conventional discounting cannot do. In industries prone to having everyone rush to the same space, the opportunity arises for a smart company to gain market share by doing something completely different. In highly homogenised industries, a differentiated loyalty program can provide a sustainable competitive advantage which can help companies gain valuable market share.

Avis and Budget

The rental car industry is highly homogenised, with the top companies all providing similar products, service, and experiences. One case study provides insight into how a differentiated loyalty program can deliver significant market share gains.

Up until late 2010, Qantas Frequent Flyer Points could be earned at Hertz, Avis and Budget in Australia. In November 2010, an exclusive deal was negotiated between Avis and Budget, and Qantas Frequent Flyer, which meant Hertz could no longer offer their customers Qantas Points, a currency highly desired by business travellers.[125]

This had a significant positive impact on Avis' revenue, which grew in 2012 by 4.6 per cent and in 2013 by a further 8.7 per cent. For

---

Ohio State University.

125 Qantas, 'News', 2010, https://www.qantas.com/fflyer/dyn/program/news/2010/aug/changes-to-car-hire, accessed 15th May 2019.

the same period, Hertz' revenue declined year-on-year in 2012 by 2.9 per cent, with a further decline in 2013 of 4.3 per cent.

IbisWorld reported 'Avis (and Budget Rent A Car) have benefitted from strategic partnerships with tourism service operators over the past five years, such as the partnership between Avis and the Qantas Frequent Flyer program. These partnerships have provided the brands with a competitive edge over other passenger car rental companies, particularly in highly competitive positions within airports.'[126]

Principle 7: Cost-effective

While loyalty programs can deliver a range of benefits to companies, they require investment. A best-practice program is operated with clarity on the costs and net gains, and delivers a positive return on investment.

Identifying and tracking the true costs associated with a loyalty program can be a challenging task. Over time, various accounting, actuarial, and regulatory models have emerged, as well as differing views on recognising and measuring loyalty program benefits and costs.

According to PWC[127], the costs involved in operating a program include reward redemption and accrued liability, soft benefits (e.g., perks, recognition, member events), program communications (e.g., advertising, mailings, email), technology, enterprise training and support (e.g., call centres), business unit overhead (e.g., staffing payroll and benefits), and research and development. To this can be added legal fees, and security and fraud monitoring.

126 Whytcross, D., 2014, 'IBISWorld Industry Report: L6611 Passenger Car Rental and Hiring in Australia,' p23-25.

127 PricewaterhouseCoopers LLP, 2013, 'Loyalty analytics exposed: What every program manager needs to know'.

Being cost-effective is often specific to the program and the company running it. Some programs can generate positive returns by conferring generous benefits on all members because there is sufficient margin in the business. An example is the cinema industry, where loyalty programs can return 10 per cent of spend in benefits, which can include free tickets and candy bar products.

Other programs focus on just the top spenders to remain cost-effective, with an understanding that it is unprofitable to confer benefits on lower value, non-loyal (or less loyal) members. This approach may include status tier programs which provide more valuable rewards to customers buying more premium products and generally spending more.

Some companies take the opposite approach, and allocate most of their loyalty budget to high churn-risk customers in an attempt to improve their retention rate. This leads to the somewhat ironic situation of ignoring the most loyal customers, with the assumption they will remain loyal without any further investment. An example is health insurance funds, which may provide rewards and incentives to newer members (a typically high-churn segment) while ignoring members who have been loyalty for many years (and have comfortably low churn rates).

Having a clear understanding of the financial return of a program can support its evolution. Berman (2006)[128] argued that the development of an effective loyalty program requires an appetite to take corrective action in the event the program is not performing as expected. This necessitates some level of insight into its commercial performance, which can support the identification of cost issues, as well as track improved performance over time due to enhancement initiatives.

Wansink (2003)[129] developed a basic mathematical model to determine the cost-effectiveness of loyalty programs:

$$\text{Gain/Loss} = (U_a * P) - D - (U_w * P) - A$$

---

128 Berman, B., 2006, 'Developing an effective customer loyalty program', California Management Review, Vol 49, Iss 1, p123.

129 Wansink, B., 2003, 'Developing a cost-effective brand loyalty program', Journal of Advertising Research, Vol 43, Iss 3, pp301-309.

Unit sales after program implementation = Ua

Price per unit = P

Dollar amount of coupons or other incentives used = D

Unit sales before program = Uw

Administrative costs of program = A

British Airways Avios

In January 2015, British Airways adjusted their Avios loyalty program[130] to provide more valuable rewards to members who buy more premium products and who generally spend more. This approach included reducing the Avios (their loyalty currency) earn rate for economy class tickets by 75 per cent, while boosting business, first-class and flexible-ticket earn by as much as two-thirds.

At the same time, British Airways increased the amount of Avios required for reward seats by as much as 100 per cent.

The move simultaneously reduced the operating costs of the program and tipped the value-equation to provide greater benefit to premium customers. The strategy was designed to lock-in the loyalty of a small percentage of premium customers (who generate a comparably significant percentage of total flight revenues) and do it in a cost-effective way.

A similar strategy has been implemented by multiple frequent flyer programs globally.

---

130 Collinson, P., 2015, 'BA airmiles now offer a worse deal for economy class passengers', The Guardian, https://www.theguardian.com/business/2015/jan/28/british-airways-airmiles-avios-changes, accessed 12 June 2020.

Principle 8: Evolving

Loyalty program designers can utilise best-practice principles, market research, sophisticated commercial modelling, advanced technology and cutting-edge marketing strategies when creating a program, however it is only post-launch that they will be able to determine how members respond.

It is recommended for companies developing a new program to launch a Minimal Viable Product (MVP) version, with an ambition to evolve it into a full program based on how members respond to the basic design. Companies should also be more considered about the type of technology platform they procure to ensure the program can continuously evolve to suit consumers changing needs and desires over time, without the need to invest in continual platform development.

Budget is required post-launch to provide the opportunity for the program to be further developed, ideally based on quality analytics, a customer feedback loop and iterative testing.

Berman (2006)[131] identified two characteristics of an effective program; firstly, investment in the development of an appropriate company to plan, implement, and fine-tune the program, and secondly, an appetite to take corrective action in the event the program is not performing as expected.

For a company launching a new loyalty program, the ongoing operational effort required can sometimes be overlooked, leading to a situation where the team required to run the program is underfunded, and their ability to make necessary adjustments to optimise member engagement is curtailed by competing business priorities. It is important to incorporate the future needs of the operational team into project planning and financial modelling to ensure the potential for the evolution of the program is preserved.

---

131 Berman, B., 2006, 'Developing an effective customer loyalty program', California Management Review, Vol 49, Iss 1, p123.

Vodafone Voxi Drop

Voxi is the youth brand of Vodafone, aimed at under-thirties customers who have heavy data usage. Voxi provides members with unlimited social media use, unlimited phone calls/texts, and a new monthly Voxi Drop gift to encourage recharging.

Voxi Drop is essentially a rebranding of Vodafone's existing VeryMe program which has been adapted for the youth segment. Inspired by the 'drop culture' which stems from the world of fast fashion, Voxi Drop appeals to the younger consumers desire for spontaneity, excitement, and consistent evolution. Members do not earn points or any recognised loyalty currency (something some younger demographics have negative connotations about), but Vodafone would be covertly measuring and managing customer segments, keeping score behind the scenes.[132]

Not only has the program evolved to speak the language of their members and meet their changing needs, the program gift also continuously evolves each month, maintaining member engagement. Voxi Drop gifts have ranged from restaurant vouchers, concert tickets, festival queue jumps, and other entertaining and contextually relevant surprises which appeal to their consumers.

Sephora Beauty Insider

Sephora's loyalty program is constantly being developed, updated and improved to suit members changing needs, proving that they are truly invested in generating long-term loyalty.

Since Beauty Insider launched in 2007, it has regularly been celebrated by retailers everywhere for its attention to the customer experience, desired rewards, and longevity.[133]

132 Ehredt, C., 'Innovators Break The Mould, At The 2020 Loyalty Magazine Awards', Currency Alliance, https://www.linkedin.com/pulse/innovators-break-mould-2020-loyalty-magazine-awards-charles-ehredt/, accessed 18 June 2020.

133 Lion, 2019, 'Successful loyalty programs: Sephora gives its loyalty program a makeover', accessed 16 June 2020.

In early 2019, a major redesign introduced a stronger focus on personalisation and special tier perks for higher tiers. It delivered a balanced combination of tangible, instant gratification benefits like discounts, as well as ways for members to build long term emotional connections with Sephora through makeovers, access to beauty inspiration, free gifts and VIB Beauty Event access.

In May 2020 (amid the Covid-19 pandemic), Sephora announced the next evolution to their program. Allegra Stanley, Vice President of Loyalty for Sephora, said that the changes were made to match the needs and wants of their customers. She explained how the changes were part of a multi-year journey that seeks to keep shaking things up.

'We've seen that members are craving value more than ever, which speaks to the role that the Beauty Insider program can continue to play in their beauty journey', said Stanley. 'The thing we hear most often from members is that they want to use points in new ways and earn points in new ways.'

'We try to think about our brand holistically, and it is not just about the value-back component. There are different components of the program that customers value more than others. This is just a starting point for us.'

In June 2023, Sephora made further program changes, including the introduction of 'Beauty Insider Cash' which allows members to instantly earn US$10 off at the checkout once 500 points are reached, plus two additional member shopping events (one for access to further discounts and one for access to points multipliers on purchases).[134]

---

134 Cara Salpini, June 2023, 'Sephora updates loyalty program for the third time in as many years' https://www.retaildive.com/news/sephora-updates-loyalty-program-for-the-third-time-in-as-many-years/579054/ accessed June 2023.

Key insights

- Loyalty & Reward Co's Essential Eight™ are Simple, Valuable, Stimulating, Emotional, Complementary, Differentiating, Cost-effective and Evolving.

- The essential principles framework can be used to guide the strategic design and ongoing development of a best-practice loyalty program.

Suggested reading

- Shiri D. Vivek, Sharon E. Beatty & Robert M. Morgan, 2012, 'Customer Engagement: Exploring Customer Relationships Beyond Purchase', Journal of Marketing Theory and Practice, Vol 20, Iss 2, pp122-146.

- Nunes, J. C. and Drèze, X., 2006, 'Your Loyalty Program Is Betraying You,' Harvard Business Review, https://hbr.org/2006/04/your-loyalty-program-is-betraying-you, accessed 2 Feb 2020.

- Hull, C. 1934, 'The rats' speed of locomotion gradient in approach to food', Journal of Comparative Psychology, Vol 17, pp393-422.

- Veloutsou, C., 2015, 'Brand evaluation, satisfaction and trust as predictors of brand loyalty: the mediator-moderator effect of brand relationships', Journal of Consumer Marketing, Vol 32, Iss 6, pp405-421.

- Tajfel, H. & Turner, J. C., 1978, 'An Integrative Theory of Intergroup Conflict', The social psychology of intergroup relations, pp33-47.

- Söderlund, M., 2019, 'Can the label 'member' in a loyalty program context boost customer satisfaction?', The International Review of Retail, Distribution and Consumer Research, Vol 29, Iss 3, pp340-35.

- Berman, B., 2005, 'How to delight your customers,' California Management Review, Vol 48, Iss 1, pp129-151.

CHAPTER 5

LOYALTY PSYCHOLOGY

*'... people provided with artificial advancement toward a goal
exhibit greater persistence toward reaching the goal.'*

- Joseph Nunes & Xavier Drèze, 2006 [135]

Focus areas

This chapter will address the following questions:

- What are the main consumer psychology theories and studies relevant for loyalty programs?

- How is consumer psychology used to guide loyalty program design and operation?

CONSUMER PSYCHOLOGY HAS heavily influenced the design of loyalty programs.

Feldman[136] stated, 'The real currency of any loyalty program lies in its

135 Nunes, J. & Drèze, X., 2006, 'The Endowed Progress Effect: How Artificial Advancement increases Effort', Journal of Consumer Research, Vol 32, Iss 4, pp504-512.
136 Feldman, D., 2016, 'The psychology of loyalty programs,' https://www.linkedin.com/pulse/psychology-loyalty-programs-david-feldman-gaicd?trk=v-feed, accessed 10 April 2019.

ability to drive changes in consumer behaviour'. Consumer psychology provides a solid, research-based foundation to guide the program design in a way which will maximise its chances of successfully influencing the desired behavioural changes.

This chapter reviews a wide body of consumer psychology academic research and theory, illustrating its practical application within loyalty programs.

The Law of Effect and the Law of Exercise

Edward Thorndike was a prominent psychology professor at Colombia University. He was elected president of the American Psychological Association in 1912 and became one of the very first psychologists to be admitted to the National Academy of Sciences in 1917.

Thorndike is famous in psychology for his work on learning theory. He experimented with cats by placing them in puzzle boxes. The cats were encouraged to escape to claim a piece of fish placed outside, while Thorndike timed how long the escape took.

Thorndike observed that the cats would experiment with different ways to escape the puzzle box, and eventually trigger a lever which opened the cage. In successive trials, the cats would adapt their behaviour and become increasingly faster at pressing the lever.

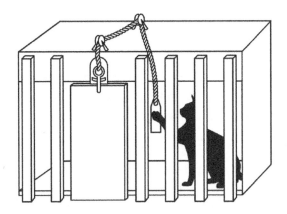

Figure 2: Thorndike Puzzle Box. Thorndike would record how long it would take for a cat to escape by using the lever to open the cage. Adapted from 'Animal intelligence: an experimental study of the associative processes in animals' by E.L Thorndike, 1898, Figure 1, p 8[137].

The study led to 'Animal Intelligence' (1911),[138] a publication which detailed two important laws relevant to loyalty programs; the *law of effect* and the *law of exercise*.

The law of effect stated: '*Of several responses made to the same situation, those which are accompanied or closely followed by satisfaction to the animal will, other things being equal, be more firmly connected with the situation, so that, when it recurs, they will be more likely to recur; those which are accompanied or closely followed by discomfort to the animal will, other things being equal, have their connections with that situation weakened, so that, when it recurs, they will be less likely to occur. The greater the satisfaction or discomfort, the greater the strengthening or weakening of the bond.*'

The law of exercise stated: '*Any response to a situation will, other things being*

137 Thorndike, E. L., 1898, 'Animal intelligence: an experimental study of the associative processes in animals', New York, Macmillan, Figure 1, p8, https://archive.org/details/animalintelligen00thoruoft/page/8/mode/2up, accessed 16 July 2020.

138 Thorndike, E. L., 1911, 'Animal Intelligence', Laws and hypotheses for behavior laws of behavior in general,' Chapter 5, https://psychclassics.yorku.ca/Thorndike/Animal/chap5.htm, accessed 12 June 2020.

equal, be more strongly connected with the situation in proportion to the number of times it has been connected with that situation and to the average vigor and duration of the connections.'

Thorndike demonstrated that behaviour that resulted in a pleasant outcome was likely to be repeated, while behaviour that resulted in an unpleasant outcome was not likely to be repeated. And behaviour that is repeated may develop a habitual attachment to the situation.

For a loyalty program operator providing rewards to members to stimulate repeat purchase behaviour, Thorndike's research should be regarded as the foundation of loyalty psychology.

Ritual Rewards

Originally launching in Toronto, and now in 4 countries (US, Canada, Australia and UK), Ritual Rewards[139] is a restaurant-based rewards app which enables members to order through any restaurant or café in the Ritual network and earn points for their spend.

Points can be redeemed at any restaurant or café within the Ritual network.

Ritual Rewards focuses on rewarding repeat behaviour with the aim to build intrinsic member habits. Some of the ways Ritual Rewards encourages the formation of habits include:

- Attaching rewards to known habits like daily coffees and lunches.

- Bonus rewards for visiting the same place twice.

- Bonus rewards for transacting for dinner as well as lunch.

- Personalised points challenges which reward consecutive daily transactions with incremental bonuses.

---

139 Ritual, https://en-ae.rituals.com/reward-points/, accessed 27 April 2023.

Operant Conditioning

B.F. Skinner was a psychology professor at Harvard University who was ranked by the American Psychological Association as the 20th century's most eminent psychologist. He built on the work of Thorndike to develop a theory of *operant conditioning* (1948).[140]

Skinner introduced two new terms into the law of effect; *reinforcement* and *punishment*. He used these to identify three key insights which expanded on Thorndike's work:

- Behaviour can be increased or maintained by the addition of pleasant stimuli or the removal of aversive stimuli (Reinforcement).

- Behaviour can be decreased by the removal of pleasant stimuli or the addition of aversive stimuli (Punishment).

- Behaviour which is reinforced tends to be repeated (i.e., strengthened), while reinforced behaviour which is no longer reinforced tends to extinguish (i.e., weaken).

Skinner's first experiment studied the behaviour of pigeons provided with access to food at regular intervals. The study identified that the pigeons tended to learn whatever response they were making when the food appeared (e.g., coincidentally flapping its wings at the time food appeared influenced the pigeon to start flapping its wings whenever it wanted food to appear). Skinner suggested that 'the experiment might be said to demonstrate a sort of superstition. The bird behaves as if there were a causal relation between its behaviour and the presentation of food, although such a relation is lacking.' The pigeon made an illogical association between its behaviour and the consequence of being provided with food.

Inspired by Thorndike's puzzle boxes, Skinner invented a box which contained a lever (for rats) or a key (for pigeons) that the animal could operate to either obtain food or water (as a positive reinforcer) or stop a small electric shock (as a negative reinforcer). The box was connected to electronic equipment

---

140 Skinner, B. F, 1948, '"Superstition" in the pigeon, Journal of Experimental Psychology, Vol 38, Iss 2, pp168–172.

that recorded the animal's actions, thus allowing for the precise quantification of the behaviour. A simple experiment involved the animal pushing the lever and receiving a pellet of food, thereby reinforcing the behaviour that pushing the lever would result in a reward.

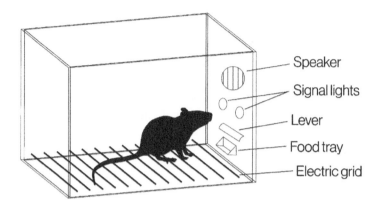

Figure 3: Skinner Box. Several stimuli including lights, images and sounds were used to measure responses. Adapted from 'The Behaviour of Organisms: An Experimental Analysis' by B.F Skinner, 1938, Figure 1, p 49[141].

Substituting a rat or pigeon with a consumer, if the purchase of a product or service earns points, and the points are redeemed for a desirable reward, the consumer may be more likely to repeat the behaviour, as it has been reinforced with a positive consequence. This effect can be reinforced further with good-quality CX design and marketing which informs and reminds the member of the benefits they have accessed, similar to a slot machine ringing bells and flashing lights each time a gambler wins.

Similarly, threatening the removal of rewarding stimulus (such as removing access to status tier benefits for not earning sufficient status credits) can motivate the member to reduce their stagnant engagement behaviour.

Finally, by removing the reward altogether, program operators can expect a weakening (extinction) of the purchase behaviour.

---

141 Skinner, B. F., 1938, 'The Behaviour of Organisms: An Experimental Analysis', Cambridge, Massachusetts, Figure 1, p49, http://s-f-walker.org.uk/pubse-books/pdfs/The%20Behavior%20of%20Organisms%20-%20BF%20Skinner.pdf, accessed 16 July 2020.

Hilton Honors

Hilton Honors[142] members unlock benefits for reaching 'nights stayed' thresholds (i.e., a member will reach silver status and unlock a range of additional benefits after they stay 10+ nights). This is an example of 'fixed ratio reinforcement' whereby a reward is offered when a behaviour is performed a certain number of times.

Members are encouraged to continue engaging in this behaviour to unlock an even more desirable set of rewards. This includes complimentary breakfast, bonus points and access to potential room upgrades after 40+ nights stayed when Gold status is unlocked.

Hilton also reinforce behaviour through the application of punishment. That is, members who do not stay enough nights to maintain their status tier will be relegated to a lower tier. With that reduction in status comes the loss of tier privileges, signalling to the member that they must maintain their higher visitation levels to avoid these negative consequences.

Social Identity Theory

Psychology has demonstrated that consumers do not just feel emotional connections to preferred brands, but they adopt them as part of their identity.

Tajfel (1978) [143] proposed *social identity theory*, whereby a person's sense of who they are is based on their membership of different groups. Tajfel theorised that groups which people belonged to as social classes (such as sporting teams, families, groups of friends, workplaces, etc.) were an important source of pride and self-esteem. He determined that groups give individuals a sense of social identity and a sense of belonging to the social world.

---

142 Hilton, Hilton Honorshttps://www.hilton.com/en/hilton-honors/member-benefits/ , accessed 29 April 2023.
143 Tajfel, H. & Turner, J. C., 1978, 'An Integrative Theory of Intergroup Conflict', The social psychology of intergroup relations, pp33-47.

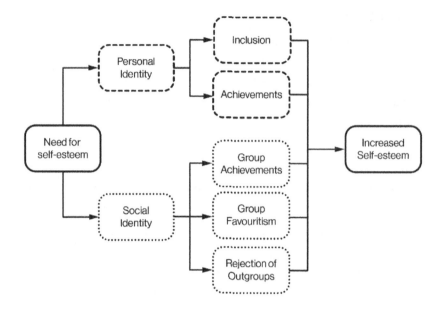

Figure 4: Under social identity theory, the sense of self is based on both personal identity and a collective social identity. Adapted from 'Group Dynamics 3c Identity and Inclusion: Social Identity (Part 3)' by D.R Forsyth, 2014.[144]

Bhattacharya and Sen (2003) [145] expanded this further by exploring social identity theory as it related to brands. They proposed that 'strong consumer-company relationships often result from consumers identification with those companies, which helps them satisfy one or more important self-definitional needs'. In other words, consumers connect with brands in much the same way they connect with their social class, sporting teams and friendship groups, and the brand plays a critical role in making them feel better about themselves by increasing their self-esteem.

As detailed in Chapter 4, a program which serves to make members feel

---

144 Forsyth, D. R., 2014, 'Group Dynamics 3c Identity and Inclusion: Social Identity (Part 3)' from the book 'Group Dynamics', https://www.youtube.com/watch?v=XPIJjcJUw7w, accessed 14 October 2019.

145 Bhattacharya, C. B. & Sen, S., 2003, 'Consumer-Company Identification: A Framework for Understanding Consumers' Relationships with Companies', Vol 67, pp76-88.

a sense of exclusivity and belonging can play a central role in the member adopting the brand (sub-consciously or otherwise) as an element of their own self-definition.

Many loyalty programs incorporate status tiers in an attempt to tap into the power of social identity theory. For example, many major beauty brands and high-end retailers provide their VIP members with custom makeovers, personal styling sessions and private store access to make them look and feel confident and beautiful, blurring the lines between brand and self.

As detailed in Chapter 4, Söderlund (2019)[146] identified that simply labelling customers as 'member' versus 'non-member' was sufficient to stimulate a higher level of sense of belonging and customer satisfaction.

Ivanic (2015)[147] identified that high status tier members engage in status-reinforcing behaviours, even if doing so offers no material or social signalling benefit, and even if it incurs costs, as engaging in these behaviours generates elevated feelings of prestige. When high status is noticeable, members demonstrate a greater propensity to engage in status-reinforcing behaviours. By contrast, members who reported as already having a reinforced sense of status were less likely to engage in status-reinforcing behaviours. Ivanic concluded that this suggests that utilising status privileges serves as a reinforcing behaviour, even in the absence of a status threat.

The most common application of this theory can be seen within airline, hotel and bank programs where tier benefits are a formidable driver of member stickiness and retention.

---

146 Söderlund, M., 2019, 'Can the label 'member' in a loyalty program context boost customer satisfaction?', The International Review of Retail, Distribution and Consumer Research, Vol 29, Iss 3, pp340-35.

147 Ivanic, A., 2015, 'Status Has Its Privileges: The Psychological Benefit of Status-Reinforcing Behaviors', Psychology & Marketing, Vol 32, pp697-708.

Thai Airways Royal Orchid Plus

A Platinum Royal Orchid member (or an equivalent frequent flyer status level within the Star Alliance partner network) is provided with a range of benefits when flying with Thai Airways including free lounge access, priority boarding/check-in/baggage handling and complimentary upgrades. By recognising and rewarding members, while making them feel they belong to something meaningful, Thai Airways provide a boost in self-esteem which can lead to the formation of an emotional connection with the brand.

Cairns and Galbraith (1990)[148] suggested that, 'frequent flyer schemes may generate switching costs for travellers' through the awarding of status tiers which confer benefits on the member which they would lose if they moved their business to another airline'. According to Social Identity Theory, the loss for some would also include a loss of self-esteem, feeling of importance and sense of belonging. This makes the stickiness effect of Royal Orchid and similar frequent flyer programs particularly powerful.

Endowed Progress Effect

Many loyalty programs tap into a psychological phenomenon known as the *endowed progress effect*. This was demonstrated by Nunes and Drèze (2006) [149] in a research study which involved a stamp card loyalty program at a car wash. Members could earn a free wash by collecting stamps.

Nunes and Drèze divided participants into two groups; for the first group, members needed to collect eight stamps (and did not receive any free stamps). The second group had to collect ten stamps, but the card already had two 'free' stamps on it. Thus, both groups required eight stamps to claim their free wash.

148 Cairns, R. & Galbraith, J., 1990, 'Artificial Compatibility, Barriers to Entry, and Frequent-Flyer Programs', Canadian Journal of Economics, Vol 23, Iss 1/2, pp807-816.

149 Nunes, J. & Drèze, X., 2006, 'The Endowed Progress Effect: How Artificial Advancement increases Effort', Journal of Consumer Research, Vol 32, Iss 4, pp504-512.

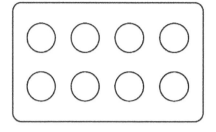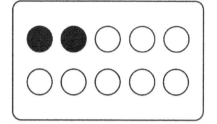

Figure 5: the two stamp card models used within the car wash program experiment by Nunes and Drèze. The right side exhibits two 'free' stamps. Adapted from the research paper 'The Endowed Progress Effect: How Artificial Advancement increases Effort' by J. C Nunes and X Drèze, 2006.[150]

The second group with two 'free' stamps recorded a reward redemption rate of 34 per cent and transacted more often. The first group saw a redemption rate of just 19 per cent. The conclusion — members provided with artificial advancement toward a goal exhibit greater persistence toward reaching the goal. In other words, when consumers feel like they have started on the journey towards a reward, they feel compelled to complete the journey to claim the reward.

Nunes and Drèze[151] wrote: '*Research has proven that the further along members are in a loyalty program, the more they use it. By contrast, at the outset of their membership, their involvement is irresolute. Because they have not yet made any progress, the rewards seem far away. Worse, they have little sense of how easy it will be to achieve the goals. Rather than lose a customer's interest right out of the gate, the best designed programs provide what we've termed 'endowed progress', a little push to get things moving.*'

Miles, points and stamps serve to drive repeat purchase because the member is accumulating with each transaction, giving them a sense they are progressing towards a goal. Loyalty program operators take advantage of this drive in a variety of ways: by providing bonus currency to new members to

---

150 Ibid.

151 Nunes, J. C. and Drèze, X., 2006, 'Your Loyalty Program Is Betraying You,' Harvard Business Review, accessed 2 Feb 2020.

get them started on the journey, by communicating to members their progress towards their goal (via progress trackers) and by promoting the desirable reward they will earn if they complete the journey.

The Beard Club

The Beard Club[152] is a premium American and Canadian online retailer offering a range of beard care products such as oils, balms, shampoos, and combs to help men maintain their best-looking beard.

New customers who sign up to The Beard Club Rewards program receive 15 points after joining the program, immediately placing them 15% of the way towards earning their first $10 reward product. There are additional ways members can boost their points balance from the outset prior to making a purchase including 'liking' the Beard Club Facebook page (5 points) and following on YouTube (5 points) or Instagram (5 points). This initial progress creates a sense of momentum and can encourage members to continue along the reward journey by making a purchase ($1 = 1 point), reviewing products (25 points) or reaching a streak of 4 purchases (100 points), which are all desirable loyal behaviours The Beard Club are looking to incentivise and reinforce via The Beard Club Rewards program.

Goal Gradient Effect

First reported by Hull (1934),[153] the *goal gradient effect* states that the tendency to approach a goal increases with proximity to the goal. Hull found that rats in a straight alley ran progressively faster as they proceeded from the starting box to food.

---

152 The Beard Club, https://thebeardclub.com/pages/rewards, accessed 14 June 2023.

153 Hull, C. L., 1934, 'The rats' speed of locomotion gradient in approach to food', Journal of comparative psychology, Vol 17, pp393-422.

Kivetz et al (2006) [154] demonstrated the presence of this phenomenon in loyalty programs. They utilised a coffee card reward program experiment to measure the effect on consumers, and reported that members of the program were prone to purchase coffee more frequently the closer they were to earning a free coffee.

The same phenomenon can be observed in loyalty program status points earn, where members have been seen to increase their consumption (more flights, more stays, more rentals) as they approach the next status tier in order to achieve it sooner (so called 'status runs' or 'mileage runs').[155] Loyalty programs have been observed to capitalise on this insight by promoting bonus status points or miles offers to members as they approach a tier threshold in order to stimulate a boost in discretionary purchase behaviour.

Dollard and Miller (1950)[156] built on Hull's research, identifying gradients of approach (which become steeper the nearer the desired object) and gradients of avoidance (where the tendency to avoid a feared stimulus is stronger the nearer the subject is to it). They found that the gradient of avoidance is steeper than that of approach, indicating the desire to avoid something is greater than the desire to obtain something. This may help explain the effectiveness of status tier programs in generating member stickiness.

Drèze & Nunes (2011)[157] used data from a major frequent flyer program to demonstrate that success in achieving a goal contributes to an increase in effort by the member in consecutive attempts to reach the next goal. They replicated the effects in a laboratory study that showed that the impact of success

154 Kivetz, R., Urminsky, O., & Zheng, Y., 2006, 'The Goal-Gradient Hypothesis Resurrected: Purchase Acceleration, Illusionary Goal Progress, and Customer Retention', Journal of Marketing Research, Vol 43, pp39-58.

155 Graham, M., 2018, 'Five Qantas Status Runs', The Australian Frequent Flyer, https://www.australianfrequentflyer.com.au/qantas-status-runs/, accessed 9 April 2019.

156 Dollard, J., & Miller, N. E., 1950, 'Personality and psychotherapy; an analysis in terms of learning, thinking, and culture', McGraw-Hill.

157 Drèze, X & Nunes, J., 2011, 'Recurring Goals and Learning: The Impact of Successful Reward Attainment on Purchase Behavior', Journal of Marketing Research, Vol 48, pp268-281.

is significant only when the goal is challenging. Importantly, they identified that progress enhanced perceptions of self-efficacy, with successful completion of the tasks providing an added boost.

Huang and Zhang (2011)[158] investigated the mindset difference when a consumer is near vs far from a reward and the implications of this on loyalty program design and communications. They argued that when progress towards attaining a goal is low, consumers are primarily concerned with the question 'Can I get there?', however when consumers have achieved sufficient progress and their attainment of the goal is relatively secured, they become more concerned about the question 'When will I get there?'. Understanding the consumer mindset and communicating based on this mindset can influence motivation:

- 'Can I get the reward?' mindset is focused on the individual's belief in their ability to achieve the reward. Members with this mindset may question their capacity to accumulate enough points, complete the necessary tasks, or maintain the required engagement level to obtain the reward. This mindset is closely related to self-efficacy, which affects motivation and persistence. In this instance, signals which tell the member that the reward is in reach, clear tips or advice on how to get there faster and access to bonus earn offers are welcome as the faster they feel they are making progress, the more motivated they become

- 'When will I get the reward?' mindset is concerned with the time it takes to achieve the reward. Customers with this mindset may be more focused on the speed of their progress and the expected timeline to reach the reward. This mindset is aligned with the concept of perceived velocity. In this instance, slower progress speed actually increases motivation because members already know they will get

---

158 Huang, S.C. and Zhang, Y., 2011, 'Motivational consequences of perceived velocity in consumer goal pursuit', Journal of Marketing Research, 48(6), pp.1045-1056, referenced by Loyalty Science Lab, 'What happens When People Get Closer to a Reward?', accessed via https://loyaltysciencelab.medium.com/what-happens-when-people-get-closer-to-a-reward-636123070daa.

there, but reducing the amount of time remaining to get there is their focus. Offering personalised progress updates and 'fast track' options to create a sense of momentum and the perception of faster progress will be well received

Koo and Fishbach (2021)[159] identified the way progress towards a goal is monitored and communicated can significantly influence motivation. Their research on the Small Area Hypothesis found that members are more motivated when focusing on whichever segment is smaller in terms of how far they have come vs how far they have to go. One of the studies reported was conducted using a 'buy 10 meals, get one free' stamp/punch card loyalty program design at a sushi restaurant. Two types of loyalty program cards were issued:

- **Backward-looking card:** the card involved stamping sushi images onto empty spaces to fill the card for the free reward. The sushi images emphasised what had already been earned.

- **Forward-looking card:** this card required punching out pre-printed sushi images from the card. So the remaining sushi images on the card reminded members how many more meals were still needed to earn the reward.

The results supported the small area hypothesis. For low-progress members, the backward-looking card brought people back to the restaurant faster, reducing average between-visit time by about 4 days compared with the forward-looking card.

The opposite was the case for high-progress members. The forward-looking card was more effective than the backward-looking card design, reducing between-visit time by 1 day.

---

159 Koo, M. and Fishbach, A., 2012. The Small Area Hypothesis: Effects of progress monitoring on goal adherence. Journal of Consumer Research, 39(3), pp.493-509., referenced by Loyalty Science Lab, 'What happens When People Get Closer to a Reward?', accessed via https://loyaltysciencelab.medium.com/ what-happens-when-people-get-closer-to-a-reward-636123070daa.

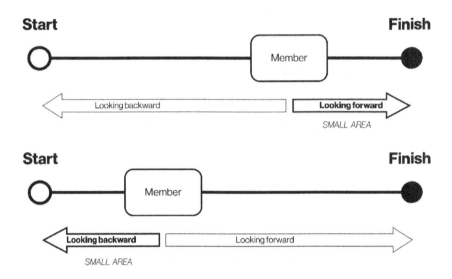

Figure 6: the Small Area Hypothesis from a looking backward and looking forward perspective. Adapted by Loyalty Science Lab, 'What happens When People Get Closer to a Reward?'[160]

Gutt et al (2020)[161] explored whether the phenomenon of self-efficacy associated with goal progression also extended to status tiers. They found evidence to suggest that members would increase their base level of effort after achieving a tier as long as the difficulty of obtaining a tier kept increasing. If the difficulty to reach the next tier was lower than or equal to the previous level, members were observed to hold their base level of effort constant. This indicated the existence of a positive effect of tier achievement on subsequent member contribution levels through increased self-efficacy, but only as long as the achievement of tiers remained challenging.

160 Loyalty Science Lab, 'What happens When People Get Closer to a Reward?', accessed via https://loyaltysciencelab.medium.com/what-happens-when-people-get-closer-to-a-reward-636123070daa.

161 Gutt, D., Rechenberg, T.V., & Kundisch, D., 2018, 'Goal Achievement, Subsequent User Effort and the Moderating Role of Goal Difficulty'. Journal of Business Research, Vol 106, pp277-287.

Starbucks Rewards

The Starbucks Rewards[162] app uses a combination of visual progress communications (how far a member has come) and Goal Gradient communications (how far the member has to go), to motivate members to increase their frequency of transactions to unlock more rewards.

Members are informed within the app how many more stars they need to earn to access a reward. For example, '1 Star Until Next Reward'. This maintains the members' focus on the goal to stimulate transaction momentum.

Starbucks capitalise on the goal gradient effect by providing members with additional opportunities to earn stars so they can reach their goal faster. Examples include bonus star promotions and ability to earn stars on Starbucks products (packaged coffee, pods, syrups, cookies, etc.) bought at petrol stations and grocery stores.

Customer Delight and Decision Affect Theory

Customer delight is a powerful technique for driving deeper member engagement. Psychological studies suggest that when a customer's expectations are met, they will be satisfied and when a customer's expectations are exceeded, they will be slightly more satisfied, but when a customer is unexpectedly delighted (commonly referred to as 'surprise and delight' in the loyalty industry) their satisfaction levels will be substantial.

Debate exists in academic circles about the definition of delight. A literature review by Barnes & Krallman (2019)[163] indicated there were initially two major viewpoints:

- Delight as an extreme form of satisfaction, measured by the extreme end point of customer satisfaction scales.

---

162 Starbucks, Starbucks Rewards, https://www.starbucks.com/rewards/, accessed 29 April 2023.

163 Donald C. Barnes & Alexandra Krallman (2019) Customer Delight: A Review and Agenda for Research, Journal of Marketing Theory and Practice, 27:2, 174-195.

- Delight as a distinct construct, defined as a profoundly positive emotional state resulting from having one's expectations exceeded to a surprising degree. This builds from Plutchik's (1980)[164] work on emotions, with delight being comprised of two primary emotions, surprise and joy.

The majority of delight researchers support the second definition, using established scales to measure delight.

Further studies have found customer satisfaction and customer delight to be empirically different, despite their strong correlation.

The debate has since shifted to whether surprise is necessary for delight. Some studies argue that surprise is essential, while others suggest that delight can occur without surprise, depending on the product's nature and the presence of cognitive and affective routes.

More recent research explores including other positive emotions such as gratitude to expand the definition of customer delight.

In earlier research, Schwarz (1987)[165] ran a study to test the impact of a positive event occurring on a subject's overall life satisfaction. He placed a small coin on a photocopier for the next user to find. He then conducted an interview with those who found the small coin about their life perspective. 'Those who found the coin were happier, more satisfied and wanted to change their lives less than those who didn't find a coin', reported Schwarz.[166] The value of the coin appeared to be irrelevant; it was significant that something positive and surprising happened to them.

There is evidence to suggest surprise and delight activity can improve a person's liking towards another. Regan (1971)[167] ran a study where a participant

164 Plutchik, R. (1980). Emotion: A psychoevolutionary synthesis, New York, NY: Harper and Row.

165 Schwartz, N., 1987, 'Stimmung als Information (Mood as information)'.

166 Ager, S., 1999, 'A dime can make a difference,' The Baltimore Sun, https://www.baltimoresun.com/news/bs-xpm-1999-08-22-9908240363-story.html, accessed 11 June 2020.

167 Regan, R., 1971, 'Effects of a favor and liking on compliance', Journal of

provided an unexpected bottle of Coca-Cola to the subject. Subjects reported liking the person giving the free Coke more than when no Coke was provided.

Mellers et al (1997)[168] explored the power of surprise and delight by looking at the difference between expected and unexpected positive outcomes. Their *decision affect theory* demonstrated that unexpected outcomes have a greater emotional impact than expected outcomes, even when the reward was of lower value. Their study required students to complete a task. The students were either told how much they would be rewarded prior to undertaking the task, or were surprised with a reward after completing the task. Smaller, surprising wins were shown to be more elating than larger, expected wins. For example, the researchers found a surprise $5 reward was rated as more enjoyable by subjects than an expected $9 reward.

Oliver et al (1997)[169] developed a *customer delight model* which hypothesised the loyalty psychology underpinning this effect. They found evidence that positive surprise and delight experiences elicit pleasure, joy and elation. They also proved that delight is a positively valanced state reflecting high levels of consumption-based affect, and the experience of delight creates a desire for future recurrences of the sensation via the repetition of consumption, which creates loyalty.

Most importantly, delighted customers have been proven to demonstrate higher loyalty to a company. Berman (2005)[170] reported significantly higher levels of loyalty from delighted versus satisfied customers. The findings also noted other potential positive consequences of delight to 'include lower costs due to increased word-of-mouth promotion, lower selling and advertising costs, lower customer acquisition costs, higher revenues due to higher initial

Experimental Social Psychology, Vol 7, Iss 6, pp627-639.

168 Mellers, B.A., Schwartz, A., Ho, K. & Ritov, I., 1997, 'Decision Affect Theory: Emotional Reactions to the Outcomes of Risky Options', Psychological Science, Vol 8, No 6, pp423-429.

169 Oliver, R. L., Rust, R. & Varki, S., 1997, 'Customer Delight: Foundations, Findings, and Managerial Insight', Journal of Retailing, Vol 73, Iss 3, pp311-336.

170 Berman, B., 2005, 'How to delight your customers,' California Management Review, Vol 48, Iss 1, pp129-151.

and repeat sales, and long-term strategic advantages due to increased brand equity and increased ability to withstand new entrants.' Berman cites one study where 'Mercedes-Benz USA found that the likelihood that a client who is dissatisfied with the service at a retailer will buy or lease from the same retailer is only 10 per cent. Mere satisfaction produces a 29 per cent likelihood of rebuy or re-lease. However, the likelihood of a delighted client rebuying or re-leasing is 86 per cent.'

Turning to neuropsychology, Pagnoni et al (2002)[171] found evidence that an unexpected event (such as surprise and delight) can powerfully stimulate the *nucleus accumbens* (the 'pleasure centre' of the brain), releasing dopamine into the blood stream, a hormone related to addiction. Subjects underwent MRI scans while having fruit juice or water squirted into their mouths through a tube either in a predictable or unpredictable pattern. The study found the *nucleus accumbens* responded much more strongly when the liquid was unanticipated, even with water. 'The region lights up like a Christmas tree on the MRI', said study co-author Dr Montague. 'That suggests people are designed to crave the unexpected.'[172]

Applications of surprise and delight campaigns within loyalty programs are extensive. They may include airline, hotel, rental car and banking programs sending premium members surprise gifts, telecommunications customers being invited to select from a range of unexpected rewards or meal kit delivery customers receiving something extra in their box. Surprise and delight case studies detailed in Chapter 4.

As the research shows, if executed correctly, surprise and delight can be an extremely powerful tool used to generate an emotional connection with a company or brand, to drive purchase behaviour and to create genuine member loyalty. In order to execute surprise and delight effectively it should be unexpected (i.e., telling a member they will receive a $10 voucher on their

---

171 Pagnoni G., Zink C. F., Montague P. R. & Berns G. S., 2002, 'Activity in human ventral striatum locked to errors of reward prediction', Nat Neuroscience, Vol 5, pp97-98.

172 Sommerfield, J., 2002, 'Human brain gets a kick out of surprises', MSNBC, http://www.ccnl.emory.edu/Publicity/MSNBC.HTM, accessed 11 June 2020.

birthday is not surprise and delight), be viewed as a gift, hold a perceived value and focus on the customer, making them feel truly special and recognised in that moment.

Mastercard Priceless Surprises

Mastercard US have been running a long-term campaign which drives their social media presence called 'Priceless Surprises'.[173] The campaign surprises cardholders with spontaneous gifts ranging from specialty cupcake deliveries, concert tickets and seat upgrades to celebrity meetings.

The #PricelessSurprises campaign has surprised almost 100,000 cardholders spanning 25 countries, with Mastercard enjoying the benefits of masses of user-generated social media content which they also use to connect with potential cardholders.[174]

They have even inspired existing members to gift their own surprises to family and friends, further expanding their reach and advocacy.

Norm of Reciprocity

The *norm of reciprocity* refers to an expectation that people will help those who helped them (Gouldner, 1960). [175] For example, one person buys another lunch, and the other person feels a compulsion to return the favour.

Regan's (1971)[176] study (where subjects reported liking a person giving them a free Coke more than when no Coke was provided) also studied the

---

173 Mastercard, Priceless Surprises, https://www.priceless.com//, accessed 28 April 2023.

174 Age, 'Best Practices: How Brands Can Build Loyalty With 'Surprise-and-Delight' Efforts', https://adage.com/article/digitalnext/brands-build-loyalty-surprise-delight-strategies/298425, accessed 29 June 2020.

175 Gouldner, A. W., 1960, 'The norm of reciprocity: A preliminary statement', American Sociological Review, Vol 25, pp161–178.

176 Regan, R., 1971, 'Effects of a favor and liking on compliance', Journal of Experimental Social Science Research, Vol 5, pp627-639.

effects of reciprocity. It found that providing a subject with a free Coke made them more willing to comply with a request from the provider to buy a raffle ticket. Subjects reported that it was not because they liked the provider more, but because they felt obligated to return the favour.

Regan's experiment built on the earlier study of Goranson and Berkowitz (1966),[177] who found evidence that conferred favours generate feelings of obligation and the desire to reciprocate. They provided a large group of female students with a dull task, and informed them the successful completion of the task would win a cash prize for their supervisor. Subjects who received voluntary help from the supervisor were observed to work harder than those who did not.

Studying the power of reciprocity, Kunz and Woolcott (1976)[178] examined whether people would send a Christmas card to a complete stranger who sent them one. For Christmas 1974, they sent 578 Christmas cards to strangers, and received an overall response rate of an astonishing 20 per cent. A follow-up study by Kunz (2000)[179] found the same 20 per cent response rate. Fifteen years later, a similar study by Meier (2015)[180] received just a 2 per cent response rate. A second study by Meier indicated two potential reasons for the low response rate; perceived threat/suspicion and high e-mail use (something which was not mainstream during the Kunz study period).

Reciprocity does have its limits. Although a person may feel obligated to return a favour, they do not always carry through with the intent. Brehm and Cole (1966)[181] found that the desire to reciprocate does not always correlate with the actual behaviour.

177 Goranson, R. E., & Berkowitz, L., 1966, 'Reciprocity and responsibility reactions to prior help', Journal of Personality and Social Psychology, Vol 3, Iss 2, pp227–232.

178 Kunz, P. R. & Woolcott, M., 1976, 'Season's greetings: From my status to yours', Social Science Research, Vol 5, Iss 3, pp269–278.

179 Kunz, J., 2000, 'Social Class Difference in Response to Christmas Cards', Perceptual and Motor Skills, Vol 90, Iss 2, pp573–576.

180 Meier, B., 2015, 'Bah Humbug: Unexpected Christmas Cards and the Reciprocity Norm', The Journal of Social Psychology, p156.

181 Brehm, J. W. & Cole, A. H., 1966, 'Effect of a favor which reduces freedom',

There is evidence that reciprocity translates to customer loyalty. Morias et al (2004)[182] studied tourism operators and found that if customers perceived that a provider was making an investment in them, they in turn made a similar investment in the provider, and those investments led to measurable loyalty. This suggests that investments of love, status, information and time are more closely associated with loyalty than investments of money (e.g., points and miles earn). They concluded that their findings explain how well-designed loyalty programs may lead to increased psychological attachment to the brand and company.

Hertz Gold Plus Rewards

Hertz Gold Plus Rewards[183] capitalise on the norm of reciprocity by giving their members free vehicle upgrades when better vehicles within their fleet are available. This gesture generates very little incremental cost to Hertz, however having happy customers drive away in a vehicle that is more valuable, advanced, spacious and stylish than what they originally booked can generate incremental benefits for Hertz thanks to the norm of reciprocity.

The member is likely to feel positively about the relationship and may feel inclined to find ways to give back in the form of purchasing additional add-ons (GPS, full insurance or an extra day), repeat business, social sharing, a positive review, or persuading a friend to join, even when there may be cheaper alternatives available.

Free upgrades can provide a fantastic ROI for Hertz as they can be conferred at little or no incremental cost and lay the foundations for future business, referrals and long-term loyalty.

Journal of Personality and Social Psychology, Vol 3, Iss 4, pp420–426.

182 Morais, D. B., Dorsch, M. J. & Backman, S. J., 2004, 'Can Tourism Providers Buy their Customers' Loyalty? Examining the Influence of Customer-Provider Investments on Loyalty', Journal of Travel Research, Vol 42, Iss 3, pp235–243.

183 Hertz, Hertz Gold Plus Rewards program Benefits https://www.hertz.com.au/rentacar/misc/index.jsp?targetPage=membership_benefits.jsp, accessed 27 April 2023.

Behavioural and Attitudinal Commitment Theory

Day (1969)[184] identified that methods used to gauge loyalty in the 1960s were flawed because they only measured purchase behaviour, and neglected to consider whether the behaviour may be due to lack of choice, long-term offers or better product positioning rather than true loyalty. He argued that many consumers who identified as 'loyal' lacked any attachment to the brand, and could easily be captured by competitors offering better deals or product promotion. Day hypothesised that loyalty should be measured by both *behavioural commitment* (where a customer repeatedly purchases a product or brand) and *attitudinal commitment* (when a customer chooses to be loyal because of a positive brand preference).

Beatty and Kahle (1988)[185] argued that *brand commitment* is conceptually similar to brand loyalty. Brand commitment is an emotional or psychological attachment to a brand within a product class, and appears to result from felt concern or ego involvement with the product or purchase decision (in other words, an attitudinal attachment). They attempted to predict the type of decision-making process subjects would make about soft drink purchases based on whether they had low or high commitment to specific brands. They concluded that commitment is the emotional or psychological attachment to a brand that develops before a customer would be able to determine that their repeat purchase behaviour was derived from a sense of loyalty. In other words, commitment to a brand is a precursor to genuine loyalty.

A core feature of commitment is resistance to change. As discussed in Chapter 4, loyal members that have formed an emotional connection (or attitudinal commitment) to a brand are more resistant to discounts and promotions from competitors. Pritchard et al (1999)[186] built a model which measured

---

184 Day, G. S., 1969, 'A Two-Dimensional Concept of Brand Loyalty', Journal of Advertising Research, Vol 9, Iss 3, pp29-35.

185 Beatty, S. E., Homer, P. M. & Kahle, L. R., 1988, 'The involvement—commitment model: Theory and implications', Journal of Business Research, Vol 16, Iss 2, pp149-167.

186 Pritchard, M., Havitz, M. & Howard, D., 1999, 'Analyzing the Commitment-Loyalty Link in Service Contexts', Journal of the Academy of Marketing Science, Vol 27, pp333-348.

resistance to change as primary evidence of commitment. The model allowed for the measurement of loyalty, which accounted for both consumers' purchase behaviour and attitudinal commitment toward the brand. It indicated that resistance to change (and therefore commitment) is maximised when consumers identify with the values and images embodied by a particular brand, and have a need for consistency and confidence in their decisions.

One technique brands use to build loyalty is to invite members to declare their level of commitment, ideally in a public space. Encouraging a public 'commitment statement' is a powerful technique for generating customer loyalty as people have a bias towards maintaining consistency with what they have done or have said they will do, thus avoiding inconsistency, an undesirable trait. A common example is 25 words or less competitions, where the entrant must write something positive about the brand or product. This is also widely used within the fitness industry to encourage members to continue engaging and ultimately derive satisfying transformative results.

F45 Training

F45 Training is a gym franchise with over 1,750 studios in 45 countries across Australia/Oceania, North America, South America, Asia, Europe and Africa. As an add-on to their membership, F45 have designed regular 8-week weight loss 'challenges' for members to participate in. The challenges have been extremely popular among members as they encourage them to set and commit to goals which ultimately increase visitation frequency, create upsell opportunities, drive advocacy and deliver member satisfaction.

F45 Training apply commitment theory by allowing members to set start and finish measurement goals and use the app to track the Challenge journey by logging workouts and physical progress, helping members 'take responsibility and make the right choices in and out of the gym'[187] to achieve the goals they have committed to.

Progress updates are often shared on social media acting as an additional display of commitment.

187 F45, https://f45challenge.com/, accessed 11 May 2023.

Mattila (2006)[188] explored commitment theory as it related to loyalty programs in the hospitality industry. Her analysis suggested that the accumulation of points and accessing of rewards at major hotel programs such as Hilton Honors, Hyatt's Gold Pass and Marriott Rewards were not sufficient to create loyalty. She argued that what was needed instead was to foster an emotional bond between the member and the brand, which is driven by both affective (attitudinal) commitment and calculative commitment (a sense of being locked into a service provider due to the economic costs of leaving). Calculative commitment may be confused with resistance to change, but scrutiny indicates it is more related to boosting resistance by introducing switching costs.

According to the more recently published 2022 Digital Consumer Trends Index[189], 67% of consumers indicated they buy frequently from the same company but are not loyal to that brand, highlighting that highly-profitable consumers may easily switch to competitors.

These are important insights for loyalty program operators to consider when analysing their base of 'loyal' members. Behavioural commitment may be perceived as true loyalty, but without attitudinal commitment (ideally reinforced by calculative commitment), the program is at risk of rapidly losing members if a better product or service offering makes itself available.

Blockbuster and Netflix

In 2000, Blockbuster led the video rental industry globally, with thousands of retail locations, millions of customers and substantial marketing budgets. According to Holmgren (2006),[190] engagement with their loyalty program Movie Pass was one measure of

188 Mattila, A. S, 2006, 'How affective commitment boosts guest loyalty (and promotes frequent-guest programs)', Cornell Hotel and Restaurant Administration Quarterly, Vol 47, Iss 2, pp174 -181.

189 2022 Digital Consumer Trends Index, Cheetah Digital, https://www.cheetah-digital.com/report/digital-consumer-trends-index-content-hub-2022/, accessed 22 June 2023

190 Holmgren, L., 2006, 'An Inside Look at Blockbuster, Inc.', The University of Michigan.

store productivity, alongside revenue and active members. Movie Pass was designed to offer benefits and enhance customer loyalty by encouraging customers to rent movies only from Blockbuster stores. Blockbuster utilised a customer relationship management (CRM) strategy to segment their customer base as a way to build relationships with new members and preserve higher-value member relationships.

From a loyalty measurement perspective, Blockbuster senior management may have been led to believe they had been successful in developing a vast, highly loyal member base. In retrospect, it can be argued that the majority of the base was primarily demonstrating behavioural commitment (such as consistent rental behaviour week after week) but not attitudinal commitment. This meant that Blockbuster's business model was at risk of significant disruption from potential competitors if a better customer experience could be successfully offered.

Famously, Netflix provided that disruption by solving a range of inherent problems with Blockbuster's offering; they did not charge late fees (Blockbuster's late fees had become such an important part of their revenue model that the company's profits were highly dependent on them),[191] their movies were always available (according to the company's own figures, members could not get popular movies at Blockbuster stores up to 75 per cent of the time)[192] and they did not require two trips to a store to watch a movie (pick-up and drop-off).

Could attitudinal commitment have saved Blockbuster? It is unlikely it could have saved their business model, however if Blockbuster had been more successful in generating true emotional loyalty from

---

191 Satell, G., 2014, 'A Look Back At Why Blockbuster Really Failed And Why It Didn't Have To,' Forbes, https://www.forbes.com/sites/gregsatell/2014/09/05/a-look-back-at-why-blockbuster-really-failed-and-why-it-didnt-have-to/#34e8927b1d64 accessed 21 June 2020.

192 Nash, K. S., 2009, 'How Blockbuster Plans to Beat Netflix,' CIO, https://www.cio.com/article/2430765/how-blockbuster-plans-to-beat-netflix.html accessed 21 June 2020.

their members, it may have slowed their demise, allowing them to transition to a new business model, such as their own streaming service. They would have been in a position to promote it to an engaged audience and grow more rapidly than Netflix, thereby offering genuine competition in an emerging market.

Expectancy Theory of Motivation

Expectancy theory of motivation (Vroom, 1964)[193] proposes that people are motivated to behave because they believe their actions will lead to their desired outcome. This can provide loyalty program operators with a foundation on which to build a better understanding of ways to motivate members to engage.

The theory states that individuals will be motivated if they believe that there is a positive correlation between efforts and performance, and that favourable performance will result in a desirable reward. This makes the desire to satisfy the need strong enough to make the effort worthwhile.

Vroom outlined three core variables in his theory; *expectancy, instrumentality* and *valence*.

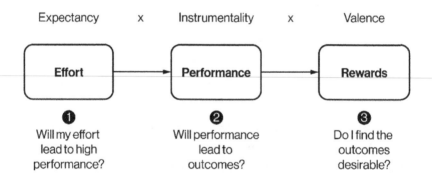

Figure 7: three components of expectancy theory by V.H Vroom, 1964. Reprinted from iEdunote[194] with permission.

193 Vroom, V.H., 1964, 'Work and motivation', New York: Wiley.

194 iEdunote, 'Expectancy Theory of Motivation', https://www.iedunote.com/expectancey-theory, accessed 16 July 2020.

Expectancy involves the belief that increases in effort leads to increases in performance. Instrumentality involves the belief that an appropriate reward will be received for the right performance. Valence is the importance a person places on the outcome that is expected.

Specific to a loyalty program, a member will be motivated to engage if they have the expectancy that their efforts will move them forward on a pathway towards accessing a reward (instrumentality) that satisfies an important need (valence).

For loyalty program design, expectancy theory is a useful tool for empathising with the members point of view. Focusing on the three core areas critical for motivation can help to clarify important and non-essential features, supporting the development of a simple yet sophisticated design. It is equally valuable when auditing existing programs, by directing the attention of the program operator to deficient aspects of the program which either block motivation, or do not motivate sufficiently.

Sharma and Verma (2014)[195] examined the application of motivation theory to influence a consumer's intention to enrol in a loyalty program. They identified several motivational factors relevant to program design:

- **Goal proximity**: how near the goal is from joining, which is positively related to intent to enrol in a rewards program.

- **Perceived effort**: how much work will be required to achieve the goal, which is negatively related to intent to enrol.

- **Reward valence**: how much the member values the reward, which is positively related to intent to enrol.

- **Customer reactance**: resistance to attempts to control behaviour or limit freedom of choice, which is negatively related to the intent to enrol.

---

195 Sharma, D. & Verma, V., 2014, 'Psychological and economic considerations of rewards programs', Journal of Retailing and Consumer Services, Vol 21, Iss 6, pp924-932.

Sharma and Verma argued a balance between all four factors is needed for a loyalty program to be successful, noting that their research suggested reward valence has the strongest positive effect and perceived effort has the strongest negative effect.

Sharma and Verma provide two examples to illustrate the application of their model; Delta Airlines and Citibank:

Delta Airlines Skymiles

In 2004, Delta Airlines revamped their Skymiles[196] program after identifying they were rewarding members who were not even covering the costs of delivering the transportation. They readjusted the Goal Proximity for discount economy passengers by providing only one quarter of the mileage reward that was being given to higher paying members. This adjustment ensured they stopped rewarding members for behaviour that was detrimental to the company's goal of profitability and instead rewarded those members which increased revenue and profits.

Citibank

Citibank[197] launched a credit card where members could earn American Airlines AAdvantage miles. To boost enrolments, Citibank offered 10,000 free miles just for opening a new account (equivalent to US$10,000 in purchases). Detrimentally, a significant percentage of customers signed up for the card, earned the free miles, and defected to the next deal being offered from a similar bank. This is an example of members being enticed by too high a level of reward valence and too low a level of perceived effort, with the unfortunate outcome being no measurable loyalty and large campaign costs.

---

196 Delta, https://www.delta.com/apac/en/skymiles/overview, accessed 15 June 2023.

197 Citi, https://www.citi.com/credit-cards/citi-aadvantage-platinum-elite-credit-card, accessed 15 June 2023.

Cognitive Dissonance Theory

Festinger (1957)[198] proposed that human beings strive for internal psychological consistency to function mentally in the real world. A person who experiences internal inconsistency tends to become psychologically uncomfortable and is motivated to reduce their *cognitive dissonance*.

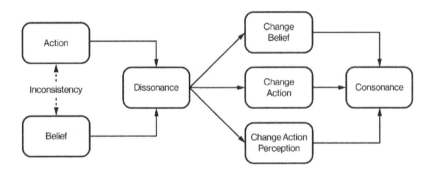

Figure 8: the development of cognitive dissonance. Adapted from 'A Theory of Cognitive Dissonance' by L Festinger, 1957.[199]

From a consumer perspective, cognitive dissonance may arise post-purchase, where buyer's remorse (or post-purchase regret) is experienced. A study by Skelton and Atwood (2017)[200] found 82 per cent of adults in Great Britain have regretted a purchase in the past. This was shown to be particularly prevalent for takeaway food, clothing and footwear. They estimated the annual expenditure on regretted purchases to be £5-25bn, equivalent to 2-10 per cent of annual consumer spending on goods in Great Britain.

Sharifi and Esfidani (2014)[201] conducted a study on mobile phone customers to test whether it was possible to mitigate cognitive dissonance in the

198 Festinger, L., 1957, 'A theory of cognitive dissonance', Stanford University Press.
199 Ibid.
200 Skelton, A. C. H. & Allwood, J. M., 2017, 'Questioning demand: A study of regretted purchases in Great Britain', Ecological Economics, Vol 131, pp499-509.
201 Sharifi, S. & Esfidani, M., 2014, 'The impacts of relationship marketing on cognitive dissonance, satisfaction, and loyalty: The mediating role of trust and cognitive dissonance', International Journal of Retail & Distribution Management, Vol 42.

post-purchase stage through relationship marketing activities. They identified that post-purchase cognitive dissonance discouraged satisfaction and loyalty, therefore addressing it was important for customer retention. Relationship marketing activities included direct marketing, database marketing, quality management and services marketing, which aimed to communicate messages of trust, commitment, co-operation and shared values. They found that targeting customers with relationship marketing activities after a high-involvement purchase reduced severe cognitive dissonance.

Customers tend to try to reduce dissonance on their own, and marketing managers can accompany such inherent efforts after the purchase to support the customer. Such personalised marketing efforts should be a standard campaign approach for companies focused on building customer loyalty.

There is a clear role for loyalty programs to play in reducing cognitive dissonance, and thereby building customer satisfaction and encouraging loyalty. This may include rewards tied to the transaction ('I spent all this money, but look how many points I earned!'), post-purchase communications efforts which strive to make the member feel they have made the right decision, and invitations to join clubs and communities which provide the customer with a sense of belonging and exclusivity, while connecting them to other like-minded customers.

Bentley Continental Club

A loyalty program by British heritage car brand Bentley likely acts to reduce the cognitive dissonance which may be associated with investing in such a high value purchase.

The Continental Club offers a range of rolling benefits which 'kick in as the car leaves the comfort zone of the manufacturer's warranty',[202] reducing the feeling of uncertainty which may arise at this key time.

Members of the Continental Club are entitled to substantial

202 Chilli Pepper, Top Marques, https://chillipepper.ie/top-marques/, accessed 29 June 2020.

discounts on their car services and maintenance work, free 'while you wait' oil top-up, car wash and tyre pressure checks, as well as additional aspirational benefits like access to exclusive launch events for new models.[203]

Key insights

- Consumer psychology provides a solid, research-based foundation to guide loyalty program design in a way which will maximise chances of successfully driving the desired behavioural changes.

- An extensive body of consumer psychology theories and studies exist which are immediately relevant for loyalty programs. These include the law of effect and the law of exercise, operant conditioning, social identity theory, endowed progress effect, goal gradient effect, customer delight and decision affect theory, norm of reciprocity, commitment theory, expectation theory of motivation and cognitive dissonance theory.

Suggested reading

- Skinner, B. F, 1948, 'Superstition' in the pigeon', Journal of Experimental Psychology, Vol 38, Iss 2, pp168–172.

- Ivanic, Aarti, 2015, 'Status Has Its Privileges: The Psychological Benefit of Status-Reinforcing Behaviors', Psychology & Marketing, Vol 32, pp697-708.

- Nunes, J. & Drèze, X., 2006, 'The Endowed Progress Effect: How Artificial Advancement increases Effort', Journal of Consumer Research, Vol 32, Iss 4, pp504-512.

- Kivetz, R., Urminsky, O., & Zheng, Y., 2006, 'The Goal-Gradient Hypothesis Resurrected: Purchase Acceleration, Illusionary Goal Progress, and Customer Retention', Journal of Marketing Research, Vol 43, pp39-58.

---

203 Ibid.

- Schwartz, N., 1987, 'Stimmung als Information (Mood as information)'.

- Regan, R., 1971, 'Effects of a favor and liking on compliance', Journal of Experimental Social Psychology, Vol 7, Iss 6, pp627-639.

- Mellers, B.A., Schwartz, A., Ho, K. & Ritov, I., 1997, 'Decision Affect Theory: Emotional Reactions to the Outcomes of Risky Options', Psychological Science, Vol 8, No 6, pp423-429.

- Oliver, R.L., Rust, R. & Varki, S., 1997, 'Customer Delight: Foundations, Findings, and Managerial Insight', Journal of Retailing, Vol 73, Iss 3, pp311-336.

- Sharma, D., & Verma, V., 2014, 'Psychological and economic considerations of rewards programs', Journal of Retailing and Consumer Services, Vol 21, Iss 6, pp924-932.

- Festinger, L., 1957, 'A theory of cognitive dissonance', Stanford University Press.

CHAPTER 6

BIASES AND HEURISTICS

This chapter was co-written by **Stacey Lyons** (Loyalty Director, Loyalty & Reward Co)

> *'... people rely on a limited number of heuristic principles which reduce the complex tasks of assessing probabilities and predicting values to simpler judgmental operations. In general, these heuristics are quite useful, but sometimes they lead to severe and systematic errors.'*
>
> *- Tversky, A. and Kahneman, D, 1974*[204]

Focus areas

This chapter will address the following questions:

- What are heuristics and biases?

- How are heuristics and biases relevant for loyalty programs?

- Which heuristics and biases are utilised by loyalty programs to influence member behaviours?

LOYALTY PROGRAMS AIM to influence consumer behaviour. Therefore, understanding how consumers make decisions and the factors that influence decision

---

204 Tversky, A. & Kahneman, D., 1974, 'Judgment under Uncertainty: Heuristics and Biases', Science, Vol 185, Iss 4157, pp1124–1131.

making is an important area of research for loyalty program designers and operators.

One area of psychology which warrants more comprehensive review is the effect of *heuristics* and *behavioural biases* which underpin the way consumers inherently behave.

A heuristic is defined as a mental shortcut that allows people to solve problems and make judgments quickly and efficiently. Heuristics form because consumers do not have the capacity, time or motivation to recognise and evaluate all the available information in their complex environment.[205]

Psychological biases, or cognitive biases, are defined as thinking patterns based on observations and generalisations that may lead to memory errors, inaccurate judgments, and faulty logic (Evans et al,) [206], causing consumers to make decisions without looking at the bigger picture.

While the influence of biases and heuristics can introduce information asymmetries and inaccuracies, and may lead to irrational decisions, they are deemed necessary to reduce the complexity of everyday decision-making processes by reducing the effort associated with cognitive tasks. Shah and Oppenheimer (2008)[207] stated that effort reduction relies on at least one of the following principles; examining fewer cues, reducing the difficulty associated with retrieving and storing cue values, simplifying the weighting principles for cues, integrating less information and examining fewer alternatives.

In the early 1970s, Kahneman & Tversky[208] introduced their foundational studies on biases and heuristics. They identified the concept of heuristics, and

205 Changing Minds, The Size Heuristic, http://changingminds.org/explanations/decision/size_heuristic.htm, accessed 29 May 2019.

206 Evans, J. St. B. T., Barston, J. L. & Pollard, P., 1983, 'On the conflict between logic and belief in syllogistic reasoning. Memory & Cognition, Vol 11, Iss 3, pp295-306.

207 *Shah, A. K., Oppenheimer, D.M., 2008, 'Heuristics made easy: An effort-reduction framework'*, Psychological Bulletin, Vol 134, pp207–222.

208 Tversky, A. & Kahneman, D., 1974, 'Judgment under Uncertainty: Heuristics and Biases', Science, Vol 185, Iss 4157, pp1124–1131.

how cognitive biases stem from the reliance on judgemental heuristics. They proposed a number of heuristic principles which explain the ways in which people assess probabilities and predict values to arrive at their choices.

Three primary heuristics were identified:

- **Representativeness heuristic**: occurs when people compare and categorise objects based on a limited number of similarities, rather than using objective statistics or knowledge.[209] One example of the representativeness heuristic relates to the judgement of value and size, where consumers misjudge the relationship between the two, thinking one directly resembles the other. To calculate how big something is, consumers may categorise this as 'lots', mistaking 'lots' for 'big'. For example, a pile of one thousand 1c coins can somehow seem more than a ten dollar note.

- **Availability heuristic**: states that people are inclined to retrieve information that is most readily available when making a decision (Redelmeier, 2005).[210] Tversky and Kahneman[211] offered the availability heuristic as an explanation for 'illusory correlations' in which people wrongly judge two events to be associated with each other, explaining that people judge correlation on the basis of the ease of imagining or recalling the two events together. If information comes to mind easily then consumers may overestimate the likelihood of an experience occurring. For example, if people have a vivid memory of being in a car accident or missing a flight, they are more likely to rate the odds of it happening again much higher than base rates would indicate.

- **Anchoring and adjustment heuristic**: occurs when people are estimating quantities. It states that they will arrive at an initial judgement

---

209 Kahneman, D. &Tversky, A., 1972, 'Subjective probability: A judgment of representativeness', Cognitive Psychology, Vol 3, Iss 3, pp430–454.

210 Redelmeier, D. A., 2005, 'The cognitive psychology of missed diagnosis', *Annals of Internal Medicine, Vol 142, Iss 2*, pp115-120.

211 Tversky, A. & Kahneman, D., 1973, 'Availability: A Heuristic for Judging Frequency and Probability', Cognitive Psychology, Vol 5, Iss 2, pp207–232.

based on an estimate (anchor) and then adjust this number based on additional information obtained. In Tversky and Kahneman's[212] experiments, subjects did not shift sufficiently far away from the anchor number to make a large enough adjustment to accurately reflect the real value. For example, a real estate agent may provide an opening bid well above the fair value price as a way of providing an anchor for negotiations. With a higher anchor, the final price will tend to be higher.

These concepts identified by Kahneman & Tversky have been refined and built upon over time, with huge bodies of research and hundreds of different behavioural biases identified since. Some are immediately relevant to specific loyalty programs, some are more closely related to general marketing functions and others do not apply to loyalty programs at all.

Loyalty programs can be designed to appeal to consumer reliance on specific biases and heuristics. The following theories are discussed in relation to practical applications within loyalty programs to influence member decisions and behaviours.

Representativeness heuristic

The *representativeness heuristic* identified by Kahneman and Tversky is utilised by points and miles programs. Program operators appeal to this heuristic by attempting to make the value of a reward appear bigger than it really is. For example, if a member spends $100 with a retailer and that retailer rewards them with 1 per cent of the total spend, then the member will receive $1 of value back, which may not sound very rewarding to the member. But if it is part of a loyalty program, the member can earn one hundred points (at 1c per point, which is equal to $1). By applying the representativeness heuristic, 'one hundred' points may be perceived as significantly bigger than 'one' dollar, making the member feel that the reward they have received is bigger than in reality.

The reverse is also true. Research on consumer processing of pricing information by Coulter and Coulter (2005)[213] determined that consumers are

212 Ibid.

213 Coulter, K. & Coulter, R., 2005. 'Size Does Matter: The Effects of Magnitude

frequently unaware of how their price and value inferences are derived. They may typically be unable to articulate the exact reasons why some aspect of the way price is presented translates into lower (or higher) perceived value. Their research determined that consumers could perceive product prices to be smaller simply by displaying the price in a smaller font size.

United Mileage Plus and Chase

In January 2023, United Mileage Plus and Chase[214] launched a competition offering MileagePlus members the chance to win 1 million miles.

Members could enter the competition for free simply by visiting a promotional website hosted by Chase.

The campaign was designed to support the launch of Timeshifter, the Jet Lag app developed by scientists to help travellers beat jet lag.

While one million points sounds like a lot to giveaway (it almost sounds like 1 million dollars), the cost would have likely been in the order of $10,000 or less. These types of promotions are an effective way for programs to drive strong engagement for a very low cost.

Time (hyperbolic) discounting bias

Frederick et al (2002)[215] coined *time discounting* (otherwise referred to as *hyperbolic discounting*) to refer to differences in the relative valuation placed on rewards by comparing value at different points in time. Their research suggested present rewards are weighted more heavily than future ones. If reward

Representation Congruency on Price Perceptions and Purchase Likelihood', Journal of Consumer Psychology, Vol 15, pp64-76.

214 Geoff Whitmore, 2023, 'United Airlines And Chase Are Giving Away 1 Million Miles', https://www.forbes.com/sites/geoffwhitmore/2023/01/24/united-airlines-and-chase-are-giving-away-1-million-miles/?sh=7299f0175789 accessed June 2023.

215 Frederick, S., Loewenstein, G. & O'Donoghue, T., 2002, 'Time discounting and time preference: A critical review', Journal of Economic Literature, Vol 40, pp351-401.

availability is very distant in time, it ceases to be valuable. In their study, subjects chose a $100 reward they could receive immediately over a $120 reward they could access in one month.

Building on time discounting is *present-biased preference*, where consumers have the inclination to prefer a smaller present reward to a larger later reward, but reverse their preference when both rewards are equally delayed. Chakraborty (2017)[216] provided the following example to illustrate:

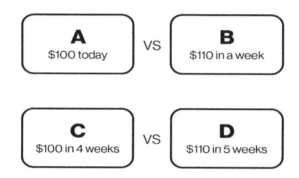

Figure 9: the example options provided within 'present-biased preference' research by A Chakraborty, 2019, p1.[217]

Most subjects chose A over B, but D over C, despite the time differences being the same.

These biases provide direction for loyalty program operators to structure their program to deliver to specific objectives:

- **To encourage points redemption**: offer lower value rewards which can be instantly accessed via website or app redemptions.

- **To encourage points accumulation**: set higher minimum points requirements for product redemptions and delay access to the reward.

---

216 Chakraborty, A, 2019, 'Present Bias,' University of California, Davis.
217 Ibid.

Chipotle Rewards

Chipotle[218] have designed their rewards program to encourage more frequent visits from members looking to unlock instant, lower value rewards.

Small amounts of points can be redeemed for free entrées. Program communications are focused on encouraging members to buy a meal in order to access their free entrée before it expires within 60 days.

This design seeks to take advantage of the time discounting bias.

Choice Privileges

The Choice Privileges rewards program encourages members to accumulate points by setting a minimum points requirement for redemption.

Members must redeem a minimum of 8,000 points within the hotel network or transfer a minimum of 5,000 points when exchanging for airline miles.[219]

This applies a time-delay on accessing the benefit to offset the present-biased preference.

Endowment Effect bias

An *endowment effect bias* occurs when people irrationally overvalue an object they own, regardless of its objective market value, whereby 'people often demand much more to give up an object than they would be willing to pay to acquire it' (Thaler, 1980).[220]

---

218 Chipotle, https://www.chipotle.com/order/rewards, accessed 8 June 2023.

219 Choice Hotels, Terms and Conditions, https://www.choicehotels.com/en-au/choice-privileges/rules-regulations#general, accessed 18 June 2020.

220 Thaler, R., 1980, 'Toward a Positive Theory of Consumer Choice,' Journal of Economic Behavior and Organization, Vol 1, pp39-60.

Kahneman et al (1991)[221] ran a series of experiments to test the endowment effect. In one experiment, 77 students were randomly assigned roles as buyers or sellers, with sellers provided with university-branded coffee mugs. Few trades ensued, with sellers asking for an average $7.12 for a mug, while buyers only wanted to pay an average $2.87. The experience suggested that the low volume of trade was primarily produced by the seller's reluctance to give up their endowment, rather than by buyers' unwillingness to spend their cash.

Figure 10: the results derived by Kahneman et al in their experiment, with the right side exhibiting the impact of the endowment effect bias on subjects overvaluing an object they own. Adapted from findings within research paper 'Anomalies: The endowment effect, loss aversion, and status quo bias' by D Kahneman et al, 1991.[222]

Qatar Airways Privilege Club

Qatar Airways utilised the endowment effect bias to attract and retain high-value customers from competitors. They provided non-members with instant access to a premium tier, hoping to make the new members feel a sense of ownership over their status, and hence value it more than if they were simply aspiring to achieve it.

In May 2020, Qatar Airways launched their first ever status match campaign.[223] Status matching allows loyal members of one pro-

221 Kahneman, D., Knetsch, J. L. & Thaler, R. H., 1991, 'Anomalies: The endowment effect, loss aversion, and status quo bias', Journal of Economic Perspectives, Vol 5, Iss 1, pp193-206.

222 Ibid.

223 Ollila, J., 2020, 'Qatar Airways Privilege Club Status Match Campaign May 2020', https://loyaltylobby.com/2020/05/18/qatar-airways-privilege-club-status-match-campaign-may-2020/, accessed 1 July 2020.

gram to access equivalent benefits with another program for a set period.

Qatar Airways offered silver, gold and platinum frequent flyers from Emirates, Etihad, Singapore Airlines, South African Airways, Turkish Airlines and Virgin Australia the corresponding status within their Privilege Club, without having to build up status credits.

By bestowing instant premium status on a new Privilege Club member for a full year, and creating a feeling of ownership, Qatar Airways hoped members would be motivated to fly more with Qatar (and less with competitors) in order to retain their status.

Loss Aversion bias

Loss aversion suggests that the pain of losing something feels twice as powerful as the pleasure of gaining the same thing.

Kahneman and Tversky (1979)[224] conducted a series of experiments where subjects were asked to choose between more or less risky propositions which provided the potential to win or lose money (e.g., an equal chance of winning or losing $100). They found 'the aggravation that one experiences in losing a sum of money appears to be greater than the pleasure associated with gaining the same amount', and that most people find symmetric bets of that form to be distinctly unattractive.

---

224 Kahneman, D. & Tversky, A., 1979, 'Prospect Theory: An Analysis of Decision under Risk', Econometrica, Vol. 47, Iss 2, pp263-9.

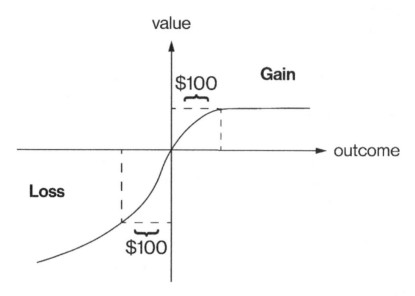

Figure 11: the findings by Kahneman and Tversky, showing the fear of losing $100 is twice as powerful as the prospect of gaining $100. Adapted from 'Prospect Theory: An Analysis of Decision under Risk', D Kahneman and A Tversky 1979.[225]

These findings have led to the development of strategies whereby workers and students have been motivated by penalties rather than rewards. Hossain & List (2012)[226] determined that framing outcomes as penalties resulted in improved performance in a Chinese production factory. Fryer et al (2012)[227] demonstrated that exploiting the power of loss aversion, where teachers were paid in advance and asked to give back the money if their students did not improve sufficiently, increased math test scores by more than one standard deviation.

225 Ibid.

226 Hossain, T. & List, J., 2009, 'The Behavioralist Visits the Factory: Increasing Productivity Using Simple Framing Manipulations', National Bureau of Economic Research, Inc, NBER Working Papers, Vol 58, Iss 12, pp2151-2167.

227 Fryer, R. G., Levitt, S. D., List, J. & Sadoff, S., 2012. 'Enhancing the Efficacy of Teacher Incentives through Loss Aversion: A Field Experiment,' NBER Working Papers 18237, National Bureau of Economic Research, Inc.

People appear to be more willing to take risks or behave dishonestly to avoid a loss than to make a gain. A study by Schindler & Pfattheicher (2016)[228] used a die-under-the-cup game and a coin-toss task, with the opportunity for participants to engage in dishonest behaviour either to avoid a loss or to approach an equivalent gain. Their results found that people showed more dishonest behaviour to avoid a loss.

Loss aversion is used extensively in loyalty programs (and marketing strategies more widely) to stimulate member engagement. Programs can provide members with something which they feel ownership for and value, and then establish conditions whereby they might have ownership removed. This can act as a motivational force to compel the member to continue transacting. This includes:

- The threat of status tier members losing their benefits if they fail to earn enough status credits.

- Members facing the risk of their points expiring if they do not engage with the program on a regular enough basis (or redeem them in time).

- Members not being able to access desirable rewards (reward seats, hotel rooms, etc.).

- Members having to spend a greater amount of points if they do not book early enough.

According to Ries (2012),[229] some private fitness centres allow people to invest their own money in weight-loss incentives (e.g., by putting in $200 and receiving a portion back as they achieve incremental weight-loss goals). Websites like www.stickK.com operate on the same basis in the online environment. They help people achieve goals via a 'commitment contract'; a binding

---

228 Schindler, S. & Pfattheicher, S., 2017, 'The frame of the game: Loss-framing increases dishonest behavior', Journal of Experimental Social Psychology, Vol 69, pp172-177.

229 Ries, N. M., 2012, 'Financial incentives for weight loss and healthy behaviours. Healthcare policy = Politiques de sante', Vol 7, Iss 3, pp23–28.

agreement which involves putting money on the table to ensure the user follows through with their intentions using loss aversion.

Loyalty programs also build in benefits which minimise the risk of loss aversion. For example, offering members money back guarantees, extended returns, free returns or automatic refunds if prices reduce on purchased items. These program benefits can provide the member with an extra sense of security by lowering the perceived risk of losing money.

Mileage Runs

A 'mileage run' or 'status run' involves members of a frequent flyer program taking a flight with the sole purpose of earning enough status credits to ensure their status tier is maintained. The destination or the number of frequent flyer points earned for the trip can be secondary considerations.

If a member has not flown enough in a calendar year to qualify or re-qualify for a premium status, sometimes they will engage in a mileage or status run due to the high value placed on the benefits they stand to lose.

Many websites and forums exist for frequent flyer members to research or discuss how a member can book a flight with the necessary status credits for the lowest cost. For example, one forum, Flyertalk, has tens of thousands of threads related to mileage run discussions.[230]

After recognising the patterns of mileage runners, airlines may adjust their promotions by offering more frequent status credit promotions on certain routes rather than offering sale prices (i.e., double status credits).

---

230 Flyertalk, https://www.flyertalk.com/forum/mileage-run-discussion-627/, accessed 18 June 2020.

Framing of Attribute Information bias

The *framing of attribute information bias* (Levin and Gaeth, 1988)[231] states people will react to a particular choice in different ways depending on whether it is presented as a loss or a gain. More specifically, people tend to avoid risks when a positive frame is presented but seek risks when a negative frame is presented, a bias which has links to loss aversion.

Levin and Gaeth asked subjects to rate several qualitative attributes of ground beef that framed the beef as either 75 per cent lean or 25 per cent fat. Subjects provided more favourable evaluations of the beef labelled 75 per cent lean.

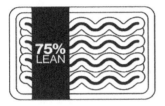 

Figure 12: the experiment run by Levin and Gaeth, showing the effects of framing of ground beef attributes on subjects. Adapted from 'How Consumers Are Affected by the Framing of Attribute Information Before and After Consuming the Product', Levin, I and Gaeth, G, 1988.[232]

Diamond and Campbell (1988) tested subjects in a laboratory simulation which compared monetary promotions (such as discounts) with non-monetary promotions (such as free goods or extra amounts of the product) using the same referenced price value. Subjects rated non-monetary promotions as making them feel that they are 'gaining something extra'. In contrast, subjects rated monetary promotions as making them feel that they were 'losing less than usual'.[233] In short, non-monetary promotions were framed as gains and

---

231 Levin, I. & Gaeth, G., 1988', 'How Consumers Are Affected by the Framing of Attribute Information Before and After Consuming the Product', Journal of Consumer Research, Vol 15, pp374-78.

232 Ibid.

233 Diamond, W. D. & Campbell, L., 1988, 'The Framing of Sales Promotions:

monetary promotions were framed as reduced losses, indicating non-monetary promotions are viewed more favourably.

This hypothesis was again tested in an experiment specifically involving supermarket coupons.[234] The test demonstrated that supermarket shoppers presented with redeemable coupons were significantly more likely to choose a test promotion if it were framed as a gain (buy a spaghetti sauce and get a free soup valued at 49c) than if it were framed as a reduced loss (buy a spaghetti sauce and a soup and get 49c off the bill).

Framing provides important direction for communication positioning within a loyalty program. Program operators can utilise framing in a variety of ways:

- Position rewards as additional perks that are provided to loyal customers at the company's expense (O'Malley and Prothero, 2002).[235]

- Use progress trackers, which highlight the progress made towards the completion of a goal and unlocking of a reward. Despite the need for a member to make further transactions, the progress tracker enables communications to be framed as a gain (e.g., earn just 200 points more to unlock a free flight) rather than a loss (e.g., $200 spend is required to unlock a free flight). The goal may be access to a reward product or the achievement of a status tier.

- Tailor messages to loyalty program members to emphasise their special status and acknowledge the importance of the relationship with the brand (Shugan, 2005).[236]

Effects on Reference Price Change', https://www.acrwebsite.org/volumes/6862/volumes/v16/NA-16, accessed 29 June 2020.

234 Diamond, W. D. & Sanyal, A., 1990, 'The Effect of Framing on the Choice of Supermarket Coupons',http://www.communicationcache.com/uploads/1/0/8/8/10887248/the_effect_of_framing_on_the_choice_of_supermarket_coupons.pdf, accessed 29 June 2020.

235 O'Malley, L., & Prothero, A., 2002, 'Beyond the frills of relationship marketing', Journal of Business Research, Vol 57, Iss 11, pp1286-1294.

236 Shugan, S. M., 2005, 'Brand loyalty programs: Are they shams?', Marketing

- Implement a points plus pay option as part of the standard purchase flow, allowing members to reduce the amount of cash they spend by subsidising the cost with points. Examples include airlines which allow members to reduce the total cost of the fare by paying with a combination of cash and frequent flyer points (a positive frame). Drèze & Nunes (2004)[237] conducted research which delivered a mathematical proof that a combination of cash and points can be superior to a standard, single-currency price by lowering the psychological or perceived cost.

Returning to Levin and Gaeth's study on lean vs fat beef, they reported that the magnitude of the framing effect lessened when subjects actually tasted the meat, suggesting a diagnostic product experience dilutes the impact of framing. This is an important consideration which cautions that while consumers may be influenced by framing, they will be influenced more by the actual experience of consumption. A focus on delivering a customer experience that is consistent with, or exceeds, expectations must be a priority in the pursuit of genuine member loyalty.

Rakuten

Rakuten[238] is a marketplace that allows shoppers to earn cashback online and offline through their app, browser extension or rakuten. com. Rakuten boasts more than 3,500 participating stores that pay them a commission for directing buying shoppers to their stores or websites. Rakuten utilises the commission to reward members with cashback when they purchase.

By magnifying the gain (cashback), rather than the loss (financial), Rakuten are framing the program as positive, with their website stating 'Get paid for shopping at all your favourite stores'.

Science, Vol 24, pp185-93.

237 Drèze, J. & Nunes, J., 2004 'Using Combined-Currency Prices to Lower Consumers' Perceived Cost.' Journal of Marketing Research, Vol. 59, pp. 59-72.

238 Rakuten, https://www.rakuten.com/, accessed 9 June 2023.

Informational Social Influence (social proof) bias

Sherif (1935) ran a famous study using optical illusions to test the influence of social conformity. When looking at a stationary point of light in a dark room, the light appears to move back and forth. Sherif found that when subjects were tested alone, they established their own range for judging the distance the light was perceived to move and used this as an anchor to guide future judgements. When subjects were tested in a group, there was clear convergence on the range with group norms being established. Even when later tested alone, group norms persisted. When subjects within this study were asked if they were influenced by the judgements of other people in the group, only 25 per cent of subjects reported they were, showing that social conformity occurs sub-consciously.

In an equally famous study, Asch (1951)[239] conducted a series of experiments which utilised a similarly clever approach to explore the effects of social conformity. Asch placed a subject in a room with seven actors who had been instructed to provide specific answers. A line length judgement test was used, where a target line was presented, followed by three other lines (labelled A, B and C). Each participant took turns to state which line was most like the target line in length across 18 different tests. The actors deliberately said the wrong answer for 12 of the 18 tests. On average, subjects conformed to the incorrect answers on 32 per cent of the tests, with 74 per cent of subjects conforming on at least one obvious test. This is an astonishing result considering the correct answer was generally obvious.

Cialdini (1984)[240] built on this insight with the concept of *social proof*, where individuals mimic the actions of others in ambiguous social situations, irrespective of whether that behaviour is appropriate and logical. Cialdini hypothesised that 'one means we use to determine what is correct is to find out what other people think is correct'. This is based on the bias that when a lot of people are doing something, it is likely the correct thing to do.

Specific to loyalty programs (and the wider field of marketing), the digital

---

239 Asch, S. E., 1951, 'Effects of Group Pressure on the Modification and Distortion of Judgments', In Guetzknow, H., Ed., Groups, Leadership and Men, Pittsburgh, PA, Carnegie Press, pp177-190.
240 Cialdini, R. B., 1993, 'Influence: The Psychology of Persuasion'.

age has made it easier to observe what others are doing, at scale and over vast geographies. Social media, review websites and word of mouth have all been identified as powerful influencers of consumer behaviour and attitudes towards brands and products. They establish group norms and stimulate mass conformity in ways not previously possible.

A loyalty program can play a role in building a positive brand presence across these promotional channels in four ways:

- Building the member base and developing a positive relationship with members to increase their propensity to become advocates. This is best supported via a comprehensive lifecycle management strategy, which is covered in Chapter 15.

- Utilising gamification techniques to encourage members to engage with the channels (e.g., awarding bonus points for following a brand on social media). Gamification is covered in Chapter 9.

- Prompting members who have recently transacted to provide their feedback via review, and responding to that review, whether it is positive or negative (studies have shown that nearly 95 per cent of shoppers read online reviews before making a purchase[241] and 97 per cent of shoppers say reviews influence buying decisions[242]).

- Providing members with access to a referral program (as covered in Chapter 8), where both the member and their family members or friends can earn a bonus reward for joining the loyalty program.

This approach of gamifying social media engagement can deliver additional benefits. Rehnen et al (2017)[243] ran a field study where subjects earned

241 Spiegal Research Centre, 2017, 'How Online Reviews Influence Sales', https://spiegel.medill.northwestern.edu/online-reviews/, accessed 12 May 2020.

242 Fan and Fuel, 2016, 'No online customer reviews means BIG problems in 2017', https://fanandfuel.com/no-online-customer-reviews-means-big-problems-2017/, accessed 12 May 2020.

243 Rehnen, L., Bartsch, S., Kull, M. & Meyer, A., 2017, 'Exploring the impact of rewarded social media engagement in loyalty programs, Journal of Service Management, Vol 28, pp305 – 328.

loyalty points for social media engagement. The results showed significantly higher attitudinal commitment to the program and the brand than that of members who earned points solely through transactions. They concluded that rewarding customers for social media engagement can be a beneficial way of boosting active participation in loyalty programs, however they cautioned that the experience needs to be enjoyable and self-determined.

There is also a large movement towards social responsibility which aligns with social proof, as people want to be seen to be doing the right thing, with social media the enabler. The market has long been full of programs providing the option for members to donate their points to charity (e.g., Amex, Singapore Airlines and *Flybuys* to name a few), and while this premise usually tests well among consumers in market research, it rarely materialises into consumer action. So, when there is no social pressure or social gain attached to doing the right thing, there is far less incentive to attract consumers to continue engaging in this way.

However, if loyalty programs can leverage the power of social media to support social movements, then the results can be powerful. For example, some brands are designing programs around the wellness social movement. Nike Training Club[244], Lorna Jane Active Living[245] and Gap Athletawell[246] not only sell activewear but also incorporate rewards for fitness, nutrition, training and wellness, with results able to be shared on social media as a form of social proof.

Klook

Online travel agent (OTA) Klook rewards members for providing reviews after they have made a booking.[247]

Klook state, 'Your joy matters to us: Leave a review to earn credits and save on your next booking.'

---

244 Nike, https://www.nike.com/au/ntc-app, accessed 17 July 2023.

245 Lorna Jane, https://www.movenourishbelieve.com/active-living-program/, accessed 17 July 2023.

246 Gap, Athletawell, https://community.athletawell.com/, accessed 17 July 2023.

247 Klook, https://www.klook.com/, accessed 17 July 2023.

> Reviews are posted against the travel and experience offers available, providing members with the ability to see what others thought about the experience prior to deciding whether to make their own booking.
>
> Rewarding members with credits aims to stimulate the number of reviews available, harnessing social proof to drive more bookings.
>
> Credits can be used as a discount for future bookings.

Moral Self-Licensing bias

A *self-licensing effect* occurs when past good deeds 'liberate individuals to engage in behaviours that are immoral, unethical, or otherwise problematic, behaviours that they would otherwise avoid for fear of feeling or appearing immoral' (Merritt et al, 2010).[248] That is, if a person performs a behaviour which they perceive to be moral, they allocate themselves a 'moral surplus' which they justify as licence to subsequently behave immorally, bringing them back to a state of moral equilibrium. A simple example would be a dieter rewarding themselves with a 'naughty treat' for sticking to their meal plan.

Effron et al (2009)[249] tested the impact that voicing support for Barack Obama just before the 2008 election would have on subjects making ambiguously racist statements. Subjects were asked to play the role of a sheriff recruiting either a black or white officer to a police department. On average, subjects said that a police force job was equally well suited for both white and black candidates. By contrast, subjects who were provided with an opportunity to express their support for Obama prior to conducting the main part of the experiment were more likely to say the job was better suited for a white candidate. The self-licensing effect is said to have occurred because the subjects who expressed support for Obama made them feel that they no longer needed to prove their lack of prejudice.

---

248 Merritt, A. C., Effron, D. A. & Monin, B., 2010, 'Moral Self-Licensing: When Being Good Frees Us to Be Bad', Social and Personality Psychology Compass, Vol 4, pp344-357.

249 Effron, D. A., Cameron, J. S. & Monin, B., 2009, 'Endorsing Obama Licenses Favoring Whites', Journal of Experimental Social Psychology, Vol 45 pp590-593.

This study replicated an original study by Monin & Miller (2001),[250] who tested the self-licensing effect on racist attitudes as well as sexist attitudes, finding subjects who were provided with the opportunity to demonstrate they were not racist or sexist were more inclined to demonstrate racist or sexist decisions.

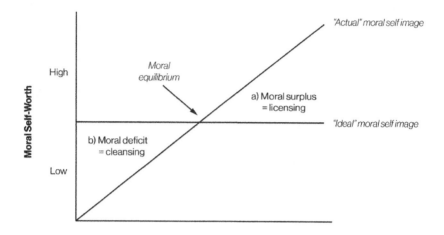

Figure 13: the process of moral self-regulation, demonstrating that when people engage in moral or immoral actions, this may lead to a surplus or deficit from their ideal state which licenses them to engage in subsequent immoral or moral behaviour respectively to re-establish equilibrium. Adapted from 'The limits of Moral Licensing' by Y Hertzman and D Stolle, 2013, Figure 1, p 4.[251]

Kivetz and Simonson (2002)[252] identified a self-licensing effect in loyalty programs. They conducted research on the effort members invested to obtain different types of rewards. They found that a higher level of effort tended to shift member preferences from necessity to luxury rewards. They hypothesised this was the result of a self-licensing effect where the higher efforts required to earn enough points acted to reduce the guilt often associated with choosing

250 Monin, B. & Miller, D. T., 2001, 'Moral credentials and the expression of prejudice', Journal of Personality and Social Psychology, Vol 81, pp33–43.

251 Hertzman, Y. & Stolle, D., 2013, 'The limits of Moral Licensing', https://rubenson. org/wp-content/uploads/2013/11/TPBW_StolleHertzman.pdf, accessed 16 July 2020.

252 Kivetz, R. & Simonson, I., 2002, 'Earning the Right to Indulge: Effort as a Determinant of Customer Preferences Toward Frequency Program Rewards', Journal of Marketing Research - J MARKET RES-CHICAGO, Vol 39, pp155-170.

luxuries over necessities. Providing further evidence for the self-licensing in loyalty programs, they also identified that the effect was stronger on members who tended to feel guilty about luxury consumption. For example, many frequent flyer program members refuse to pay for business class seats but are comfortable redeeming points for business class upgrades. Members may justify or give themselves moral license to indulge on a business class seat by detaching loyalty currencies from money, or mentally accounting a reward as being 'free', whereby guilt is also mentally detached.

This is reflective of Nunes and Drèze (2006),[253] who argued the more successful loyalty programs feature less functional and more pleasure-providing rewards as 'consumers love to be given a treat they would not splurge on with their own money.'

Mastercard Pay With Rewards

Rather than offering rewards which a member could easily buy themselves, Mastercard have moved towards experiential rewards to align with the changing desires of their members. Pay With Rewards gives cardholders the flexibility to use their points however they desire.[254]

They have focused on providing rewards options which add an extra level of service across a member's lifestyle to deliver a complete end-to-end experience. For example, a member can use Pay With Rewards to splurge on a night out which can include everything from the ride there, the restaurant, the movies and the ride home, making the entire experience rewarding at every touchpoint.

This structure gives members the chance to enjoy indulging in luxuries, holidays, or even groceries they may not have given themselves license to buy otherwise.

---

253 Nunes, J. C. & Drèze, X., 2006, 'Your Loyalty Program Is Betraying You', Harvard Business Review, https://hbr.org/2006/04/your-loyalty-program-is-betraying-you, accessed 2 Feb 2020.

254 Mastercard, https://www.mastercard.com.au/en-au/issuers/products-and-solutions/grow-manage-your-business/loyalty-solutions/pay-with-rewards.html, accessed 29 June 2020.

Priming bias

Priming is a psychological technique whereby exposure to a certain stimulus may influence the response to a subsequent stimulus. North et al (1999)[255] investigated the extent to which stereotypically French and German music could influence supermarket customers selecting of French and German wines. Over a two-week period, French and German music was played on alternate days from an in-store display of French and German wines. French music led to French wines outselling German wines, whereas German music led to German wines outselling French wines. Responses to a questionnaire suggested that customers were unaware of these effects of music on their product choices.

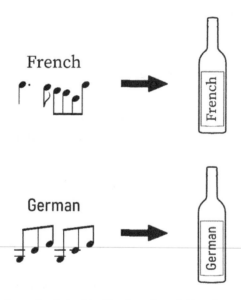

Figure 14: the results derived by North et al, with French music positively impacting the purchase of French wine and German music positively impacting the purchase of German wine. Adapted from findings within 'The influence of in-store music on wine selections' by A.C North et al, 1999.[256]

255 North, A. C., Hargreaves, D. J. & McKendrick, J., 1999, 'The influence of in-store music on wine selections.' Journal of Applied Psychology, Vol 84, Iss 2, pp271-276.

256 North, A. C., Hargreaves, D. J. & McKendrick, J., 1999, 'The influence of in-store music on wine selections.' Journal of Applied Psychology, Vol 84, Iss 2, pp271-276.

Priming can have different effects on different people. A study by Rick et al (2008)[257] tested the effect of priming on subjects who experienced different levels of anticipatory mental pain when paying for products ('Spendthrifts', who experience low pain vs 'Tightwads', who experience high pain). When primed with sad music, the Spendthrifts indicated they would spend more, while the Tightwads indicated they would spend less. Both strategies aimed to make them feel better: Spendthrifts cheered themselves up by going shopping, while Tightwads made themselves feel more in control by managing their budget. This provides some evidence for the need for segmentation strategies when utilising these types of approaches.

For loyalty programs, understanding whether members respond better to bonus earn promotions, bonus redemption promotions or discount offers will increase the effectiveness of priming members to take a desired action. For example, informing the member they will earn bonus points for a transaction may act to reduce the mental pain of the member spending money.

Another application of priming is the use of status tier labels invoking value (e.g., Gold, Platinum, Emerald and Diamond). Drèze and Nunes (2009)[258] found that using status-laden colours (Gold and Silver) primed members to form a perception of a pyramid-shaped hierarchy without them needing to specify the percentage of customers in each tier. This was not the case when the colours Blue and Yellow were used.

Woolworths Everyday Rewards

Product placement within physical supermarkets is a primary driver for influencing purchase behaviours, and Everyday Rewards have found a way to deliver the same effects digitally by priming their member base.

---

257 Rick, S. I., Cryder, C. E. & Loewenstein, G., 2008, 'Tightwads and spend-thrifts', Journal of Consumer Research, Vol 34, Iss 6, pp767–782.
258 Drèze, X. & Nunes, J., 2009, 'Feeling Superior: The Impact of Loyalty Program Structure on Consumers' Perceptions of Status', Journal of Consumer Research, Vol 35, pp890-905.

Woolworths prime their program members to try new products that they usually would not purchase by strategically placing them alongside commonly purchased products within personalised emails. In this way, members become familiar with products that they have never even considered.

As an example of the type of insight they have learned and applied to grow member spend, Everyday Rewards identified that 'new products sandwiched between familiar products or brands are more likely to be bought and tried by consumers'.[259]

Sunk Cost Effect bias

Arkes and Blumer (1985)[260] identified the *sunk cost effect* as greater tendency to continue an endeavour once an investment in money, effort, or time has been made. They conducted a field study where customers who had initially paid more for a season subscription to a theatre series attended more plays during the next six months, presumably because of their higher sunk cost in the season tickets.

Sunk costs are deemed a fallacy because they are irrecoverable investments that should not influence decisions, which should be made on the basis of expected future consequences.

Sweis et al (2018)[261] identified that rats, mice and humans are all sensitive to sunk costs after they have made the decision to pursue a reward. They suggested this indicates the sensitivity to temporal sunk costs lies in a vulnerability distinct from deliberation processes, and that this distinction is present across species.

259 Maes, I., cited in Croft, L., 2018, 'We must treat data as a precious gift', says Woolies Exec', http://www.bandt.com.au/marketing/must-treat-data-precious-gift-says-woolies-exec, accessed 10th April 2019.

260 Arkes, H. R. & Blumer, C., 1985, 'The psychology of sunk cost', Organizational Behavior and Human Decision Processes, Vol 35, pp124-140.

261 Sweis, B. M., Abram, S. V.,Schmidt, B. J., Seeland, K. D., MacDonald III, A.W., Thomas, M. J. & Redish, A. D., 2018, 'Sensitivity to "sunk costs" in mice, rats, and humans', Science (New York, N.Y.), pp178-181.

Ashley et at (2015)[262] identified a sunk cost effect in subscription loyalty programs by running a study which demonstrated consumers who pay a fee to participate in a loyalty program have more favourable attitudes, and more positive evaluations of value for the money and benefits than non-paying members.

Whilst the sunk cost effect can provide benefits for subscription-based loyalty program operators, it is important for them to also manage the issue of 'subscription guilt'. For Love or Money 2019[263] explores the reality of 'subscription guilt', revealing that 30 per cent of members who participate in loyalty programs with a subscription have *felt guilty for not using or accessing enough of the benefits offered through that subscription*. This effect increases to 46 per cent of women aged between 18-45, indicating different generational and gender cohort impacts.

Club Pret

Popular UK food chain Pret A Manger launched its subscription product post Covid-19, offering up to five barista-made drinks a day (including coffee, iced products and speciality teas), plus 10 per cent off the entire menu for £15 for the first month and £30 thereafter.

The program successfully generated 15,000 subscribers by 3pm the first day, with the attention that followed focused around the value of the program, rather than the subscription cost. A Twitter calculator emerged which allowed users to input their Pret order and see how much they would save with their subscription. The creator of the calculator, Jonathan Allenby, found he would recoup £62.77 a month, however, if someone ordered five frappés a day, seven days a week, they would benefit from a monthly saving of £556.33.

262 Ashley, C., Gillespie, E. A. & Noble, S. M., 2015, 'The effect of loyalty program fees on program perceptions and engagement', Journal of Business Research, Vol 69, Iss 2, https://digitalcommons.uri.edu/cgi/viewcontent. cgi?article=1051&context=cba_facpubs, accessed 26 April 2020.

263 Point of Loyalty, 'For Love Or Money 2019', https://thepointofloyalty.com.au/subscription-guilt-myth-or-reality/, accessed 5 May 2020.

> The subscription has been extremely successful for Pret in growing recurring revenue, acquisition of younger demographics, habitual data sharing (what Pret describe as their 'first digital relationship with their customers'), repeat visits, and retention from subscribers who view the program as a money saver.[264]

Scarcity bias

Worchel et al (1975)[265] stated the *scarcity effect* as when an item is more difficult to acquire, it will be valued more highly. They conducted experiments where students were asked to rate the value and attractiveness of cookies that were either in abundant or scarce supply. They found that when the same cookies were labelled as in scarce supply, subjects rated them as more desirable than cookies labelled as in abundant supply. In addition, cookies were rated as more valuable when their supply changed from abundant to scarce, than when they were constantly scarce.

In economics, the scarcity effect is reflected in the water-diamond paradox; water is cheap, but necessary for survival, while diamonds are expensive, but not required for survival. This indicates that object value is not merely determined by usefulness, but also by availability.

Song et al (2019)[266] conducted research on credit card loyalty programs using the scarcity effect as part of their marketing strategy. They studied how different messages motivated engagement of the associated reward referral program and found limited-quantity messages had the highest positive impact on consumers' behavioural intentions.

Airline and hotel loyalty programs utilise scarcity to drive desire for reward products. Airlines only have a limited number of available reward seats, and

264 Lewis, T., 2021, 'From coffee to cars: how Britain became a nation of subscribers', The Guardian, https://www.theguardian.com/lifeandstyle/2021/may/09/from-coffee-to-cars-how-britain-became-a-nation-of-subscribers, accessed 11 May 2023.

265 Worchel, S., Lee, J., & Adewole, A. (1975). Effects of supply and demand on ratings of object value. Journal of Personality and Social Psychology, 32(5), 906–914.

266 Song, C., Wang, T. & Hu, M., 2019, 'Referral reward programs with scarcity messages on bank credit card adoption', International Journal of Bank Marketing, Vol 37.

hotels only have a limited number of available reward rooms. In addition to members feeling fortunate when they manage to access such a reward, programs also allocate a proportion of their inventory to status tier members, making them feel a heightened sense of exclusivity by being able to secure rewards that lower or non-status members cannot.

From 2017-2019, a number of companies launched cryptocurrency loyalty programs (Shelper, 2019).[267] The essence of the programs was to reward members with a loyalty currency which had a finite supply, denoting scarcity. Thus, as more and more members joined the program and earned, the currency would increase in value. The majority of these programs collapsed relatively quickly, primarily due to the fact that they were unsuccessful in generating sufficient member engagement to stimulate enough demand to drive the value of the cryptocurrency higher. However, some programs rewarding members with major cryptocurrencies, such as Bitcoin, are succeeding and growing.[268]

Wyndham Rewards

Members of Wyndham Rewards[269] earn points and status credits when they spend with Wyndham hotel brands across 22 countries, with partner brands or with their Wyndham Rewards Visa card. Members can redeem points within the Wyndham hotel network, as well as on gift cards, merchandise and airline miles.

Another way for members to redeem points is at a Wyndham Auction. Typical auction items include experiences such as a chance to see Jennifer Lopez's show in Las Vegas, family passes to Legoland or a two-night getaway at a luxury Wyndham hotel. Like eBay, members may bid on multiple auctions simultaneously, and

267 Shelper, P., 2019, 'Blockchain Loyalty: Disrupting Loyalty and reinventing marketing using blockchain and cryptocurrencies - 2nd Edition'.

268 Kahatri, Y., 2020 'Bitcoin rewards startup Lolli raises $3 million in new funding,' Yahoo! Finance, https://finance.yahoo.com/news/bitcoin-rewards-startup-lolli-raises-133312938.html accessed 17 July 2020.

269 Wyndham Rewards, https://www.wyndhamhotels.com/en-ap/wyndham-rewards, accessed 1 July 2020.

track the history of their bids to assess the effectiveness of their bidding strategy. Auctions run for 2-3 weeks and winners are notified via email.[270]

The auction feature places a fresh spin on redemption, capitalising on the scarcity bias due to the limited nature of auction items. The scarcity element has helped Wyndham Rewards to generate sustained engagement with the program, motivating members to continue earning points for more chances to win desired auction items.

Lucky Loyalty Effect

The Lucky Loyalty Effect is a cognitive bias that tells us that loyal customers believe they are more likely to win random promotions run by a program because they have invested more time, money and emotion into the brand than other customers.

Reczek, Haws and Summers (2014) investigated the effect of random gamification elements such as sweepstakes on loyal customers through their research on the Lucky Loyalty Effect[271]. The studies concluded that loyal customers reported a higher perceived likelihood of winning random rewards such as sweepstakes and competitions (i.e., they feel more lucky) because they feel they deserve special treatment and recognition for their loyalty. The work demonstrated that loyal individuals feel they can 'earn' something which is unearnable through effort, even when effort and outcome are unrelated. The Lucky Loyalty effect was found to occur under specific conditions:

- The member has made high actual earn efforts previously

- The promotion is directly associated with the program/company the member is loyal to

270 O'Neill, S., 2017, 'Wyndham Hotels Debuts Online Auctions for Loyalty Program Redemption', Skift, https://skift.com/2017/07/26/wyndham-hotels-debuts-online-auctions-for-loyalty-program-redemption/, accessed 1 July 2020.

271 Reczek, R.W., Haws, K.L. and Summers, C.A., 2014. Lucky Loyalty: The Effect of Consumer Effort on Predictions of Randomly Determined Marketing Outcomes. Journal of Consumer Research, 41(December), pp.1065-1077.

- The member is comparing themselves with other lower effort customers

The consequences associated with the Lucky Loyalty Effect include higher participation from loyal members in random promotions because they feel luckier. However, less effort is input into maximising their chances of winning as loyal members rely on their luck alone. Another consequence is member disappointment when they do not win after feeling lucky about and deserving of a win.

For program operators, communications are key to managing member expectations associated with the Lucky Loyalty Effect bias, particularly post the announcing of the winner. For example, sending loyal members a message sympathising with them after not winning, but recognising their loyalty by providing them with a personalised special offer or benefit can help curve their disappointment and maintain the valuable relationship.[272]

LEGO VIP Rewards

In honour of Star Wars Day ('May the 4th Be With You') LEGO VIP Rewards went live with a sweepstake offering members the chance to win a one-of-a-kind Star Wars minifigure accompanied by a picture autographed by the actor of the character. Members could enter up to 50 times, with 50 points required per entry.

Because of the Lucky Loyalty Effect, theoretically loyal customers may have perceived their chances of winning were greater, thus increasing the likelihood they would enter.[273]

---

272 Loyalty Science Lab, 2021, The Lucky Loyalty Effect, https://bettermarketing.pub/the-lucky-loyalty-effect-f809550d5fc6, accessed 11 May 2023.

273 Loyalty Science Lab, 2021, The Lucky Loyalty Effect, https://bettermarketing.pub/the-lucky-loyalty-effect-f809550d5fc6, accessed 11 May 2023.

Key insights

- Heuristics are mental shortcuts that allow people to solve problems and make judgments quickly and efficiently.

- Biases are thinking patterns based on observations and generalisations that may lead to memory errors, inaccurate judgments, and faulty logic, causing consumers to make decisions without looking at the bigger picture.

- Loyalty programs can be designed to appeal to consumer reliance on heuristics and the prevalence of biases.

- An extensive body of heuristics and biases theories and studies exist which are immediately relevant for loyalty programs. These include the representativeness heuristic, elimination-by-aspects heuristic, commitment bias, time (hyperbolic) discounting bias, endowment effect and loss aversion bias, framing bias, social proof bias, moral self-licensing bias, priming bias, sunk cost effect bias, scarcity bias and the lucky loyalty effect bias.

Suggested reading

- Tversky, A.; Kahneman, D., 1974, 'Judgment under Uncertainty: Heuristics and Biases', Science, Vol 185, Iss 4157, pp1124–1131.

- Shah, A.K., Oppenheimer, D.M., 2008, 'Heuristics made easy: An effort-reduction framework', Psychological Bulletin, Vol 134, pp207–222.

- Tversky, A., 1972, 'Elimination by aspects: A theory of choice', Psychological Review, Vol 79, Iss 4, pp281–299.

- Jacoby, J. and Kyner, D. B., 1973, 'Brand Loyalty vs Repeat Purchasing Behavior', Journal of Marketing Research, Vol 10, Iss 1, pp1-9.

- Thaler, Richard, 1980, 'Toward a Positive Theory of Consumer Choice', Journal of Economic Behavior and Organization, Vol 1, pp39-60.

- Schindler, S., & Pfattheicher, S., 2017, 'The frame of the game: Loss-framing increases dishonest behavior', Journal of Experimental Social Psychology, Vol 69, pp172-177.

- Levin, Irwin & Gaeth, Gary, 1988, 'How Consumers Are Affected by the Framing of Attribute Information Before and After Consuming the Product', Journal of Consumer Research, Vol 15, pp374-78.

- Thorndike, E. L., 1920, 'A constant error in psychological ratings', Journal of Applied Psychology, Vol 4, pp25-29.

- Asch, S. E, 1946, 'Forming impressions of personality', The Journal of Abnormal and Social Psychology, Vol 41, Iss 3, pp258–290.

- Cialdini, R.B., 1993, 'Influence: The Psychology of Persuasion'.

- Merritt, A.C., Effron, D.A. and Monin, B, 2010, 'Moral Self-Licensing: When Being Good Frees Us to Be Bad', Social and Personality Psychology Compass, Vol 4, pp344-357.

- North, A. C., Hargreaves, D. J. & McKendrick, J., 1999, 'The influence of in-store music on wine selections', Journal of Applied Psychology, Vol 84, Iss 2, pp271-276.

CHAPTER 7

REWARDS

This chapter was co-written by **Stacey Lyons** (Loyalty Director, Loyalty & Reward Co)

'Recent investigations suggest that the firing of dopamine neurons is a motivational substance as a consequence of reward-anticipation. This hypothesis is based on the evidence that, when a reward is greater than expected, the firing of certain dopamine neurons increases, which consequently increases desire or motivation towards the reward.'

- Oscar Arias-Carrión and Ernst Pöppel, 2007 [274]

Focus areas

This chapter will address the following questions:

- Why are consumers motivated to join a loyalty program?

- What are the different classifications of rewards used in loyalty programs?

- Which types of rewards are best suited for different circumstances and situations?

- Which industries are best able to provide efficient rewards?

- How are rewards supplied and fulfilled within large loyalty programs?

274 Arias-Carrión, O. & Pöppel, E., 2007, 'Dopamine, learning, and reward-seeking behavior', Acta neurobiologiae experimentalis, Vol 67, pp481-8.

The critical importance of rewards

Academic literature emphasises the critical role rewards play in driving member acquisition and engagement with loyalty programs.

Sharma and Verma (2014)[275] hypothesised that members are motivated to join loyalty programs in order to access desirable rewards, therefore 'the nature of reward offered can influence the outcomes of the loyalty program'.

Mauri (2003)[276] identified that customers become members of a loyalty program if the expected rewards are higher than the expected costs. This was reinforced by Reinares and Garcia-Madariaga (2007)[277] who found that the main cause of non-members' refusal to join a program was because they perceived the rewards to be inadequate in comparison to the effort required.

Johnson et al (2003)[278] determined that rewards and benefits provide the foundation for the development of switching costs, which create a certain degree of calculative commitment or stickiness in customer relations with the company.

Roem et al (2002)[279] found that the reward that is offered in a loyalty program is important to whether the program succeeds or fails at building brand loyalty.

275 Sharma, D. & Verma, V., 2014, 'Psychological and economic considerations of rewards programs', Journal of Retailing and Consumer Services, Vol 21, pp924–932.

276 Mauri, C., 2003, 'Card loyalty. A new emerging issue in grocery retailing', Journal of Retailing and Consumer Services, Vol 10, Iss 1, pp13–25.

277 Reinares, P. & Garcia-Madariaga, J., 2007, 'The importance of rewards in the management of multisponsor loyalty programmes', The Journal of Database Marketing & Customer Strategy Management, Vol 15.

278 Johnson, M. D., Gustafsson, A., Andreassen, T.W., Lervik, L. & Cha, J., 2001, 'The evolution and future of national customer satisfaction index models', Journal of Economic Psychology, Vol 22, Iss 2, pp217–245.

279 Roehm, M., Pullins, E. & Roehm, H., 2002, 'Designing Loyalty-Building Programs for Packaged Goods Brands', Journal of Marketing Research - J MARKET RES-CHICAGO, Vol 39, pp202-213.

Reward type classifications

Loyalty program rewards can be classified in several different ways:

- **Tangible vs intangible**: tangible rewards are concrete, visible, and easily measurable (such as a consumer product), while intangible rewards are relatively less observable and measurable (such as a status tier or recognition).

- **Immediate vs deferred**: an immediate reward is accessed instantly (such as a discount or bonus product), while a deferred reward may require the accumulation of value over time to redeem for a reward (such as building up a points balance to unlock a consumer product or a free flight).

- **Direct vs indirect**: direct rewards support the value proposition of the brand (such as free product samples), while indirect rewards have no obvious linkage with the brand (such as a third-party product discount).

- **Efficient vs inefficient**: efficient rewards are inexpensive compared to the perceived value by the member (such as a free flight which costs the airline little but is valued highly by the member), while inefficient rewards are worth the same to the member and the company (such as cashback which costs the company the same amount as the perceived value by the member).

- **Monetary vs non-monetary**: a monetary reward might be a cash or a cash-equivalent reward (such as an account credit), while a non-monetary reward is not a cash reward (such as a consumer good or an experience).

- **Visible vs invisible**: a visible reward might be something which people can present to others, sometimes with attached trophy value and self-esteem boost (such as priority boarding), while an invisible reward is generally not seen by others (such as a discount or cashback credit).

- **Utilitarian vs hedonic:** utilitarian rewards are useful or practical rewards (such as a toaster), while hedonic rewards are pleasure-producing rewards (such as a luxury spa experience).

- **Owned vs unowned:** owned rewards are a unique asset that the member has certified and verified proof of ownership over (such as an NFT where ownership is tracked on a blockchain), while unowned rewards are inferred upon a member without being unique or owned by them (such as a number of rewards points displayed within a member account). Research has shown different reward types may be better suited to generating engagement in different circumstances.

Yi and Jeon (2003)[280] found that in high-involvement situations (where the customer invests time in researching options), direct rewards are preferable to indirect rewards, while in low-involvement situations (where the product is not of utmost concern to the member), immediate rewards are more effective in building value-perception than deferred rewards.

As detailed in Chapter 6, Kivetz and Simonson (2002)[281] identified that a higher level of effort invested in earning a reward tends to shift member preferences from necessity (utilitarian) to luxury (hedonic) rewards. They argued this self-licensing effect occurs when the higher efforts required to access the reward acted to reduce the guilt often associated with choosing luxuries over necessities.

Ruzeviciute and Kamleitner (2017)[282] conducted research which suggested that monetary rewards are more attractive than non-monetary rewards. They found that 'across different industries, the monetary loyalty program was

280 Yi, Y. & Jeon, H., 2003, 'Effects of Loyalty Programs on Value Perception, Program Loyalty, and Brand Loyalty', Journal of The Academy of Marketing Science - J ACAD MARK SCI, Vol 31.

281 Kivetz, R. & Simonson, I., 2002, 'Earning the Right to Indulge: Effort as a Determinant of Customer Preferences Toward Frequency Program Rewards', Journal of Marketing Research - J MARKET RES-CHICAGO. Vol 39, pp155-170.

282 Ruzeviciute, R. & Kamleitner, B., 2017, 'Attracting new customers to loyalty programs: The effectiveness of monetary versus nonmonetary loyalty programs', Journal of Consumer Behaviour, Vol 16, Iss 6, pp113-124.

consistently perceived as more attractive, and it was more likely to inspire intentions to join the program. Even in light of variations in consumption goals (hedonic vs. utilitarian), the effect persisted'.

Despite this, non-monetary rewards, such as achieving status tiers, appear to play a critical role in generating brand engagement. Braesher et al (2016)[283] found that non-monetary benefits from loyalty programs can promote brand engagement by inducing customers' feelings of status and belonging in a company-initiated community. Ivanic (2015)[284] identified that members who hold high status in a loyalty program engage in status-reinforcing behaviours, even when doing so offers no material or conspicuous social signalling benefit, and in fact causes them to incur some costs.

In a study of employee benefits programs, Jeffrey (2004)[285] argued that cash is not always the best extrinsic incentive to use and that tangible non-monetary incentives may accomplish a firm's objectives better than a cash award of equal market value. One of the reasons provided by Jeffrey included that a tangible non-monetary incentive enhances social utility because it is a visible prize that others will know about, making it unnecessary for the employee to advertise that they earned the prize. In other words, a visible, desirable reward delivers 'trophy' value which a monetary payment fails to deliver.

Subconsciously, people may blend the cash reward with their everyday cash and use it to make utilitarian purchases (Kelly et al, 2017),[286] which conse-

283 Brashear, T., Kang, J. & Groza, M., 2015, 'Leveraging loyalty programs to build customer–company identification', Journal of Business Research. Vol 69.

284 Ivanic, A., 2015, 'Status Has Its Privileges: The Psychological Benefit of Status-Reinforcing Behaviors', Psychology & Marketing, Vol 32, pp697-708.

285 Jeffrey, S., 2004, 'The Benefits of Tangible Non-Monetary Incentives', Incentive Research Foundation, https://theirf.org/research/the-benefits-of-tangible-non-monetary-incentives/205/, accessed 15 June 2020.

286 Kelly, K., Presslee, A. & Webb, A., 2017, 'The Effects of Tangible Rewards Versus Cash in Consecutive Sales Tournaments: A Field Experiment, Accounting Review, Vol 92, Iss 6, cited by Incentive Research Foundation in 'Award Program Value & Evidence White Paper, 2018, https://theirf.org/research/award-program-value-evidence-white-paper/2455/, accessed 29 March 2020.

quently derive little meaning or appreciation (Dunn et al, 2014).[287] As these are unmemorable and unemotional transactions, any positive associations between the member and the brand that provided the benefit are lost quickly (Allen et al, 2003;[288] Eisenberger et al, 2001[289]). This is a particularly large risk associated with cashback, credit and discount loyalty program design frameworks (reviewed in Chapter 8).

Fun, enjoyable experiences stimulate a part of the brain that cash does not.[290] Within this area, there has been an uplift in loyalty programs offering experience-based rewards such as holidays, tickets to live sporting events or music concerts, theatre and cinema tickets as well as 'money cannot buy' experiences, such as celebrity meet-and-greets. These go beyond standard rewards to build lasting memories and positive emotional connections, acting to develop attitudinal commitment.

287 Dunn, E., Aknin, R. & Norton, M., 2014, 'Prosocial Spending and Happiness Using Money to Benefit Others Pays off', Current Directions in Psychological Science, Vol 23, Iss 1, pp41-47, cited by Incentive Research Foundation in 'Award Program Value & Evidence White Paper, 2018, https://theirf.org/research/award-program-value-evidence-white-paper/2455/, accessed 29 March 2020.

288 Allen, D., Shore, L. & Griffeth, R., 2003, The Role of Perceived Organizational Support and Supportive Human Resource Practices in the Turnover Process, Journal of Management Vol 29, Iss 1, pp99-188, cited by Incentive Research Foundation in 'Award Program Value & Evidence White Paper, 2018, https://theirf.org/research/award-program-value-evidence-white-paper/2455/, accessed 29 March 2020.

289 Eisenburger, R., Armeli, S., Rexwinkel, B., Lynch, P. & Rhoades, L., 2001, Reciprocation of Perceived Organizational Support, Journal Applied Psychology , cited by Incentive Research Foundation in 'Award Program Value & Evidence White Paper, 2018, https://theirf.org/research/award-program-value-evidence-white-paper/2455/, accessed 29 March 2020.

290 Kelly, K., cited by Incentive Research Foundation, 2018, 'Award Program Value & Evidence White Paper', https://theirf.org/research/award-program-value-evidence-white-paper/2455/, accessed 15 June 2020.

Friends of Laphroaig

Laphroaig say that 'our acres of peat fields are not only essential to produce the most richly flavoured of all Scotch whiskies, they are a tangible reward for our global community.'[291]

When a customer purchases a Laphroaig Whisky, they are invited to become a Friend of Laphroaig.

A Friend of Laphroaig is given their own honorary square foot of land from the Laphroaig fields. All members who wish to visit their land are welcome whenever they wish and are each given a map to direct them to their plot of land. Those who make the pilgrimage can collect 'rent' from their plot of land during their visit, which is a dram of Laphroaig from the distillery. Friends of Laphroaig can also contact their 'neighbour' online, which serves to strengthen the Laphroaig Whisky community.

By attaching the reward (which is highly efficient and inexpensive to deliver) to a unique and positive experience, Laphroaig are creating lasting memories from visitors who feel attitudinal commitment to the brand through ownership of their piece of the land. As shown by the endowment effect (reviewed in Chapter 6) people over-value the things they feel ownership for.

NFT's (Non-Fungible Tokens) further capitalise on asset ownership by providing brands with a new means of creating and issuing unique digital assets to members as rewards. NFT's have exploded over the last two years with the market reaching $41 billion at the end of 2022, with $80 billion expected to be reached by 2025[292].

Digital assets and NFT's are making their way into more loyalty programs globally, with many innovators and industry leaders enjoying significant

---

291 Laphroaig, https://www.laphroaig.com/en/islay/our-plots#joinfol, accessed 20 April 2023.

292 Varma, V., 2022, Entrepreneur, 'How NFT's Drive Brand Engagement and Opportunity', accessed 11 April 2023.

revenue gains[293] in addition to benefits across acquisition (access to new audiences driven by hype), engagement (new ways to interact and access community) and retention (driven by recognition and exclusivity)[294]. The ways that NFT's are being used within loyalty programs is discussed in detail within Chapter 12.

Roehm et al (2002)[295] conducted a series of experiments to investigate the effects of loyalty programs on generating loyalty towards packaged goods brands. They identified that:

- Tangible rewards are more appropriate than intangible when influencing short-term buying behaviour.

- Intangible rewards are more effective in reinforcing relations between the company and the member soon after joining.

- Immediate rewards are better suited to changing short-term behaviour.

- Deferred rewards are better suited to establishing a long-term relationship and stable modification of consumer behaviour.

In a study of coalition programs, Reinares and Garcia-Madariaga (2007)[296] identified that there are significant differences in the evaluation of rewards between members and non-members, indicating a risk that not offering certain rewards in the catalogue may condition non-members to avoid participation.

---

293 Varma, V., 2022, Entrepreneur, 'How NFT's Drive Brand Engagement and Opportunity', accessed 11 April 2023.

294 Harrison, S., 2022, 'NFTs: The Next Evolution of Rewards and Loyalty Programs', https://loyaltyrewardco.com/nfts-the-next-evolution-of-rewards-and-loyalty-programs/, accessed 11 April 2023.

295 Roehm, M., Pullins, E. & Roehm, H., 2002, 'Designing Loyalty-Building Programs for Packaged Goods Brands', Journal of Marketing Research - J MARKET RES-CHICAGO, Vol 39, pp202-213.

296 Reinares, P. & Garcia-Madariaga, J., 2007, 'The importance of rewards in the management of multisponsor loyalty programmes', The Journal of Database Marketing & Customer Strategy Management, Vol 15.

O'Brien and Jones (1995)[297] argued that a rewards range should include five characteristics: cash value, choice, aspirational value, relevance, and convenience. Cash value relates to how much the member perceives its cash equivalent to be, while choice means ensuring a wide enough range of options to inspire the member. Aspirational value refers to rewards that motivate a customer to change their behaviour over a longer period of time, while relevance and convenience focus on ensuring the member can access something meaningful in a way that is adequately accessible.

Loyalty program operators are increasingly including opportunities for members to support causes within their program. This may be providing the ability to redeem points for a charity donation or a promise to plant a tree if a certain spend threshold is reached.

According to The Future of Loyalty Report, '51 per cent of all consumers and 65 per cent of those under the age of 35 agree that brand support for environmental issues matters in their loyalty decision (while) 57 per cent of consumers under 35 have actively looked for information about the environmental friendliness/sustainability of the brand they are loyal to. Three other social causes – social justice, equity, and diversity, well-being of vulnerable populations, and poverty and hunger – are important to a similar degree...' [298]

Dialog Star Points

Dialog Axiata, is Sri Lanka's leading quad-play connectivity provider with a customer base of over 17m and has been ranked the Most Valuable Brand in Sri Lanka by Brand Finance, UK.

The Dialog Star Points is a loyalty program designed to reward its members with points for Dialog bill payments, reloads or top-ups. Members can also earn and redeem points across an extensive network of 1000+ partner merchant outlets across Sri Lanka to access

297 O'Brien, L. & Jones, C., 1995, 'Do Rewards Really Create Loyalty?', Harvard Business Review, May–June 1995 Issue.

298 Loyalty Science Lab at Old Dominion University, 2023, 'The Future of Loyalty Report', accessed 18 July 2023.

exclusive offers and discounts. Dialog Star Points services can also be accessed via Alexa Voice assistant and Dialog Futureverse where members can check their points balance and offer details.

Star Points is closely linked to Dialog's Voice of Customer (VOC) and Net Promoter Score (NPS) studies to identify customer pulse continuously and drive further improvements to the loyalty program. Star Points program is also a part of Dialog's internal employee engagement activities, enabling employees to earn Star Points for sports events, quiz competitions, entertainment events and more.

For those members looking for an opportunity to give back to communities, they can donate their points to a range of charities including UNICEF, Little Hearts, HelpAge, World Vision, SOS and more.

In discussion with Loyalty & Reward Co, Ayomal Gunasekera, Head of Loyalty Business at Dialog, said, "When crafting a loyalty program it is vital to consider the social impact the program can deliver with its members. The end result of any loyalty program is the sense of satisfaction by way of value, appreciation, recognition and the opportunity to 'make a difference'."

Dialog Star Points won the Gold Trophy for Best Loyalty Strategy – Telecommunications at the Loyalty & Engagement Awards 2023.

Efficient vs inefficient rewards

Certain companies and industries are better positioned to provide rewards aligned with O'Brien and Jones' criteria than others. The ability for a company to access low-cost, high-perceived value rewards (efficient rewards) and provide these to their members has a material bearing on the program design which will best suit their business.

Efficient rewards (vs inefficient rewards) are clearly a preferred option in delivering cash value and aspirational value in particular. Few industries provide the opportunity for companies to establish the appropriate business structure to deliver truly efficient rewards. The industries which can deliver them tend to dominate the loyalty industry, reinforcing the critical role rewards play in an overall program's attractiveness. For example:

- Frequent flyer programs can access empty seats on flights and provide them to members in exchange for points, at a cost to the program of 5-10 per cent of the ticket price. Free upgrades to business class can also be provided at very low additional cost to the airline.

- Hotels can provide members with empty rooms in exchange for points, costing them little more than cleaning and toiletry expenses. Free room upgrades can also be provided with little cost impact.

- Car rental firms can provide members with a free rental of an unrented car, paid with points, with no cost other than wear and tear. Car upgrades can also be provided at a relatively small cost.

- Cinemas can provide members with free tickets (no cost) and candy bar items (with around 90 per cent margin on most products).

- QSR's can provide members with free food or drink, or a size upgrade, at very low cost to their business.

- Cosmetics retails can provide members with free samples funded by suppliers.

A challenge faced by some of these companies, particularly in travel and hospitality, is limited reward inventory. While free flights and hotel rooms are highly desirable, they rely on accessing supply which the company cannot sell directly (which would generate a more profitable outcome). Thus, high-demand travel periods, and popular routes and locations, tend to offer the least amount of reward inventory, causing member dissatisfaction.

Oneworld Alliance

Oneworld Alliance is a partnership network of 13 member airlines – plus Oneworld connect partner, Fiji Airways. Oneworld also has 24 affiliated airlines operating across over 170 countries, carrying over 500 million passengers a year.[299] While the alliance was set up

---

299 About the oneworld Alliance, https://www.oneworld.com/about-the-oneworld-alliance, accessed 20 April 2023.

to serve international travellers by allowing frequent flyer points and miles to be redeemed for reward seats with any partner airline, it is also the cause of some member disappointment.

The disappointment stems from the sheer volume of members wishing to redeem for the limited available reward seats, which are subject to capacity controls and route restrictions.

Some programs apply different restrictions to manage the needs of their more valuable members. For example, Finnair only make business class award seats available to members of partner frequent flyer programs 60 days in advance at most, prioritising Finnair Plus members over Oneworld alliance members.[300]

Other industries do not provide such opportunities for efficient rewards, meaning companies may be required to source rewards from third parties (e.g., gift cards which cost the operator almost as much as their face value). Many consumer goods retailers operate on small margins, making it exceedingly difficult for them to provide members with access to free products. Utilities such as gas, electricity, and telecommunications, are similarly challenged in providing members with efficient rewards as part of a formal loyalty program. Banks have limited opportunities, as do companies operating in the insurance, superannuation, health, and real estate industries.

NatWest

NatWest bank have negotiated partnerships with cinema chains in the UK to provide their members with discount ticket access.[301]

Silver and Platinum account holders can take advantage of up to 40 per cent off the price of cinema tickets at over 250 UK cinemas including Vue, ODEON and Showcase.

---

300 One Mile At A Time, 2020, https://onemileatatime.com/finnair-blocking-business-class-awards/, accessed 20 April 2023.

301 https://www.natwest.com/current-accounts/existing-customers/Cinema-discount.html accessed 12 June 2023.

> The benefit for NatWest customers provides attractive value in a form which NatWest could never afford to fund as a direct discount.

Reward aggregators

Loyalty program members globally earn hundreds of billions of points, miles and other loyalty currencies each year. These are redeemed on flights, hotel rooms, cash discounts on supermarket shopping, experiences, consumer goods, gift cards, movie tickets and more. As the loyalty programs have expanded their reward ranges, a parallel industry has developed to service the demand.

Loyalty program operators tend to avoid directly sourcing and warehousing thousands of consumer goods and hundreds of gift cards for their members. This is not their core capability and would involve significant incremental cost to the business, both from a logistics perspective, but also for warehousing and stock management. For example, Lufthansa' Miles & More World Shop offers over 3,000 consumer goods and gift cards which members can access by redeeming points. For Miles & More to purchase and warehouse all those products would not be feasible, particularly when some of the products will see little or no redemption activity, while others will be superseded by new versions. It is safe to say that modern loyalty programs are not structured to operate in the same way that the big stamps programs of old were run.

Instead, most programs have developed relationships with large product and gift card aggregators whose core business is to source and warehouse stock which they can deliver on demand via a drop-ship model, or provide digital goods such as gift cards to order. For example, if a member redeems points for a case of wine on an online store hosted by the loyalty program, an order will be sent to a third-party wine supplier that will pick, pack and dispatch the wine to the member. On completion of the order, the wine supplier will invoice the loyalty program for the wholesale cost of the wine. One additional advantage of this partnership is the loyalty program does not need to hold a liquor license, as this is covered by the wine supplier.

There are many reward product suppliers operating around the world that specifically support loyalty programs by offering large consumer product or gift card ranges, while other companies have developed new divisions to support the reward demand.

In rare instances, a larger loyalty program may request exclusivity for a particular product in order to attempt to gain a competitive advantage. In other instances, the brand or product supplier may insist they only want to have their product ranged with a specific loyalty program or a small selection of loyalty programs which they feel are aligned to their brands positioning in the market.

These aggregators tend to support competition in the loyalty program industry. A program can very quickly develop a large and attractive range of consumer goods and gift cards to offer to their member base as rewards.

RewardOps

RewardOps[302] are a rewards supply aggregator that have networked with dozens of reward suppliers offering millions of reward products across multiple categories (gift cards, merchandise, discounts, donations, music, movies, magazines, events, travel and more).

A loyalty program can connect to the RewardOps platform, curate their own rewards catalogue, manage their reward store, distribute rewards, and track redemptions and browsing activity.

Invoicing is also managed entirely by RewardOps, so the company only needs to pay one single monthly invoice to RewardOps for their entire reward store, allowing them to focus on their core business.

PointCheckout

Point Checkout[303] is a payment gateway for loyalty points. They have relationships with thousands of merchant partners. This allows program members to pool their loyalty points from existing programs and spend them through participating merchant apps and online stores in real time.

302 RewardOps, https://rewardops.com/, accessed 20 April 2023.
303 PointCheckout, https://www.pointcheckout.com/en/ accessed 20 April 2023.

Concierge services

In instances where a member may not be able to find a reward that appeals to them, some loyalty programs offer basic concierge services. This allows the member to request the sourcing of a specific product or service they desire. The concierge will calculate a price in points for procurement, and if the member chooses to progress with the redemption, the concierge will process the points transaction and organise fulfilment of the order.

Other programs have expanded the concierge concept to provide additional services. This may include a dedicated phone number, website and app which allows members to request travel bookings, restaurant bookings, event and show tickets, private shopping events, golf course bookings and rental car bookings. Members can also access additional perks, including flight, car and room upgrades, access to sold-out events, exclusive restaurants and airport lounges, and priority discounts.

Alternatively, a company with an existing call centre can potentially train their team accordingly and in turn divert some internal resources to managing the concierge service at a lower cost than outsourcing may deliver. The benefits and challenges associated with insourcing and outsourcing are detailed in Chapter 19.

AMEX Platinum Card Concierge

American Express offers complimentary concierge services[304] for their premium card members.

Platinum card holders enjoy a concierge service to act as an agent to make purchases or book services on the member's behalf. Services include hotel or restaurant reservations, event tickets for entertainment (like concerts or sports games), pet care and more.

American Express has access to VIP shows, luxury hotels and sometimes sold-out events. Access is not guaranteed, but the concierge service will try to accommodate members as best they can.

---

304 Amex, https://www.americanexpress.com/in/articles/life-with-amex/benefits/what-is-a-concierge-service.html, accessed 9 June 2023.

> The concierge can even help cardholders in emergencies, such as lost baggage during travel or missed flights during medical emergencies.

With the existence of a multitude of reward options, loyalty program operators need to select the type of reward which fits the specific behaviour they are seeking to influence. Different reward types tend to correlate to specific loyalty program design frameworks. For example, monetary rewards may be suited to discount and credit frameworks, whilst non-monetary rewards may be better suited to status tier, member benefits, and surprise and delight frameworks. Achieving the optimal balance between valuable and cost-effective rewards is also critical.

Key insights

- Consumers are motivated to join loyalty programs to access desirable rewards, and therefore the nature of rewards offered can influence the effectiveness of the loyalty program. Consumers will be more likely to become members of a loyalty program if the perceived rewards are higher than the perceived costs.

- Rewards that are offered in a loyalty program are important to whether the program succeeds or fails at building behavioural and attitudinal commitment. A reward range should include five characteristics: cash value, choice, aspirational value, relevance, and convenience.

- Rewards can be tangible vs intangible, immediate vs deferred, direct vs indirect, efficient vs inefficient, monetary vs non-monetary, visible vs invisible and utilitarian vs hedonic.

- Some rewards types are better suited to influencing certain behaviours. Research suggests that tangible rewards are more appropriate than intangible when influencing short-term buying behaviour; intangible and visible incentives are more effective in reinforcing relations between the company and the member soon after joining; immediate rewards are better suited to changing short-term behaviour, while deferred incentives are better suited to establishing a long-term relationship and stable modification of consumer behaviour.

- Industries which can provide members with efficient rewards have a natural advantage in delivering value and tend to dominate the loyalty industry. This includes airlines, hotels, car rental companies and quick service restaurants.

- Product and gift card aggregators source and warehouse stock which they can deliver on demand via a drop ship model, or provide digital goods such as gift cards to order. Reward aggregators have grown their businesses to specifically support loyalty programs by offering large consumer product or gift card ranges, while other companies have developed new divisions to support demand.

Suggested reading

- Sharma, D. & Verma, V, 2014, 'Psychological and economic considerations of rewards programs', Journal of Retailing and Consumer Services, Vol 21, pp924–932.

- Mauri, C., 2003, 'Card loyalty. A new emerging issue in grocery retailing', Journal of Retailing and Consumer Services, Vol 10, Iss 1, pp13–25.

- Roehm, Michelle & Pullins, Ellen & Roehm, Harper, 2002, 'Designing Loyalty-Building Programs for Packaged Goods Brands', Journal of Marketing Research - J MARKET RES-CHICAGO, Vol 39, pp202-213.

- Kivetz, Ran & Simonson, Itamar., 2002, 'Earning the Right to Indulge: Effort as a Determinant of Customer Preferences Toward Frequency Program Rewards', Journal of Marketing Research, Vol 39, pp155-170.

- Ruzeviciute, Ruta & Kamleitner, Bernadette, 2017, 'Attracting new customers to loyalty programs: The effectiveness of monetary versus nonmonetary loyalty programs', Journal of Consumer Behaviour, Vol 16, Issue 6, pp113-124.

- Jeffrey, Scott., 2004, 'The Benefits of Tangible Non-Monetary Incentives', Incentive Research Foundation, https://theirf.org/research/the-benefits-of-tangible-non-monetary-incentives/205/

- O'Brien, L. and Jones, C., 1995, 'Do Rewards Really Create Loyalty?', Harvard Business Review, May–June 1995 Issue.

CHAPTER 8

LOYALTY PROGRAM DESIGN FRAMEWORKS

'Good design is good business.'

- Thomas Watson Jr,
second president of IBM, 1973

Focus areas

This chapter will address the following questions:

- What are the different types of design frameworks utilised in loyalty programs?

- What are the benefits and challenges of each design framework type?

- How are different design frameworks combined to create a more comprehensive loyalty program?

THIS CHAPTER PRESENTS a range of loyalty program (and member engagement program) design frameworks. While companies may utilise a single design, it is common practice to combine elements from a number of frameworks to create a more comprehensive program design.

The conceptual frameworks and variations presented throughout this chapter aim to provide guidance in considering different design approaches.

Certain designs may not be suitable in delivering to a specific company's needs and objectives. Strategically working through a range of design options will help ensure the framework adopted by a company is well considered and appropriate.

As discussed in Chapter 7, specific rewards will influence and motivate members in varying ways and will generate engagement in different circumstances. Certain rewards are also more appropriately suited to specific loyalty design frameworks.

Punch and stamp cards

Model

The most pervasive loyalty program design in the world is the punch/stamp card. A member collects punches/stamps for purchases, and after earning enough to complete the card, a reward is unlocked, which is usually a free product, such as a coffee.

Paper cards are cost-effective to produce and the reward provided is generally high margin, making the program affordable to implement and run. The card itself acts as a visual progress tracker, taking advantage of the endowed progress effect and goal gradient effect. The commercial model is a smart design. For example, a café wanting to sell more coffee can decide to offer a 10 per cent discount, but loyal and non-loyal customers will access it equally. The punch/stamp card essentially gives loyal customers a 10 per cent cumulative delayed discount (buying ten coffees and getting one free is worth roughly the same as a 10 per cent discount on each of 10 cups), while one-off and irregular customers will pay full price, protecting the café from unnecessary discounting.

Over the past decade, the introduction of digital punch/stamp cards has provided convenience for customers (one less card in their wallet) and a better ability for cafes to track usage, including the ability to collect some customer data (a key limitation of a paper card).

In exploring punch/stamp card programs, three design variations are considered; basic, complex and multi.

1. Basic punch/stamp cards:

The basic model involves the member earning a stamp/punch for each transaction to unlock a set reward. It is effective when the price of the product being purchased is relatively consistent, such as a cup of coffee or a car wash. Each time a specific item is purchased, the punch/stamp card is marked, and the customer is one step closer to accessing that item for free once the card is completed.

Costa Coffee Club

For every cup of coffee purchased, Costa Coffee Club members earn one bean. Eight beans will earn the member a free drink.[305]

Members can join by picking up a card in-store which is scanned each time they purchase, or by downloading the Costa Coffee app which displays a digital coffee card.

To support sustainability, each time members use a reusable cup in store, they earn an extra bean.

2. Complex punch/stamp cards:

A more complex punch/stamp card model allows members to be rewarded for purchases which have a wider variability in cost. When the member has earned the required number of stamps for their transactions, the total amount spent is calculated, and a percentage of the total is provided as the reward.

---

305 Costa Coffee Club, https://www.costa.co.uk/costa-club, accessed 12 June 2023.

Target Shop+

The Target Shop+ program[306] rewards members for shopping online. Members who purchase Target products via the Target app or website earn stamps for each individual transaction.

For every second stamp collected, members unlock a mystery reward in the form of a digital voucher or coupon.

The rewards change as the member earns more stamps to keep the mystery alive.

3. Multi-punch/stamp cards:

When a program incorporates multiple punch/stamp cards within a single program framework. Members can track progress towards unlocking rewards from each individual card simultaneously.

This model is commonly used when a company has multiple products at differing price points, or when a company has multiple partners offering different reward values. Both case studies below reflect each of these scenarios respectively.

GREGGS ON TAP

GREGGS is the largest British bakery chain in the UK. The GREGGS ON TAP program enables members to unlock freebies across multiple popular categories including sandwiches, bakes, hot drinks and sweets.[307] Members are required to collect a total of 9 stamps within each category to receive the 10th item for free.

Members can track the number of stamps earned across each individual category via progress trackers located on the app home page.

---

306 Target, https://www.target.com.au/target-shop-plus, accessed 9 June 2023.
307 GREGGS, https://www.greggs.co.uk/app, accessed 12 June 2023.

Loyalty currencies

Model

The evolution of loyalty currencies over several centuries was detailed in Chapter 2, where it was shown that trade marks, checks, tickets, coupons, certificates, stamps, miles, points, cryptocurrencies and tokenised assets have all been used throughout the ages. In the current age, the dominant loyalty currencies globally are points and miles. Other variations include Stars (Starbucks), Tokens (Subway), Deli Dollars (Jason's Deli), Beefsteak Bucks (Beefsteak), as well as Bitcoin (Lolli), tokenised shares (Bits of Stock) and tokenised real estate (BrickX).

Loyalty currency frameworks are flexible, allowing them to be used across many different company types and industries to reward members. To earn the currency, members are required to identify at each transaction, enabling valuable data capture opportunities.

Loyalty currency programs are more complex than punch/stamp cards, and typically require a technology system to manage, but are still sufficiently simple.

To simplify illustrating loyalty currency design frameworks and their benefits, loyalty currencies will be referred to as 'Points', with the understanding that this can be substituted for any alternative currency name.

In exploring loyalty currency programs, two design variations are considered: basic and coalition. There are many sub-variations of the two main models.

1. Basic loyalty currency program:

This basic model involves a single brand providing the ability for members to earn points by transacting with them. Commonly, the points are redeemable on the company's products. The program may also provide the option for members to redeem points for third-party products, although this is less common because it can result in higher program costs.

An attractive feature of this design is the ability for a company to control the associated costs. For example, if a member earns one point for every dollar they spend, and 1,000 points is equal to a $10 reward, the retailer is contributing 1 per cent return on each dollar spent. Irrespective of whether the member spends more, or less, the 1 per cent cost remains constant, allowing the company to manage their program spend to budget.

PetSmart Treats

Members of PetSmart earn eight points for every US$1 spent on PetSmart products and services in-store and online.[308] Members can redeem points on any product or pet service for up to 12 months with no exclusions. Treats start at 1,000 points for a redemption.

Additional *Treats* built into the program include special bonus points offers.

Allowing points to be redeemed only on PetSmart products and services makes the program operation more cost-effective, as PetSmart only pay wholesale cost for a product which the member values at the retail price.

---

2. Coalition loyalty currency program:

As referenced in Chapter 1, a coalition loyalty program allows members to earn points across multiple partners, such as airlines, banks, supermarkets, utilities, retailers and hotels. These programs are primarily controlled by a single company, which is responsible for distribution of points as well as management of member accounts, marketing and program rules. Many coalition programs generate sizeable profits, utilising sophisticated commercial models which will be explored in Chapter 16.

---

308 Petsmart, https://www.petsmart.com/treats-rewards.html, accessed 20 July 2020.

Rather than starting their own points program, a company may instead choose to join a coalition as a program partner, allowing them to offer coalition points as a reward to their customers. This can deliver a range of benefits, including access to an effective marketing database, attracting new customers and retaining existing customers by rewarding with an already desirable loyalty currency, and using the coalition to turbocharge member acquisition. They may also face challenges, such as insufficient marketing support, excessive costs for purchasing points, and a lack of tangible results and exclusivity.

Alaska Airlines Mileage Plan

Alaska Airlines' Mileage Plan program allows members to earn when they spend with Alaskan Airlines, but also across thousands of everyday retail partners online and in-store. Retail partners include the likes of Disney, Sephora, Adidas, Macy's, Costco, FedEx and Jimmy Choo.

Partners leverage the Mileage Plan platform to market promotions to the large Mileage Plan member base as an effective advertising channel.

Promotions change regularly and range from 0.5 Miles per US$1 spent up to 25 Miles per US$1 spent.[309]

---

309 Alaska Mileage Plan, https://www.mileageplanshopping.com/b.htm, accessed 19 June 2020.

Status tiers

Model

As detailed in Chapter 2, the first modern status tier structure appears to have been introduced by AAdvantage in 1982, when they launched Gold status to recognise their most loyal members. Many programs now segment members based on spend via overt or covert tiers that deliver a range of exclusive tangible and intangible benefits.

With overt tiers, the member is aware of their tier they have achieved and can proactively access the communicated benefits. With covert tiers, the member is placed in a tier and treated accordingly but is unaware of their status.

The tiering approach is loosely aligned to the Pareto Principle, whereby a small number of customers can account for a sizeable amount of a company's revenue (the so called 80/20 rule). While this does not occur across all companies (e.g., utilities, subscription companies and insurance companies do not appear to have such a pronounced effect within their consumer bases), it does manifest elsewhere (such as airlines, hotels and car rental companies) providing the conditions by which a status tier program can be usefully applied.

Pareto Principle conditions are favourable for the success of status tier programs, as tiering is most effective when a relatively small number of high-value customers are concentrated into elite hierarchies and provided with disproportionate attention and benefits. This is only cost-effective when the number of elites is small, because if the tier population is too big, the program operator will not be able to afford to bestow the generous benefits which make status tiers successful. Furthermore, research shows larger tier populations appear to make existing tier members feel less special (Drèze and Nunes, 2009).[310]

---

310 Drèze, X. & Nunes,J., 2009, 'Feeling Superior: The Impact of Loyalty Program Structure on Consumers' Perceptions of Status', Journal of Consumer Research, Vol

In exploring status programs, two design variations are considered: stand-alone and within program.

1. Stand-alone status tier programs:

This model involves status tiers with set benefits provided to members at each tier level.

Members can progress tiers in two ways:

- Member engagement: when a certain amount of currency is accumulated (based on spend or other activities), a new tier is unlocked for the member. The currencies (i.e., status credits) themselves cannot be redeemed on any rewards, but are specifically designed to track progress towards the next tier.

- Purchasing a tier subscription: allow members to pay a monthly or annual fee to instantly access one or a selection of tiers, with accompanying benefits.

This model can deliver the same engagement benefits as a points program; members are motivated to identify at each transaction to ensure they continue to progress towards the next tier, utilising the endowed progress effect and goal gradient effect. More valuable members are automatically recognised and rewarded with elite benefits and status titles, helping to develop their brand loyalty via social identity theory.

Subscription tier members are also likely to experience the sunk cost effect bias, where they will feel compelled to engage more with the program to realise a return on their spend.

35, pp890-905.

Swarovski Club

Swarovski have embraced a status tier design for their loyalty program, Swarovski Club.[311] Member spend is tracked annually, with automatic progression to higher tiers when spend thresholds have been reached.

Swarovski Club encompasses four status tiers:

- Bronze: (A$0 spend)

- Silver: (from A$400 spend)

- Gold: (from A$1000 spend)

- Platinum: (from A$2000 spend)

This structure makes it relatively easy to access the higher tiers, with A$2,000 spend unlikely to be perceived as excessive for a Swarovski obsessive.

Benefits improve by tier, and include exclusive pre-sales, birthday vouchers, free shipping, VIP events, and extra Gold/Platinum discounts and gifts.

2. Within program status tiers:

A more common application of status tiers is within a broader loyalty currency program, such as an airline, hotel, car rental or bank program. The design segments members by their value to the business, and provides them with incremental benefits to recognise their loyalty. It reinforces the endowed progress effect and goal gradient effect, whereby members can track their progress towards a reward (with points or miles) and track a parallel pathway to a status tier (with a different loyalty currency, such as status credits).

The most common structure is four tiers (e.g., Bronze, Silver, Gold and Platinum), although some major coalitions have extended to five (a super elite tier above the previous top tier). Drèze and Nunes' (2009)[312] study found that

---

311 Swarovski Club, https://www.swarovski.com/en_GB-AU/club/, accessed 20th August 2020.

312 Drèze, X. & Nunes, J., 2009, 'Feeling Superior: The Impact of Loyalty Program Structure on Consumers' Perceptions of Status', Journal of Consumer Research, Vol 35, pp890-905.

a three-tier program is more satisfying to all members of a program than a two-tier program (Gold and no-status), even to those who do not qualify for elite status. It is unusual that they did not extend their study to four-tier programs.

IHG One Rewards

IHG One Rewards[313] is the hotel loyalty program of The Intercontinental Hotel Group (IHG). Members earn points which can be redeemed for 'Reward Night' stays at more than 6,000 of their hotels and resorts globally, on merchandise or experiences from partners, for frequent flyer points from over 40 airline partners or for car rentals, and other rewards.

Alongside points, IHG One Rewards has four membership tiers which unlock valuable benefits based on nights stayed:

- Club Member: ten points for every US$1 spent, points for Reward Nights, member rates, member promotions, free internet and late checkout.

- Silver Elite (10 nights): Club benefits plus an additional 20 per cent bonus on base points and points do not expire.

- Gold Elite (20 nights or 40,000 points): Silver Elite benefits plus additional 40 per cent bonus on base points earn rate and rollover nights to help maintain status.

- Platinum Elite (40 nights or 60,000 points): Gold Elite benefits plus additional 60 per cent bonus on base points earn rate, guaranteed room availability and complimentary room upgrades, Reward Night discounts, welcome amenity (i.e., points or drink/snack) and early check-in.

- Diamond Elite (70 nights or 120,000 points): Platinum Elite benefits plus additional 100 per cent bonus on base points earn rate, a dedicated support team and a welcome amenity (i.e., free breakfast, points or drink/snack)

---

313 IHG, https://www.ihg.com/onerewards/content/us/en/home, accessed 15 June 2023.

Member benefits

Model

Many companies do not earn sufficient margin, or do not have customers spending enough at an individual level, to support a loyalty currency program or status tier program that delivers adequate value to drive consistent member engagement. A popular alternative is a member benefits program, which provides members with access to a range of benefits simply by joining, by spending over a certain threshold, or by purchasing a subscription. These may be provided by the company, but primarily tend to be sourced from third-party partners.

Members may access benefits by presenting a membership card or voucher, by calling a dedicated phone number, or by accessing a website or app.

Member benefits programs are particularly prevalent across specific industries, such as utilities, telecommunications, insurance and pension funds/superannuation, where large member bases spend relatively small amounts at an individual level, but the companies are wealthy enough to invest in quality partnerships to access desirable benefits. These are companies where customers tend to make regular periodic payments and where there is a dedicated focus on reducing customer churn.

Membership may be provided as complimentary as a way to reward members for being a customer. Alternatively, program access may be provided as part of a subscription model.

In exploring member benefits programs, three design variations are considered: company-provided, supplier-provided and third-party provided.

1. Company-provided member benefits program:

Under the company-provided member benefits design, members are provided with access to desirable benefits which are products or services of the company.

The strategic imperative is to offer members a bundle of benefits which they value highly but cost the company little to deliver. This may include free samples, extended warranties, charity donations and other benefits that make it worthwhile enough for the member to identify when transacting, or sticky enough to reduce their propensity to churn.

The challenge for companies is being able to deliver program benefits of significant appeal to their wider population of customers.

IKEA Family

Members of IKEA Family[314] are encouraged to swipe their card at the checkout each time they transact to access a bundle of benefits. This differs by country, but can include free insurance to cover the transport of the product from the store to assembly at home, an extended returns policy, member discounts on products and food, entry into a draw to win IKEA gift cards, and a small donation to a local charity.

The bundle is perceived by members as good value, stimulating membership card swipe behaviour, and allowing IKEA to capture important member transaction data, while the cost of running the program equates to a fraction of a per cent of revenue per transaction.

In reality, members are unlikely to return a product if they have not already done so under the standard non-member 3 months returns policy. The claims associated with store-to-home insurance are estimated to be exceedingly small. The gift card prizes cost each store a few thousand dollars per year, and likely stimulate incremental revenue by persuading winning members to spend more

---

314 IKEA, https://www.ikea.com/au/en/ikea-family/, accessed 29 June 2020.

than the value of the card. The small charity donation is capped, allowing IKEA to manage the cost because once the limit has been reached, member card swipes no longer generate a donation until it resets at the end of the year.

While the cost to IKEA is likely incredibly low, when presented as a carefully constructed stack of contextually relevant benefits, the value to the member feels greater.

2. Supplier-provided member benefits program:

Certain companies are fortunate enough to access product samples or rewards from suppliers, which they can incorporate into loyalty programs. Accessing free samples is a fantastic way for members to try new products without having to commit to a purchase. Under this model, members receive access to a selection of regular samples, combining the delivery of relevant rewards with surprise and delight, as members do not know what specifically they will receive. This enables a dynamic where the member places a high value on a reward which costs the company little, an approach which is particularly prevalent in the beauty and cosmetics industries.

Priceline Sister Club

Priceline Sister Club program is the rewards program of Priceline, with over 8 million members.[315] Priceline Sister Club is primarily a points-based program; however they have introduced tiers which unlock a number of benefits including access to secret sales, VIP events and competitions. The most valuable reward advertised, to which all members are encouraged to strive for, is the Pink Diamond Gift which is available to their highest tier Pink Diamond Members.[316]

The Pink Diamond Gift is a complimentary gift box provided every

---

315 Australian Pharmaceutical Industries Limited, Annual report 2017, p11. No membership figures were listed in the Annual report 2018.

316 Priceline, https://www.priceline.com.au/about-priceline, accessed 17 May 2023.

quarter containing 3-4 sample products. The samples are provided by Priceline suppliers who use this as an opportunity to get their brand and product lines in front of the company's most engaged and loyal shoppers.

3. Third party-provided member benefits program:

Where benefits cannot be sourced internally, or provided via supplier samples, a company may develop relationships with a range of third-party partners to provide member benefits. This is the most prevalent member benefits design in market.

While company and supplier-provided member benefits programs stand-out for their cost-efficiency, third-party provided member benefits programs can be more expensive to run, particularly if the company is seeking exclusive, best-in-market offers. These types of offers can require annual licensing fees, reciprocal marketing support and other concessions. For example, a company wishing to provide their customers with access to discount event tickets may need to pay an annual fee to the ticketing partner for the rights, as well as promoting certain events to their member base.

In instances where the rewards represent a lack of contextual relevance or a lack of perceived value, the ability to drive member engagement can be challenging.

Irrespective, there are a number of successful programs globally utilising this model.

O2 Priority

O2 Priority,[317] the loyalty program of UK telecommunications company O2, provide rotating benefits to members across over thirty exclusive categories, including discount event tickets, discounts at major brands such as The Body Shop, free cookies and crisps, free Uber rides and generous discounts on new technology. The pro-

---

317 O2 Priority, https://priority.o2.co.uk/, accessed 29 June 2020.

gram also offers regular prize draws which members can opt-in to win products, VIP experiences, concert tickets and more.

The rotation of the offers keeps them fresh, compelling members to continually check-in to ensure they do not miss a bargain.

Discounts

Model

Discounting is used extensively in loyalty and member engagement programs by providing members with offers which are not accessible to non-members (exclusivity).

In exploring discount programs, five design variations are considered: basic, delayed, tiered, bundled, and third-party.

Access to discount programs is normally free, however some companies may charge a subscription fee.

1. Basic discount program:

This is one of the simplest program designs, whereby members who join are entitled to a set discount off every purchase for in-store and online transactions. This type of design is simple to understand and engage with, and can drive high participation rates (with members not wanting to miss out on their discount), ensuring substantial member data is captured.

While useful in generating behavioural commitment, it may be questionable whether discounting can drive attitudinal commitment. Anyone can access the discount (one-time and truly loyal members), making it potentially expensive to operate. If a member can access a better price or discount at a competitor, there are no exit costs if they switch, meaning the design may be limited in its ability to generate stickiness.

That being said, there are many examples of loyalty programs successfully operating this model, especially in high-margin industries where attractive discounts can be readily provided and a quality service experience can ensure members feel positive about returning.

Beyond+

The Beyond+ program from Bed Bath & Beyond is a paid yearly membership program (US$29 per year) which gives all members access to 20 per cent off their entire purchase made at any Bed Bath & Beyond store in the US or online during the year of membership, plus members also receive free shipping.[318]

Incorporating the ongoing member discount and benefit within a yearly subscription is a sound strategy to leverage the sunk cost effect bias and generate stickiness from members looking to make the most of their US$29 membership.

The membership fee is also another revenue stream for the program.

---

2. Delayed discount program:

Delayed discounts are a more sophisticated version of a basic discount program, where a member transacting above a certain amount earns a discount to use on a future purchase. For example, 'spend $50 and save 10 per cent on your next visit'.

This design is simple to understand and engage with, and has the added advantage of locking the customer into a future purchase to access the discount. An expiry date can be applied to the discount to stimulate FOMO (fear of missing out) and encourage the member to transact more quickly than they may have been intending. One-time customers will not access the discount, helping to manage program costs.

---

318 Bed Bath & Beyond, Beyond+, https://www.bedbathandbeyond.com/store/loyalty/beyondplus, accessed 29 June 2020.

My Cub Rewards

My Cub Rewards[319] offers a delayed discount on fuel for all members who refuel at participating Holiday Station stores.

For every US$100 a member spends at Cub, they get ten cents off per gallon of fuel the next time they fill up at any participating location. Frequent shoppers can redeem up to US$1.50 per gallon which would save them US$24 on a 16-gallon tank.

This strategy takes advantage of the loss aversion bias where members are motivated to avoid losing their benefit before it expires, resulting in repeat purchases.

3. **Tiered discount program:**

With a tiered discount, the level of discount provided increases based on the cumulative value of spend. For example, a member may start by receiving a 2 per cent discount, which increases to 4 per cent when they spend a cumulative $2,000 over a one-year period, and further increases to 6 per cent for $5,000 cumulative spend.

It can be argued this is a simple version of a status tier program, with status resetting at the end of the period. This approach is unique amongst the discount program designs in supporting the endowed progress effect and goal gradient effect.

Home Depot Pro Xtra Paint Rewards

Pro Xtra Paint Rewards[320] by Home Depot is a tiered discount program. Cumulative spend with Home Depot accrues and once certain spend thresholds are reached, the discount off purchases increases thereafter. Members who reach Bronze level (after spending US$1,000) get 10 per cent off everything, members who reach Silver level (after spending US$3,500) get 15 per cent off

---

319 Cub, https://www.cub.com/savings/fuel-rewards.html, accessed 29 June 2020.

320 Home Depot, Pro Xtra, https://www.homedepot.com/c/Pro_Xtra, accessed 29 June 2020.

everything, and members who reach Gold level (after spending US$6,500) get 20 per cent off everything.

Since all purchases are counted towards the total spend, members are reluctant to give up the progress they have made towards unlocking higher discounts by shopping at a competitor.

4. Bundled discount program:

Bundled discounts involve members being provided with a set discount off all products or services when a minimum number of products or services are purchased. For example, a member takes out three different insurance products with a single insurance company, earning them a 10 per cent discount off all insurance products.

Like a basic discount program, this design is simple to understand and engage with, however it also has some additional advantages. The discount is only provided to members who have a minimum amount of product or service consumption (indicating some level of brand loyalty), and program stickiness is built-in, because if a member reduces the number of product or services they access, they will lose their discount across all products (a clear exit cost). For example, if the member reduces their insurance products from three to two, they will lose the 10 per cent discount on the remaining two products.

NRMA

NRMA is an insurance provider offering a loyalty discount[321] to members.

Members can use their online loyalty discount calculator to determine the amount they could save across all policies based on how many eligible policies the member has taken out and how many consecutive years the member has been with NRMA.

The loyalty discount is re-calculated at each renewal and is adjusted based on how many active policies the member has at that time.

---

321 NRMA, https://www.nrma.com.au/loyalty-discount, accessed 29 June 2020.

5. Third-party discount program:

Under the third-party discounting model, brands provide discounts which can be used at third-party companies. For example, 'spend $50 and earn a 10 per cent discount voucher to use at brand X'. This may be because the company does not have sufficient margin to offer its own discounts. It may also be because it is an independent program which relies on sourcing third-party offers for its reward pool.

This program design faces some challenges. It is more complicated to understand. It assumes members transacting with them will also be interested in transacting with the company honouring the discount. It involves the company promoting another brand, which may be positive (a halo effect could eventuate) or negative (marketing efforts focus on promoting another brand). There may be costs to access the third-party partner's discounts.

AIA Vitality

AIA Vitality[322] is a third-party rewards program aimed at improving the health of members by rewarding them for meeting health goals. The cost of rewards to members aims to be offset by a reduction in AIA insurance claims on the premise that members will have reduced their health risks and thus their liability to the company.

Members earn AIA Vitality Points for committing (commitment bias) to making healthy choices like healthy eating, going to the gym, going for a health check or completing a set number of steps. Members can redeem points for third-party rewards like discounted movie tickets, spa vouchers or shopping vouchers.

The AIA Vitality program is offered as an AIA Vitality branded rewards program for members of a range of companies across banking, insurance, healthcare and other industries.

---

322 AIA Vitality, https://www.aiavitality.com.au/vmp-au/, accessed 29 June 2020.

Credits

Model

Closely related to the discount program design is the credit program; where members earn a credit amount for future spend on the company's products. This may be in the form of a voucher or be held in their account.

The program is typically structured such that the margin required to cover the cost of the credit is built into the price of the product. Thus, the member perceives they are receiving incremental value, while the company can control the costs of the program.

One advantage credits have over discounting is they may be more likely to be perceived as something tangible (a specific dollar amount visible in the member's account vs an unallocated percentage). A credit which the member has earned and feels ownership over may be more likely to tap into the endowment effect and loss aversion biases, meaning the member may be more reluctant to lose access to their credit compared to a discount.

An additional advantage is that credits avoid creating a negative precedent (i.e., members expect to see the same thing next time and hold off purchasing until another discount becomes available) or lower perceived value in the same way that discounts can generate.

A study by Vana et al (2018)[323] found evidence that credit programs increase the probability that consumers will make an additional purchase and increase the size of the spend. Loyalty & Reward Co theorise that members

323 Vana, Prasad and Lambrecht, Anja and Bertini, Marco, Cashback Is Cash Forward: Delaying a Discount to Entice Future Spending (May 17, 2018). Journal of Marketing Research, Vol. 55, No. 6, 2018.

engage in mental accounting of the available credit and association with the brand, so they are more easily able to justify spending more money there.

A challenge with a credit program is the cost of the credit may need to be a greater value than a loyalty currency to excite the member (i.e., offering 1 per cent return on $100 spend in the form of 100 points can work, but a cash equivalent credit of $1 may not sound valuable enough to motivate the member). In addition, the credit may be mentally combined with the price, neutralising the feeling of goodwill that a loyalty program should engender, although this is less likely to be the case than with discounts.

In exploring credit programs, three design variations are considered: delayed credit, interest payments and lowest price guarantee.

1. Delayed credit program:

This is an identical model to the Delayed discount program, however instead of being provided with a discount, the member is awarded an account credit which they can apply to their next purchase.

Modern Market Rewards

As a join bonus, customers who sign up to Modern Market Rewards[324] receive US$2 credit into their account aimed at immediately encouraging them to spend at Modern Market to take advantage of their credit.

Every time the member dines at Modern Market they progress towards earning their next US$10 credit. A US$10 credit is triggered ready for redemption each time a US$100 spend threshold is reached, encouraging continuous earn activity to progress towards more credits.

Accumulated value can be redeemed by activating the credit and presenting it to the cashier at checkout.

---

324 Modern Market, https://modernmarket.com/rewards, accessed 29 June 2020.

2. Interest payments credit program:

This model involves inviting members to pay money into a holding account to apply against future purchases. Members are rewarded with 'interest' on their deposits, which acts as an account credit.

The program design may appear complex, but the core proposition messaging is simple, and when compared to the low rates of interest provided by banks, can be quite compelling. The credit is typically applied against high margin products which can support generous discounts, making it cost-effective. One advantage is members may feel they are being provided with additional spending power, which can act to stimulate their desire to transact, particularly when this builds over time.

The approach requires investment in technology systems to manage member accounts, organise direct debit transactions, present clear transaction records and provide robust security to protect against breaches.

Virgin Wines UK

Virgin Wines UK have created a wine credit service called WineBank[325] which allows members to save a chosen amount within their WineBank account each month (from £15 to £100) to spread the cost of buying wine and maintain consistent wine bills.

For every £5 a member saves in their WineBank account, an extra £1 interest is added to the account by Virgin Wines. This acts as a 20 per cent discount when the member chooses to spend their WineBank credits.

---

3. Lowest price guarantee credit program:

Lowest price guarantee credits are a structure which provides an automatic credit to members in the event they purchase a product which later reduces in price. This is typically confined to a fixed period of time post-purchase, with the difference between what the member paid and the new price credited to

---

325 Virgin Wines, https://www.virginwines.co.uk/winebank, accessed 29 June 2020.

their account. For example, 'if the price reduces within two weeks of purchase, you will receive the difference as an account credit'[326]. The member can access the credit on their next transaction.

This strategy is based on a similar premise to a lowest price guarantee company committing to matching or beating competitor prices in order to give customers confidence they are always accessing the cheapest price available. Best price guarantee companies constantly study the competition and adjust prices to remain the low-cost leader. In the instance that a customer finds a better price from a competitor, they will honour and potentially even beat it with a committed discount. This strategy aims to reduce comparison shopping by customers, representing a form of loyalty.

The systems required to operate a lowest price guarantee company are already relatively sophisticated. Extending these systems to support a price guarantee credit program will require investment in platform development. For companies with large product ranges and constantly changing prices, the operational complexities of such a program may be too onerous. Customer service support requirements to provide adequate responses to member enquiries may also require investment.

Super Cheap Auto Club Plus

The Super Cheap Auto Club Plus Membership[327] offers members several benefits including a 'Get Credit Back' promise. That is, 'if an item you just purchased goes on sale, we will automatically credit you the difference!'.

The join fee to sign up to Club Plus is A$5 per member with members receiving an automated A$10 credit into their online account once it is activated. This program design helps create a lock-in effect for members who have paid (sunk cost bias), provides instant gratification whilst familiarising members with using credits, and

---

326 Supercheap Auto, https://www.supercheapauto.com.au/p-supercheap-auto-club-plus-membership/900440.html, accessed 10 September 2020.
327 Ibid.

gives them confidence they will always be accessing the cheapest promotional discount.

If a member buys a catalogue item and the price is reduced within two weeks, the difference is credited to their account. Members have 30 days to spend the credit or it expires, harnessing the loss aversion bias.

Referrals

Model

A referral program is a structured framework which makes it simple and rewarding for a customer to refer a brand or product to someone they know. Berman (2016)[328] indicates referral programs rely on 'motivating satisfied/delighted customers as a referral base, seeking current customers that can provide referrals with a high lifetime value, using referral-based marketing programs to augment traditional promotions, and developing a compensation system for referrals based on either direct payment or increased visibility'.

In exploring referral programs, two design variations are considered: within program and standalone.

1. Referrals within an existing program:

Referrals can be a feature within an overarching program. As an option to earn bonus rewards, members can invite friends to participate in or engage with the program. This is a common component built within many best-practice loyalty programs.

---

328 Berman, B., 2015, 'Referral marketing: Harnessing the power of your customers', Business Horizons, Vol 59.

DiDi

Chinese rideshare giant DiDi[329] leverage their member network to further grow their member database through a referral program within their app and email communications.

Members can easily share their unique referral link with as many friends as they desire in order to give their friends $20 worth of DiDi ride value and receive $20 of DiDi ride value in return when they take their first trip.

The referral feature is prominently positioned on the homepage of the member app and within the onboarding email and push notification series.

2. Referrals as a standalone program:

If operating as a standalone program, members are rewarded for referring family and friends with product credits, discounts, vouchers or third-party rewards. This approach is particularly useful for B2B programs, where a referral for a loyal client can lead to a substantial revenue boost from new clients.

Tesla

Tesla created a successful referral program to capitalise on the loyal sentiment of Tesla owners, with 97 per cent reporting that their next motor purchase will also be a Tesla.[330]

The program was originally designed in a way which ranked referrers (gamification) by the amount of successful referrals they created, with those at the top of the leader board able to obtain exclusive invites to the Tesla factory, attend the launch of new models and receive early access to purchase new models (social identity theory). The first referrer to achieve 10x referrals in North America,

329 Didi, https://australia.didiglobal.com/, accessed 10 September 2020.

330 Luckerson, V., 2015, 'Tesla's Elon Musk responds to Consumer Reports Model S criticism', Fortune, https://fortune.com/2015/10/22/tesla-musk-consumer-reports/, accessed 2 June 2020.

Europe and Asia would receive a free Tesla SUV. The referrer was also able to give up to 10x friends a US$1000 discount as a reward for the referee.

One referrer was responsible for selling 188 Tesla cars in just two months (at an average of US$85,000 per car) equating to almost US$16 million in revenue, and costing Tesla US$188,000 in referrer rewards and a further US$188,000 in referee rewards (representing an ROI of 42x on every dollar spent).[331]

It has been claimed that all referrers combined were responsible for selling about 5,000 new Model S cars during this iteration of the referral program with a total value of US$425 million.[332]

Tesla are continually evolving their referral program. They initially leveraged their loyal customers to grow sales to new heights, including best-selling luxury car in the US and the best-selling electric car in the world. The company has more recently decided to shift the referral program focus towards driving the sales of specific car models and product releases. They stated that although the previous program was successful, it came at significant costs.

The latest iteration rewards both the referrer and referee with credits. The credits can be redeemed for free ultra-rapid Supercharger access or merchandise, including hats, T-shirts, wall chargers, roof racks and more.

It is likely the program design will continue to evolve.

---

331 Toledano, E., 2016, 'How Tesla's Magnetic Referral program Delivered Over 40x ROI in Q4 2015', Business 2 Community, https://www.business2community.com/loyalty-marketing/teslas-magnetic-referral-program-delivered-40x-roi-q4-2015-01450250#BLybFfug4kCUkp0K.97, accessed 2 June 2020.

332 Ibid.

Merchant funded

Model

A merchant funded program involves a third-party partner (or merchant) covering the cost of the benefits provided to the member. This is generally because of the loyalty program promoting the third-party partner to the member, leading to the member transacting with that partner.

A number of programs have built their entire strategy around affiliate, recruiting members to spend online via advertisers to earn cashback. Most major coalition programs, particularly frequent flyer programs, have adopted affiliate earn as part of their wider program offering.

In exploring merchant funded programs, three design variations are considered: affiliate, card-linked and gift card-linked.

1. Affiliate merchant funded program:

Affiliate is a digital business model connecting thousands of advertiser and publisher companies globally. The publisher business publicises the advertiser to their marketing database. The members click through to the advertiser's online store and transact. The advertiser pays a percentage of the total amount spent by the member to the publisher, known as affiliate marketing revenue. The publisher rewards the member with cashback or points funded by the affiliate marketing revenue.

The percentage return provided in the form of affiliate marketing revenue can range from 1 per cent up to 20 per cent and even more, making it an attractive bonus earn opportunity for points programs where the average earn rate may only be a 1 or 2 per cent return. Advertisers often run short-term promotional campaigns which increase the percentage return, making it increasingly attractive.

Two challenges faced by program operators utilising this affiliate marketing framework include payment delays (to avoid situations where members return items after affiliate marketing revenue is paid, many advertisers align the affiliate marketing payment with the official refund period, which can be up to 90 days) and onerous member processes (members must remember to follow a certain process to ensure they earn their cashback or points which commonly requires the member to sign into their program account, find the logo of the relevant brand and click through to their online store to transact).

ShopBack

Shopback[333] have partnerships with over 15,000 large brands which pay a commission for any purchases made on their ecommerce stores which are linked to Shopback members.

Shopback shares the commission with the member that made the purchase in the form of a cashback. Cashback accumulated in a member's ShopBack account can be withdrawn into a member's bank account via Paypal.

Shopback also have a 'Toolkit' for members to install so they 'Never miss a Shopback opportunity' and do not have to remember to go to the Shopback website and click through to the brands site to gain the cashback. The toolkit includes either a Google Chrome or Firefox browser extension which enables an automated pop-up when a member visits the online store of a participating advertiser. Members click an 'activate' button to link their Shopback account prior to transacting to access the cashback on their purchase.

The browser extension approach used by Shopback has been instrumental in boosting member engagement with affiliate programs.

However, there is mixed feedback among the advertisers, with some opting out as they believe they would have gained the member sale (with the member already on their website when the browser

---

333 Shopback, https://www.shopback.com.au/how-we-work, accessed 29 June 2020.

extension pop-up notifies them to activate) without the need to pay commission to Shopback, thus unnecessarily eating into profits.

2. Card-linked or bank account-linked merchant funded program:

This approach involves the linking of a credit/debit card or bank account to a member account.

For card-linking, when the member uses the registered card to transact with a participating merchant, the transaction data is routed from Mastercard, Visa or Amex to the program operator, and an agreed percentage of the total transaction is retained (similar to affiliate marketing revenue). The program operator can use the retained revenue to re Wansink rd the member with points, cashback or credits etc.

For bank account-linking, any transaction made via the member's bank account is redirected to the program operator, allowing them to identify transactions made with participating retailers, and apply the relevant reward. The participating merchant can then be invoiced for the cost of the reward at some time in the future.

This approach provides some advantages over affiliate marketing. The benefit is provided to the member real-time (or at the latest within 24 hours) instead of having to wait up to 90 days. The member can spend online, but more importantly in-store, expanding the flexibility of shopping options. The member does not need to follow specific processes to earn, but simply pays with the registered card or bank account.

Dosh

Dosh[334] is a US card-linked cash back program which enables members to earn automatic cash back when they shop, dine and book hotels with over 100,000 partners.

Members are required to download the app and link their credit card. Unlike most cash back programs, Dosh does not require members to activate their offers. Upon swiping their card with

---

334 Dosh, https://www.dosh.com/, accessed 9 June 2023.

eligible brands, Dosh will automatically deposit the cash back into the member's digital wallet within 4 weeks.

Members receive up to 40 per cent cash back on purchases.

3. Gift card-linked merchant funded program:

Gift cards are typically sold to loyalty programs (and other retailers such as supermarkets) at a discount to the face value amount. Loyalty programs have developed app solutions which allow members to register a credit or debit card and purchase a variable value gift card for a specific brand in real-time. The gift card barcode displays in the app and can be scanned at the checkout, completing the sale. The member pays the face value amount for the gift card (i.e., $20 for a $20 gift card), with the gift card discount used to reward the member with points or miles. Discounts can range from 1 per cent up to 15 per cent for different brands.

United MileagePlus

United MileagePlus offers MileagePlus X,[335] a payments app which allows members to earn miles across hundreds of retailers across the US.

Members register their credit/debit card in the app. When they are transacting, they search for the participating retailer and enter the amount they wish to spend. In the back end, the system purchases a digital gift card of the same variable amount, and presents a QR code in the app for the member to scan to complete the purchase.

MileagePlus buy the gift cards at a discount. They use the discount to cover the cost of the miles they award to the member, making the rewards cost neutral.

The model is clever in two ways; firstly, the discounts provided on gift cards are often quite generous (5-10 per cent or more can be common), meaning the member receives a healthy miles bonus,

---

335 United, https://www.united.com/ual/en/us/fly/mileageplus/earn-miles/mileage-plus-x.html, accessed 29 June 2020.

and secondly, gift card affiliate suppliers have already negotiated the relationships with the gift card providers, making it easy for MileagePlus to build out a rapid expansion of their coalition without having to negotiate individual agreements.

MileagePlus X offer over 1,100+ popular brands, such as Adidas (earn 3 miles), Levi's (earn 1 miles), Sephora (earn 2 miles), Apple (earn 1 miles), and Walmart (earn 1 miles).[336]

Surprise and delight

Model

The surprise and delight model focuses on providing members with periodic surprise gifts to elicit positive emotional responses and build attitudinal commitment. Reciprocity also plays a role in the effectiveness of this design approach.

Extensive consumer psychology research indicates unexpected delight can develop an emotional connection between members and a brand and can be cost-effective (as detailed in Chapter 5). However, maintaining the element of surprise over a long period of time and measuring the direct effects of surprise and delight can be challenging.

In exploring surprise and delight programs, three design variations are considered: basic, member journey and touchpoint.

---

336 United, https://shopping.mileageplus.com/b_____.htm, accessed 9 June 2023.

1. Basic surprise and delight program:

A basic model involves providing the member with an unexpected reward as part of their purchase and consumption journey in the hope it will trigger an emotional response which stimulates the member to seek a repetition of the experience.

This may be provided when the member transacts, when they receive their product or independent to a specific consumer action.

Marley Spoon

Marley Spoon[337] attempt to surprise and delight their customers by providing a small gift in meal kit boxes. This may be a wooden spoon, an apron or a tea towel, ensuring members feel extra delighted when they receive and open their box.

Having Marley Spoon branding on these items which are utilised within their member's kitchens reinforces the generosity of Marley Spoon.

2. Member journey surprise and delight program:

Some customer purchase journeys are complex and involve a series of steps. This creates an opportunity for a company to provide their customers with unexpected treats at each step.

This approach reinforces the customer service focus of the company and increases the likelihood that the customer will proceed to the next step. It also increases the propensity for a customer to wish to repeat the journey in the future, as well as promote the company to family and friends.

---

337 Marley Spoon, https://marleyspoon.com.au/, accessed 29 June 2020.

Frasers Property Care & Rewards

Loyalty & Reward Co worked with this major property development company to use the program as a way to establish emotional connections with customers and maintain relationships which result in single property owners becoming multiple property owners with the company.

One thing Frasers do is reinforce the member's decision to buy a property with the aim to reduce any uncomfortable feelings which can often be attached to making such a large investment. This element of the program provides gifts to customers at strategic times throughout the customer journey to help them proceed to the next step and reflect on their decision favourably and with certainty.

The major gifting milestones for customers include when they purchase a property, when they sign the papers, when their build progresses to the next stage, when they get the keys, when they move in and on their first anniversary since moving in etc.

Attaching these key moments to gifts accompanied by messages of encouragement work to reduce any incidence of cognitive dissonance associated with the purchase while simultaneously building attitudinal commitment.

As a result of the program, 24% of all stock is sold to existing members. Of the sales to members, 43% are repeat purchasers and the remaining 57% were referrals.

3. Touchpoint surprise and delight:

The touchpoint model ensures the customer is delighted at each interaction with the company. It is more relevant for service companies, and requires heavy investment in staff training, quality management, systems and processes.

The desired outcome is a service culture which makes customers feel as if they are the centre of the company's universe. This approach is less of a formalised program design and more of a brand actualisation. It is arguably the most sophisticated application of surprise and delight.

Waldorf Astoria

This luxury hotel corporation executes surprise and delight at an extremely advanced level with the aim to make every interaction unique, personalised, unforgettable and delightful.

The hotel famously allocates two staff members for each guest. Staff members are encouraged to learn small amounts of information about each guest, from the coffee they drink, the type of sheets they prefer, the flowers they love, the newspaper they read and the activities they like which can be drawn upon to deliver delightful experiences which deepen connections with members.

Examples of the lengths Waldorf Astoria go to make members feel like they are the centre of the universe are showcased through thousands of positive member reviews online, most of which refer to these special moments.[338] Many of these guests also mention that the thoughtful surprises, amazing service and personal gifts are the reason they felt compelled to provide a positive review online and will be returning for another stay.

4. Subscription surprise and delight:

The pandemic saw a rise in surprise subscriptions where members subscribe to receiving a monthly package containing unspecified products from the parent company. Many of these surprise subscription services have emerged in the UK and are said to be aimed at open-minded 'culture vultures', with subscriptions around receiving retro comics, games, records or cassettes available[339].

For members, this model builds a sense of excitement each month as

338 Reviews published on TripAdvisor, https://www.tripadvisor.com.au/ Search?q=waldorf%20astoria&searchSessionId=652F5BE9932CC9714793C827891 B82BB1593407950594ssid&searchNearby=false&geo=295424&sid=8446226E978 364D404979EFB35960817159340797 1976&blockRedirect=true, accessed 29 June 2020.

339 Lewis, T., 2021, 'From coffee to cars: how Britain became a nation of subscribers', The Guardian, https://www.theguardian.com/lifeandstyle/2021/may/09/from-coffee-to-cars-how-britain-became-a-nation-of-subscribers, accessed 11 May 2023.

members anticipate their next surprise delivery, and for the company, it allows them to lock-in recurring revenues and tactfully manage inventory.

Domaine-Thomson Mystery Wine Society

New Zealand residents can sign up to receive a mystery case of 6 wines each quarter from Domaine-Thomson vineyards.[340]

For NZ$199, members receive their case, plus other benefits including priority access to limited-edition wines from Burgundy and Library Stock/Museum Release vintages, priority access to Magnums and large format offers, and invitations to The Mystery Wine Society members-only events at Domaine-Thomson and around New Zealand.

Domain-Thomson take advantage of the scarcity effect by limiting the society to just 200 members at any time.

Gamification

Model

Gamification is the use of elements of gameplay in non-game contexts to stimulate specific behaviours. Gamification can play a key role in loyalty programs because of its ability to make a mundane task less boring and can stimulate members to engage in extremely specific, desirable behaviours.

The potential of gamification, the consumer psychology supporting it and the applications in real-world loyalty programs are extensive. As a result, the following chapter has been dedicated specifically to the application of gamification and games and how they can be used within different program design variations.

---

340 https://domainethomsonwines.com/wine-club/ accessed 12 June 2023.

Volkswagen Group BONEO

The Volkswagen Group designed the BONEO program with the aim to encourage weekly interaction with customers, a particularly challenging task due to the frequency by which consumers purchase cars. [341]

The gamified BONEO app provides members with their own car avatar during onboarding. Members can overcome challenges or interact digitally with other members to improve or upgrade their avatar. They can also earn other rewards such as a free drive in a Porsche or Audi, plus occupy virtual sectors of territory on the in-app map.

Members can win virtual Lootboxes which are distributed periodically to encourage habitual engagement with the app. These prizes may be tangible (but contextually relevant) rewards like a free car wash, a free coffee at a petrol station, or a free weekend with a Porsche.

Combining frameworks / hybrid models

There are clear benefits and challenges associated with each design framework, however, brands do not need to commit to just one framework. Many loyalty programs are a combination of multiple frameworks, creating a hybrid model that is better suited to delivering to the business objectives. These programs are more difficult to operate and communicate, but provide a much richer pool of assets from which to incentivise members, a more meaningful way to communicate with members ongoing, more opportunities and flexibility to deliver value to members, and more opportunities to collect and apply data insights to drive incremental visits and spend.

Strategically combining frameworks to create an original and unique loyalty program is the true art and science of loyalty program design. The possibilities are truly infinite. Engaging experienced loyalty consultants is recommended to ensure the final design is optimised to deliver to core objectives and stimulate desirable member behaviours.

---

341 The Octalysis Group, Case Studies, https://octalysisgroup.com/case-studies/, accessed 19 June 2020.

e.l.f Beauty Squad

e.l.f[342] integrate a combined total of seven different design frameworks within their Beauty Squad program.

These include:

- Points: members receive 100 points as a join bonus and continue to earn points with every purchase. Points can be redeemed for dollars off e.l.f products.

- Tiers: the amount of points a member has accumulated directly determines the members tier. 'Fan' is the base tier level, 'Pro' tier requires 1000+ points and 'Icon' tier requires 2000+ points to qualify.

- Member benefits: different tiers unlock access to different member benefits such as access to a birthday gift, bonus points offers, double points events, free shipping, early access to sales, new product launches and bonus vouchers and discounts.

- Discounts: one of the benefits enjoyed by members of the Pro and Icon tier is personalised discounts based on previous purchases and recommendations.

- Referrals: members can refer their friends by giving them a US$10 reward. When the friend joins and spends, the referrer also receives a $5 reward.

- Surprise and Delight: e.l.f send their valued members periodic surprise gifts (i.e., samples within their orders), bonus offers and discounts to recognise, reward and delight them.

As part of the design, e.l.f also have native receipt scanning functionality within the app where members are encouraged to submit receipts from purchases made at Walmart, Target and Amazon, allowing members to earn bonus points. In return, e.l.f receive valuable insights about members, such as other products they are buying, and where they are shopping.

---

342 E.l.f, https://www.elfcosmetics.com/e.l.f.-beauty-squad/, accessed 21 July 2020.

Ekta Chopra, VP of Digital at e.l.f. stated, 'If I think about 2020, my single goal is take that data, harness it in a way that we can make every single loyalty consumer experience very, very relevant.'[343]

While complex in design, the Beauty Squad program is simple for members to understand and engage with. The value of points, status levels and member benefits are all clear.

Through a hybrid of frameworks and rewards, e.l.f benefit from being able to deliver instant gratification through immediate tangible rewards, whilst building attitudinal commitment through status tiers and carefully curated experiential, visual and delightful rewards.

Most importantly, they harness rich member data collected from multiple touchpoints to support the delivery of hyper-personalised member experiences and relevant communications and rewards.

Key insights

- There are many distinct types and sub-types of design frameworks utilised in loyalty programs.

- The overarching design framework models are loyalty currencies, status tiers, member benefits, discounts, credits, referral, merchant funded, surprise and delight, and gamification.

- Certain designs may be better suited to delivering to a specific company's needs and objectives, with each model providing different benefits and challenges, and some models dictating the rewards which are offered. Working through a range of design options and conducting thorough market research will help ensure the framework adopted is appropriate.

- Many programs use a combination of multiple frameworks, creating a hybrid model which is better suited to delivering to the

---

343 Serna, I., 'Loyalty Designed For Authentic And Brand Driven Experience Commerce With Insights From E.L.F. Cosmetics', Annex Cloud, https://www.annex-cloud.com/blog/annex-cloud-elf-cosmetics-glossy-summit/, accessed 21 July 2020.

short term and long-term business objectives which is the art and science of loyalty program design.

Suggested reading

- Drèze, Xavier & Nunes, Joseph., 2009, 'Feeling Superior: The Impact of Loyalty Program Structure on Consumers' Perceptions of Status', Journal of Consumer Research, Vol 35, pp890-905.

- Berman, B., 2015, 'Referral marketing: Harnessing the power of your customers', Business Horizons, Vol 59.

CHAPTER 9

GAMIFICATION AND GAMES

*'In every job that must be done, there is an element of fun.
You find the fun and snap! The job's a game.'*

- Mary Poppins

Focus areas

This chapter will address the following questions:

- What is the difference between gamification and games?

- How is gamification used in loyalty programs to motivate specific member behaviours?

- How are games used in loyalty programs to drive deeper member engagement?

GAMIFICATION IS DEFINED as the use of elements of gameplay in non-game contexts to stimulate specific behaviours.

Games are defined as 'an activity that one engages in for amusement or fun', and 'a complete episode or period of play, ending in a final result'.[344]

These distinctions are important. Gamification and games are different

---

344 Oxford dictionary.

approaches but are often confused as the same thing when applied within loyalty programs.

In modern loyalty programs, both gamification and games are being used to drive deeper member engagement. Applied intelligently, gamification and games can support the stimulation of a wide range of desirable member behaviours, including personal data collection (to support analytical modelling and hyper-personalised communications), advocacy and referrals (to grow the member base and promote tactical offers), and incremental visits and spend.

Approaches are becoming increasingly sophisticated and more prevalent. Momentum is building in both areas as companies are inspired by the efforts of their competitors and other loyalty program operators, while technological advances (smartphone market penetration and better white-label software platforms) support lower cost execution of gamification and games strategies.

While much has been written about the potential of gamification within loyalty programs, digital games are booming, rapidly developing into one of the loyalty industry's mega-trends.

Gamification

Gamification can play a key role in loyalty programs by making mundane actions fun, as well as motivating members to engage in desirable behaviours. Gamification incorporates a range of useful tools to facilitate engagement; points, badges, levels, leaderboards, progress trackers and challenges. It can be argued that many loyalty programs are gamification programs. Members are motivated to complete specific tasks in non-game contexts to accumulate points, earn badges and move up levels (status tiers), climb leaderboards and complete challenges (e.g., shop at new coalition partners to earn bonus points).

The term gamification was first coined by games designer Nick Pelling. He launched a company in 2003 which focused on 'applying game-like accelerated user interface design to make electronic transactions both enjoyable and fast.'[345] Pelling claims his vision was a decade too early for its time, and the

---

345 Pelling, N., 2011, 'The (short) prehistory of "gamification"', https://nanodome.

company was closed in 2006. To his credit, gamification has blossomed, with Pelling identifying Apple as the company which has run furthest with it by embracing 'the underlying idea of gamification – making hard things easy, expressive, near-effortless to use.'

During that same period, others in the gaming industry were also contemplating the expansion of game thinking into non-game areas, such as technology use and work environments. Much of the conceptual focus was on fun and enjoyment. Brandtzaeg et al (2004)[346] explored a theoretical model for understanding the components and nature of enjoyment, and how designers could use their model to predict and evaluate enjoyment. McCarthy and Wright (2004)[347] wrote of feeling attached to technology brands which had provided them with a sense of 'enchantment' when using their products. Anderson et al (2004)[348] proposed using tools for market research that were both provocative and aesthetically pleasant to involve people in engaging experiences as a way to access their intimate sphere and collect revealing data. Overbeeke et al (2004)[349] argued that technology could be made more engaging by appealing more to the senses to make the interaction more tangible.

In 2008, Currier[350] argued that 'there is no more consistent way to predictably induce desired behaviour in humans than engaging them in a context that uses game mechanics such as leader boards, levelling, currencies, stored value,

---

wordpress.com/2011/08/09/the-short-prehistory-of-gamification/, accessed 22 May 2020.

346 Brandtzæg, P. B., Følstad, A. & Heim, J., 2004, 'Enjoyment: Lessons from Karasek', Funology; From Usability to Enjoyment, Springer.

347 McCarthy, J. C. & Wright, P. C., 2004, 'The enchantments of technology', Funology; From Usability to Enjoyment, Springer.

348 Anderson, K., Jacobs, M. & Polazzi, L., 2004, 'Playing Games in the Emotional Space', Funology; From Usability to Enjoyment, Springer.

349 Overbeeke, K., Djajadiningrat, T., Hummels, C., Wensveen, S. & Pens, J., 2004, 'Let's make things engaging', Funology; From Usability to Enjoyment, Springer.

350 Currier, J., 2008, 'Gamification: Game Mechanics is the New Marketing', Oogalabs, https://blog.oogalabs.com/2008/11/05/gamification-game-mechanics-is-the-new-marketing/, accessed 19 April 2020.

privileges, super-powers, status indicators, random reward schedules, etc.' He provided examples of Tencent in China, where members could be sold virtual medicine for their virtual pets if they became sick, and MyCokeRewards, where members could engage with a virtual currency, leaderboards, quests and each other.

The Loyalty360 Expo in Hollywood, Florida in 2009 featured a presentation on gamification by Barry Kirk and Tim Crank of Maritz.[351] 'Games tap into competition, status, flow, play, reward, achievement and mastery—primal psychological needs', Kirk was quoted as saying. He provided a long list of game mechanics, including points, tiers, collecting (e.g., badges), leaderboards, exchanges (sharing gifts on social media), customisation (encouraging members to invest in creating their profile, as it develops exit barriers), feedback (progress tracking), randomness (elements where the member does not know when an event will occur), spectators and bosses (those who climb to the highest tiers). Of interest is that more modern gamification theory tends to focus on a more refined list (points, badges tiers, leaderboards and challenges), indicating that along the way the full scope of gamification appears to have been watered down.

Earlier that year, Foursquare (acknowledged as one of the first mass-market applications of gamification) had been unofficially launched at the SXSW conference in Austin.[352] Creators Dennis Crowley and Naveen Selvadurai spent the conference walking around showing attendees the app and grew the member base in the space of a few days from one hundred to over four thousand. The iPhone app let members explore cities, check-in at restaurants and bars (to let friends know where they were), read and write reviews, and access special offers. Gamification elements included the ability to earn points and badges, achieve status levels and become 'mayor' of a particular venue (for checking in multiple times in a set period). Inspired by Dodgeball (a texting app launched in 2000, which allowed users to check-in, and view crushes, friends, friends of friends, and interesting venues nearby), Foursquare demonstrated to a much

---

351 Loyalty Management Magazine, 2009, Loyalty 360, Vol 3, Iss 1.

352 McKracken, H., 2009, 'Foursquare's first decade, from viral hit to real business and beyond', Fast Company, https://www.fastcompany.com/90318329/foursquares-first-decade-from-viral-hit-to-real-business-and-beyond, accessed 14 April 2020.

wider, global audience the potential of gamification in the new age of smartphones and increasingly sophisticated internet applications.

Deterding et al (2011)[353] reported that Foursquare helped gamification gain rapid traction in interaction design and digital marketing, with numerous applications developed across productivity, finance, health, education, sustainability, news and entertainment media, and software service layers just two years later.

A 2019 whitepaper from Bunchball[354] expanded on the concept of game mechanics by also focusing on 'game dynamics' or desires. They argued that through the application of game mechanics, companies could create an experience that drives behaviour by satisfying one or more desires. These included status, reward, competitive nature, altruism, self-expression and achievement. Bunchball maintained that these desires are universal, crossing generations, demographics, cultures, and genders.

Club Rip Curl

Surf fashion brand Rip Curl launched Club Rip Curl[355] in 2022. Members earn points for shopping, receive birthday gifts, and access free shipping and returns.

The program incorporates a very unique gamification feature. Rip Curl allow members to earn bonus points for surfing waves which capitalises on the unique selling proposition of the brand.

To earn, members need to link their account to a Rip Curl Search

---

353 Deterding, S., Dixon, D., Nacke, L. E., O'Hara, K. & Sicart, M., 2011, 'Gamification: Using game design elements in non-gaming contexts', Paper presented at the 2011 Annual Conference Extended Abstracts on Human Factors in Computing Systems (CHI EA'11), Vancouver, BC, Canada.

354 Bunchball Whitepaper, 2019, 'Gamification 101: An Introduction to the Use of Game Dynamics to Influence Behavior', https://www.bunchball.com/gamification101, accessed 5 May 2020.

355 Rip Curl, https://www.ripcurl.com/au/explore/club-rip-curl.html, accessed 15 June 2023.

GPS Watch (driving purchase of additional Rip Curl products). This watch records top speed, distance paddled, wave count and session time. Members can review their surfing stats live from the line-up as the watch connects to satellites and calculates speed, duration and distance.

The wave count data is automatically fed into their loyalty platform which calculates the bonus points earned and credits them to the member's account.

Waze

Waze[356] is a peer community of users who aim to 'outsmart traffic together'. They use their pool of crowdsourced information to allow Waze to adapt to traffic patterns, avoid traffic jams, avoid police, regulate roads, and generally get around faster and more efficiently.

Waze achieved the critical scale of users necessary to make their user generated sharing economy succeed by employing gamification tactics to reward user participation. Wazers (drivers) can earn points and achieve a higher ranking (5 levels) for anything which will improve the map data and make the roads safer for other drivers. These rewardable actions include reporting incidents, reporting hazards (e.g., roadkill), mapping new roads, updating house numbers or marking police sightings on the map.

Wazers can see other Wazers on the road (as well as their ranking) and can send notifications thanking other Wazers for sharing useful traffic information which helps increase their ranking further. Having the rank visual and being appreciated by peers are both powerful motivators from a consumer psychology perspective, reinforcing the idea that users feel accepted, important and useful to the group (social identity and social proof biases).

A model which is widely applied to gamification theory is the 'Fogg

---

356 Waze, https://www.waze.com/about/, accessed 15 June 2023.

Behavior Model', developed by Stanford professor B.J. Fogg.[357] The model proposed that three elements (Motivation, Ability and a Prompt) must converge at the same moment for a behaviour to occur.

To illustrate, if a loyalty program operator aims for members to increase spend at a particular coalition partner, the model provides guidance on how to stimulate the base. Specifically:

- **Motivation**: the key motivation of the community is their desire to earn more points and status credits.

- **Ability**: most members of the community will have the ability to access the partner via a retail store or online.

- **Prompt**: the program operator can prompt the behaviour with bonus points and status credits for spending with the partner and promoting their purchase on social media.

The 'Fogg Behaviour Model' further elaborates on Prompt types, which can differ in effectiveness dependent on the level of motivation and ability of the member:

- **High motivation-low ability**: a Facilitator Prompt is required, where the member is provided with a higher level of support to commence and complete the behaviour. For example, a short training video on how to progress status tiers.

- **High motivation-high ability**: a Signal Prompt is required, where the member simply requires a cue to commence the behaviour. For example, a text message that the campaign has commenced.

- **Low motivation-high ability**: a Spark Prompt is required, where the member requires additional motivation to commence the behaviour. For example, double status credits for purchases made in a defined period.

---

357 http://www.behaviormodel.org/. Reproduced with permission Professor B.J. Fogg.

Uber and Lyft

Ridesharing companies around the world utilise sophisticated gamification strategies to motivate drivers to keep driving and build loyalty to their brand.

Both Uber[358] and Lyft[359] have implemented achievement and badge gamification features. Drivers can see how they rank compared to other drivers in their region and can earn badges for accomplishments such as completing a certain number of rides or maintaining high ratings. This creates a competitive atmosphere and fosters a sense of achievement aimed at boosting driving time, ensuring a steady supply of rides for passengers.

To further incentivise drivers to stay on the road, both Uber and Lyft offer streak bonuses. These bonuses reward drivers for completing consecutive rides without logging off or declining a ride request. Streak bonuses act as an incentive for drivers to remain active and engaged whist avoiding switching between rideshare companies.

Taylor Swift

Taylor Swift launched a 'Taylor's Biggest Fan'[360] program in 2017, pitching to her fans that she was committed to getting tickets into the hands of her most committed fans (not scalpers or bots) through the exclusive program. Using the 'verified fan' system introduced by Ticketmaster, fans could watch and repost her latest music video, buy her new album or buy Taylor Swift merchandise to increase their chances of accessing tickets. Those fans with the highest motivation (with some fans reportedly buying the same

358 Uber, https://www.uber.com/au/en/, accessed 15 June 2023.

359 Lyft, https://www.lyft.com/, accessed 15 June 2023.

360 Hann, M., 2017, 'Bad blood! Is Taylor Swift's 'verified fan' system a way to reward followers – or rip them off?', The Guardian, https://www.theguardian.com/music/2017/aug/31/bad-blood-is-taylor-swifts-verified-fan-system-a-way-to-reward-followers-or-rip-them-off, accessed 20 July 2020.

album multiple times from different stores to boost their chances) were rewarded with ticket access.

The program received significant criticism due to all fans not having the same financial means to prove they were Taylor's biggest fan, earning the program a derogatory name of 'Taylor's Richest Fan'. Although the intention was to reward motivation, the campaign design was weighted towards those with high financial ability to purchase more products.

Gamification has since extended into many areas, not just limited to loyalty programs. But does gamification work? A literature review of 25 empirical studies by Hamari et al (2014)[361] where the principal research question was 'Does gamification work?' found that the majority of the programs produced positive effects and benefits. It is important to note that most of the programs studied were for education and learning or for intra-organisational systems. Hamari et al were surprised that none of the studies were conducted on marketing gamification, despite the wide range of applications already in market by that time, and that no studies focused on the relationship between gamification and purchase behaviour.

Sailer et al (2017)[362] reported support for gamification in a study where they deliberately varied different configurations of game design elements, and analysed them in regard to their effect on the fulfilment of basic psychological needs. They found that badges, leaderboards and performance graphs positively affected competence need satisfaction, as well as perceived task meaningfulness, while avatars, meaningful stories and teammates affected experiences of social relatedness. Their conclusion was that specific game design elements have specific psychological effects.

This insight is important for loyalty program designers seeking to apply

361 Hamari, J., Koivisto, J. & Sarsa, H., 2014, 'Does Gamification Work? – A Literature Review of Empirical Studies on Gamification', In proceedings of the 47th Hawaii International Conference on System Sciences, Hawaii, USA, January 6-9, 2014.

362 Sailer, M., Hense, J., Mayr, S. & Mandl, H., 2017, 'How gamification motivates: An experimental study of the effects of specific game design elements on psychological need satisfaction', Computers in Human Behavior. Vol 69, pp371-380.

gamification, indicating they should have clarity on the types of psychological and emotional reactions they are attempting to arouse to guide their use of the appropriate game elements.

Hwang and Choi (2019)[363] conducted a study of U.S. consumers responding to gamification elements within app-based loyalty programs. The results confirmed that gamified loyalty programs increased consumer loyalty towards the program, which in turn enhanced consumers' participation intention and app download intention. The findings also suggested that gamified loyalty programs can help companies differentiate their program from other conventional programs, acting to improve overall member loyalty.

Central Group – 'The 1'

The Central Group is a conglomerate based in Thailand, with interests in multiple industries such as retail, real estate, hospitality, and food.

'The 1' is Central Group's loyalty program[364] which is the country's most popular program serving over 20 million members.

The program incorporates gamification via 'The 1 Mission' feature. This enables members to participate in addictive and interactive challenges that unlock a digital badges and points when completed. For example, the 'Snack Time' mission involved buying snacks for 3 days at Tops or Tops online to unlock 50 points. Missions include progress tracker bars and congratulatory messaging when completed.

Since introducing this feature into 'The 1', The Central Group has reported impressive results. This includes 6000M THB (approx. US$177.5 million) in incremental sales, 200M THB (approx. US$5.9

363 Hwang, J. & Choi, L., 2020. 'Having fun while receiving rewards?: Exploration of gamification in loyalty programs for consumer loyalty', Journal of Business Research. Vol 106, pp365-376.

364 Central Group, https://www.centralgroup.com/en/our-business/the-1, accessed 15 June 2023.

million) worth of rewards issued, 6x more purchase frequency from mission participants than non-participants, 60 per cent increase in app engagement, and 15 per cent more spend from participants.

Central Group won the 'Best Use of Gamification to Enhance Loyalty' for 'The 1' at the 2022 International Loyalty Awards in conjunction with loyalty platform provider SessionM.

TripAdvisor (B2B gamification)

TripAdvisor[365] awards each business (e.g., hotels, restaurants, tour companies) a ranking within their specific category and overtly display this ranking to users. For example, if a user searches for restaurants within their city, the list is showcased to them in the order of the restaurant rank together with a label on each restaurant displaying the rank (i.e., as of April 2023, Route Twenty-Six is #14 of 1,605 restaurants in Zurich).

This is aimed at motivating companies to rally their customers to provide positive reviews, with the reward to the business being an improved ranking, exposure to new customers, and an increased likelihood of attracting additional business. TripAdvisor have built out subcategories to further rank companies (i.e., Route Twenty-Six is #1 of 22 Steakhouses in Zurich).

This strategy encourages companies to consider the elements which contribute to a positive review (food + service + value) and improve certain aspects of the customer experience to ensure they work towards progressing and/or maintaining their valuable ranking.

TripAdvisor uses a ranking/leaderboard system to stimulate companies to promote TripAdvisor and leverage their customer bases to drive acquisition and engagement on the TripAdvisor platform.

---

365 Tripadvisor, 'Tripadvisor Popularity Ranking: Key Factors and How to Improve', https://www.tripadvisor.com/TripAdvisorInsights/w722#:~:text=Your%20 Tripadvisor%20Popularity%20Ranking%20is,when%20they%20search%20 your%20area., accessed 30 June 2020.

Games

According to the Entertainment Software Association (ESA), in 2019, '164 million adults in the United States play video games and three-quarters of all Americans have at least one gamer in their household.'[366] The ESA also identified that smartphones are the most common device for playing games (60 per cent) compared to personal computers (52 per cent) and dedicated game consoles (49 per cent). There is only minimal gender imbalance, with 46 per cent of gamers being female.

Assuming similar statistics in other modern or modernising countries, this represents a sizeable population of consumers who are likely to be open to engaging with quality games provided through a loyalty program.

Games can be both entertainment in themselves and a pathway towards a reward, making them a useful tool. Members can be invited to play a physical or digital game, enjoy the experience and unlock a prize, reinforcing the positive experience.

Lazzaro (2004)[367] conducted a comprehensive study of the role of emotions in video games. She identified four key emotion-based reasons why people play games:

- **Hard fun**: players like the opportunities for challenge, strategy, and problem solving.

- **Easy fun**: players enjoy intrigue and curiosity. Players become immersed in games when it absorbs their complete attention, or when it takes them on an exciting adventure.

366 Entertainment Software Industry, 2019, '2019 Essential Facts about the Computer and Video Game Industry', https://www.theesa.com/wp-content/uploads/2019/05/ESA_Essential_facts_2019_final.pdf, accessed 15 June 2020.

367 Lazzaro, N., 2004, 'Why we Play Games: Four Keys to More Emotion without Story', Game Dev Conf, http://twvideo01.ubm-us.net/o1/vault/gdc04/slides/why_we_play_games.pdf, accessed 2 June 2020.

- **Altered states**: players treasure the enjoyment from their internal experiences in reaction to the visceral, behaviour, cognitive, and social properties.

- **The people factor**: players use games as mechanisms for social experiences.

Lazzaro reported being surprised by the 'dramatic contrast in emotional displays between one vs. several people playing together. Players in groups emote more frequently and with more intensity than those who play on their own. Group play adds new behaviours, rituals, and emotions that make games more exciting.' This insight should be of particular interest to loyalty program operators that are contemplating games, as campaigns which stimulate group and social discussion may tap into this greater intensity to the benefit of the operator.

When considering whether to implement a game into a loyalty program, the company must consider the simplicity of the game, its contextual relevance to the program, how stimulating the game would be, and whether it will help achieve the company's objectives.

Industry observation indicates many brands are adopting them on a shorter-term promotional basis, as maintaining long term engagement with one game may be challenging.

Brands can enjoy some valuable benefits from providing members with access to compelling games:

- **Acquisition:** if a consumer is required to join the program to play the game, they are provided with an additional motivation to join. If an existing member needs to download an app to play, they are provided with an incentive to complete that action.

- **Brand exposure**: members playing a game will focus their attention for an extended period of time on a field or game board which will likely contain overt branding, as well as subtle brand associations. This can tap into a psychological bias known as the mere-exposure effect. Zajonc (1968)[368] found that mere repeated exposure of individuals to a stimulus object enhances their attitude toward it. His study focused on exposure to images such as foreign words, Chinese characters and faces of strangers. Later research has replicated the effect across paintings, colours, flavours, geometric shapes and people.[369] Baker (1999)[370] found the effect also works for brands, and recommended that advertisers should place a higher priority on maximising the prominence of the brand name and package in advertisements to capitalise on the effect.

Games provide an engaging medium for intense, repeated exposure. Examples of luxury brands which have embraced games as promotional channels include Louis Vuitton, Guerlain, Dior, Hermes, Burberry, Gucci and Chanel.[371]

Dior

To drive hype around a new store opening in Shanghai, Dior created a playful, competitive, interactive game on their WeChat account.

Dior invited users to collect six Dior branded in-game tokens via an interactive treasure hunt, allowing them to launch a virtual hot air balloon into the sky upon successful completion. Launching a balloon gave shoppers the opportunity to win tickets to the store's grand opening.

Dior gave repeated exposure to their logo within the game, while effectively using it to meld online and offline engagement experiences.

368 Zajonc, R. B., 1968, 'Attitudinal effects of mere exposure', Journal of Personality and Social Psychology, Vol 9, Iss 2 Pt.2, pp1-27.

369 Moreland, R. L. & Beach, S. R., 1992, 'Exposure effects in the classroom: The development of affinity among students', Journal of Experimental Social Psychology, Vol 28, Iss 3, pp255–276.

370 Baker, W. E., 1999, 'When Can Affective Conditioning and Mere Exposure Directly Influence Brand Choice?', Journal of Advertising, Vol 28, Iss 4, pp31-46.

371 Page, R., 2020, 'Game on: 7 brands getting into gaming', CMO, https://www.cmo.com.au/article/670396/game-7-brands-getting-into-gaming/, accessed 4 April 2020.

- **Education**: according to Tulleken,[372] games provide a unique opportunity for brands to represent their values and involve their customers in their mission. He cites the examples of Chipotle (who used a game called Scarecrow to allow customers to save produce and animals from industrial food corporations) and Burger King (who created their Sneak King game to incorporate their promise to 'feed your hunger' by having players feed hungry people). Loyalty programs can further utilise this approach by better educating members on how to extract more value from the program.

Porsche

Porsche consolidated their brand values and commitment for fast cars with the launch of their racing game *Need For Speed: Porsche Unleashed*[373]. The game let users race with different Porsche sports car models, bringing to life the history of the Porsche designs and how they have been refined and evolved over time with each model.

With speed and style always at the core, the game is a classic portrait of the brand and its values, with the game itself now a collector's item.

Boost Juice Vibe Club

Boost Juice launched two games in two years for their Vibe Club loyalty program members to play within their app. The games educate members on the healthy fruit contained within Boost drinks and incorporate elements of their brand story and founder. They also allowed members to win prizes which stimulate an incremental visit or spend.

Boost Juice said in a statement that their first 'Free the Fruit' app

---

372 Tulleken, H., 2019, '5 ways games increase brand awareness', Plinq, https://www.plinq.co/blog/5-ways-games-increase-brand-awareness, accessed 4 April 2020.

373 Fandom, Need for Speed, https://nfs.fandom.com/wiki/Need_for_Speed:_Porsche_Unleashed, accessed 15 June 2023.

saw over 329,889 downloads and 225,970 prizes given away, while reaching number one on the Apple App Store and remaining in this position for four weeks.[374]

During this time, Vibe Club members spent close to 56 million minutes of gameplay at an average 173 minutes per user. This level of app engagement (which rewarded members with digital discount vouchers), drove high traffic into their bricks and mortar stores and resulted in significant sales uplifts.

The game was quickly followed by a second game 'Find the Fruit', capitalising on the success of Free the Fruit.

- **Advocacy**: games are effective in generating word of mouth promotion. In 2009, The NDP Group revealed that 41 per cent of all gamers report that they rely on word of mouth to obtain information on video games.[375]

  Further research from Poretski et al (2019)[376] found that word of mouth increases game consumption, particularly for online games. Loyalty program operators that develop games with a 'talkability' factor can benefit from generating a buzz amongst social groups.

KFC

KFC utilise games extensively around the world. Two examples include KFC China and KFC UK and Ireland.

- **KFC China**: KFC China identified that the country's 564

---

374 McGilloway, C., 2018, cited in 'Boost Juice launches new "Find the Fruit" game app', Inside FMCG Magazine, https://insidefmcg.com.au/2018/04/19/boost-juice-launches-new-find-the-fruit-game-app/, accessed 16th May 2019.

375 The NPD Group, 2009, 'Gaming Device Profiles'.

376 Poretski, L., Zalmanson, L. & Arazy, O., 2019, 'The Effects of Co-Creation and Word-of- Mouth on Content Consumption - Findings from the Video Game Industry', Fortieth International Conference on Information Systems Munich 2019, https://aisel.aisnet.org/cgi/viewcontent.cgi?article=1639&context=icis2019, accessed 15 June 2020.

million gamers were a core target market which was key to achieving their goals of connecting with the youth population. They strategically partnered with the most popular Esports gaming franchise in China, League Of Legends, to create an AI commentator (which they called Colonel KI) that predicted outcomes of League of Legends tournaments in real time. Fans could log into the KFC app to track predictions throughout the match. During the most exciting moments in the match, the Colonel would virtually distribute QR coupons to fans inviting them to order KFC online and enjoy fried chicken during the game.

Results generated impressive metrics in both social buzz and sales. There were 203 million viewers on League of Legends live streams, 35 million topic views on Weibo, 1.9 million on screen comments, 100 per cent of coupons accepted and 25 per cent of coupons redeemed (2,500 per cent above the benchmark).[377]

To increase talkability further, KFC also themed some of their restaurants with League of Legends branding, and saw a 35 per cent uplift in sales in themed stores.[378]

- **KFC UK and Ireland**: KFC launched Rewards Arcade to members in 2022. This new loyalty program gives KFC app users a chance to win prizes such as a Popcorn Chicken or a Bargain Bucket every time they spend £3 or more in a KFC store.

  KFC Arcade also invites members to play a game called 'Hammer Time' where members swing a digital hammer to try and ring a bell at the top of the screen.

  Hammer Time resembles the classic retro festival-style game where players 'swing to win'. KFC had indicated that they will

377 The Esports Ads, Colonel KI campaign, https://theesportsads.com/campaigns/colonelki, accessed 27 May 2020.

378 Thomas, P., 2019, Digital Driving Growth in KFC China, Global Convenience Store Focus, https://www.globalconveniencestorefocus.co.uk/features/digital-driving-growth-in-kfc-china/, accessed 14 January 2020.

- **Social sharing**: gamers are increasingly sharing their experiences and successes on social media. According to Minguez,[379] this commenced with interactive browser-based Facebook games like Zynga Poker, Mafia Wars and FarmVille, where it was observed that 'players not only loved to play against one another, but also liked the bragging rights that came with getting high scores or passing a particularly tough level'. Loyalty programs which develop more comprehensive, challenging games have the opportunity to tap into social sharing, and even harness it by making it easy to share (via strategically positioned buttons) and rewarding the behaviour (by providing incremental rewards).

Lidl Slovakia

In a bid to differentiate itself from other major supermarkets and to drive customer engagement, Lidl Slovakia launched a short-term collectible campaign called The Fresh Heads[380]. With every purchase over €20, customers would receive a pack containing one of 24 collectible marble characters.

Each pack also contained a unique QR code that could be scanned with The Fresh Heads app.

The app allowed customers to digitally track their collection, play in-app maze games with their favourite characters, create their

---

379 Minguez, K., 2014, 'The Merging of Social Media and Gaming', Social Media Today, https://www.socialmediatoday.com/content/merging-social-media-and-gaming, accessed 14 January 2020.

380 Magneds, https://magneds.com/the-fresh-heads-marbles-lidl-slovakia-2021/, accessed 15 June 2023.

own maze levels to share with friends, and earn a special 25th character with the chance to win an electric scooter if all 24 collectibles were collected. By adding social functionality to the app, such as trading digital marbles with friends and publishing the top 10 levels shared each week, Lidl was able to build engagement and promote the app to a wider audience.

The campaign was a resounding success, with over 110,000 users (26 per cent of the target group) and more than 1 million marbles digitised. Additionally, 20 per cent of users traded digitally, and over 40,000 levels were created.

The social aspect of the app helped to drive engagement and organic promotion of the campaign, while also providing Lidl with the ability to track customer engagement, a traditionally difficult metric to measure in such campaigns.

Chipotle

Chipotle took advantage of digital games and social sharing during National Burrito Day by launching a metaverse experience called Chipotle Burrito Builder on the gaming platform Roblox[381].

The game transported players back to a 90s-themed Chipotle restaurant, and the first 100,000 players to successfully build a virtual burrito earned in-experience currency called 'Burrito Bucks'. Players could exchange these Bucks for a free entrée code, which could be redeemed via the Chipotle app. This incentivised players not only to engage in the game but also to download the app.

To further increase engagement and social buzz, the game featured a real-time leaderboard to inspire competition. The top five players at the end of the promotion won free burritos for a year. The community was also involved in building a collective go-to burrito via a poll on Twitter, with the winning community-built burrito becoming

---

381 Kelly, C., MarketingDive, https://www.marketingdive.com/news/chipotle-roblox-burrito-bucks-rewards-metaverse/621566/, accessed 15 June 2023.

a real-world menu item exclusively for Chipotle Rewards members during the promotional period.

To enhance the tie-in with the Chipotle Rewards program, members could exchange Reward points for one of 10,000 Roblox gift cards (valued at 400 Robux - Roblox's in-game currency). Additionally, Chipotle gave away one million Robux to participating fans.

This entire effort created an incredible amount of social buzz, which was the key driver for the campaign's success. The free promo codes were claimed within 30 minutes, and the Roblox experience amassed over 15 million visits. By leveraging the power of a game and social sharing, Chipotle was able to create a memorable experience that resulted in increased app downloads, member acquisition, and overall customer engagement.

Chipotle followed up this campaign in 2023 with a Capcom partnership.[382] Members were provided with the opportunity to earn Street Fighter 6 in-game currency Fighter Coins as a reward for purchases via app and website.

- **Habit formation**: games can be used to generate more sustained and habitual behaviour. A program operator may apply simple, low skill and randomness elements to turn their delivery of offers into a game. This provides the opportunity for a member to reveal a new offer every day by playing, exposing them to the brand on a frequent basis and entering their consideration set frequently and consistently.

382 PYMTS, 2023 " Chipotle Leverages Video Game Rewards for Deeper Connection With Diners", https://www.pymnts.com/restaurant-innovation/2023/chipotle-leverages-video-game-rewards-for-deeper-connection-with-diners/ accessed 27 June 2023

Maccas Mini Games

'Maccas Mini Games', a 2020 promotion provided by McDonald's[383], gave players one opportunity per day to unlock a prize by playing an in-app game. Players could choose to dunk a chicken nugget, play mini-golf or run through a maze, where everyone won a prize.

On successful completion of the game, an offer was presented to the player which expired within 16 hours, generating engagement urgency.

The player could revisit the app and play again the next day, helping to develop habitual behaviours.

- **Endowment effect**: as detailed in Chapter 6, Thaler, (1980)[384] identified that consumers place a greater value on things once they have established ownership. The endowment effect can be harnessed by loyalty programs when distributing offers as prizes. A member who earns an offer after successfully completing a game is likely to value it more than a member who has just been provided with the offer. As a result, they are potentially more likely to use the offer.

T-Mobile PrePaid Surprise

T-Mobile Netherlands (supported by mobile marketing, customer retention and content solutions agency Velti) run an innovative digital game, PrePaid Surprise, to drive customer retention and higher revenues.[385]

Customers that top-up their PrePaid account receive a free PrePaid Surprise code in an SMS with a unique link to play a 'Find the hidden

---

383 McDonalds, https://mcdonalds.com.au/sites/mcdonalds.com.au/files/MaccasMiniGames_%20February2020.pdf, accessed 15 June 2023.

384 Thaler, R., 1980, 'Toward a Positive Theory of Consumer Choice,' Journal of Economic Behavior and Organization, Vol 1, pp39-60.

385 PrePaid Surprise, T-Mobile Netherlands https://prepaidsurprise.t-mobile.nl/ accessed 6 July 2023

object' game. Algorithms randomly select two items for them to find in the shown image within a specific time frame.

Depending on how many items are found, the customer earns 'Wheel of Fortune' spins to win a digital or physical prize.

In 2019, PrePaid Suprise was reimagined by incorporating an Augmented Reality (AR) game. Using their mobile phone camera, customers take a photo that will then become the canvas of the 'Find the hidden object' game.

Additional games have been added where players complete missions while being incentivised to share marketing consent and a verified email address.

In the missions campaigns, Velti has observed that incorporating a game element and offering customers a chance to win premium rewards before receiving an instant reward leads to higher conversion rates compared to not including a game. The redemption rate with a game is approximately 45 per cent higher compared to the redemption rate without a game.

This indicates that members who win an offer are likely to value it more (and hence be more likely to redeem it) than members who are simply provided with an offer.

In an interview with Loyalty & Reward Co, Mariëtta Robbé Groskamp of Velti said, 'By integrating digital games, T-Mobile is experiencing extended customer loyalty, higher buyer frequency and a higher value of top-ups. The message is clear: when you make customer journeys enjoyable, customers stay engaged, play along, and everyone wins.'

With all these benefits, it is important to acknowledge that developing a compelling, engaging, likeable and shareable game within a reasonable budget can be challenging. Phan et al (2016)[386] developed a Game User Experience

---

386 Phan, M., Keebler, J. & Chaparro, B., 2016, 'The Development and Validation of the Game User Experience Satisfaction Scale (GUESS)', Human Factors: The Journal of the Human Factors and Ergonomics Society, Vol 58, Iss 8.

Satisfaction Scale (GUESS) to comprehensively measure video game satisfaction based on nine key factors; usability/playability, narratives, play engrossment, enjoyment, creative freedom, audio aesthetics, personal gratification, social connectivity and visual aesthetics. Developing a game which measures highly across most or all factors would be challenging, although it should be recognised that games developed for short-term loyalty program promotional campaigns are likely not going to be judged in the same light as a major label release.

To support loyalty programs interested in experimenting with games, platform providers have evolved offering white-label game solutions specialising in rapid, low-cost development, deployment and analytics.

Key insights

- Gamification and games are different approaches which deliver different outcomes within loyalty programs.

- Gamification is the use of elements of gameplay in non-game contexts to stimulate specific behaviours.

- Games are defined as 'an activity that one engages in for amusement or fun', and 'a complete episode or period of play, ending in a final result'.

- It can be argued that loyalty programs are gamification programs. Gamification incorporates a range of useful tools to facilitate engagement within loyalty programs; points, tiers, collecting, leaderboards, progress trackers, exchanges, customisation, feedback, randomness, spectators and bosses.

- Games can be used to acquire new members, expose consumers to the brand for extended periods, be used to promote company values and mission, generate word of mouth promotion, stimulate social media sharing, generate habitual behaviours and make members value offers more highly than if they are simply conferred.

Suggested reading

- Lazzaro, Nicole., 2004, 'Why we Play Games: Four Keys to More Emotion without Story', Game Dev Conf, http://twvideo01.ubm-us.net/o1/vault/gdc04/slides/why_we_play_games.pdf.

- William E. Baker, 1999, 'When Can Affective Conditioning and Mere Exposure Directly Influence Brand Choice?', Journal of Advertising, Vol 28, Iss 4, pp31-46.

- Pelling, N., 2011, 'The (short) prehistory of 'gamification'', https://nanodome.wordpress.com/2011/08/09/the-short-prehistory-of-gamification/.

- McKracken, H., 2009, 'Foursquare's first decade, from viral hit to real business and beyond', Fast Company, https://www.fastcompany.com/90318329/foursquares-first-decade-from-viral-hit-to-real-business-and-beyond.

- Sailer, Michael & Hense, Jan & Mayr, Sarah & Mandl, Heinz., 2017, 'How gamification motivates: An experimental study of the effects of specific game design elements on psychological need satisfaction', Computers in Human Behavior, Vol 69, pp371-380.

CHAPTER 10

BUSINESS-TO-BUSINESS (B2B) PROGRAMS

'By registering and joining Club Clipsal you'll start earning points and be able to access Club Clipsal benefits and rewards. Gain access to customised tools, resources and support for all your business needs.'

- Schneider Electric's Club Clipsal registration page for electricians and electrical business owners[387]

Focus areas

This chapter will address the following questions:

- How are B2B loyalty programs different to B2C programs?
- Does loyalty play as important a role in B2B industries as B2C industries?
- Who within a company should the B2B loyalty program attempt to engage?
- What are the main design frameworks utilised within B2B loyalty programs?

---

387 Club Clipsal https://www.clipsal.com/register accessed 18 July April 2023.

The importance of loyalty within B2B industries

Most of the academic focus and societal awareness around loyalty programs relates to consumer-focused programs (B2C). Business-to-business (B2B) programs can also work to drive desirable behaviours from business customers; increased spend, repeat purchase, data capture, relationship development and advocacy.

This chapter provides a focus on B2B programs; academic research, similarities and differences compared to consumer programs, and framework designs supported by case studies.

Research supports the importance of customer loyalty as part of a B2B relationship.

Haghkhah (2013)[388] stated that retaining a companies current customers and making them loyal is a critical component for a company to be successful. 'With loyal customers, companies can maximise their profit because loyal customers are willing to purchase more frequently; spend money on trying new products or services; recommend products and services to others; and give companies sincere suggestions. Thus, loyalty links the success and profitability of a company.'

Asgarpour (2013)[389] argued that customer loyalty is essential if a company is going to retain its current customers and that client loyalty is one of the most sought-after objectives of B2B companies today.

Eakuru and Mat (2008)[390] indicated that the ultimate goal of companies is to build customer loyalty, which is achieved via the mediating influence of

---

388 Haghkhah, A., 2013, 'Commitment and Customer Loyalty in Business-To-Business Context', European Journal of Business and Management, Vol 5, Iss 19, pp156-164.

389 Asgarpour, R., Abdul Hamid, A. B., Mousavi, B. & Jamshidy, M., 2013, 'A Review on Customer Loyalty as a Main Goal of Customer Relationship Management', Jurnal Teknologi (Sciences and Engineering), Vol 64, pp109-113.

390 Eakuru, N. & Mat, N. K. N., 2008, 'The Application of Structural Equation Modeling (SEM) in Determining the Antecedents of Customer Loyalty in Banks in South Thailand', The Business Review, Vol 10, No 2, pp. 129-139.

customer trust. This acts to enhance the impact of corporate identity, corporate image, and the reputation of the company.

B2B loyalty program characteristics

There are a range of options for companies to develop loyalty amongst B2B customers which do not include a formal loyalty program. This includes providing superior products and services, attractive pricing and exclusive discounts, quality account management, supportive post-sales customer service, events and conferences, and education courses.

That being said, companies are increasingly embracing formal B2B loyalty programs as a method to build customer loyalty. Krafft et al (2017)[391] identified that in recent years more B2B companies have implemented customer relationship management (CRM) practices and, increasingly more B2B companies are introducing loyalty programs to build stronger relationships with, and lock in, their best customers.

Examples of companies that have introduced B2B loyalty programs globally include MailChimp, HP, American Express, Schneider Electric, Ingram Micro, Trend Micro, WeWork, Lenovo, IBM, Thomas Cook, Fujitsu, Countrywide, Cisco, Nufarm, Uber, The Iconic and Mercedes-Benz.

The characteristics of B2B programs tend to be different to B2C programs in six fundamental ways.

- **Member base size**: B2B programs generally have smaller member bases than B2C programs. Not surprisingly, this is because B2B companies have access to a smaller pool of customers from which to draw members. This provides B2B program operators with an advantage; a smaller member base makes personalisation of communications and services much more achievable. B2B relationships tend to involve a greater level of intimacy than B2C models, with face-to-face meetings, social events, tailored services and post-purchase

---

391 Viswanathan, V., Sese, F. J. & Krafft, M., 2017, 'Social Influence in the Adoption of a B2B Loyalty Program: The Role of Elite Status Members', International Journal of Research in Marketing, Vol 34, Iss 4, pp 901-918.

support. This provides a good opportunity to build a positive brand connection and attitudinal commitment.

- **Member base spend**: on average B2B programs generally provide greater value to members than B2C programs. This is because B2B customers tend to spend more than B2C customers, allowing the company to return more value to the business customers as rewards. For example, a program providing 1 per cent return on one million dollars of business spend will be able to provide a much more generous reward that a program where a consumer spends one thousand dollars. This is an important distinction; as value is a key principle in generating program engagement, B2B programs have a natural advantage over B2C programs.

- **Purchasing drivers**: companies have different purchasing approaches to consumers, which necessitates variations in program design. According to Kaushik (2019),[392] consumers buy based on family needs, fashion and social necessity, they make fast and simple decisions, receive relevant marketing primarily via mass market channels (internet, social media, radio, TV, newspaper ads, etc.) and are reasonably sensitive to technological changes. By comparison, companies buy to enhance profitability, productivity, payback, and operational ease and maintenance, make slow and complex decisions, receive relevant marketing primarily via direct one-to-one presentations and discussions, and are overly sensitive to technological changes. Thus, the factors which influence a consumer to be positively influenced by a loyalty program are distinct to the factors which will influence a business decision. Adequate client research is essential to identify those factors and tailor the design accordingly.

- **Relationships**: the complexity of the buying relationship is greater for B2B than B2C, meaning the program needs to cater for multiple member relationships within a single account. Kaushik (2019)[393]

---

392 Kaushik, P., 2019, 'B2B Marketing,' Lecture series, Atharva Institute of Management Studies.

393 Kaushik, P., 2019, 'B2B Marketing,' Lecture series, Atharva Institute of Management Studies.

highlighted that while a B2C relationship is generally one-to-one, a B2B relationship may be between multiple participants, including owners, initiators, influencers, deciders, users, buyers and gatekeepers. This can make it incredibly challenging to design an effective program. For example, a B2B program which rewards the business owner or leader may fail to influence purchase behaviour if procurement decisions are made by buyers. A program which rewards buyers may not be effective if they are following the product-selection direction of the users. A program which rewards users may not be effective if their decisions are often overruled by the gatekeepers. Research of individual companies is required to ascertain which participants the program is best targeted towards. Flexibility within the program design to adjust the targeting for different companies is also important, as is understanding that different stakeholders will have different agendas and objectives which they believe a loyalty program should deliver to.

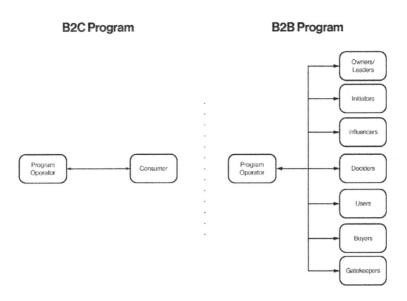

Figure 15: the different relationships between program operators and stakeholders/members within both B2C and B2B loyalty programs.

A side-effect of this dynamic is that B2B programs which deliver rewards based on spend tend to be better suited to targeting smaller businesses (small-to-medium enterprises or SMEs) than large companies. SME's are more likely to be able to receive and distribute rewards within the business, while this is more challenging within large companies due to the greater number of engaged stakeholders.

- **Fundamental challenges**: the design of a B2B program needs to accommodate three fundamental challenges; ethical, communications and employee longevity. For *ethical,* a program needs to ensure it is not influencing decision-making in a way which delivers a poorer outcome for the business or their customers. For example, if a buyer decides to purchase a service from one business over another because they will receive a loyalty program reward, ethical challenges arise if the service is more expensive or delivered at a lower quality. In this instance, the loyalty program could be viewed as a form of bribery. For *communications*, the program design needs to identify which participants within the customer business should receive program information, and the nature of that information. For *employee longevity*, the program operator needs to quickly identify when a participant leaves the business and update the membership status to accommodate new participants. This can be particularly challenging for larger member programs.

- **Reward variations**: B2B programs tend to have different reward ranges than B2C programs. While they may incorporate consumer goods and gift cards, they also tend to include the company's own products, direct discounts, free education courses, access to events and conferences, and other benefits more suited to the needs of particular customers.

B2B customer commitment

In the same way that commitment (measured as resistance to change) leads to loyalty within B2C programs, B2B programs should strive to build customer commitment to the brand. Gilliland and Bello (2002) identified that attitudinal commitment by a client towards another business motivates specific actions to manage and advance ongoing relationships. This includes a greater willingness to use relational, over contract-based mechanisms to keep behaviours consistent with the contractual agreements. They hypothesised that attitudinal commitment for B2B relationships consists of two components: a rational, economic calculation (calculative commitment) and an emotional, social sentiment (loyalty commitment).

Gilliland and Bello identified three important characteristics specific to loyalty commitment within B2B relationships; it makes it difficult to exit the relationship, partially because loyalty sentiments motivate participants to work out problems rather than leave; it suggests a preference for one company over their competitors when making supply decisions; and, it maintains the relationship even if the decision may be economically irrational. These are clearly desirable and valuable relationship characteristics for a business to generate with a customer.

A well-designed B2B loyalty program can help develop loyalty commitment in order to support the realisation of these benefits.

B2B program design frameworks

B2B loyalty program designs are diverse, although less so than B2C programs. They often mimic B2C designs, but with some variations. The remainder of this chapter presents a range of program design frameworks used by B2B loyalty programs. As with B2C, it is common for a B2B program to combine elements from a number of frameworks to create a more comprehensive design.

Loyalty currencies and status tiers

Members earn points for transactions, which can be redeemed on a set reward range. Members can also achieve status tiers to unlock greater benefits.

Schneider Electric Club Clipsal

Schneider Electric is a multinational company providing energy and automation digital solutions, and Clipsal is a subsidiary brand providing electrical accessories.

Club Clipsal is Australia's largest loyalty club for the electrical industry with over 8,000 members in the rewards program.[394] Operating on a four-tiered membership basis, the program offers members the ability to earn points by purchasing Clipsal products from their selected wholesalers. The program features an earn accelerator, where the higher the tier, the higher the earn rate per dollar spent. Points can then be redeemed via a rewards store for a variety of gift cards and consumer goods.

Members of Club Clipsal also access exclusive functions for networking, social gatherings, and getaways. In addition to the earn accelerator, higher tiers have access to some additional member perks such as discounts on insurance, business management services, and fleet purchases.

Member benefits and discounts

Members can access a bundle of desirable benefits, which may include some form of preferred discounting structure, preferred payment terms, credit lines or invitations to exclusive conferences and events.

Allianz Blue Eagle Program

Allianz is a German multinational financial services company with their core businesses covering insurance and asset management. The Allianz Blue Eagle Program[395] exists to engage and reward their

---

394 Schneider Electric, Clipsal, https://www.clipsal.com/club-clipsal, accessed 6 April 2023.

395 Allianz, https://www.einsure.com.au/wb/blueeagle-welcome.html, accessed 6 April 2023.

broker network, primarily through networking, educational and celebratory events.

The program offers one point of call for all the information brokers require, such as program news, policy and claims information, online training, and product quoting and binding. An important aspect of the program is to build a sense of community between brokers and the brand, and Allianz do so by organising a variety of initiatives to get members involved.

These networking initiatives include:

- Annual Allianz Blue Eagle Awards: an exclusive celebratory event rewarding highly distinguished Blue Eagles for their achievements, while offering an opportunity to network with fellow members.

- Young Eagle program: designed to educate insurance brokers on how to operate an effective insurance company. Young brokers are regularly brought together to learn and compete in team-based scenarios, coached by members of the Allianz board.

- Blue Eagle Ladies Day: celebrating female brokers and Allianz staff, providing an opportunity to network and build broker-staff relationships.

- Tipping competitions: the Blue Eagle community can compete in annual tipping competitions for grand prizes such as overseas holidays.

Merchant funded

Members can accumulate value by transacting with third-party partners, with the cost of the reward covered by the third-party partner.

Nufarm Priority Partnerships

Nufarm is an agricultural chemical company which provides an extensive range of agricultural and crop protection products around the globe.

Nufarm's B2B loyalty program[396] allows members to accumulate points when purchasing eligible Nufarm products and transacting with relevant Nufarm suppliers. Points can be redeemed via the Priority Partnerships reward store which hosts over 5,000 rewards including a selection of consumer goods, travel, sporting equipment, events and more.

Rewarding members for ordering through verified third-party suppliers and partners provides an additional purchase incentive to build the feedback loop and reinforce client commitment both with Nufarm and its suppliers.

Surprise and delight

Members receive unexpected delights to recognise and reward them for their business and to build an emotional connection.

Influitive

Influitive is a SaaS product and professional services company which specialises in providing customer marketing platforms and tools to drive customer advocacy and engagement.

In December 2016, Influitive created a personalised video messaging tool which allowed their customers to deliver a surprise 1:1 holiday season message to their customers and business partners via one of three fun characters.

The videograms were delivered to each recipient via Twitter, personally addressing both the sender and receiver, designed to

---

396 Nufarm, Priority Partnership, http://www.prioritypartnership.co.nz/pp_app/page_public.php?page=about_priority_partnership, accessed 6 April 2023.

'pack a bigger emotional punch with them'[397] and show customers they care.

This surprise and delight initiative cost 'a few hundred dollars in costumes, décor and a few new video cards',[398] but the effort and personalisation is what made the most impact, strengthening the relationship and increasing retention by making both Influitive customers and their customers feel special.

Education, training and mentoring

Members may be able to access online and classroom courses relevant to their industry and career progression. They may also be able to access mentoring support from leaders in the industry.

Know Your IBM (KYI)

IBM's primary B2B loyalty program, KYI[399] targets resellers in its distribution channel with rewards structured around two key components:

- Learn and Earn: provides points to members who undertake educational activities and modules, learning about various IBM products and solutions, including skill enhancement courses and certifications.

- Sell and Earn: allows members to earn points for selling eligible IBM products, services, or solutions.

Members can redeem their points for products and gifts from participating merchants.

Periodically, IBM drives member engagement and retention by

---

397 Influitive, 2016, 'The Secret to Delighting B2B Customers in 30 Seconds This Holiday Season', https://influitive.com/blog/secret-delighting-b2b-customers-30-seconds-holiday-season/, accessed 6 April 2023.

398 Ibid.

399 IBM, https://www.ibm.com/partnerworld/resources/manage/incentives-promotions, accessed 6 April 2023.

integrating gamification into e-learning. An example of this is KYI Badge Bingo, which involves members completing specific e-learning modules to be given the opportunity to share in a KYI points pot, as well as compete on leaderboards for bonus points.

Results published by Moviforce[400] indicate that KYI's 2018 results broke all previous year's records. In addition, the 15 per cent of IBM's B2B channel that participated in KYI generated 62 per cent of IBM's overall revenue for all products and services that were incentivised in KYI.

They also stated that KYI participants outperformed similar profiled non-participants (same geography, similar size and turnover) by a record 800 per cent.

Due to these impressive results, further IBM divisions such as IBM Watson and IBM Security asked to join the program in 2019.[401]

Referrals

Members may be able to unlock benefits by referring other companies.

American Express Partner Plus

Partner Plus[402] is a referral-based partnership program with American Express. Akin to most referral programs, members are rewarded if they successfully refer a business contact to American Express' Global Commercial Services.

Partners can track the status of submitted leads at any time through a partner portal and receive support from an appointed

400 Motivforce, 2019, 'Motivforce wins best B2B Loyalty Program with IBM for second year running at Loyalty Magazine Awards', https://www.motivforce.com/blog/back-to-back-award-winning-b2b-loyalty-program#:~:text=Know%20Your%20IBM%20(KYI)%20is,as%20sales%20of%20eligible%20solutions., accessed 6 April 2023.

401 Ibid.

402 American Express, Partner Plus, https://corporateforms.americanexpress.com/PartnerPlusCompetitionAU, accessed 6 April 2023.

sales representative. When successful, members reap the benefits as a percentage of the new account volume.

Simple and straightforward for members to understand, the program creates a win-win situation for existing and new members.

Corporate social responsibility initiatives

Members may be able to participate in activities which contribute to social causes.

HP Planet Partner Rewards

HP Planet Partner Rewards[403] is available in over 76 countries and territories worldwide, with the objective to reward companies for returning used HP print cartridges, supporting HP's recycling initiative. The program goes beyond rewards, enabling companies to contribute towards social and environmentally responsible actions, and earn HP points in the process.

The design is simple, with HP leveraging their partnerships with collection agencies to make the pick-up and recycling processes seamless and convenient. Points are awarded based on the quantity of returns, with more points awarded per item for scale. Points can be redeemed by partners for HP gift vouchers which can be used to purchase HP products from selected channel partners.

The program has a threefold impact, where partners save resources and get rid of empty cartridges for free, partners earn points to save money on future purchases, and they contribute to a cleaner environment by opting for safe and responsible recycling.

---

403 HP Planet Partners Return and Recycling Program, http://www.hp.com/hpinfo/newsroom/press_kits/2010/ecoachievement/HP_PP_Recycling_Program.pdf, accessed 6 April 2023.

Key insights

- B2B loyalty programs are similar to B2C programs, however there are a number of characteristics which differ; smaller member bases, higher spend, different purchasing approaches, more complex buying relationships, reward range variations, and ethical, communication and employment longevity challenges.

- Loyalty is a critical component for the success and profitability of a company. The ultimate goal of companies is to build customer loyalty, which is achieved via the mediating influence of customer trust. This acts to enhance the impact of corporate identity, corporate image and the reputation of the company.

- In recent years more B2B companies have implemented customer relationship management (CRM) practices and, increasingly more B2B companies are introducing loyalty programs to build strong relationships with their best customers.

- A B2B relationship may be between multiple participants, including owners, initiators, influencers, deciders, users, buyers and gatekeepers, which can make it incredibly challenging to design and operate an effective loyalty program with appropriate rewards.

- The main B2B design framework categories are loyalty currencies, status tiers, member benefits, discounts, merchant funded, surprise and delight, education, training and mentoring, and corporate social responsibility initiatives.

Suggested reading

- Haghkhah, A., 2013, 'Commitment and Customer Loyalty in Business-To-Business Context', European Journal of Business and Management, Vol 5, Iss 19, pp156-164.

- Asgarpour, R., Abdul Hamid, A. B., Mousavi, B. and Jamshidy, M., 2013, 'A Review on Customer Loyalty as a Main Goal of Customer Relationship Management', Jurnal Teknologi (Sciences and Engineering), Vol 64, pp109-113.

- N. Eakuru and N. K. N. Mat, 2008, 'The Application of Structural Equation Modelling (SEM) in Determining the Antecedents of Customer Loyalty in Banks in South Thailand', The Business Review, Vol 10, No 2, pp. 129-139.

- Krafft, Manfred & Viswanathan, Vijay & Sese, F. Javier., 2017, 'Social Influence in the Adoption of a B2B Loyalty Program: The Role of Elite Status Members', International Journal of Research in Marketing, Vol 34, Iss 4, pp 901-918.

PART 2
LOYALTY PROGRAM ENABLEMENT

PART 2 COVERS loyalty program enablement, detailing the critical elements required to effectively launch a loyalty program and support ongoing operational execution.

Loyalty & Reward Co have developed a digital transformation framework called the Member Engagement Ecosystem™. The model illustrates that a loyalty program is a major component of a wider member engagement strategy, and in order to deliver the best results, the loyalty program needs to be supported by the right technology, data collection practices, reporting and analytics structure, member lifecycle management strategy, and omnichannel personalisation approach.

A loyalty program also requires support from many business functions including administration, marketing, finance, IT, customer care, analytics, legal and security.

Part 2 answers the *how* behind implementing and operating a successful loyalty program.

CHAPTER 11

LOYALTY TECHNOLOGY AND INNOVATION

This chapter was co-written by **Max Savransky** (ex-COO, Loyalty & Reward Co)

'Technology advancements enable consumers to interact with more brands and more channels than ever before. With more interactions, brands must manage the increasing opportunity for comparisons and higher expectations. The increasing emphasis to meet customer needs on digital channels is rapidly shifting their expectations and, therefore, businesses' priorities.'

- Michele Carlson

Focus areas

This chapter will address the following questions:

- What role does technology play in the execution of best-practice loyalty programs?

- What are the types of technology solution providers available?

- What capabilities does a world-class loyalty platform incorporate?

- What are some of the emerging and major trends driven by technology within the loyalty industry?

THE SELECTION, IMPLEMENTATION and use of loyalty technology continues to be a critical element in the delivery of best-practice loyalty programs. The industry has made great strides over the past few years, increasingly moving towards more modular and flexible technology solutions which can be integrated with other platforms to deliver the required capabilities.

The main trend for loyalty technology over the past decade has been a move to headless systems where companies are able to select best of breed components and combine them into a custom application built for specific business needs.

This chapter explores what an ideal loyalty technology stack looks like, and dives into technological innovations which are made possible by various technology platforms, including the ever-increasing use cases enabled by machine learning/AI platforms.

Loyalty technology platforms

Loyalty platforms have traditionally been expensive and inflexible, but more recently a range of high-quality, cost-effective platforms have entered the market, delivering companies the ability to better realise their innovative visions, while making the loyalty technology industry increasingly competitive.

These newer platforms have been designed for easy Application Programming Interface (API) integration with other systems and provide highly complex campaign capabilities, app and digital wallet support, automated machine learning capabilities, and extensive analytics functionality.

The purpose of the technology

A loyalty platform is ultimately a rules engine. Best-practice platforms can support complex rules supporting all manner of earn, redeem, expiry, progression, regression, referral and promotional campaign rules. The loyalty program operator can feed in available transaction data (such as the date and time, product Stock Keeping Unit (SKU), cost and retailer), personal data (such as a member identifier, demographic data and status tier) and offers, and the platform can apply a range of rules in real time to deliver a variety of specified outcomes designed to generate member engagement. This may be bonus points, cashback, new status tiers, product discounts, or many other rewards.

Types of loyalty technology solution providers

Loyalty platform solution providers can be categorised into four main groups:

- **Full-service loyalty solutions**: provided by specialised loyalty agencies which deliver everything required to run the loyalty program as part of an outsourced approach. Services include delivery of a loyalty program website and/or app with the client's branding, the back-end platform holding member accounts and points balances, status tier and profile data, customer service support, analytics processing, supply of reward products, account management, consulting services for the future evolution of the loyalty program, full lifecycle marketing management (including trigger emails at key points of the member journey) and customer care support. With this type of solution, the client rarely has direct access to the platform itself, as it is generally limited to agency personnel.

- **Partial service loyalty solutions**: focused more on the technology rather than a full-service offering, but with the option to provide additional support if required. This solution usually allows the clients to have direct access to their platform, with the platform enabling the running of the loyalty program, rather than the service provider actually running it. The agency (usually a smaller agency) may also provide some marketing strategy formulation and execution, reward support co-ordination and customer care support, as required.

- **Off-the-shelf loyalty solutions (SAAS)**: come with an extensive array of features and functions that will deliver to the technical needs of a client looking to launch a loyalty program or replace the legacy platform of their existing loyalty program. They are designed to be user-friendly, self-service and configurable to minimise the amount of additional client support required post-launch. This type of platform is suitable for program operators seeking maximum control over their operations.

- **Niche loyalty solutions**: may provide a partial solution which solves a specific problem. Niche agencies specialise and excel in their area of expertise, with the ability to solve an issue effectively and efficiently, however additional technical solutions will likely be required to run the complete loyalty program. An example is a company providing a solution to support the collection of member transaction data across multiple disparate point of sale (POS) systems or from third-party retailers.

Ideal loyalty technology stack

With loyalty being a lucrative and complex industry, significant investment has been made in developing technology.

A trend emerged several years ago where all-in-one platforms were developed. In additional to supporting a loyalty program, these platforms also provided marketing, CRM (customer relationship management), CDP (customer data platform), analytics and data warehouse capabilities. While an impressive vision, the platforms ultimately failed to gain meaningful market share due to the fact that none of the components were ultimately best-practice.

A more recent trend, and one which is likely to dominate for the next decade, is headless loyalty technology. These platforms integrate with separate best-practice CRM, CDP, marketing engine, data lake/warehouse and Business Intelligence (BI) tools. They will also API integrate into website, app, Point of Sale (POS), customer care module, and any other relevant front-end systems.

The benefits of this approach are numerous. The company gets to choose the best of everything, individual platforms can be integrated one-by-one to take the place of outdated legacy technology, and if a single platform requires replacement it can be done without impacting the other systems.

A champion of this approach is the MACH Alliance, a not-for-profit industry body that advocates for open and best-of-breed enterprise technology ecosystems. MACH stands for Microservices based, API-first, Cloud-native SaaS and Headless. The organisation exists as a vendor-neutral institution that provides resources, education and guidance through industry experts to support companies on their journey.

Other organisations also exist to promote this technology industry standard, with a range of loyalty platforms delivering exceptional platforms that can form a critical part of a modern stack.

Best-practice loyalty platform capabilities

Best-practice loyalty platforms contain a wide-range of sophisticated functions:

- **Loyalty rules, offer and promotional engine**: a configurable engine which can accept member identifier and transactional data, then apply complex rules to determine the benefits to be awarded. The types of rules and promotions supported may cover earn, burn, expiry, tiers, discounts, gamification, and referrals.

  Additional types of offers and promotions include discount based (e.g., $5 off or 10 per cent off), product based (e.g., double points on product x), time based (e.g., triple cashback during the first week of September), spend based (e.g., free gift with any purchase of over $100) and location based (e.g., 50 per cent off your first drink at a specific bar or pub).

- **Redemptions**: an additional set of configurable rules which support the redeeming of stored value. This may be via integration into the website and app, or via a white-label reward store (an eCommerce store for members to use their points (or any other loyalty currency) to redeem for a range of reward options).

  While a popular feature several years ago, many modern loyalty platforms are choosing not to include reward store capability as a feature. This is partly due to client requirements where the reward store will be built into an existing website or app, with the loyalty platform only needing to API/SDK in to support redemptions. It is also due to the rise of standalone reward store operators that can API into a loyalty platform if required.

For those platforms that do provide a reward store, it is typically designed in the same style as an eCommerce platform with a range of rewards, a shopping cart, and the ability to pay with points, cash or a combination (points plus pay).

- **Reporting and analytics:** a reporting engine with pre-built loyalty metrics and customisable dashboards which can be viewed within the platform or exported in multiple file formats.

  While many loyalty platforms provide this capability, larger companies tend to export the data into their own BI tool where it can be combined with other data to develop more comprehensive reporting and analytical insights.

  For currency-based programs, the loyalty platform can be used as a mini-ledger to manage reporting covering earn, burn and expiry of points, providing the finance team with the data they need to accurately manage deferred liabilities and support program audits.

- **User interfaces:** permissioned access portals for different users within the business. Typical users would include:

  - Administration, for the configuration of program and campaign rules.

  - Marketing, for the development of segments/cohorts for targeted promotions.

  - Customer Service, to facilitate member queries by reviewing account details to resolve issues and provide relevant support.

  - Operations, to add/remove reward products and adjust pricing, as well as manage reward fulfilment and delivery issues.

  Super-admin users will also be able to adjust permission levels for other users to maintain security access as required.

- **Multi market:** capability which supports global programs via a multi-language back-end and the ability to display and transact in multiple currencies.

Sometimes different instances of the loyalty platform will be set-up to manage the program across different geographies.

- **Segmentation**: the ability of the loyalty platform to group members using transactional data, like member recency, frequency and spend, along with any demographic data.

- **Security and fraud monitoring:** automated and manual monitoring to identify potential security breaches and instances of fraud. Ideally, the platform will automatically lock an account when suspicious activity is detected and trigger alerts to a dedicated team to quickly investigate.

- **Helpdesk and technical support:** vendor support to ensure the platform runs consistently and the client has access to required support to optimise use of the features and functions.

Integrations capabilities:

Best-practice platforms lead with an API-first approach to allow the ability to easily connect to any other platform within the stack:

- **Application programming interface (API's):** a set of programming code that enables data transmission between the loyalty platform and other systems. It also contains the terms of the data exchange.

- **Out of the box vendor integrations**: many loyalty platforms have existing integrations to other CRM, CDP, marketing engine, data lake/warehouse, BI tool and eCommerce platforms.

- **Software development kit (SDK)**: an installable package which can be integrated into a client app to provide a gateway to all platform capabilities. The same can also be achieved via an API.

Types of systems a loyalty platform may need to integrate with include:

- **CRM:** a platform used to manage interactions and relationships with members via centralised data storage. CRM platforms allow program operators to track, manage, automate, and synchronise member interactions. They can provide detailed insights into member behaviour and help anticipate member needs and desires.

- **CDP:** a platform that collects and organises data from various sources to create a unified member database. A CDP can consolidate and integrate member information from multiple sources, including websites, apps, email, social media, and more, to provide a single, comprehensive view of each individual member. A key feature of a CDP is that it is designed to be managed and used by marketers who want to understand and predict member behaviour, as well as personalise and optimise member experiences. It can handle structured and unstructured data.

- **Marketing engine:** a platform that helps companies orchestrate and optimise member engagement across various marketing channels. These platforms typically offer features for creating, managing, and measuring marketing campaigns, and they use member data to enable dynamic personalised, real-time interactions with members. They generally have capabilities in mobile engagement, email, in-app messages, and push notifications. They are increasingly incorporating machine learning/AI to analyse member data and predict future behaviour, enabling companies to deliver personalised and timely messages to their members.

- **Data lake/warehouse:** a data lake is a large, scalable storage repository that holds a vast amount of raw data in its native format until it is needed. Data lakes are designed to provide maximum flexibility and are capable of storing virtually any type of data, including structured data from relational databases (rows and columns), semi-structured data (CSV, logs, XML, JSON), unstructured data (emails, documents, PDFs), and binary data (images, audio, video). The key difference between data lakes and data warehouses is that a data lake stores data that is unstructured or semi-structured, and the schema is only defined when the data is ready to be used, while a data warehouse stores data in a structured and often processed form.

- **BI Tool:** a platform that helps companies analyse and interpret data to make informed decisions. BI tools gather, process, and present data in a way that is easy to understand, often through visualisations like charts, graphs, and dashboards. BI tools can handle large amounts of structured and sometimes unstructured data to identify, develop, and create new strategic business opportunities. They provide historical, current, and predictive views of business operations, using data gathered into a data lake/warehouse.

- **Customer care platform:** a platform that helps companies manage and enhance their interactions with members, with a primary focus on providing support and resolving issues. These platforms aim to streamline the process of handling member inquiries, complaints, or problems, and they provide tools to facilitate efficient and effective customer service. Key features include ticketing systems to track and manage member support requests, live chat or messaging capabilities, knowledge bases for self-service support, call centre integration, social media management, member feedback tools, and analytics to track and measure member satisfaction and agent performance.

- **Front-end systems:** platforms including websites, apps, Point of Sale systems and chatbots that members interact with directly or that support transactional interactions.

- **Social media monitors:** an automated monitoring tool which can be integrated with major social media networks to support campaigns and data collection.

- **Reward supply partners:** integration with established reward supply partners to support automatic fulfilment (e.g., gift cards, movie vouchers) or order submission and tracking (e.g., consumer goods). This may extend to third-party partners where members can redeem points in real-time when transacting online or in-store.

Technological innovation and emerging capabilities

Extensive innovation and the evolution of trends within the loyalty industry has led to the development of a wide range of complimentary technology solutions. These are used to enhance existing platforms or implement different types of engagement strategies altogether.

This section reviews loyalty trends and technology, with supportive examples of how they are being applied.

Utilising machine learning/AI within loyalty programs to deliver members more relevant experiences and communications is a major emerging trend.

Machine learning and AI

Machine learning involves creating algorithms that can recognise patterns in large, evolving data sets, and drawing conclusions from past experience by using that data.[404]

Artificial intelligence is the field of computer science that is associated with the concept of machines 'thinking like humans' to perform tasks such as learning, problem-solving, planning, reasoning and identifying patterns.[405]

Autonomous decisioning engines powered by machine learning/AI can process models such as affinity, propensity, churn risk, market and basket analysis, offer optimisation, Next Best Action and more. For marketing, the models can be designed to identify and send the right offer to the right member at the right time, then learn from the member's response to enable adjustment of approach for future campaigns. Very few loyalty platforms provide full AI, with most operating machine learning modules which require manual intervention to train and evolve. The launch of platforms provided by OpenAI, Google, Amazon and more will fast-track evolution for the loyalty industry at scale.

Since writing the first edition of this book, machine learning/AI applications

---

404 Burnett, S., 2018, 'Customer Loyalty Trend: Artificial Intelligence' Customer Insight Group, https://www.customerinsightgroup.com/loyaltyblog/loyalty-marketing/loyalty-trend-artificial-intelligence accessed 13 April 2023.
405 Ibid.

within loyalty programs have expanded rapidly, supported by advances in member personal data collection techniques, data science and computing.

These allow specialised data agencies working on behalf of loyalty programs to develop, analyse and monetise datasets, generate insights, create decision support tools and embed automated decision engines into loyalty platforms. These agencies employ teams of actuaries, statisticians, data scientists, product leaders, strategy consultants, software engineers, delivery managers, industry experts, designers, and futurists to capture, process and apply data on behalf of large loyalty programs seeking deeper member engagement, optimisation of marketing spend and a competitive edge. Some of the services provided include in-depth analysis of brand and product performance, advertising effectiveness analysis, identifying high-priority shoppers and profiling their behaviour, developing unique member profiles, and delivering individualised marketing communications to millions of members.

Ways in which machine learning/AI is being employed to power loyalty programs are numerous.

AI-powered marketing communications

While mass market offers (e.g., double points bonuses) can be highly effective in driving incremental visits and spend, they can also be costly and inefficient (e.g., the member may have already been intending to transact anyway, hence the additional promotional cost was unnecessary). An opportunity exists to optimise promotional activity to reduce overall program spend.

Machine learning/AI-powered marketing execution can automatically construct and send individualised communications to members across a variety of channels, then track responses and evolve future communications to optimise engagement potential. Their ability to serve up individualised communications to members across a variety of channels makes them highly effective, while helping to reduce marketing costs.

For example, marketing communications supplemented by AI can run thousands of automated A/B tests and multi-variate email message tests for multi-step campaigns, uncovering new customer segments and buyer personas.

The capability can also manage frequency of contact and optimise the send time for each contact, so the members receives the email at the right time.

AI platforms can tailor brand copy. The platform can be briefed as a copywriter, guided by previous communications, tone, brand guidelines and campaign focus.

AI-powered marketing execution is primarily the domain of larger loyalty programs due to the cost and the enormous amount of data required to optimise the algorithms, however this is set to change with the launch of publicly available AI platforms, making personalisation at scale much more achievable for a larger number of brands.

Jason Nathan, *dunnhumby*'s global managing director, directly referred to using member data to personalise communications and offers as a way for retailers to fight disruptive challengers like Aldi in the supermarket space. 'If you are up against somebody selling 2000 products at 10 per cent cheaper then clearly you have to do something different, and that something different is going to be able to stay in a personalised conversation with your customers.'[406] Personalisation of communications, offers and experiences Is detailed further in Chapter 15.

The Nordy Club

Since 2015, Nordstrom[407] have been making conscious decisions to invest in digital. They began their phased approach to using AI by focusing first on identifying potential customer cohorts which shop with Nordstrom's discount brand (Nordstrom Rack) who may be willing to pay for full price Nordstrom items.[408] Converting the right

406 Hatch, P., 2019, 'Winning your loyalty: Australia's retail data war is heating up', Sydney Morning Herald, https://www.smh.com.au/business/companies/winning-your-loyalty-australia-s-retail-data-war-is-heating-up-20181221-p50npy.html, accessed 14 April 2023.

407 Nordstrom, https://shop.nordstrom.com/, accessed 14 April 2023.

408 Townsend, T., 2018, 'How Nordstrom tapped into a century's worth of customer data', https://venturebeat.com/2018/08/21/

customers from their existing member base was a way of improving product margins and decreasing customer acquisition costs.

Early in 2018, Nordstrom invested in the BevyUp and MessageYes platforms to continue their momentum in the AI space by delivering style advice and personalised messages to members at strategic times, from which they can purchase items.[409]

Nordstrom now leverage AI technology across both online and brick-and-mortar stores with a focus on personal shopping, style advice and local order collection services, with AI integrated across fulfilment, distribution, customer experience and loyalty.

AI-powered personalised digital experiences

AI platforms are being applied to hyper-personalise member experiences and communications across websites and apps.

AI platforms can identify individual members when they are engaging with a range of digital channels, access their profile information (encompassing hundreds of datasets) and automatically trigger a relevant promotion to stimulate a desired behaviour from the member.

The platforms use cookies, member logins, app tracking software and other methods to track browsing and shopping behaviour. AI is then harnessed to determine the right offer to provide to the member at the right time to maximise the chances of generating a specific outcome, which in most cases will be the purchase of a featured product, an increase in overall spend, or the completion of check-out. The approach is designed to optimise advertising spend by ensuring budgets are invested in activities which have the maximum impact.

how-nordstrom-tapped-into-a-centurys-worth-of-customer-data/#:~:text=Nordstrom%20is%20looking%20to%20continue,had%20bought%20BevyUp%20and%20MessageYes., accessed 14 April 2023.

409 Ibid.

Spotify

Hundreds of millions of Spotify users receive new playlists tailored to their own tastes every single week, all generated by AI and machine learning. The brand uses a recommendation engine, a system which processes data to help subscribers find what they want and identify things they might be interested in based on preferences and previous behaviours.

Spotify's engine uses a combination of three models: collaborative filtering (analysing and comparing an individual's behaviour to other people's taste), natural language processing (analysing text from the lyrics and the internet for key terms that describe a song or artist), and audio modelling (processing the raw audio of a song and matching it with songs of similar likeness). By combining this information, the engine can recommend new songs with a strong certainty of user interest.[410]

Features like Discover Weekly and the Daily Mix lend to the popularity of Spotify, as they provide more personalised experiences and unexpected delights. These engage the member and encourage repeat usage of the platform, leading to the formation of habitual behaviour.

Affectiva

Affectiva use 'computer vision, speech analytics, deep learning and a lot of data'[411] to analyse human states in context. Having analysed close to ten million faces and expressions, their AI-powered algorithm can detect human emotions, cognitive states, behaviours, activities and objects people use in real time.

Large scale analysis of emotional responses can be valuable to a loyalty program in providing predictive analytics, purchase intent

---

410 Sen, I., 'How AI helps Spotify win in the music streaming world', https://outsideinsight.com/insights/how-ai-helps-spotify-win-in-the-music-streaming-world/, accessed 14 April 2023.

411 Affectiva, https://www.affectiva.com/, accessed 14 April 2023.

recognition or friction point detection for each member, with the ability to adapt and tailor the member experience in real time based on their emotions.

AI-powered in-store personalisation

Some retail stores have begun to experiment with AI in ways which have the potential to change the traditional retail experience for good. AI is being applied directly to the in-store experience, whereby members can receive real-time recommendations, virtual assistants, and test products without physically trying them on. This level of hyper-personalisation in-store enriches the member experience and aids purchase decision stimulation.

Retail stores can enable platforms that specialise in analysing sentiment, dwell time, visitor count and demographics via high-resolution videos that are installed in the required locations, usually throughout the store. These solutions do not specifically identify individuals, meaning there are no privacy considerations. However, they can identify males vs females and can track unique age groups, which might be 0-20, 20-40, 40-60, 60+, usually with around 95 per cent accuracy. This is certainly enough to be able to extract insights and use them for further enhancing the in-store experience.

Alibaba

Alibaba has built a 'FashionAI' store in Hong Kong[412]. AI is used in intelligent clothing tags which carries item specific info and will detect when it is touched or moved.

Smart mirrors work in conjunction with the clothing tags and use AI to suggest complementary items, help locate products and request other sizes/colours.

Data is captured throughout the entire process.

---

412 McIlvaine, H., 2018, Inside Retail, https://insideretail.com.au/news/alibaba-opens-ai-powered-fashion-boutique-201807, accessed 15 June 2023.

Kroger

Supermarket chain Kroger partnered with Microsoft to create a personalised shopping experience with smart shelves.[413]

With the Kroger app open on their phone, members can walk down the aisle and sensors will highlight products the member might be interested in buying based on account information and previous shopping history.

It also provides dynamic personalised pricing and will display relevant ads, making the shopping experience efficient and convenient.

7-Eleven

7-Eleven has introduced facial recognition technology to its 11,000 stores in Thailand.[414]

The technology is used to identify loyalty members, analyse in-store traffic, monitor stock levels, recommend products and measure emotions while in the store.

This type of approach is not always permitted. The Office of the Australian Information Commissioned (OAIC) found that when 7-Eleven conducted a trial on this in Australia in 2020/21, it breached Australian privacy laws.[415]

Subsequently, 7-Eleven was ordered to cease all activities and destroy every faceprint it collected.

---

413 Retail Insight, 2019, 'Kroger and Microsoft to launch new connected store concept', https://www.retail-insight-network.com/news/kroger-microsoft-connected-store/, accessed 14 April 2023.

414 Chan, T., 2018, '7-Eleven is bringing facial-recognition technology pioneered in China to its 11,000 stores in Thailand', Business Insider, https://www.businessinsider.com.au/7-eleven-facial-recognition-technology-introduced-in-thailand-2018-3?r=US&IR=T, accessed 14 April 2023.

415 OAIC, 2021, 'OAIC finds against 7-Eleven over facial recognition', https://www.oaic.gov.au/newsroom/oaic-finds-against-7-eleven-over-facial-recognition, access June 2023.

In-store personalisation can also be delivered via other technologies outside AI which also work to ensure the shopping experience for members is as hassle-free and convenient as possible. Members can choose to be identified, or self-identify, when they enter a store to be provided with a customised experience.

Additional non-AI technology utilised to identify members includes RFID, Wi-Fi tracking, beacons, facial recognition software and iPads.

Musti Group Finland

Musti Group Finland[416] have invented a world first member recognition program for pets. 'Biscuit' is a smart collar with an RFID chip that recognises the pet, rather than the owner, when they walk into a pet store.

This gives staff access to 'personal dog data' including their name and birthday, favourite treat, and shopping history. A picture of the dog flashes up on a screen when they enter the store as a personalised welcome.

The program works to build an emotional connection with pet owners through pet owners deep emotional connection with their pets.

AI-powered predictive modelling

As already established, AI is able to process incredibly large volumes of data. Once analysed, there is capability to help many companies understand the next steps that should be taken from a promotional standpoint. Use cases such as predicting trends related to the types of clothing that customers might want in the future across retail (greatly enhancing the member experience), or using transactional credit card data to predict and then recommend rewards that customers will like in financial services programs exist today and will only improve in sophistication in the future.

---

416 Musti Group, https://www.mustigroup.com/, accessed 14 April 2023.

H&M

H&M uses AI for predictive modelling of clothing trends[417].

This means analysing store receipts, returns in the store, and loyalty-card data.

In addition, the algorithms look at blog posts and search engines to gather more information about fashion trends. It is also used to calculate optimal pricing based on a variety of factors, such as cost of raw materials, currency fluctuations and unsold stock.

AI-powered virtual try-ons

Consumer brands are rolling out virtual try-on technology to allows members to try on clothes, shoes, cosmetics and more using the webcam on phones or laptops, or screens installed in stores.

The technology allows brands to load thousands (or even millions) of items into the platform for members to try. More advanced platforms can utilise member data to generate general recommendations, as well as suggesting items which complete their wider wardrobe.

Zeekit

Zeekit have developed the first dynamic virtual fitting room technology now adopted by large retail clothing brands including ASOS, Macy's, Modcloth, Net-a-Porter, Adidas and more.

Based on real-time image processing, Zeekit can map a member's image into thousands of segments with the equivalent points mapped against each piece of clothing to simulate how the garment and fabric will fit and fall.[418]

Members are provided with ultra-convenience, whilst retail brands are provided with a large amount of additional data and upsell/

---

417 Kotorchevikj, I.,2020, Towards Data Science, https://towardsdatascience.com/ai-driven-retail-how-h-m-group-does-it-c9606597f7bc, accessed 15 June 2023.

418 Zeekit, https://zeekit.me/, accessed 14 April 2023.

cross-sell opportunities. This became particularly relevant with the Covid-19 pandemic when physically trying clothing on in-store was not possible, allowing retailers to not only stay alive, but to thrive.

Yael Vizel, the co-founder of Zeekit, reported that 'shoppers who use the company's artificial intelligence to virtually try on clothing are five times more likely to purchase the item'. She also notes that member's 'are also more likely to keep what they buy with a reduction in return rates from 38 per cent to about 2 per cent'.[419]

Zeekit was acquired by Walmart in 2021, further boosting Walmart's capabilities in the digital try-on space.[420]

Conversational AI

Conversational AI refers to the use of messaging and speech-based virtual assistants to automate communications and create personalised customer experiences at scale. These technologies are fuelled by the rise of messaging apps, voice assistant platforms and general advancements in AI, including deep learning and natural language understanding.

The most rudimentary form of conversational machine learning/AI currently in use is chatbots. Chatbots are primarily language text interfaces designed for a specific purpose. They typically follow linear-driven interaction based on predefined rules and are therefore restricted by the bot's limited understanding of conversation and inability to learn. Many online retailers and airlines have recognised the benefits of chatbots particularly in terms of improved efficiencies for customer support. However, since the rules are handwritten, developers must anticipate all scenarios of human interaction, and this presents some obvious problems.

True conversational AI is the next step where machines will be capable

---

419 Bhattarai, A., 2020, 'Virtual try-ons are replacing fitting rooms during the pandemic', https://www.washingtonpost.com/business/2020/07/09/virtual-try-ons-are-replacing-fitting-rooms-during-pandemic/, accessed 14 April 2023.

420 Sara Perez, 2021, 'Walmart acquires virtual clothing try-on startup Zeekit' https://techcrunch.com/2021/05/13/walmart-acquires-virtual-clothing-try-on-startup-zeekit/ accessed 12 June 2023.

of understanding and responding to human language and behaviour in real-time, learn from these experiences, and then apply these learnings to future conversations. These intelligent assistants will not be limited by the functions anticipated by a programmer. This technology will present new ways for brands to appear more lifelike, respond contextually and personally at scale, and shift the brand-customer dynamic from many-to-one to one-to-one.

In practice, there are AI platforms that greatly assist sales teams, especially those that have hundreds or thousands of inbound leads. The quality leads are identified and given to the sales team; the others are handled by the AI, until such time that the criteria for what constitutes a quality lead has been achieved.

KLM's BlueBot

KLM Royal Dutch Airlines implemented an AI-powered assistant, named BlueBot or BB, as a sustainable solution which supports the scale of its servicing team.[421]

Available across all existing conversational platforms and virtual assistants, BB automates simple member queries like finding a destination, booking a flight, and providing holiday preparation tips.

BB helps make the member journey as stress-free as possible and frees up time for human assistants to focus efforts where required.

Nestle's NINA

Nestlé India has built NINA (Nestlé India Nutrition Assistant), an AI-powered nutrition assistant.[422]

Available via an online platform name AskNestlé, parents can track

421 Future Travel Experience, 2017, https://www.futuretravelexperience.com/2017/09/klm-new-ai-powered-bluebot-enables-flight-booking-via-messenger/, accessed 30 May 2023.

422 Deoras, S., 2019, Nestlé India Introduces NINA, A Virtual Nutrition Assistant In Association With Senseforth', Analytics India, https://analyticsindiamag.com/nestle-india-introduces-nina-a-virtual-nutrition-assistant-in-association-with-senseforth/, accessed 14 April 2023.

how their children are growing in relation to a paediatric database, get answers to daily nutrition questions and tips, and receive custom meal plans based on regional preferences and allergies.

The system is designed to help parents and their children with real-time, personalised advice on nutrition which is relevant and accessible.

Rose, the Hotel Chatbot

The Cosmopolitan of Las Vegas is a luxury casino and resort which encourages hotel guests to interact with their virtual assistant during their stay.

The hotel chatbot, known as Rose, is designed with a unique voice with over 1,000 conversation threads to offer guests ways to book experiences such as restaurant reservations, spa treatments, events tickets, and other exciting adventures.

Rose can provide recommendations based on what the guest desires and provide insider information like secret menu items to drive guests to specific bars, clubs, and restaurants. For example, a guest can ask 'What should I have to drink?' and Rose may make a special drink recommendation which is not on the menu, both assisting and delighting the guest.[423]

AI-powered security and fraud monitoring

In addition to enhancing the member experience, machine learning/AI are being applied to protect programs and their members from security breaches and fraud. The advantage of an algorithm-based monitoring approach is speed, volume of account reviews, and the ability to learn and adapt to changing circumstances.

---

423 Brecker, J., Behance, https://www.behance.net/gallery/108722507/The-Cosmopolitan-of-Las-Vegas-Rose-the-Hotel-Chatbot, accessed 30 May 2023.

GetPlus Loyalty

GetPlus, a leading coalition loyalty program in Indonesia, utilise a fraud-management system powered by AI. With GetPlus OCR within the membership mobile app, members can scan their receipts from participating merchants to earn GetPlus reward points at their convenience.

According to Adrian Hoon (COO of Global Point Indonesia), the leading operator of the GetPlus program in Indonesia),[424] the AI system includes configurable, action-based scoring rules to evaluate the risk of loyalty fraud in real time. If a high-risk earn order is identified, it is suspended to be reviewed by human operators, or is automatically cancelled.

The fraud-detection capability also provides reports to be actively monitored, and orders can be analysed by risk status. It can also make modifications to scoring algorithms as patterns of fraud change.

Machine learning/AI limitations and challenges

While the potential of machine learning/AI is significant, there are also some limitations and other challenges which need to be considered:

- **Data**: there is a direct relationship between the richness of data and the capability of a machine learning/AI application, meaning large volumes of clean data is critical. If the loyalty program systems are unable to provide this, the quality of the output will be compromised.[425]

---

424 Hoon, A., 'How AI can drive customer loyalty programs', The Jakarta Post, Feb 2020, https://www.thejakartapost.com/life/2020/02/20/how-ai-can-drive-customer-loyalty-programs.html accessed 14 April 2023.

425 Roetzer, P., '6 Limitations of Marketing Artificial Intelligence, According to Experts', Marketing Artificial Intelligence Institute, June 2017, https://www.marketingaiinstitute.com/blog/limitations-of-marketing-artificial-intelligence accessed 14 April 2023.

- **Marketing stack**: the primary limitation of applying machine learning/AI to a marketing function lies in system constraints. These primarily come from the inputs into the model, the algorithms available to the model and/or the actions the model is capable of driving. Disparate, disconnected marketing systems can present a major obstacle. With no connection between data points, the machine learning/AI algorithms are only able to assess some behaviour in aggregate versus individual use cases. Delays in gathering data (e.g., batch process) will also limit the ability to act in real time or near real time.[426]

- **Responsiveness to rapid changes**: machine-learning/AI execution is not always operationally smooth and can be sensitive to changes in human behaviour. For instance, at the start of the Covid-19 pandemic, the top selling products on Amazon switched from phone cases, phone chargers and Lego to toilet paper, hand sanitiser and face masks. According to a MIT Technical Review article, this caused issues for the AI algorithms powering marketing, inventory management, and more. 'Machine-learning models are designed to respond to changes. But most are also fragile; they perform badly when input data differs too much from the data they were trained on.'

  Loyalty & Reward Co received reports from a number of loyalty programs operators which utilise AI for marketing who faced similar challenges at the start of the Covid-19 pandemic. Some stated they needed to turn their AI systems off for a period as the systems could not cope with the rapid change in member transaction behaviour, which had led them to generate illogical marketing campaign activity.

- **Ethical considerations**: some AI systems (particularly 'deep learning' platforms) work to solve problems and complete tasks, but data scientists are not really sure how they work. According to some commentators, AI systems that are unexplainable should not be

---

426   Ibid.

acceptable. They argue that explainable AI needs to be part of the equation to ensure the AI system can be trusted. [427]

Deep learning relies heavily on training data, thus biased training data can lead to biased AI systems. Testing and monitoring are essential to identify and address any biases in the system.

- **Climate considerations:** The process to build an AI model – a program or algorithm trained to recognise patterns or features in data to make systems such as Apple's Siri or Amazon's Alexa, or to augment human decision-making, or to teach a self-driving car to identify objects in its path – consumes enormous amounts of energy. Data centre networks carrying the large-scale computation required for AI model-making and cloud computing platforms such as the massive Amazon Web Services are among the world's largest consumers of electricity. Naturally, the more AI is used within loyalty program applications, the higher the total consumption will be.

- **Risk to humanity:** AI could eventually pose an existential threat to humanity. This includes the possibility of an AI system becoming super-intelligent, surpassing human intelligence in all practical aspects. If such an AI's goals are not perfectly aligned with human values, it could take actions detrimental to humanity to achieve its goals.

The convergence of loyalty and payments

A major industry trend is the convergence of loyalty programs and payments. This enables more ways for members to earn and redeem, plus makes the transactional process more seamless, helping to improve adoption.

Card-linking and bank-account linking

Two ways that loyalty and payments have converged is via card-linking and bank account-linking.

---

427 Walch, K., 'Ethical Concerns of AI,' Forbes, Dec 2019, https://www.forbes.com/sites/cognitiveworld/2020/12/29/ethical-concerns-of-ai/#573ac23823a8 accessed 26 April 2023.

Card-linked platforms have direct relationships with the major card payment providers (such as Visa, MasterCard and Amex) and allow retailers to set-up offers which can be linked to a consumer's credit or debit card. When a consumer spends in-store or online with a participating merchant using their credit or debit card, the offer (predominately cashback or points earn) is automatically triggered and applied without them having to also scan their membership card.

Bank account-linking platforms access authorised feeds of transactions from member accounts. This approach is more comprehensive than credit card linking because it provides all of the transaction data from an account, not just the transactions made with participating retailers. Thus, a member can access offers even if they do not pay with a specific credit card, while the program operator accesses significantly more member transaction data.

Some companies provide the option for participating merchants to access a portal to configure their own offers. The offers are sent to customers, who can click to activate them. This ties the offer to their card or bank account, ready to be unlocked when they transact with the merchant.

Bits of Stock

Bits of Stock[428] is a brand loyalty and investment app which allows members to receive a cashback reward in the form of fractional shares of stock.

Members can shop with participating brands and earn a cashback amount. They can then select which companies to invest the cashback in and receive a small amount of shares in the company they choose.

This vested interest may also increase the propensity for the member to contribute to the brand through repeat purchases, potentially because they might feel a stronger bond with the brand in which they own a stake.

---

428 Bits of Stock, https://www.bitsofstock.com/, accessed 12 June 2023.

Affiliate marketing platforms

As detailed in Chapter 8, advertisers can reward publishers (or 'affiliates') with a set amount of commission for each customer that they refer to their online store (and increasingly, physical stores). This may be for a visit, but more commonly it is for a transaction.

Affiliate marketing platforms have evolved to act as middlemen to track transactions and attribute the correct affiliate to the sale. They track member progress using cookies or APIs and organise the transfer of the affiliate marketing revenue from the third-party retailer to the loyalty program.

Partnerize

Partnerize[429] work with over 300 of the world's leading brands to track online sales and pay commissions to affiliate marketers. The company has developed their Partner Management Platform (PMP), a SaaS-based solution which streamlines the process of managing affiliate partnerships.

Brand partnerships are complex and fragmented across different networks and channel partners (e.g., loyalty programs, cashback programs, bloggers, influencers, resellers, and brand alliances).

The traditional model of building affiliate partnerships would require a loyalty program operator to establish and manage ongoing relationships with brands on an individual basis, which is costly and onerous.

Partnerize solves this issue by acting as the intermediary, allowing a loyalty program operator to create, build and manage brand relationships, affiliate revenue, and integrate partnership insights via a single platform.

---

429 Partnerize, https://partnerize.com/, accessed 26 April 2023.

Payment apps

Loyalty programs can introduce payments and digital wallet capabilities via app solutions which allow members to pay and earn or redeem in a single transaction.

Some apps allows members to use their loyalty account as an all-in-one wallet, which can support any established currency such as fiat currency, loyalty currencies and even a range of cryptocurrencies.

The member can connect a bank account or a credit card to facilitate instant payments. The payments capability lets the member pay via their smartphone app after selecting the funding source.

Australian Venue Co

Loyalty & Reward Co client Australian Venue Co (AVC) own 200+ bars and pubs across Australia and NZ.

In 2022, they launched The Pass, a loyalty and payments app. Members download the app, then they are invited to register and store a credit or debit card.

When they visit a venue, members can sit at a table and scan a QR code. This opens The Pass app and allows them to order and pay for food and drinks, which are delivered directly to their table.

Every dollar spent earns points, which can be redeemed for digital vouchers to be spent on future orders.

Members can also buy, send and redeem gift cards.

To give back to the community, Australian Venue Co allow members to nominate their local sports team which receives a percentage of what they spend as a rebate.

Australian Venue Co won three trophies for The Pass at the 2023 Loyalty & Engagement Awards; Best Loyalty Strategy - Food & Beverage, Best Use of Mobile, and Best Loyalty Strategy – Consumer.

Some loyalty apps allow members to redeem their points anywhere as a form of payment using new technology.

CoinBridge by Nayax

CoinBridge[430] is a patented solution that converges payments and loyalty by converting digital assets such as points, vouchers, rewards, gift cards, and miles into real purchase transactions over the credit card schemes.

This innovative approach allows users to pay for goods and services at any shop or website worldwide via the loyalty program's app.

CoinBridge offers seamless implementation into any existing loyalty program mobile app through its mobile SDK (Software Development Kit).

This easy-to-integrate solution enables transactions via a Tap and Go experience (NFC/EMV) at any shop worldwide. The SDK is opaque to the end-user and does not affect the look and feel of the mobile app.

The back-end connector can link any loyalty platform with CoinBridge systems, allowing CoinBridge to verify each transaction against the customer's balance and the retailer's spending policies.

Upon completion of each purchase, CoinBridge forwards transaction data to the loyalty platform, providing a valuable data set retailers can use to better understand their member's spend behaviour across different retailers and industries – outside their outlets.

CoinBridge facilitates NFC/EMV transactions through its Mastercard issuer license, and by issuing a virtual pre-paid card, which is tokenised into the CoinBridge SDK, for the seamless use of each customer at the point of sale.

---

430 Nayax, 2022, https://www.nayax.com/resource/nayax-launches-a-unique-solution-for-the-conversion-of-any-virtual-asset-into-real-cash-transactions-and-purchases-across-the-world/, accessed 15 June 2023.

Currency exchange

A member of a loyalty program may earn points, miles or another currency in one program, but desire to redeem them in another program. For example, a member may earn points from a credit card program but wish to redeem them with a travel or retail program.

A member may also simply wish to consolidate all their existing loyalty currencies into a single account.

Currency exchanges (also known as points exchanges, miles exchanges and loyalty marketplaces) provide platforms and API integrations to support currency transfers.

Members can access their loyalty account or a separate online portal, choose how many points or miles they wish to transfer and the transaction will be processed at a set exchange rate.

The currency exchange platform will manage settlement by collecting the value of the points in a denominated fiat currency from the transferring program to the receiver, enabling them to cover the deferred liability.

Typically, the currency exchange platform will collect a flat and or percentage fee for the transaction.

Currency Alliance

To facilitate points and miles exchanges, Currency Alliance provide a platform solution that connects brands, merchants, retailers and small-to-medium businesses.

Members of any programs which are connected via the exchange can transfer their points or miles to another program at a set conversion rate.

Currency Alliance provides connectivity but does not behave as an intermediary. This means loyalty programs are provided with control and transparency over all collaborations, agreements and loyalty operations.

Payment terminal software

New software solutions allow companies to run basic loyalty programs directly from payment terminals.

A new generation of smart terminals running Android software have enabled the ability for loyalty companies to develop a range of different program designs including stamp cards, cashback and even games with the primary identifier being a secure derivative of the customer's payment card.

When a customer makes a payment with a retailer using a specific card for the first time, the card is recognised as new. The terminal displays a screen inviting the member to join the program. Subsequent payments advance the customer towards a reward.

When a reward is unlocked, the terminal displays an option for the member to redeem and apply against their current transaction.

A back-end user interface enables the retailer to configure different program types, add branding and view engagement reporting.

Payment Loyalty

UK-based software company Payment Loyalty has developed a patented solution that embeds loyalty into the existing payment process.

They have removed the need for loyalty cards, requests for customer data, mobile app downloads or point of sale integration, making it easy for individual or chain retail businesses to quickly launch a loyalty program with custom design, branding and campaign mechanics.

Retailers can configure their own program design via a wizard in the user portal. Loyalty program design options include stamp cards (e.g., spend £10 five times to earn a £5 reward) or simple competitions (e.g., pick a card to win a percentage or £value discount on your next transaction).

To engage with the program, customers simply need to pay as

normal (via card / mobile / wearable etc), then use the same payment method for future transactions.

Removal of friction for customers has enabled Payment Loyalty to deliver high engagement rates, with opt-in levels averaging 70-90 percent across client programs.

Stock keeping unit (SKU) capture platforms

New hardware solutions allow loyalty program operators to capture SKU data (i.e., a line-by-line summary of what items the member has purchased). Traditionally, this capability has been available primarily to supermarket programs and other retail programs which capture all the transaction data of individual members. Coalition loyalty programs, such as frequent flyer programs and bank programs, do not normally have access to this data as the supermarkets and retailers do not share it with them.

SKU data allows the loyalty program to not only understand where a member is spending and how much they are spending, but also what they are spending on. They can use this information to build a more comprehensive profile of the member, as well as promote offers tied to the products they like, to stimulate increased visits and spend. The loyalty program can also provide data services to third-party suppliers who are interested to understand the profile of their customers.

PiCo

Hardware and software provider, PiCo,[431] has created a black-box solution which plugs into any Point of Sale (POS) system to capture the SKU data.

The data is sent to the cloud, where it can be fed into the loyalty program's platform for processing.

The solution can also input personalised member discounts directly into the POS, and support earn and redemption activity, all without any direct POS integration.

---

431 PiCo, http://picolabs.co/, accessed 26 April 2023.

Digital receipt software

With a move towards more sustainable retail practices, many companies are introducing the option for digital receipts to replace paper.

This provides an opportunity for loyalty program integration. With the member providing their mobile phone number, the options exists to also provide them with discount vouchers and other benefits when the digital receipt is delivered (assuming relevant capture of privacy and marketing permissions).

The communications may also include a link which they can click to register for the company's loyalty program.

Weezmo

Weezmo is digital receipt software that integrates with over 300 POS systems.[432] In addition to providing digital receipts, it uses a unique member identifier (such as mobile phone number) to connect multiple attribution points (social channels, eCommerce store, physical stores, and digital receipts) to provide retailers with full visibility into customer journeys.

It also turns these touchpoints into engagement opportunities by providing the ability to present exclusive offers to the member and invitations to register for loyalty programs.

In addition, Weezmo can support online-to-offline conversion by enabling retailers to accurately measure the impact of their digital ads on in-store revenue.

Receipt scanning apps

Receipt scanning capabilities allow a member of a loyalty program to take a photo of the entire receipt via their smartphone once a transaction has been made. In the back end, the information is broken down and translated into a digital record, all of which is stored against a member profile, thus providing insightful product purchase information. The loyalty program not only verifies

---

432 Weezmo, https://weezmo.com/, accessed 12 June 2023.

that the member purchased their product, but also captures details of all the products the member bought in the same transaction.

Loyalty programs can use this to personalise communications and offers to a product level, rather than just a transaction level. The member can be provided with rewards for their entire spend, or for buying specific products.

---

myWorld

myWorld members are invited to scan their shopping receipts using the program app to earn myWorld benefits.[433]

Members open the app, select the participating partner, scan the receipt and submit.

Members earn cashback and shopping points for every purchase at a local myWorld Partner.

Loyalty card apps

A range of apps allow consumers to store all their loyalty cards digitally, removing the need to carry plastic versions in their wallet. This allows quick access to any membership card that the member requires when transacting with a loyalty program.

Some apps have API connections to certain loyalty programs, allowing them to access their points balances within the same app.

As they hold the membership card for millions of members of different loyalty programs, the app companies may provide marketing services to the loyalty programs by sending offers directly through the app to members.

Stocard

Stocard allows users to store all their reward cards in one app on their smartphone and collect points and rewards without having to carry around plastic loyalty cards. Their 50m users across 11

---

433 myWorld, https://www.myworld.com/gb/scanandgo accessed 12 June 2023.

countries access the app on average every eight days, with over 500m plastic cards digitised. Users can add their loyalty cards into Stocard by scanning the barcode or entering the member number manually.

Users can also access discount offers from participating partners, who pay advertising fees to Stocard to promote their brands to users.

Stocard was purchased by Klarna in 2021.

Third-party aggregators

With member benefits programs increasing in prevalence and popularity (where loyalty programs provide third-party offers to their members such as discount movie tickets, gift cards, accommodation, experiences and more), an industry has developed to provide support. Third-party aggregators have evolved to provide both a white-label transaction platform and the relationships with the third-party partners, such as gift card providers, cinemas, travel companies and experience companies.

This can save a program operator years of work as the establishment of many relationships can be time-consuming and expensive. Aggregators typically charge a per member annual fee or a flat rate annual fee for a certain number of members.

The Ambassador Card

The Ambassador Card[434] is a large, third-party aggregator providing a white-label platform that includes over 3,500 offers in one solution. The Ambassador Card network gives brands an effortless way to provide their loyal customers and member base with instant discounts and exclusive offers on a wide range of goods and services from restaurants, hotels and cinemas to tourist attractions, accommodation, and health and wellbeing resources.

---

434 The Ambassador Card, https://www.ambassadorcard.com.au/, accessed 26 April 2023.

As a white-label solution, The Ambassador Card provides a high degree of scalability and customisation, which allows loyalty program operators to tailor offers and communications to their audience and objectives.

New offers, partnerships and platform features are continuously developed by The Ambassador Card, which evolves the platform and thus extends the overall value given to loyalty program operators and their members.

Digital games platforms

Games act as entertainment in themselves and can provide a pathway towards a reward as part of a loyalty program. They are fun, experiential, rewarding, and reinforcing.

Games are typically delivered by self-service SaaS platforms that allow creation of interactive content, competitions, gamified experiences and rich media with no coding required.

These platforms can be connected to a loyalty platform in the same way that other platforms can, enriching and stimulating the overall member experience. The platforms enable program operators to create interactive content to embed within an app or website.

There are many different types of games that can be delivered by gaming platforms. The more robust platforms will have well known games that would ordinarily be available via the App Store or Google Play and may include Pacman, Bubble Shooter, Soccer (penalty shoot outs), Memory Cards, Connect Four, Crosswords and more. These games are white labelled and support the application of loyalty program branding.

Program operators seeking to incorporate games into their loyalty program can take one of three approaches:

- **Self Service:** the operator can create games on their own via a user-friendly interface.

- **Hybrid:** the games platform provider can assist the operator on their journey, starting from the creation process to the final set up of the game.

- **Full Service:** the operator submits a brief to the games platform provider, who does the complete design and build.

Next best action platforms

By creating rich member profiles, loyalty programs provide a foundation for the installation of a Next Best Action (NBA) platform. These are primarily used in call centres and prompt the call centre agent or sales agent to recommend a specific product to the member at the end of the call.

For example, a member may call their bank to address an issue with their account, and at the end of the call the NBA system will prompt the call centre agent to recommend that the member consider applying for a credit card which enables them to earn loyalty points. The recommendation provided by the NBA platform is based on all the data held against the member's profile, including their propensity for loyalty program engagement, their credit card usage history and current cards, their credit score, their preferred loyalty points (bank or airline) and many other datasets.

According to Deloitte,[435] 'NBA is focused on using sophisticated rules, analytics and algorithms to better predict customer needs and in turn, present more relevant actions and offers leading to improved wallet share and loyalty'. The NBA approach enables companies to shift from a product-centric view to a customer-centric focus with product offerings tailored to the individual.

---

435 White, D., 2017, 'Customer loyalty: A relationship, not just a scheme', The Deloitte Consumer Review, https://www2.deloitte.com/tw/en/pages/consumer-business/articles/gx-consumer-review.html, accessed 12 June 2023.

Financial Times

The Financial Times (FT) adopted an NBA model[436] to make communication with members more efficient by using the model to prioritise and potentially limit product promotions based on each reader's needs.

Their research team investigated correlations between reader engagement and specific member actions with FT products (e.g., Newsletters, Gift links, FT App, MyFT Feedpage), identifying reader habits that are more frequent with engaged users. These member actions and habits were given values based on the expected impact and probability of engagement to ultimately determine a reader personalised Next Best Action.

The implemented model increased reader engagement by suggesting actions that an individual was more likely to take based on existing habits and engagement.

Geolocation tracking

Geolocation systems capture user location data (once permission has been enabled) and then use that data to enable targeted marketing communications based on a range of criteria. Tracking the location of a member adds a valuable layer of data to the member's profile which helps to provide a better understanding into their lifestyle, habits, interests and motivations.

Tracking a member's location can be done through several channels, with apps and Wi-Fi being the most prevalent channels. This can be done in several ways:

- **Geofencing**: the program operator can set a virtual boundary around a location, together with a specific offer, so that if a member comes within the boundary, the offer is triggered. For example, an offer could be strategically triggered when a member is within 500m of a

---

436 Kastrinakis, G., 'How we calculate the Next Best Action for FT readers', https://medium.com/ft-product-technology/how-we-calculate-the-next-best-action-for-ft-readers-30e059d94aba, accessed 26 April 2023.

retail location to entice them to visit, or near a competitor's location to entice them to switch.

- **Geotargeting**: the program operator can segment members based on the location data stored within their profile and target them with a specific offer aimed at driving a desired behaviour. Geotargeting does not need to be based on the real-time location of a member, it can also be based on historical location. For example, the retailer may wish to target members who usually travel within a 1km radius of a store between 12 noon-2pm with a lunch offer.

- **Wi-Fi tracking**: Wi-Fi platforms can be used to capture personal details, send targeted and real-time offers and promotions to an individual when they are at a specific location (via geolocation tracking), and track the movement of members and non-members around stores. A retailer's existing Wi-Fi network could be effectively leveraged to drive incremental sales by tracking a member's connection time and sending a curated offer to stimulate an additional purchase if they have been in-store for a specified period of time.

- **Beacons**: working in a comparable way to Wi-Fi tracking platforms, beacons allow for more localised engagement. A beacon is essentially a small Bluetooth radio transmitter. A Bluetooth-equipped device like a smartphone can 'see' a beacon once it is in range. The key capability of this type of platform is to send coupons and offers to consumers via an app. The beacon sends out its ID number about ten times every second (sometimes more, sometimes less, depending on its settings). A nearby Bluetooth-enabled device picks up that signal. When a dedicated app recognises it, it links it to an action or piece of content stored in the cloud and displays it to the consumer. Platforms can 'teach' the app how to react to a beacon signal.

Westfield Group

Major shopping centre group Westfield[437] uses free Wi-Fi to run a customer engagement program. It captures a range of member data which they use for marketing purposes, and to find out which webpages are the most popular and where different shopper segments spend most of their time. Customers can access competitions, news, events and offers for mall retailers and get directions to any store.

Westfield also use the customer data gathered to pinpoint the types of customers within their shopping centres at any point in time. They then adjust the advertisements displayed on their digital billboards within the mall to appeal to those customers to stimulate increased buying behaviour.

For example, advertisements targeted towards mothers with young children are shown during the middle of the day.

Blockchain

Blockchain and Web3 loyalty is a dynamic area of loyalty program evolution that is worthy of its own chapter.

The following chapter explores the different ways in which blockchain technology is being used by loyalty programs to drive deeper member engagement.

*

As can be seen, the technology innovation in the multi-billion dollar loyalty industry is extensive and provides loyalty program operators with a wide range of options to deliver any manner of program designs and member engagement approaches.

---

437 Westfield Group, https://www.westfield.com/, accessed 26 April 2023.

Key insights

- Loyalty technology plays an increasingly critical role in the execution of best-practice programs, both by providing the core capabilities required to run the program, and by providing technological innovations to support emerging and major loyalty trends.

- Types of loyalty solution providers can range from full-service providers, partial service providers, off-the-shelf solutions or niche solutions, each with their own benefits and challenges.

- A loyalty platform is ultimately a rules engine. Best-practice platforms can support complex rules underpinning all manner of campaigns, earn/burn promotions and member movements between tiers. Platform capabilities are typically comprised of six overarching areas; integrations, product functionality, marketing execution, financial management, security and data protection, and account management and support.

- Extensive innovation and the evolution of trends within the loyalty industry has led to the development of a wide range of complimentary technology solutions. These are used to enhance existing platforms or implement different types of engagement strategies.

- Emerging and major trends within the loyalty industry include machine learning and AI, in-store personalisation, subscription memberships, card and bank account linking, digital wallets and payments, receipt scanning, third-party aggregators, next best action platforms, geolocation tracking, SKU capture platforms, digital receipts software, affiliate marketing and blockchain.

Suggested reading

- Heaven, W. D., 'Our weird behavior during the pandemic is messing with AI models', MIT Technology Review, May 2020, https://www.technologyreview.com/2020/05/11/1001563/

covid-pandemic-broken-ai-machine-learning-amazon-retail-fraud-humans-in-the-loop/

- Hoon, A., 'How AI can drive customer loyalty programs', The Jakarta Post, Feb 2020, https://www.thejakartapost.com/life/2020/02/20/how-ai-can-drive-customer-loyalty-programs.html

- White, D.,2017, 'Customer loyalty: A relationship, not just a scheme', The Deloitte Consumer Review, https://www2.deloitte.com/tw/en/pages/consumer-business/articles/gx-consumer-review.html

CHAPTER 12

BLOCKCHAIN AND WEB3 LOYALTY

This chapter was co-written by **Scott Harrison** (Senior Strategy Consultant, Loyalty & Reward Co)

> *'A purely peer-to-peer version of electronic cash would allow online payments to be sent directly from one party to another without going through a financial institution'*
>
> *- Satoshi Nakamoto, Bitcoin:*
> *A Peer-to-Peer Electronic Cash System*

Focus areas

This chapter will address the following questions:

- What is blockchain and Web3?
- How was blockchain first adopted by loyalty programs?
- What are all the ways the loyalty industry is utilising blockchain and Web3 to drive member engagement?
- What should brands and loyalty program operators consider as part of a Web3 strategy?

THE LOYALTY INDUSTRY has a track record of adopting new technology early to support innovative member engagement initiatives. Blockchain, a technology that was invented in 2008, is enabling new opportunities to help companies enhance engagement and improve customer loyalty.

Blockchain loyalty programs first emerged in 2017 with the use of cryptocurrencies as an alternative to points or miles. Despite market volatility and many business failures, companies have continued to experiment with the use of blockchain within loyalty programs.

This chapter explores blockchain and Web3 within the loyalty industry, delving into the novel ways loyalty operators use it to incentivise and engage members with fungible token rewards, non-fungible tokens (NFTs), Decentralised Autonomous Organisations (DAOs), and new virtual experiences in the Metaverse.

As a new technology, blockchain has enabled an additional and dynamic loyalty program feature set.

Defining Blockchain and Web3

Discussion of blockchain, cryptocurrencies and Web3 are often clouded by misunderstanding and interchangeably used buzzwords. The following definitions are designed to provide a basic framework of understanding:

- **Blockchain** is a digitally distributed ledger - a database hosted by a network of computers - that offers an unchangeable and transparent way to store information. Blockchain is the foundational technology for cryptocurrency and Web3.

- **Cryptocurrency** is a form of digital currency that does not rely on a single or central authority, such as a central bank or government. These currencies underpin a new financial system of exchanging value. Bitcoin and Ethereum are the most well-known cryptocurrencies, but there are thousands in existence.

- **Tokenisation** is a broader term that encompasses the creation of digital tokens on a blockchain that represent underlying assets and liabilities, including their characteristics, status, activity history and ownership. Tokens enable efficient trade, transfer and ownership of value. Examples include utility tokens, security tokens, stablecoins, non-fungible tokens (NFTs), and governance tokens.

- **Web3** refers to the third generation of the World Wide Web and is based on concepts of ownership, decentralisation and peer-to-peer networks, facilitated via blockchain technology. Web3 is the philosophy underpinning a new financial movement, commonly associated with ideas around transparency, interoperability and permissionless activity. Cryptocurrencies, DAOs and tokenised assets such as NFTs are all Web3 associated technologies.

In summary, blockchain is the underlying technology, cryptocurrency and tokens are the means of value exchange and incentivisation, and Web3 is the guiding vision and mindset.

Blockchain 101

Blockchain is a decentralised and digitally distributed ledger that records transactions and stores data in a secure and transparent manner. It enables peer-to-peer transactions without any intermediaries, provides immutable and tamper-proof records and allows for trustless and automated processes through smart contracts.

Here's a simple example of how a blockchain transaction works:

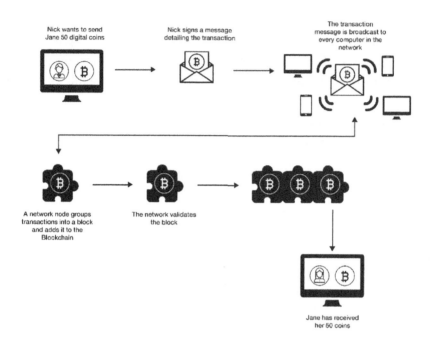

Figure 16: how a blockchain transaction works

A blockchain is a continuously growing list of records, called 'blocks', which are cryptographically secured and linked into a 'chain'. Blockchains are inherently resistant to modification of the data. This is because the data in all the blocks must match in order for a record to be valid and the blocks are held by millions of computers around the world. Blocks are a ledger which are not controlled by a central entity, hence the term decentralised ledger technology (DLT). Notably, while all blockchains are distributed ledgers, not all distributed ledgers are blockchains.

The security and integrity of a blockchain are maintained through a consensus mechanism, which determines how new blocks are added to the chain and how the network agrees on the state of the ledger. The example provided primarily represents the Proof of Work (PoW) consensus mechanism. In this mechanism, the 'millions of computers around the world' are run by miners who use special software to solve complex mathematical problems. By successfully solving these problems, miners earn rewards in the form of cryptocurrency bonuses. This creates an incentive for more people to participate in the mining process, increasing the network size and expanding the decentralisation and security of the blockchain platform.

It is important to note that while the example focuses on PoW, there are other consensus mechanisms employed by different blockchain platforms. This includes Proof of Stake (PoS), Delegated Proof of Stake (DPoS), Practical Byzantine Fault Tolerance (PBFT) and more. Each consensus mechanism has its own characteristics, advantages, and considerations regarding security, scalability and energy efficiency.

Because a healthy operating blockchain is so secure, it allows for the creation of a trustworthy digital currency, or cryptocurrency, without the need for a centralised authority (such as a bank or loyalty program) to maintain a ledger.

Prior to blockchain, a decentralised digital currency could not be trusted because there was no way for the holder to ascertain whether it had already been spent or not. Blockchain solves this problem because a transaction creates a decentralised, immutable record stored on the blockchain for everyone to see, making it easy to verify who the actual owner of the cryptocurrency is.

The first blockchain was launched in 2009, supported by a paper titled Bitcoin: A Peer-to-Peer Electronic Cash System by Satoshi Nakamoto[438]. Nakamoto has since been discovered to be a pseudonym and debate has raged ever since about who they are. For the essential history of Bitcoin, a useful book is Digital Gold by Nathaniel Popper[439].

Since the launch of the Bitcoin blockchain, a large number of blockchain platforms have been developed with different capabilities including Ethereum, Solana and Litecoin, each offering unique features and functionalities beyond the original concept of a digital currency.

---

438 Nakamoto, S., 2008, 'Bitcoin: A peer-to-peer electronic cash system', https://bitcoin.org/bitcoin.pdf, accessed 4 April 2023.

439 Popper, N., 2015, 'Digital gold: Bitcoin and the inside story of the misfits and millionaires trying to reinvent money', New York, NY, HarperCollins Publishers.

Essentially, blockchain is about *trust*. In addition to being algorithmically protected, the only way a record on a block can be altered is if all records on that block stored in all the computers in the network are altered simultaneously. If the record held by one computer differs to that held by the rest of the computers, it will be rejected. Blockchain is digital democracy in action.

For a large blockchain system containing millions of computers, hacking a block, altering the data on it and having the data accepted by the network is deemed impossible, particularly when the data on each block is protected by heavy cryptographic algorithms. This all makes for an incredibly secure and trustworthy system.

This level of trust allows companies to do things which they could not do in the past, providing fascinating opportunities for loyalty program operators. Many of these innovations have been since grouped under the term 'Web3'.

Web3 101

Web3 refers to the third generation of the World Wide Web and is based on concepts of ownership, decentralisation and peer-to-peer networks, facilitated via blockchain technology (including decentralised applications (dApps), cryptocurrencies and NFTs).

Fundamentally, Web3 is the vision of a more open, transparent and equitable internet that empowers individuals and communities to control their data, identity and assets.

One concern of many people about the current World Wide Web is that it is controlled by large technology companies such as Google and Microsoft. The promise of Web3 is that it decentralises that control and returns the internet to individuals to manage.

'Web 3.0' was first coined by Ethereum co-founder Gavin Wood in 2014. He envisioned 'a peer-to-peer web that lets you do everything you can now, except there would be no servers and authorities to manage the flow of information.'[440] As with many things in the blockchain space, the idea has evolved since then and new use cases continue to evolve.

To understand the context in which Web3 exists, it is important to understand how it is different from its predecessors. The early days of the internet were primarily a 'read-only' web experience, where users could view static web pages but had limited ability to interact or contribute. This era, known as Web1, was characterised by the development of the physical infrastructure that allowed computers to communicate with each other.

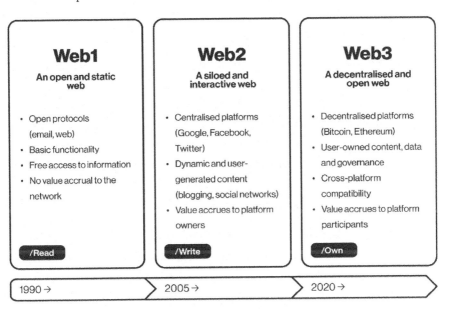

Figure 17: The evolution of the Internet

The emergence of Web2 in the early 2000s saw a shift towards user-generated content and increased interactivity, as social media platforms like Facebook and Twitter became more prominent. This 'read and write' web also saw the rise of centralised technology giants collecting and monetising user data through targeted advertising. While Web2 has facilitated the creation of

---

440 Wood, G., 2023, 'Why we need Web 3.0', Medium, https://gavofyork.medium.com/why-we-need-web-3-0-5da4f2bf95ab, accessed 6 April 2023.

new avenues for people to generate revenue, it has also led to an immense centralisation of online activity, and thus concentration of data and power.

Web3 aims to address the problems and challenges of Web2 by decentralising power and ownership. In this vision, users have greater control over their data and identities, and can directly participate in decision-making on the networks they use – in other words, users can 'read, write and own'. This is made possible through technologies like blockchain and decentralised databases, which facilitate greater transparency and immutability. Additionally, Web3 envisions a future where users are not just consumers, but also owners, with a stake in the networks they participate in.

An important distinction must be made; Web3 is not a replacement of the existing web, but rather an expansion of possibilities. The advent of social networks and new online interaction methods brought about a fundamental shift in how we socialise, obtain information and conduct business, thereby reshaping our lives in profound ways. Despite this, the essential functionality of websites and email remain the backbone of our digital landscape. This duality reminds us that as users embrace advancements, it is also important to appreciate and leverage enduring principles.

Taking this perspective into the world of loyalty programs, Web3 brings decentralisation, transparency and empowerment to the member experience. Rather than perceiving it as a threat or complete replacement for traditional loyalty models, the philosophy and accompanying technology offers supplementary approaches to enhance online interactions, the exchange of value, and the overall customer-brand relationship.

A short history of Web3 loyalty

As early as 2017, new loyalty programs emerged which rewarded members with cryptocurrencies (or crypto tokens). Members of these crypto loyalty programs were able to earn these cryptocurrencies by spending with participating merchants or engaging in gamified activities in the same way as earning points (or miles, tickets, stamps, coupons or trademarks). The key difference was that the cryptocurrencies were listed on trading exchanges, meaning speculators could buy and sell them similar to shares. This meant the value of the loyalty cryptocurrency could increase or decrease in value dependent on demand and supply, an innovation that had not been seen in loyalty programs before.

In order to raise funds to build the technology and launch the loyalty program, companies engaged in Initial Coin Offerings (ICOs). These involved creating a fixed amount of cryptocurrency, with a proportion sold to speculative investors seeking high-risk returns. Between 2017-18, a small number of companies raised US$10-12m each in successful ICO's to fund their new loyalty programs.

Around that time, Loyalty & Reward Co (in conjunction with Pico Labs and University of NSW) conducted academic research to ascertain whether cryptocurrencies could act as a viable alternative to points and miles in driving member engagement. The study involved creating a new loyalty program, Unify Rewards, which rewarded students on the university campus with Ether (the cryptocurrency of the Ethereum network) for transacting with participating merchants.[441]

The research results were encouraging for cryptocurrency loyalty programs. Participants reported that Unify Rewards was more motivating in influencing them to spend their money with participating merchants than their favourite loyalty program (7.80 vs 5.98/10). 86 per cent indicated Unify Rewards was more appealing than their favourite loyalty program. 59 per cent spent more money on campus during the trial period as a result of the loyalty program.

Despite this early enthusiasm from investors and research subjects, within a few years, all the cryptocurrency loyalty companies had failed. Where did it go wrong?

Several factors contributed to the failures.

Firstly, speculative cryptocurrency trading from 2017 to early 2018 was substantial, with billions of dollars pouring into the industry over an extended bull market driving record prices. This helped these crypto loyalty companies

---

441 Unify Rewards, 2018, 'A cryptocurrency loyalty research project', https://cdn2. hubspot.net/hubfs/2918918/Unify%20Rewards%20-%20A%20cryptocurrency%20 loyalty%20research%20project.pdf?t=1526445721137, accessed 4 April 2023.

raise their ICO funds and launch their programs. Once launched, early investors and program members watched their cryptocurrencies increase in value. The euphoria was short-lived however, with a protracted bear market starting in 2018 wiping out gains. Many loyalty cryptocurrencies dropped in value by as much as 99 per cent. With value a primary driver of loyalty programs, the majority of members saw no benefit in continuing their engagement. In addition, some of the loyalty program operators lost their main capital holding, making it challenging for them to fund the running of the program.

Secondly, the cryptocurrency program operators generally failed to achieve scale. Creating a coalition loyalty program is challenging. Today's dominant loyalty programs did not start with a loyalty program. They started with a massive base of engaged consumers and layered the loyalty program over their existing operations. Examples include frequent flyer programs, supermarket programs, hotel programs and more. The crypto loyalty program operators found that simultaneously acquiring a mass scale of members and participating merchants takes an enormous amount of time and money. While a US$10-12m raise may sound like a lot, it is a tiny fraction of what major loyalty programs invest in growing their businesses.

Finally, in 2018, sentiment turned sour on cryptocurrencies in general. Governments raised regulatory concerns, scams were rife, and the industry developed a reputation for supporting drug dealing and money laundering. This raised concerns in the minds of the generally public about the risks of personal exposure which reduced the appeal of crypto loyalty programs.

EZTOKEN

Vietnamese-based EZTOKEN raised US$10m in an ICO in late 2017-early 2018.[442] They decided to launch their program in Australia, starting in Brisbane. The launch of the program in June 2018 included a competition where members stood the chance to win a Lamborghini.

The team were successful in building a network of smaller retail

---

442 EZToken Rewards, 2018, https://www.eztoken.io/, accessed 6 May 2023.

merchants in the central business district which enabled members to earn EZT cryptocurrency. Members could also redeem EZT with the same merchants.

Initial member engagement was solid, and EZTOKEN started planning expansions to Sydney and Melbourne. The subsequent crypto bear market halted the expansion, with EZT value plummeting 99 per cent. Eventually, the cryptocurrency was delisted from exchanges and the loyalty program closed down.

Despite these setbacks, the Web3 loyalty industry has continued to evolve as technical innovations have given rise to new use cases. Market capitalisation, developer activity, and funding activity have all increased steadily over the last decade.[443] The popularisation of NFTs and DAOs in the 2020-22 bull market introduced new possibilities for loyalty program operators, including tokenisation of membership and increased community-based engagement through governance. These developments have the potential to transform traditional loyalty program models into more decentralised and participant-driven ecosystems.

What is most clear from the short history of Web3 loyalty, and the broader blockchain industry, is that each market cycle has been characterised by four core stages: product innovation, increased interest, increased volatility and market reset. Each new cycle has led to further innovation and more sophisticated use cases, and therefore greater exploration by both innovative and traditional brands.

Web3 loyalty today

This section will cover five key areas where Web3 loyalty can be used within loyalty programs; blockchain, cryptocurrencies, non-fungible tokens (NFTs), Decentralised Autonomous Organisations (DAOs) and the Metaverse.

---

443 Andreessen Horowitz, 2023, 'State of Crypto Report 2023', https://a16zcrypto. com/posts/article/state-of-crypto-report-2023/, accessed 15 May 2023.

Blockchain

A blockchain platform can be integrated with loyalty and retail partner platforms to facilitate secure, real-time, auto-reconciled transactions powered by smart contracts. Operating on the principle of 'if-then' logic, smart contracts are programs stored on a blockchain that runs when predetermined conditions are met without the need for intermediaries.

Blockchain can provide advantages over traditional technical approaches in specific instances, such as for major loyalty programs with multiple partners or brands looking to establish a new partner ecosystem.

Coalition programs can include cumbersome processes to settle earn and redemption processes. The legacy technology of some parts of the aviation industry dates back to the 1960s. Blockchain can be used to settle transactions almost instantly using smart contracts, with clean, auditable records. This on-chain approach to loyalty points issuance can be highly useful for these partner-heavy programs that need to track, settle and reconcile several cross-party transactions.

Notably, an enterprise-sized company may not want all loyalty program data on-chain for privacy and scalability reasons. In this case, a major loyalty program such as an airline or supermarket could utilise a hybrid approach where sensitive member data is kept off-chain in a secure database, while the smart contact on the blockchain handles settlement and validation of loyalty program transactions and reward distribution among partners. It is possible to also implement on a private blockchain instead, whereby the blockchain network and its data is restricted to a specific group of participants. This maintains the smart contract benefits of transparency, immutability and automation without compromising privacy, albeit in a more centralised network.

Singapore Airlines and KrisFlyer

Back in 2018, Singapore Airlines commenced the development of KrisPay - a digital blockchain wallet that allows KrisFlyer members to convert their miles and partner reward points into a digital currency for everyday spending in Singapore.[444]

Members can use their KrisPay miles to pay for items at the airline's partner merchants, including gas stations, retailers, and food and beverage outlets.

For Singapore airlines, the benefits include reducing inventory by giving members new ways to spend their miles, a decentralised network improving system resiliency, and removing third-party involvement in processing transactions.

Singapore Airlines has continued to enhance and expand the blockchain-based loyalty project, including the revamp of KrisPay to the new Kris+ wallet app.[445] It operates on a private Ethereum blockchain involving Singapore Airlines and its partners and merchants, developed in-house in partnership with KPMG.[446]

Cryptocurrencies

As detailed earlier, companies in specific niches are continuing to explore different avenues to leverage the potential of cryptocurrencies to incentivise user engagement and foster loyalty.

Many cryptocurrency exchange and trading platforms offer their own native currency as a way to incentivise user engagement. For example, Binance, one of the largest cryptocurrency exchanges, uses its native token Binance Coin

---

444 Wong, J., 2020, 'Singapore Airlines rolls out Kris+ as its new KrisPay lifestyle app', Mainly Miles, https://mainlymiles.com/2020/10/10/singapore-airlines-rolls-out-kris-as-its-new-krispay-lifestyle-app/, accessed 6 June 2023.

445 Singapore Airlines, 2023, 'Kris+', https://www.singaporeair.com/en_UK/us/ppsclub-krisflyer/use-miles/krisplus, accessed 6 June 2023.

446 Computer Weekly, 2023, 'CW Innovation Awards: SIA taps blockchain for loyalty app' Retrieved from https://www.computerweekly.com/news/252497795/CW-Innovation-Awards-SIA-taps-blockchain-for-loyalty-app, accessed 6 June 2023.

(BNB) to reward members for trading, referrals and other behaviours.[447] By using BNB, users are incentivised to trade and engage more actively on the single exchange.

A number of companies use major cryptocurrencies including Bitcoin and Ethereum as alternatives to traditional cashback rewards. For example, US-based Lolli rewards members for shopping at over 10,000 retailers with Bitcoin.[448] App-based CryptoSpend allows users to buy, send and spend cryptocurrency and also earn cashback in the form of Ripple (XRP).[449] Members of a loyalty program might prefer cryptocurrency givebacks because of its potential value appreciation and multi-purpose use, and companies may prefer them to attract and retain a specific audience, differentiate, and reduce the financial cost associated with traditional cashback.

Web3-based companies, which operate on decentralised principles, often have their own native cryptocurrencies that play a crucial role within their ecosystems. Companies such as Brave and Travala.com both utilise their respective cryptocurrency for various purposes, including using services, participating in governance, and incentivising desired behaviours. Being rewarded with a company's native cryptocurrency can foster a sense of ownership and participation, helping to build sunk costs that deepen their commitment to the brand.

Some companies offer 'staking' or 'lock-up' as an option to earn cryptocurrency rewards. This essentially involves locking a specific amount and type of cryptocurrency in a wallet to support the operations and security of a blockchain network or platform. In return for staking, users and members earn rewards in the form of additional currency (akin to an interest payment), discounts and/or access to exclusive features. For cryptocurrency-enabled loyalty programs, integrating a lock-up mechanism can lead to better market liquidity, which allows for token price stability. Lock-up mechanisms can also serve as an incentive for token holders to become active participants or perform specific actions. For example, a company may offer additional token or governance rewards for member to lock up tokens for a certain period or participate in

447 Binance, https://www.binance.com/, accessed 7 June 2023.
448 Lolli, https://www.lolli.com/, accessed 7 June 2023.
449 CryptoSpend, https://www.cryptospend.com.au/, accessed 7 June 2023.

specific activities. This encourages engagement and alignment with company objectives and desired behaviours, increasing token utility beyond simple ownership. This can lead to several benefits for both parties, including greater sunk cost commitment, positive network effects, and long-term value appreciation.

Brave

Brave Software, Inc. has developed the Brave browser, a free and open-source web browser. Its main focus is on user privacy.[450]

Most importantly, built into the Brave browser is the option for users to join Brave Rewards, a feature that enables members to earn Basic Attention Tokens (BAT), their native cryptocurrency token, for viewing advertisements in Brave.[451]

Users can personalise the types of ads they see, such as those displayed on the new tab page or through push notifications.

BAT can be used for exchanging with multiple currencies, buying gift cards, transferring to Web3 wallets, buying NFTs, and making in-app purchases. Moreover, Brave Rewards lets users support content creators by manually sending BAT contributions to their preferred sites and creators or having Brave do it automatically for them, reinforcing the value of the token.

Non-fungible Tokens

A Non-fungible Token (NFT) is a term used to describe a unique digital asset where ownership is tracked on a blockchain. Broadly speaking, non-fungible simply means that it is unique and cannot be replicated. On the flip side, something fungible is non-unique and interchangeable (e.g., you can swap $1 for another $1 in your given currency). NFTs enable scarcity, verified ownership and tradability in the digital world, elements which were not possible until the invention of blockchain.

---

450 Brave, https://brave.com/, accessed 15 May 2023.

451 Brave, 2023, 'Brave Rewards', https://brave.com/brave-rewards/, accessed 15 May 2023.

As mentioned in Chapter 7, Web3 approaches have given rise to a new reward class, 'owned' (e.g., NFT) versus 'unowned' (e.g., points) rewards. Ownership of digital assets can foster a sense of psychological ownership that can make members feel more invested in a brand, which potentially unlocks a new form of network effect through community engagement and social cohesion.[452]

There are three key features of NFTs which are important to understand:

- An NFT acts as a certificate of ownership which uniquely represents any piece of media or asset, making it possible to trade an asset

- The value of an NFT is not necessarily the media or asset itself but the proof of ownership

- NFTs can contain smart contracts, making it possible to attach additional utility to expand their purpose

NFTs are the most popular way in which brands are experimenting with Web3, arguably because of their broad application. The initial peak of NFT-mania between 2021 and early 2022 saw a lot of brands like AMC, Burger King, Clinique, Louis Vuitton and Marriott attempt to capitalise on the hype by launching campaigns whereby their members could claim or win limited-edition NFTs.[453] However, these activities were primarily focused on scarce, tradeable collectibles, rather than a deep connection to their respective loyalty program value proposition. Since this time, the loyalty industry has increasingly seen brands exploring NFTs with more advanced applications - specifically focused on expanding the value offered by pairing issued tokens with utility. An example of a utility based NFT is one that provides the holder with access to exclusive experiences, offers, or other specified benefits.

The level of consumer awareness of NFTs is on par with the number of

452 Esber, J. & Kominers, S.D., 2022, 'Why build in Web3?', Harvard Business Review, https://hbr.org/2022/05/why-build-in-web3, accessed 1 June 2023.

453 Harrison, S., 2022, 'NFTs: The next evolution of rewards and loyalty programs', Loyalty Reward Co, http://loyaltyrewardco.com/nfts-the-next-evolution-of-rewards-and-loyalty-programs/, accessed 17 May 2023.

brands that are experimenting with them. Research shows that consumer awareness of NFTs and digital collectibles is high, with 84 per cent of surveyed consumers knowing what they are.[454] However, there is still relatively limited adoption. Notably, 38 per cent of consumers consider NFTs and digital collectibles to have an impact on their loyalty decision. This percentage varies across age groups, from 60 per cent of the 25-34 age group to only 5 per cent in the 65 or over group, suggesting such tools are best suited for brands seeking to appeal to younger and more digitally native audiences.

Some of the world's most iconic brands are now exploring Web3, primarily via NFTs, including Nike, Starbucks and Reddit. A growing trend which each of these brands have followed is abstracting the technology away from the member to reduce the confusion of Web3 jargon and make the onboarding process more seamless.[455] This approach has proved significantly beneficial to adoption.

A second major trend is the rise of NFTs as a 'membership' pass. Whether free or paid, brands are experimenting with these membership tokens. For example, Latvian airline, airBaltic, has an Ethereum based NFT collection known as 'Planies', whereby ownership gives holders access to a number of benefits connected to the airlines' loyalty program.[456] Asian Street food giant, Wao Bao, launched NFTs dubbed 'CollectaBaos' to complement their existing points-based program.[457] Ownership of these NFTs unlocks access to an exclusive club with benefits such as invites to special events, cooking classes and personal meet-and-greets with the CEO.

Importantly, brands which have issued NFTs with utility and access to rewards which are complimentary to the brand (one of Loyalty & Reward Co's Essential Eight™ detailed in Chapter 4) have been the ones which have thrived.

---

454 Loyalty Science Lab at Old Dominion University, 2023, 'The Future of Loyalty Report', accessed 18 July 2023.

455 Ducoff, N., 2023, 'Blockchain, crypto, and Web3 abstraction', Blockworks, https://blockworks.co/news/blockchain-crypto-web3-abstraction, accessed 1 June 2023.

456 PlaniesNFT, https://planiesnft.com/, accessed 14 May 2023.

457 Wow Bao, https://www.wowbao.com/hot-buns-club/, accessed 30 May 2023.

It is likely that the industry will continue to see loyalty operators use NFTs across four areas:

- **Collectibles:** digital assets that are tradable and collectible, creating value for customers.

- **Membership tokens:** used as proof of membership and to grant customers access to exclusive rewards or experiences.

- **Memory tokens:** digital mementos that commemorate experiences or achievements.

- **Equity tokens:** provide voting rights or governance powers to members, allowing them to have a say in the direction of the loyalty program or wider company strategy.

AO Artball

The AO ArtBall Project is an NFT based membership created by the Australian Open (AO), a major tennis tournament held annually in Melbourne, Australia.[458]

The project allows fans to purchase digital artworks that grant them access to exclusive benefits, such as the chance to win tickets to future AO matches, Web3 educational resources, member in-person events, and collaborator benefits.

Each ball represented a 19cm square plot of tennis court randomly assigned when the NFT was minted. Every time a winning shot landed in that plot during a match at the 2022 Australian Open, the relevant NFT was updated in real time with match and ball tracking data.

Penfolds were a collaborator on six ArtBalls whereby holders received two premium wines, several wine tasting experiences and other loyalty benefits in addition to the existing ArtBall benefits.

---

458 Australian Open, 2023, 'AO ArtBall 2023', https://ao-2023.artball.io/, accessed 17 May 2023.

Nike .SWOOSH

.SWOOSH is a Web3 platform designed for Nike's fans, creators, and athletes to trade and create digital assets (NFTs) that can be worn in games, provide access to real-life events, and even unlock access to physical products.[459]

Each NFT represents something different, whether it is a piece of art, a music album, a tweet, or even a virtual real estate property. Unlike cryptocurrencies, which are interchangeable with one another and have equal value, NFTs are one-of-a-kind and have their own distinct value.

In April 2023, Nike's .SWOOSH platform released its debut NFT collection named 'Our Force 1 (OF1),' consisting of Polygon NFTs that celebrate the 40th anniversary of the iconic Air Force 1 sneakers.

Users are able to join the .SWOOSH program to collect and trade assets, with community members earning the opportunity to co-create and earn royalties on sales.

The platform will feature a Learning Centre for education on Web3 and asset creation in the future.

Nike's distribution and cultural influence has given .SWOOSH the potential to introduce millions of users to Web3, and Nike's focus on education and community-building reflects its commitment to creating a more engaging customer experience through the use of NFTs.

By implementing NFTs into their operations, SWOOSH offers Nike new revenue streams and the opportunity to create new forms of community-driven engagement with its customers.

More recently, Nike partnered with video game developer EA SPORTS to bring .SWOOSH virtual creations to the EA SPORTS gaming ecosystem, showcasing the benefits of open and transparent blockchains.[460]

---

459 Nike, https://www.swoosh.nike/, accessed 17 May 2023.
460 Nike, 2023, 'Nike Virtual Studios and EA Sports Partner to Bring .SWOOSH

Starbucks Odyssey

Starbucks Odyssey is a loyalty program that uses NFTs (called Journey Stamps) to reward members for completing a specific series of actions (i.e., Journeys).[461]

Starbucks offer a variety of Journeys to choose from. Some Journeys focus on educating members about the Starbucks brand, while others are more transactionally focused and encourage members to explore the product range. For example, the 'Doing Good' Journey requires a member to visit a Starbucks, bring your own cup three times, explore the non-dairy drinks range twice and complete a short lesson about the company's sustainability efforts.

On successful completion of each Journey, the member receives an NFT-based Journey Stamp. Each stamp unlocks a separate set of benefits, including access to exclusive experiences such as virtual coffee tastings or invites to special events. Members also earn points for each Journey activity they complete, and each Stamp they obtain. Points accumulate and can be redeemed for a variety of rewards during specific redemption windows set by Starbucks.

Whilst Odyssey's core framework fundamentally follows an advanced gamification model (as detailed in Chapter 9), the innovative element of the program is that the NFTs are integrated with the open crypto market, enabling members to freely trade on any marketplace for real money. This introduces real-world economic incentivisation into the traditional loyalty approach. Community members are now encouraged to work together and align their interests to promote Odyssey. The more people that are actively involved and promoting the program, the greater the demand (and potential value).

Virtual Creations to Future EA Sports Titles', https://about.nike.com/en/newsroom/releases/nike-virtual-studios-dot-swoosh-ea-sports-partnership, accessed 6 June 2023.

461 Starbucks, https://odyssey.starbucks.com/, accessed 15 July 2023.

Decentralised Autonomous Organisations

A Decentralised Autonomous Organisations (DAO) is a member-owned community without centralised leadership. DAOs have become very popular during the past few years, covering everything from investment management, acquisition of artwork and collectibles, awarding of grant funding, and facilitation of charity donations.

DAOs work differently to most hierarchically structured companies, with a democratic focus powered by voting rights, no central owner, and full transparency for participants. DAOs utilise blockchain technology to safely manage voting rights and transparency. DAOs generally include a digital wallet which holds group funds. The funds can only be unlocked via multiple signatures (or multi-sig) to ensure appropriate security.

The loyalty programs of the future will likely incorporate DAO-like elements to provide members with the ability to vote on specific initiatives and give members a say in how the program is run. Smart contracts will be used to automatically implement the winning decision.

Travala

Founded in 2017, Travala.com is the world's leading blockchain-based travel booking platform with over 2.2 million properties in 230 countries and territories.[462] The platform is a Booking.com-like travel site that also incorporates blockchain technology and tokenised incentives, with its native cryptocurrency (AVA) being used for payments, rewards, refunds, and as a store of value.

The platform accepts a variety of other cryptocurrencies including Bitcoin, Ethereum and Cardano, as well as traditional payment options. Interestingly, the company publicly publishes key financial and member activity metrics every month – approximately 78 per cent of all bookings are paid with cryptocurrencies, illustrating their primary audience.[463]

---

462 Travala.com, https://www.travala.com/, accessed 5 May 2023.
463 Travala.com, 2023, 'Travala.com Monthly Report: April 2023', https://www.

Travala's loyalty program entitles members to several benefits, including member pricing on travel products and giveback rewards of up to 2 per cent for each booking in the form of AVA.[464]

Travala members can also opt-in to the 'Smart Program' by locking a specific amount of AVA tokens in their account to access one of seven tier levels, scaling up with increasing benefits. Uniquely, members choose their Smart tier and lock up the required amount of AVA tokens to access the corresponding benefits. These benefits include cheaper booking rates, higher giveback rewards, payment discounts when booking with AVA and access to Travala Governance.[465]

This decentralised governance system allows Smart members to vote on proposals that affect the future of the company, with past proposals ranging from new product features, marketing campaigns and even fundamental changes in AVA's ecosystem mechanics.[466] The goal of community voting is to give users a say in the future of the company and its ecosystem. By voting on proposals, members can help to ensure that Travala.com remains aligned with their interests. The benefits of such an approach are threefold; firstly, members can see their votes and how they are impacting the company, secondly, members are more likely to support decisions that they have had a say in, and finally, members who are interested in the future of the company are more likely to keep their tokens staked and reinforce ecosystem stability.

For example, a member can lock up as low as 50 AVA (~$27.53 USD) to unlock Basic tier and up to 2,500 AVA (~$1,428 USD) to become

travala.com/blog/travala-com-monthly-report-april-2023/, accessed 10 May 2023.

464 Travala.com, 2023, 'Travala Members', https://www.travala.com/members, accessed 5 May 2023.

465 Travala.com, 2023, 'Smart Program', https://www.travala.com/smart, accessed 5 May 2023.

466 Travala.com, 2023, 'Governance Proposals – Community Voting', https://www. travala.com/governance/proposals

Platinum (the second highest tier), unlocking benefits such as a 5 per cent booking discount and 5 per cent giveback rewards.

The highest and most premium tier, Smart Diamond, is exclusively available to members who also hold a specific NFT in their wallet – the Travala.com Travel Tiger NFT - currently valued at 3.28 ETH (~$5,957 USD) at the time of writing.

Travala.com's resilience and longevity through multiple market fluctuations make it a compelling case study for an innovative approach, showcasing the potential for sustained growth and adaptation in the evolving digital landscape.

Immutable X

The IMX Rewards program is a prime illustration that showcases the power of governance and incentivisation in driving growth within an ecosystem.[467]

IMX Rewards was designed to kick-start network effects within the Immutable ecosystem (a network partnership, recognised as the leading platform for launching Web3 games and trading digital assets) ultimately benefiting the community and token holders. Its primary objective was to drive growth by generating more trading volume, leading to increased staking rewards and heightened productivity of the IMX token.

While the organisation is not a DAO, it uses DAO elements to run governance and voting.

The program was initially introduced as a 6-week campaign to stimulate trade growth and reward existing users. The true pivotal milestone was the introduction of community governance voting, allowing IMX token holders to determine how rewards were distributed. This democratic process, akin to frequent flyer miles holders deciding on status criteria, garnered 76 per cent in favour, and resulted in

---

467 Immutable X, https://www.immutable.com/, accessed 20 May 2023.

a remarkable 47 per cent increase in reward efficiency.[468] Ultimately, this enhancement benefited all IMX holders by cultivating a more sustainable and thriving ecosystem for the long term.

The program has been very successful since its launch in June 2022. Total active buyers on Immutable X have increased by over 300 per cent since the program was launched. The program has also been successful in driving engagement, with users trading more NFTs than ever before.

The success of IMX Rewards is due to its emphasis on community governance, giving users a strong say in how the program is run, thus building trust and loyalty. Its ongoing evolution and exploration of new opportunities paves the way for future programs and brands to capitalise on governance and incentivisation, fostering sustainable and thriving ecosystems in the process.

Virtual 'Metaverse' Experiences

Metaverse is used to describe a 3D iteration of the internet. The term envisions a combination of virtual reality and in real life (IRL) online interactions accessed through a browser or virtual reality (VR) headset, which allows people to have experiences in real-time. These could range from gaming, shopping or attending virtual events.

Compared with NFTs and digital collectibles, awareness about the metaverse Is slightly lower with 80% of consumers reporting familiarity with the concept. However, younger consumers (57% under the age of 44) consider the availability of metaverse brand Interactions Impactful to their loyalty decisions.[469]

Loyalty programs are starting to explore the Metaverse as a channel to engage with consumers and enhance their online virtual experiences, particularly younger audiences.

468 Immutable X, 2023, 'IMX Rewards: Web3 Disrupting Loyalty Programs', https://www.immutable.com/blog/imx-rewards-web3-disrupting-loyalty-programs, accessed 20 May 2023.

469 Loyalty Science Lab at Old Dominion University, 2023, 'The Future of Loyalty Report', accessed 18 July 2023.

Metaverse spaces that have been created to take advantage of this trend have tended to fail in generating mass scale engagement, often due to a substandard experience and low member interest. For example, shopping in Decentraland today is arguably worse than shopping on Amazon, while music concerts in Decentraland are arguably worse than they are on Zoom.

A better example of a Metaverse that is thriving is video game universe Roblox. According to gamer Erik the skeleton, 'The (Roblox) Metaverse is a virtual world that is like our real world but there are endless possibilities. You can fly a spaceship, fight with a light saber and go back in time. You can kill zombies or be a zombie. You can rob banks, arrest criminals and adopt pets. You can play classic games, prop hunts and obi's (obstacle courses). And you can make friends, play with friends and talk with friends.'[470]

Like any universe, the Metaverse requires currencies and verifiable ownership to support the buying and selling of goods and services. This provides an opportunity for loyalty programs.

Adidas Originals Into the Metaverse

Adidas has made a successful entry into the world of NFT web3 culture with their 'Into the Metaverse' collaborative project.[471]

The project emphasises the web3 concept of 'with the community, for the community' and offers holders of the 'Into the Metaverse NFT' both physical and digital benefits. With the creation of this NFT collection, Adidas has opened up new revenue streams and created a new form of community-driven engagement with its customers.

The project has been highly successful, with Adidas making over $22 million in revenue during the initial release, where 30,000 ITM NFTs were minted and sold out almost immediately upon launch.

---

470 Shelper, P., 2022, https://loyaltyrewardco.com/the-metaverse-is-coming-according-to-kids-its-already-here/, accessed 4 April 2023.

471 Adidas, https://www.adidas.com.au/metaverse, accessed 30 May 2023.

Since the release of the 'Into the Metaverse' NFT collection, Adidas has launched three phases of the project.

During Phase 1, the Adidas Originals collection was launched, and various community projects were initiated, such as the Prada resource art project and the Hot Seats with Bad Bunny. Additionally, Adidas partnered with WAGMI United and became the official kit supplier for Crawley Town FC.

Phase 2 of the project allowed holders to claim exclusive physical merchandise using their 3D NFT as a ticket. Those who kept their NFT were surprised with a mysterious airdrop in June 2022. The Capsule collection transformed into The Impossible Box on November 5, 2022, revealing the genuine meaning of Phase 2 and presenting holders with the opportunity to 'Unbox The Impossible' and reveal the contents of the capsule, which included The Adidas Virtual Gear Collection.

Considerations for loyalty practitioners

As with any new technology, there are still many considerations that companies, and the wider industry, must address when planning to implement Web3 elements into a loyalty program.

Understanding

With a great deal of negative press generated over the years about blockchain and cryptocurrencies, consumer uncertainty and ignorance still persists. In addition, sentiment tends to change rapidly in the blockchain world. For example, while NFTs were a hot marketing device in early 2022, they quickly lost favour as interest waned and crypto-trading markets crashed. Despite less hype, some of the world's biggest brands continue to explore Web3, particularly with NFTs.

As Web3 technology is still relatively new, many consumers may not fully understand how it works, or may be sceptical of its benefits. Program operators will need to educate their customers and build trust in the technology in order to successfully implement Web3-based loyalty programs.

Technical

In addition to rapid changes in sentiment, innovation in Web3 happens at lightning speed. Slow-moving, large companies tend to struggle to keep up-with the pace, and a strategic initiative that sounds exciting today may already be out of date tomorrow. Companies need to tread with caution or be prepared to move very quickly to capitalise on new advancements.

Web3 technology is constantly evolving and changing, which means that program operators will need to be adaptable and able to keep up with the latest developments in order to stay relevant and competitive.

Accessibility

As a new technology, consumer accessibility to Web3 can be challenging. Digital wallets, encrypted keys, gas, exchange accounts, KYC and other elements can be daunting and complex to navigate.

This has acted to slow mainstream adoption. Loyalty programs have a role to play by making Web3 more accessible. Members already have to register for an account, providing companies with the opportunity to weave the Web3 technology and experience into the wider loyalty ecosystem. As mentioned earlier, major companies currently exploring the usage of such technologies are focusing on the member experience, ensuring any Web3-related activities are easy to use and accessible to a wide range of customers.

Legal

Loyalty practitioners who want to use Web3 and crypto for loyalty programs need to be aware of the legal considerations. For example, ownership of some non-fungible tokens could potentially be classified as a security, and this comes with legal implications that are still yet to be fully defined in most countries. This is notably different to traditional loyalty program frameworks such as points.

It is important to consult with legal counsel familiar with these emerging technologies and monitor and comply with ever-changing regulations within the relevant jurisdiction. The US financial regulator crackdown on several major crypto platforms in 2023 demonstrated that financial regulators and institutions are still working towards regulatory certainty.[472]

Strategy

When integrating Web3 elements into loyalty programs, loyalty program operators must prioritise the underlying strategy and design as per Loyalty & Reward Co's Essential Eight™ (as detailed in Chapter 4). It is vital for companies to establish a clear guiding strategy that harnesses the potential of this technology effectively. Instead of simply attempting to fit blockchain into existing approaches, it is important to explore how this new technology can give rise to fresh use cases and innovative solutions. By adopting a forward-thinking mindset, program operators can break free from the limitations of reinventing old practices and embrace the transformative power of Web3 to create novel and impactful loyalty experiences.

Key insights

- Blockchain is the underlying technology, cryptocurrency and tokens are the means of value exchange and incentivisation, and Web3 is the guiding vision and mindset.
- Blockchain and Web3 technology is enabling an additional feature set within modern loyalty programs. It can be used within loyalty programs across five key areas; blockchain, cryptocurrencies, NFTs, DAOs and virtual experiences in the Metaverse.
- There are strong commonalities between the most popular Web3 projects and the world's most recognised and successful loyalty programs; they deliver to the essential principle of providing meaningful and ongoing value (or 'utility', as it is often referred to in the blockchain industry) to individuals.
- Around the world, brands are exploring Web3 primarily via NFTs.

---

472 Helmore, E., 2023, 'Binance, Coinbase – US targets crypto giants', The Guardian, https://www.theguardian.com/technology/2023/jun/09/binance-coinbase-us-government-cryptocurrency, accessed 30 June 2023.

This includes some of the world's most iconic brands, including Nike, Starbucks and Reddit. A growing trend which each of these brands have followed is focusing on the user experience and benefits that Web3 enables, rather than on technical jargon and processes. Abstraction away from the technology is likely to be a continuing trend towards adoption.

- Web3 brings decentralisation, transparency and empowerment to the member experience. The philosophy and accompanying technology offers supplementary approaches to enhance online interactions, the exchange of value, and the overall customer-brand relationship. However, there are several important considerations that loyalty practitioners must acknowledge across understanding, technology, accessibility, legal and strategy.

Suggested reading

- Harrison, S., 2022, 'NFTs: The next evolution of rewards and loyalty programs', Loyalty & Reward Co, http://loyaltyrewardco. com/nfts-the-next-evolution-of-rewards-and-loyalty-programs/.

- Esber, J. & Kominers, S.D., 2022, 'Why build in Web3?', Harvard Business Review, https://hbr.org/2022/05/why-build-in-web3.

- Boston Consulting Group, 2023, 'Web3 customer loyalty program opportunities', https://www.bcg.com/publications/2023/ web3-customer-loyalty-program-opportunities.

CHAPTER 13

DATA COLLECTION & STORAGE

'The practice of marketing today runs on data. Predictive analytics and AI are fueled by data. Data enables personalization. In short, marketers use data to grow customer value.

Loyalty programs are a mainstay source of the data that is foundational to marketing today. As customer protections related to data provision and use increase, the importance of loyalty programs for customer data is becoming greater.'

- Thomas F. O'Toole, Kellogg School of Management, 2023

Focus areas

This chapter will address the following questions:

- Why should companies strive to use their loyalty programs to collect member data?

- How is data collected directly and indirectly by loyalty programs?

- What are some of the privacy regulation challenges companies face with the collection of member data?

- How aware are consumers about the data being collected about them?

Loyalty programs can play a key role in the entire data value chain; facilitating the collection of member personal data, utilising loyalty platforms to analyse the data, and harnessing the insights generated to stimulate deeper member engagement by using sophisticated segmentation and lifecycle management models. This allows loyalty program operators to determine when, why and how members are engaging with the program.

This chapter focuses on how loyalty programs collect data and best-practice methods for protecting that data. It explores challenges that marketers face via the rise of walled garden data strategies and the death of cookies. It also considers the implications of certain governments around the world tightening privacy regulations to improve consumer protections regarding personal data.

Chapter 14 (the next chapter) continues the data theme by detailing the ways in which collected data is prepared, analysed and structured into reporting. This enables critical insights to be made accessible across the business to support strategic decision-making.

Before exploring the many ways loyalty programs collect member data, it is important to consider consumer opinions on data collection.

Member awareness and attitudes about personal data collection and usage

Research indicates members are becoming increasingly aware that loyalty programs are collecting personal information about them. They are also realising that their personal data has a tangible value, and they appear to be more willing to share their data with preferred brands and companies, especially those they trust. Members expect that they will be rewarded for sharing, or that the data will be used to personalise and enhance their experience engaging with the brand.

A 2022 study by Pure Spectrum found 64 per cent of US consumers said they would be willing to provide their email address for a $20 coupon or discount.[473] 31 per cent reported they would share their full name, while

473 Tinuiti, 'A Marketer's Guide to Consumer Sentiment Towards Online Privacy in 2022', Pure Spectrum, March 2022.

23 percent would share their phone number. 27 per cent said they would share nothing. Younger generations were more open to sharing their data in exchange for value.

This aligns with an earlier 2016 global report by loyalty agency Aimia which indicated consumers are 'increasingly aware of the value of their personal data' and would put a price tag from $50 (Australia) to $70 (Germany) to $120 (South Korea) on their personal data if they could.[474] Snap My Eats, a case study featured later in this chapter is an example of a transparent data exchange between members and a program for a cash-equivalent reward. The Aimia report also found 71 per cent of global respondents believed their preferred brands are good at using their data to make online shopping experiences better, yet 77 per cent would like more control over what data companies hold on them. Transparency can also work to the loyalty program's advantage. For example, while 52 per cent said they would provide their mobile phone number without any context, the figure increased to 69 per cent when companies provided an explanation as to why they were asking for it.

The data exchange does not always need to be monetary. A 2023 PwC study indicated 82 per cent of US consumers are willing to share their personal data if it leads to a better customer experience.[475] The same survey identified that many consumers are extremely or very concerned when engaging with social media (47 per cent), the media in general (41 per cent), third-party travel websites (36 per cent) and healthcare companies (34 per cent). This reduces for consumer companies (32 per cent) and retailers (30 per cent), which PwC hypothesised is because 'the return for consumers on providing data is clearer and more transparent, in the form of vouchers, discounts and special offers'.

Relevancy is increasingly desired. A 2018 report by US firm Adlucent titled 'Data Wars' determined that 'seven out of ten consumers prefer content and

---

474 Cameron, N., 2016, 'Report: Aussie consumers value their online behavioural data at $50', CMO, https://www.cmo.com.au/article/611697/report-aussie-consumers-value-their-online-behavioural-data-50/, accessed 17 April 2019.

475 PwC, 'Consumers seek frictionless experiences in a world of disruptions,' February 2023 Global Consumer Insights Pulse Survey, https://www.pwc.com/gx/en/industries/consumer-markets/consumer-insights-survey.html accessed April 2023.

advertising that is tailored to their personal interests and shopping habits', and most importantly, consumers are willing to provide 'a wide array of information ranging from name and email address to product preferences and updates on major life updates in order to get the personalized experiences they want'.[476] The challenge for loyalty programs is one of transparency. While consumers are increasingly willing to share personal data with preferred brands and programs, the Adlucent report indicated that '96 per cent want brands to be more transparent about the collection and use of their personal data'.

The Covid-19 pandemic has shifted consumer expectations about data privacy. A 2021 EY survey found 54 per cent of consumers reported Covid-19 made them more aware of the personal data they share than before the pandemic.[477] Younger generations are much more aware of privacy and sharing data than older generations, with Millennials (53 per cent) and Gen Z (47 per cent) more likely than Gen X (43 per cent) and Baby Boomers (35 per cent) to take the time to research how a company will use their personal data. Better knowledge has an inverse impact on willingness to share, with younger generations much more likely to provide data in exchange for the promise of a more personalised experience.

These findings are consistent with a much larger 2022 study by Euromonitor International which surveyed 19,000 consumers across 19 markets.[478] They identified that around 10 per cent of Baby Boomers avoid online shopping specifically because they are concerned about companies sharing their personal details. By contrast, over 50 per cent of Millennials and Gen Z respondents indicated they are not opposed to the idea of companies sharing personal data with third-parties, but they expect to receive more value in return.

---

476 McFarling, A., 2018, 'Data Wars: Information's Role in the New Era of Advertising', Adlucent, https://www.adlucent.com/blog/2018/data-wars-informations-role-in-the-new-era-of-advertising, accessed 17 April 2019.

477 Vizioli, N, 'Has lockdown made consumers more open to privacy?' Jan 2021, https://www.ey.com/en_ca/cybersecurity/has-lockdown-made-consumers-more-open-to-privacy- accessed April 2023.

478 Holmes, L, 'Generational Attitudes and Actions Around Data Privacy', Euromonitor International, July 2022, https://www.euromonitor.com/article/generational-attitudes-and-actions-around-data-privacy, accessed April 2023.

Data security concerns by consumers are justifiable. Research from Check Point identified that weekly cyber-attacks have increased worldwide by 7 per cent in Q1 2023 (with companies averaging 1,248 attacks per week).[479] With these trends likely to continue, consumer willingness to share data may be negatively impacted.

A 2019 KPMG survey measuring consumer attitudes towards data privacy in loyalty programs showed that while consumers are generally willing to share personal information with retailers for better rewards, they also expect retailers to be transparent about their data usage practices.[480]

Attitudes about sharing data differ across cultures. A 2018 Asia-Pacific survey by Mastercard reported 46 per cent of Japanese respondents would be willing to share personal information with their loyalty programs to receive more relevant experiences or benefits. This increased to 64 per cent for Australia, South Korea and Hong Kong, and up to 87 per cent for China, Indonesia and India.[481]

There is sharing and then there is taking. Research indicates members are not always aware of what type of information is being collected about them, and they seek more control and transparency over what data is collected and used. A 2017 report from the Consumer Policy Research Centre (CPRC) indicates consumers do not appear to read privacy policies which are designed to inform them of the ways in which their data is collected, used and shared.[482]

---

479 Alessandro Mascellino, 2023, 'Global Cyber Attacks Rise by 7% in Q1 2023', https://www.infosecurity-magazine.com/news/global-cyber-attacks-rise-7-q1-2023/ accessed 12 June 2023.

480 "The truth about customer loyalty", 2019, https://kpmg.com/xx/en/home/insights/2019/11/customer-loyalty-survey.html, access 12 April 2023.

481 Mastercard, 2017, 'Achieving Advocacy and Influence in a Changing Loyalty Landscape', p22, https://newsroom.mastercard.com/asia-pacific/files/2018/01/Loyalty-Solutions-Whitepaper.-AP-Region-20171.pdf, accessed 16 April 2019.

482 Nguyen, P., & Solomon, L., 2017, 'Consumer data and the digital economy – Emerging issues in data collection, use and sharing', Consumer Policy Research Centre, http://cprc.org.au/wp-content/uploads/Full_Data_Report_A4_FIN.pdf, accessed 17 April 2019.

*

In addition to considering consumer awareness and attitudes about data collection and usage practices, companies should also consider the critical importance of collecting quality customer data while building a healthy, well-managed database to support marketing efforts.

Companies such as Google, Amazon, Meta (via Facebook, Messenger and WhatsApp) and Apple have implemented, or are in the process of implementing, changes to the way they operate which will make it more expensive and restrictive for companies to manage their digital marketing.

Two areas that should be of immediate concern to most companies include the rise of walled garden data and the death of cookies.

Walled garden data

Walled garden data refers to the collection of user information and behavioural data confined within a closed digital ecosystem, where access and data sharing are restricted or controlled by the platform owner.

These walled gardens, typically operated by large technology companies like Google, Facebook, and Amazon, limit the flow of information to and from their platforms, making it challenging for companies to independently analyse and leverage the data for marketing, advertising, and personalisation purposes.

The marketing tools provided by these companies are highly effective in targeting specific segments based on defined criteria, but they can be expensive to use. While it is wise for companies to consider them as part of their overall marketing mix, too much reliance on them can negatively impact the return on investment (ROI) of campaign activity.

Companies can gain several advantages by using walled garden data tools to run marketing campaigns, including:

- **Access to large user bases:** walled gardens, such as Facebook, Google, and Amazon, have massive user bases, allowing companies to reach a wide and diverse audience. By leveraging these platforms' data tools, companies can potentially increase the reach and impact of their marketing campaigns.

- **Access to lookalike audiences:** walled gardens help reach new audiences who may share many similar attributes to a company's own customers.

- **Advanced targeting capabilities:** walled garden platforms offer sophisticated targeting options based on user demographics, interests, behaviour, and location. Companies can use these capabilities to create highly targeted and personalised marketing campaigns, increasing the likelihood of connecting with their desired audience segments.

- **Rich insights and analytics:** walled garden data tools provide valuable insights and analytics, enabling companies to measure the effectiveness of their marketing campaigns and optimise them accordingly. These insights can help companies understand user engagement, conversions, and return on investment, allowing for data-driven decision-making.

- **Native advertising formats:** walled gardens often provide native advertising formats that seamlessly blend with the platform's content. This can result in higher user engagement and better conversion rates compared to traditional display ads. Examples include sponsored posts on Facebook or Instagram, promoted tweets on Twitter, and Google Shopping ads.

- **Cross-platform integration:** many walled garden platforms offer integration across multiple devices and services. For example, Google's marketing tools can be utilised across search, YouTube, and the Google Display Network, while Facebook's advertising platform extends to Instagram and Messenger. This cross-platform integration allows companies to create cohesive and consistent marketing campaigns, reaching users at multiple touchpoints in their online journey.

Unfortunately, companies can face several disadvantages when using walled garden data tools to run marketing campaigns:

- **Limited data access and ownership:** walled gardens restrict access to user data and often do not share detailed information with advertisers. This limitation can make it difficult for companies to develop a comprehensive understanding of their target audience and to independently analyse and leverage data for marketing and personalisation purposes.

- **Dependence on platform policies:** companies relying on walled garden data tools are subject to the policies and terms of service of these platforms. Changes in policies or algorithms can have a direct impact on marketing campaigns, potentially leading to decreased visibility, reach, or effectiveness.

- **High competition and ad costs:** due to the large user bases and popularity of walled garden platforms, advertisers face high levels of competition. This can result in increased advertising costs as companies bid for limited ad space and visibility.

- **Data privacy concerns:** as consumers become more aware of data privacy issues, the use of walled garden data tools can be viewed as invasive or unethical. This perception might harm a company's reputation and lead to a loss of customer trust.

While walled garden data tools offer clear advantages for marketing campaigns, the potential disadvantages can be concerning. Striking a balance between leveraging walled garden platforms and maintaining control over data, marketing strategies, and customer relationships can help companies navigate the complex digital landscape more effectively.

Suffice to say, companies which have utilised their loyalty program to collect rich data profiles and build an engaged marketing database are better positioned to attain a balance. Firstly, they are less reliant on the use of such tools as they have the opportunity to execute promotional campaigns directly to their member base, helping to manage their marketing budget. Secondly, they have a more comprehensive data set to feed into the tools, which helps to improve their targeting ability.

Death of cookies

Cookies are small text files stored on a user's device by websites they visit. These files contain information about the user's preferences, browsing history, and other data that enables websites to remember the user and provide a more personalised experience.

Marketers rely extensively on cookies for digital campaigns as they:

- Allow tailoring of content, offers, and advertising based on a user's browsing behaviour, interests, and preferences.

- Enable marketers to deliver targeted ads to users based on their online activities.

- Support data collection on user behaviour, such as the pages visited, time spent on a website, and conversion rates.

- Enable marketers to identify users who have previously visited their website and show them relevant ads on other websites.

- Help improve the overall user experience on a website by remembering a user's preferences, such as language, location, or login information.

Despite these advantages, Microsoft, Apple, and Mozilla have banned the use of cookies via their web browsers, and Google plans to introduce a ban in 2024 (after several false starts).

The rationale behind this decision can be attributed a range of factors:

- In recent years, there has been a growing awareness and concern about user data privacy. Third-party cookies are often used to track user behaviour across websites, which has been criticised as intrusive and a violation of privacy. Google's decision to ban cookies can be seen as an effort to address these concerns and provide users with more control over their data.

- Regulatory frameworks, such as the General Data Protection Regulation (GDPR) in the European Union and the California

Consumer Privacy Act (CCPA) in the United States, have imposed strict rules on data collection and usage. By phasing out third-party cookies, technology companies aims to comply with these regulations and avoid potential legal issues or fines.

- A need exists to maintain user trust in the technology companies' products and services. By addressing privacy concerns and adopting alternative solutions, the technology companies strive to maintain their reputation as responsible and forward-thinking.

- The technology companies have been working on alternative solutions for advertising and user tracking that constitute their future walled garden data strategy. For example, Google has been developing the Privacy Sandbox, a set of proposals aimed at providing a more privacy-centric approach to digital advertising. This included the Federated Learning of Cohorts (FLoC), introduced in March 2021, which grouped users with similar browsing habits together, allowing for targeted advertising without the need for individual-level tracking. FLoC was very quickly discontinued because it still failed to provide privacy. It was replaced with Topics, announced in January 2022. Topics will use less sensitive data categories for targeting, plus provide more control to the user who will be able to customise involvement or even opt-out altogether. Even major technology companies are treading unchartered waters as privacy demands and regulations increase.

Critically, the death of cookies creates a risk where marketers are forced towards an increased reliance on the use of walled garden data tools, which will likely lead to a substantial increase in their marketing costs.

The ideal antidote to this risk is a best-practice loyalty program which is used to collect rich data profiles and build an engaged marketing database, thereby reducing reliance on such tools.

*

With clear and obvious advantages available to companies that build quality data profiles on their member bases, it is important to recognise the many ways data can be collected.

Loyalty program operators use a range of methods to collect member data both directly and indirectly.

Direct member data collection

Member personal data can be collected directly by loyalty programs via many touchpoints.

Join process

When a member registers to join a loyalty program they are required to provide personal details (e.g., their name, date of birth, email address and mobile phone number) which forms the basis of their member profile.

While it can be tempting for the loyalty program to ask for copious amounts of data as part of the join process, this can significantly reduce registration completion rates. As detailed in Chapter 4, simplicity is key.

Once the join process is complete, there may be a section or preference centre within the new account where the member is invited to share their likes and interests.

> **Flybuys**
>
> Once the registration process is completed, Flybuys [483] loyalty program invites new members to fill in a profile section.
>
> This includes fields for home and work phone, residential and postage address, number of people living in the household, including number of people under 18 years old and any pets, number of cars, whether the member owns their own business, the month of the year when they intend to review their home insurance, car

---

483 Flybuys , https://join.flybuys.com.au/desktop/fullname, accessed 29 June 2020.

insurance and mobile phone contract, how often they take flights for personal travel, which loyalty programs they are a member of, mobile phone, pay TV and internet products they use, internet shopping habits, and alcohol purchase behaviour.

This is all highly valuable information for Flybuys to build a comprehensive member profile, while for the member it is entirely voluntary.

Interactions

When and how an individual member interacts with a brand and their marketing material can be tracked at a micro level. This includes click maps or real-time user recordings across websites and electronic direct mail, and heat maps for in-store visits.

Digital assets are a particularly rich source of customer insights. This may include where a member's cursor gravitates to on a website, where in the sales funnel they take an action, what products they leave in their basket, which colour buttons they are more likely to click, what elements are confusing or missing, and which banner ad messaging resonates most. Interactions with a brand's customer service team may also be tracked and stored against the member's profile, including the nature of the call.

Cookies are used extensively to collect data, however as detailed above this option will soon not be available.

Browser extension installations are becoming increasingly popular among loyalty program members. Members install these free toolbars because they can be helpful in notifying them when loyalty points, cashback or coupons are available, and to access price comparisons. They are a valuable source of member data, providing information about the user's device, IP address, geo-location, browsing history, mouse movements and logins.

Shopkick, Swagbucks, Honey and Cashrewards

These companies are just a few examples of the range of affiliate marketing programs which allow members to collect points or cashback for online shopping via partner sites (the merchant funded framework detailed in Chapter 8).

They each have browser extensions which run across Chrome, Firefox and Safari which, when installed, allow members to shop online as normal whilst receiving pop-up notifications when they are on an affiliate partner's website.

While these programs make it very easy for their members to earn and save points/cash, members are also opening themselves up to extensive tracking of personal information, banking details, browsing activity and online shopping patterns and interactions.

For example, Cashrewards state within their privacy policy that they 'collect, use and share aggregated data such as statistical or demographic data for any purpose'.[484]

As detailed earlier, members connecting to free Wi-Fi can be tracked, even without them needing to sign-in to an account. If the member accesses Wi-Fi once and signs-in, each time they visit the same location, the Wi-Fi may automatically connect and track their activity.

This provides loyalty programs with important data on how different segments of members utilise online and locational data. For example, a retail loyalty program operator could track behaviour inside store locations in different ways; learning how they move, where they reside and how long they stay, which can all be mapped and processed to gain better member insights.

---

484 Cashrewards, privacy, https://www.cashrewards.com.au/privacy, accessed 27 May 2020.

Consumers can virtually try on clothes, shoes, cosmetics, glasses, and other goods using augmented reality technology. The experience, available online and via apps, as well as in-store, allows brands to collect valuable member data which can be used to better understand members likes and preferences.

The data includes what a member looks like, what items they try and reject, what items they place in their wishlist or shopping basket, and which items they finally purchase.

L'Oréal Paris

L'Oréal Paris[486] launched a virtual try-on feature within their app using ModiFace[487] augmented reality technology. The tool allows L'Oréal members to easily try on hundreds of different cosmetics products or change their hair colour virtually.

The patented technology uses a face-tracking algorithm that can detect 63 landmarks on a member's face, providing the member with a realistic result when trying on L'Oréal products without any cost or commitment to purchase. L'Oréal benefit from increased

---

485 Skyfii, https://skyfii.io/, accessed 15 May 2019.

486 L'Oréal Paris , https://www.lorealparisusa.com/virtual-try-on/makeup.aspx, accessed 22 July 2020.

487 ModiFace, https://modiface.com/, accessed 22 July 2020.

engagement with the app and their products, as well as detailed product preference data captured, which can then be used for hyper-personalised marketing and retargeting purposes.

This is a clear trend among the beauty industry with Maybelline, Sephora, *bareMinerals*, MAC, Bobbi Brown, Redken and others, all integrating virtual tools within their apps for members to find and easily compare different foundation, lipstick, blush or hair colour hues.

Transactions

When, where and how often a member transacts, and how much they spend, provides valuable data about the member's lifestyle, habits, interests, motivations and goals. This data is collected by loyalty programs in a variety of ways.

The most common way is the member purposefully identifying when they transact by scanning their membership card or app in-store, signing into their account online or via an app, or providing verification to a call centre agent.

For loyalty programs that offer credit cards which earn points when the member spends with the credit card, the loyalty program may receive the transaction data, such as time and date, retailer and amount spent. For example, a bank loyalty program which provides members with a credit card will receive all the member's transaction data. Other loyalty programs, such as frequent flyer programs, may not receive this data if the bank chooses not to (or is not able to) pass it on to them. Instead, they are likely to just receive the total amount the member spent for the month to facilitate the points earn calculations.

Some loyalty programs require the member to link a credit card or their bank-account when they join, with points earn or cashback automatically processed when they spend at participating retailers. This provides the program operator with a significant amount of transaction data. In the case of bank account-linking, the program operators receive details of all transactions made through the member's bank account. This approach is covered in more detail in Chapter 11.

Some retailers have implemented a process where they automatically link any credit or debit card used by the member to their profile, enabling them to capture transactions, even when the member does not scan their membership card.[488] To illustrate, a member of a supermarket loyalty program scans their membership card at the checkout, then pays using a specific credit card. The loyalty program platform automatically matches the credit card against the member's profile. If the member spends with that card at the supermarket but does not scan their loyalty card, the loyalty platform will still collect the transaction data by recognising the credit card. While cost effective for the program operator because they collect valuable member data without having to reward the member with loyalty points, this practice is being scrutinised by governments with some going so far as to demand that the practice cease.[489]

Some programs require the member to scan receipts to prove they have made a valid transaction. The loyalty platform identifies relevant data (time, date, store location, SKU, amount spent, etc.) and calculates the points earn, discount or cashback applicable. While this approach requires the member to take extra steps in the earn process (friction which inevitably leads to lower engagement rates), the platform also captures other items on the receipt, helping to build a more complete profile of the member's spend habits.

Snap My Eats

NPD Group, one of the world's biggest market research agencies, runs a reward program called Snap My Eats[490] in the UK.

Members can download the app and register, then earn up to £5 of credit per month just for taking surveys and snapping pictures of receipts from their food and drink purchases. This includes things like a snack or coffee on the go, fast food, restaurant meals, or even an impulse candy purchase.

Snap My Eats requires the member to accumulate £10 of value before they can process a redemption, ensuring the program

---

488 Australian Competition and Consumer Commission, 2019 'Customer loyalty schemes: Final report,' pg 65 https://www.accc.gov.au/publications/customer-loyalty-schemes-final-report accesses 20th August 2020.

489 Ibid.

490 Snap My Eats, https://www.snapmyeats.uk/, accessed 19 July 2020.

takes advantage of the endowed progress effect to drive ongoing member engagement, while simultaneously reducing costs.

Surveys

Loyalty programs often invite members to participate in surveys. These can be used for two purposes: to capture attitudes and opinions about the loyalty program, and, to collect additional data about the member.

Qantas Frequent Flyer

Qantas Frequent Flyer released a survey in March 2019 asking participating members a wide range of questions including:

Whether the member would recommend the Qantas Frequent Flyer loyalty program to family and friends.

Which competitor loyalty programs members belong to (from a list of 17 local and international programs) and the NPS rating and ranking for each.

How the member generally redeems points with the competitor programs.

A comparison of aspects of the Qantas Frequent Flyer program and the member's favourite competitor program across customer service, ease of use of scheme benefits, value accessed by the member, the credibility of the program, ease of accessing information, ease of accessing flight reward bookings and perceptions of the programs website.

Household income figures including how much the member spends on groceries each week, how much is spent on credit cards, how many dependent children live in the household and their ages, work status and number of employees in the member's company and whether the member flies mainly for business or leisure.

Qantas Frequent Flyer also requested permission to store the survey answers against the member's profile 'to be used for program development (including delivering program benefits to our members)'. Such data would provide the program with rich insights about that member, including attitudinal views, which can often be hard to obtain.

Apps

When a member downloads a loyalty program app, they are generally requested to provide permission for the loyalty program to gain access to certain features and data, plus the ability to track location (either all the time, or only when the app is being used). This approval can provide extensive access including precise user location, access to the member's contacts, access to phone call logs, access to the camera and microphone, ability to read contents of storage, and ability to read phone status and identity.[491]

As a result of these permissions, smartphones have grown to become a major source of member data for loyalty program operators by allowing the loyalty program to extensively track member activity even when they are not actively engaging with the loyalty program or parent company.

The number of app control settings for users have increased, however, apps still bundle a number of permissions together, making it difficult for users to make decisions. For example, it is necessary for a food delivery company to access location information to function optimally, however this permission may be bundled together with permission to share information with advertisers, something not critical for operations.

Air New Zealand Airpoints

The Air New Zealand website terms of use state the ways by which they collect, combine, use and share Airpoints member data. Privacy policies and data practices of this nature are common among loyalty programs:

'...where you are an Airpoints member, Koru member, have a myairnz login or subscribed to our grabaseat or Special Offers database, we combine the information we collect from your computer, mobile or other devices with the other information we collect about you, for example your booking history with us, your Airpoints or Koru

---

491 Cleary, G., 2018, 'Mobile Privacy: What Do Your Apps Know About You?', Symantec Corporation, https://www.symantec.com/blogs/threat-intelligence/mobile-privacy-apps, accessed 11 April 2019.

membership information, information we collect from third parties in accordance with our Privacy Statement and information that is publicly available (for example, information in public directories and publicly available social media information). We use this combined information to learn about your interests and preferences so that we can provide you with an improved and personalised online experience, improve our products and services, and identify suitable offers and promotions that you might be interested in.

We may disclose your personal information to the range of third parties identified in our Privacy Statement. For example, to our third-party business partners including marketing and advertising companies, data processing companies and data analysis companies to conduct sales, marketing and advertising research and analysis on our behalf so that we can better understand your preferences, carry out business improvement analysis, present you with suitable offers that you might be interested in, and for any of the other purpose described in the Privacy Statement.[492]

Virtual home assistants

Some companies are experimenting with the use of virtual home assistants (such as Google Assistant, Alexa, or Siri) to support new ways for customers to interact.[493]

While there is some nervousness among members of the public about the conceivably invasive nature and eavesdropping potential of these devices, their household penetration is forecast to grow exponentially over the next five years.[494] As the capability evolves to better maintain and interpret reasonable

---

492 Air New Zealand, https://www.airnewzealand.com.au/website-terms-of-use, accessed 30 June 2020.

493 Crozier, R., 2019, 'Woolworths looks to large-scale conversational AI', IT News, https://www.itnews.com.au/news/woolworths-looks-to-large-scale-conversational-ai-518016, accessed 11 April 2019.

494 Hargreaves, I., 2018, 'Voice Assistant use to grow 1000% to reach 275 million by 2023, Juniper says', PC World, https://www.pcworld.idg.com.au/article/642969/voice-assistants-use-grow-1000-reach-275-million-by-2023-juniper-says/, accessed 11 April, 2019.

levels of conversation, they have the potential to become a valuable personal data source for loyalty programs.

> ### Marriott
>
> Marriott partnered with Amazon to offer an Amazon Echo device (equipped with microphones and speakers, and connected to a network) within hotel rooms allowing the services of Alexa to bring simplicity and convenience to guests.
>
> Guests can ask Alexa for hotel information (like pool or gym open times), request guest services (like room service or a wakeup call), play music from their hotel room and more.[495]
>
> This conversational AI can help build a bond between the AI assistant and user (Shulevitz, 2018)[496] and also helps strengthen the Marriott brand through the ability to collect data, personalise experiences, influence decisions and predict future behaviour.

Social media

Tools like Facebook Connect can be used by loyalty programs to allow members to login with their existing social login credentials, with the primary benefit to the consumer being the convenience of not having to create a separate login each time they want to interact with a different loyalty program.

Facebook Connect allows sharing of data between the website and Facebook. This includes the member's name, email, birthday, relationships, friends list, education history, work history, interests, friend interactions, wall posts and comment frequency. Much of this data would be complex or arduous to collect via a loyalty program's own registration form.

---

495 Jones, V. K., 2019, 'Experiencing Voice-Activated Artificial Intelligence Assistants in the Home: A Phenomenological Approach', Public Access Theses and Dissertations from the College of Education and Human Sciences, Vol 348, accessed via https://digitalcommons.unl.edu/cehsdiss/348, 3 June 2020.

496 Shulevitz, J., 2018, 'Alexa, should we trust you?', The Atlantic, accessed via https://www.theatlantic.com/magazine/archive/2018/11/alexa-how-will-you-change-us/570844/, 3 June 2020.

Facebook also allows loyalty programs to build and target 'look-a-like audiences' based on this data to run targeted advertising.

Asics Runkeeper

When logging into the Asics Runkeeper[497] mobile app for tracking running activity, social sign-in is prompted and encouraged. Users are given the option to connect their accounts via Facebook networks.

There are both benefits to the user (faster, easier and more familiar sign-in process with a single password, single account to manage and fewer clicks) and to Asics (increase sign-ups and leverage existing social data which can improve app personalisation and marketing ability).

Loyalty psychology and behavioural biases studies show that connecting social networks can facilitate stronger levels of social motivation and engagement with the app and the brand (appealing to the social proof and commitment biases).

Households

Loyalty programs may link multiple members to a specific mailing address, allowing them to build out their data profile by matching members living in the same household. This may be spouses, children, parents or housemates.

Some loyalty programs, such as supermarket, bank and hotel programs in particular, allow members to apply for companion cards, where the member can nominate another individual to receive a secondary card of the same account to enable both card-carriers to earn points.

This household profile approach allows for the loyalty program to view a much broader consumption profile than for an individual member, providing new and relevant insights.

---

497 ASICS, https://runkeeper.com/, accessed 29 June 2020.

My Cold Stone Club Rewards

My Cold Stone Club Rewards awards members with 1 point per dollar spent at Cold Stone Creamery, with 25 bonus points for joining. Every time the account reaches 50 points, the points are automatically redeemed for a US$5 voucher.

The program allows up to seven family members to be added to the same account to help accumulate points. Each family member has their own profile and will receive individual birthday offers.

The terms and conditions warn that while household pooling allows points to be earned faster with no limits to the amount of US$5 vouchers members can accumulate, this also means family members 'can redeem your rewards'.[498]

Indirect member data collection

Member personal data can also be indirectly sourced by multiple third parties, with the data fed into the loyalty program's systems and matched against individual member profiles. This is primarily facilitated via data brokers, data exchanges and database generators.

Data Brokers

In the digital age, individual consumers are sharing unprecedented amounts of personal data — sometimes overtly and sometimes without being aware. Numerous research articles detail what Google,[499] Facebook,[500] Apple,[501]

---

498 Cold Stone Creamery, FAQ's, https://www.coldstonecreamery.com/faqs/eclub/index.html, accessed 29 May 2020.

499 Desjardins, J., 2018, 'What Does Google Know About You', Visual Capitalist, https://www.visualcapitalist.com/what-does-google-know-about-you/, accessed 15 April 2019.

500 Fried, I., 2019, 'What Facebook knows about you', Axios, https://www.axios.com/facebook-personal-data-scope-suer-privacy-de15c860-9153-45b6-95e8-ddac8cd47c34.html, accessed 15 April 2019.

501 Murphy, D., 2018, 'I Asked Apple For Everything It Knows About Me, And Here's What I Found', Life Hacker, https://www.lifehacker.com.

Amazon[502] and many other companies know about individuals, including who they are, where they go, who their friends are, what they like and dislike, their future plans, their online life and much more.

Often member personal data is publicly accessible, such as social media posts. Additional data can come from tracking software in website and apps,[503] plus Wi-Fi. More data to understand members can be sourced from consumer surveys and census data.

Data brokers accumulate masses of information about consumers. They may provide database tools for loyalty programs to help them improve their member profiling, or even provide the data directly to the loyalty program to be matched against existing member profiles. Globally, data brokers 'have highly detailed profiles on billions of individuals, comprising age, race, sex, weight, height, marital status, education level, politics, shopping habits, health issues, holiday plans, social media posts, income and more'.[504]

Data brokers can match the individual member's data against the loyalty programs' existing databases using common denominators such as name, email address and mobile number. Such a service can build a profile for an individual member from tens to hundreds of datasets overnight, making this a valuable service for loyalty programs which use machine learning/AI analytics to generate member insights and power hyper-personalised marketing campaigns.

Data brokers match data to members in three basic ways:

au/2018/12/i-asked-apple-for-everything-it-knows-about-me-and-heres-what-i-found/, accessed 15 April 2019.

502 Haselton, T., 2018, 'Here's how to find what Amazon knows about you', CNBC, https://www.cnbc.com/2018/04/05/what-does-amazon-know-about-me. html, accessed 15 April 2019.

503 Couts, A., 2019, 'Top 100 websites: How they track your every move online', Digital Trends, https://www.digitaltrends.com/web/top-100-websites-how-are-they-tracking-you/, accessed 16 April 2019.

504 Molitorisz, S., 2018, 'It's time for data brokers to emerge from the shadows', IT News, https://www.itnews.com.au/news/its-time-for-data-brokers-to-emerge-from-the-shadows-488450, accessed 16 April 2019.

- **User account integration**: a personal identifier in a member's profile (primarily an email, or name and email combination) is matched to the same identifier in the database of the data broker. This is typically anonymised via a technique called hashing.

- **Mobile ID tracking**: identifiers such as email addresses can be matched to a specific mobile device ID such as Apple's IDFA (Identifier for advertisers),[505] or Google's AAID (Google advertising Identifier),[506] which are shared by partners which also collect this information. Third-party data platform companies may also embed code within their client's apps to track the mobile phone usage of the user, further building out their unified customer data pools.

- **Cookie syncing**: data brokers rely on partners freely sharing their individual member's cookie data which they tag and match with cookies from other independent company data to create matches within their ecosystem of individual devices.

Experian

Experian, a global data broking company, state on their website that 'Consumers are creating large amounts of data every day, and you're capturing it at every moment through your brand, product and service touch points. While this information can be leveraged and used to your advantage, often it doesn't provide you with some of the most important insights you need – going beyond the customer journey to actually get to know the customer.'

They inform potential clients that their platform, 'layers comprehensive information about every household on top of your existing

---

505 Nichols, J., 2017, 'Mobile Tutorial Series – What is an IDFA or Apple Identifier for Advertisers?', Singular, https://www.singular.net/mobile-tutorial-series-idfa-apple-identifier-advertisers/, accessed 9 April 2019.

506 Google Support, 2019, 'Target mobile apps with IDFA or AAID', Authorized Buyers Help, https://support.google.com/authorizedbuyers/answer/3221407?hl=en, accessed 9 April 2019.

> data, giving you unprecedented insights into who your customers are, how they operate, and how best to reach them. Next-level segmentation brings your customers to life with pen portraits, word clouds, infographics, animations, interactive maps, bar charts and crosstabs.'[507]

As detailed earlier in this chapter, one challenge many loyalty programs struggle with is utilising the data available to them. Data brokers deliver additional value by not only providing extensive additional data but formatting it in ways that are accessible and user-friendly for programs, enabling them to be better positioned to extract value from their investment.

How trustworthy is broker data? Due to the secretive nature in which data brokers acquire information and create segmented audience data, loyalty program operators should be aware of the issue of potential inaccuracies in the information supplied. Researchers from the Harvard Business Review conducted a review of popular audience segments supplied by a range of brokers and found consumer information sold by brokers varies greatly in quality.[508] For example, demographic data such as age tiers or gender had very low levels of accuracy, whereas other target lists such as interest-based segments had an accuracy of 80 per cent. The findings indicate prospective buyers of data broker lists and audience profiles should be cautious, especially when seeking information for broad segments, which appear to be the least cost-effective.

Acxiom

Acxiom is one of the largest data brokers in the world with 'over 23,000 servers collecting and analysing consumer data, collecting up to 3,000 data points per person'.[509]

---

507 Experian, 'Mosaic', http://www.experian.com.au/mosaic, accessed 9 April 2019.

508 Neumann, N. & Tucker, C., 2020, 'Buying Consumer Data? Tread Carefully', https://hbr.org/2020/05/buying-consumer-data-tread-carefully, accessed 9 June 2020.

509 The Next Web, 2019, 'Loyalty programs cost you your personal data – are the rewards worth it?', https://thenextweb.com/insights/2019/06/12/loyalty-programs-cost-you-your-personal-data-are-the-rewards-worth-it/, accessed 1 June 2020.

They track consumers digital footprints online using invisible track-ing pixels and combine this with offline information and publicly available records to build rich data assets which they can leverage as part of their data services and solutions product offering.

Acxiom also conduct propensity modelling and sell this data. For example, whether an individual has an 'online search propensity' for a certain ailment or prescription[510] can be sold to insurance companies which are looking to flag health related risks.

Datalogix

Datalogix are a data collection company that obtains and tracks offline and online data purchasing behaviour patterns alongside information from retailer loyalty programs. Datalogix says it has 'information on more than $1 trillion in consumer spending across 1400 leading brands'.[511]

They have partnered with Facebook to track whether Facebook users who see ads for certain products end up buying the products from local stores. This allows for better understanding of consumer behaviour and improves the various layers of information across communication touchpoints.

Data exchanges and clean rooms

A data exchange is similar to a data broker but operates in a slightly differ-ent way. Data exchanges allow companies to share data collected from their customers with other selected companies. This practice can provide loyalty programs with access to many data points, which they can use to build out member profiles. Contributors have full control of what gets exchanged, over-sight of its use, and legal rights to protect against misuse. The platform ensures

510 Beckett, L., 2013, 'Everything We Know About What Data Brokers Know about You', ProPublica, https://www.propublica.org/article/everything-we-know-about-what-data-brokers-know-about-you, accessed 1 June 2020.
511 Ibid.

that the use of the data is reasonable, legal and provides a full audit trail for this to be monitored.

Data clean rooms are growing in popularity and are seen as one of the ways that companies can effectively and compliantly share data as they move away from cookie-based targeting. Data clean rooms differ from data exchanges in a few key ways. With data exchanges, the companies that have partnered share user-level data through identifying keys like cookie IDs, device IDs and IDs created from hashed email addresses. In a clean room, multiple data sources can be shared in a secure environment without having to physically exchange the data sets or compromise personal information, IP identifiers or any other form of user privacy protection.

DataCo

DataCo provide a data clean room for companies to match and share data safely and securely.[512]

Their solution enables companies to understand information about overlapping customers and link partner data sets without having to expose customer PII (personally identifiable information).

Using DataCo's Privacy Preserving Customer Matching, partner companies can perform matching without exposing customer personal information or transferring it to a third party for processing.

Furthermore, customer matching can be performed without revealing which individual customers are matched - the output is limited to summary statistics about the overlapping customers. This is useful for early-stage partnership exploration (Proof of Value) to estimate the value of a potential data partnership.

Where sufficient consent exists, DataCo can provide a new universal ID to both partners to reveal the matched audience. This unlocks basic promotional activities, such as cross-selling or can be used as an input into more advanced use cases

---

512 Dataco, https://dataco.ai/home, accessed 12 June 2023.

Database generators

A member database is highly valuable to any company, but they can be difficult to build. Some loyalty programs engage third-party database generators to grow their databases. This is achieved by partnering with other companies who offer online transactions.

For example, a member of a loyalty program may choose to purchase some tickets from the company which runs the program. At the end of the purchase journey, they are presented with offers from other companies. This may be a discount off a hotel stay, a flight, a pizza, a food delivery service, or any manner of products or services. They may also be invited to enter a competition.

The personal data which the member enters is collected by the database generator and provided to the sponsoring company to build their database. The member's personal data may be auto populated if the member is signed into their online account. The member will later begin to receive marketing communications from the company which funded the collection of the data.

The database generator uses powerful machine learning capabilities to deliver highly personalised messaging to target members as a way to boost their conversion rate.

Rokt

Rokt are a database generator operating around the globe.

Rokt state on their website they use, 'more than 2B user records during the Transaction Moment creating the ability to personalize the creative and user journey using data such as past purchases, event type and demographic.'[513] They also communicate that their algorithms 'consider 1B pieces of data every 40 milliseconds — getting smarter and more predictive with each user action—surfacing the most relevant message for each individual user.'

According to Rokt statistics, consumers making a purchase are two times more likely to engage with marketing offers (leveraging the

---

513 Rokt, https://rokt.com/, accessed 16 April 2019.

*

With significant amounts of data being collected by loyalty programs all
around the world, companies need to consider consumer privacy regulations.
These are generally designed to provide protections to the consumer on how
their personal data is collected and used.

There is a global trend of privacy regulations being increasingly restricted
to provide consumers with more control over their data.

Privacy Regulation Restrictions

Around the world, some governments are changing consumer privacy regulations to provide increasing protections to consumers.

The most well-known example of this is the European Union (E.U.) which
implemented the General Data Protection Regulation (GDPR) in 2018.[514]
GDPR was designed to safeguard personal data privacy and security. The regulation applies to organisations operating within the EU and those handling the
personal data of EU citizens, regardless of their location, meaning companies
outside the EU may also need to comply.

GDPR emphasises transparency, individual rights, and accountability, requiring companies to obtain explicit consent for data collection and
processing, ensure data accuracy, and adopt privacy-by-design principles. Non-
compliance can result in significant fines, up to 4 per cent of a company's
annual global turnover or €20 million, whichever is greater.

Businesses must adhere to several key requirements under the GDPR when
dealing with consumer data. These include:

---

514 "General Data Protection Regulation" https://gdpr-info.eu/ accessed 12 April
2023.

- **Lawfulness, fairness, and transparency:** data processing must be legal, fair, and transparent, with clear communication to consumers about how their data is being used.

- **Purpose limitation:** data must be collected for specified, explicit, and legitimate purposes, and not further processed in a way that is incompatible with those purposes.

- **Data minimisation:** data collection should be limited to what is necessary for the intended purpose, avoiding excessive or irrelevant information.

- **Accuracy:** businesses must ensure that the personal data they hold is accurate and up-to-date, and take steps to rectify or erase inaccurate information.

- **Storage limitation:** personal data should be stored only for as long as necessary to fulfill the stated purpose, and then deleted or anonymised.

- **Integrity and confidentiality:** organisations must protect personal data using appropriate security measures, including encryption and access controls, to prevent unauthorised access, disclosure, or destruction.

- **Accountability:** companies must demonstrate their compliance with GDPR principles by implementing appropriate policies, procedures, and documentation, as well as appointing a Data Protection Officer (DPO) when required.

- **Consent:** businesses must obtain explicit and informed consent from consumers for data collection and processing, allowing them to easily withdraw consent at any time.

- **Data subject rights:** companies must respect and facilitate individuals' rights, such as the right to access, rectify, erase, restrict processing, object to processing, and data portability.

- **Data protection by design and default:** organisations must integrate data protection principles into the design of their products, services, and processes, as well as ensure that privacy settings are set to the most protective level by default.

GDPR was quickly followed by the California Consumer Privacy Act (CCPA), which became effective from January 1, 2020.[515] The CCPA aims to enhance privacy rights and consumer protection for residents of California, granting them more control over their personal information collected by businesses. Once again, the regulation also applies to organisations handling the personal data of Californian citizens, regardless of their location, meaning companies outside California may also need to comply.

Other governments have, or are, following this trend. Virginia, Colorado, Utah and Connecticut have instituted comprehensive consumer data privacy laws, while four other US states have active bills at this time. The Australian government has also recommended a significant overhaul of its 1988 (pre-internet) Privacy Act.[516]

For loyalty program operators, this presents some clear disclosure, process and technical challenges. They must provide the ability for members to give (and remove) content to collect, use and share data. They must provide the ability to provide consumers with a list of data held against their profile when requested. They must ensure they can delete some, or all, of the data held against a member profile when requested. They must delete data that is no longer necessary.

These requirements place significant onus on the loyalty program operator. It can be argued that bigger companies have an advantage as they are better able to implement the required technology, processes and customer service support required to achieve compliance.

That being said, loyalty programs provide some advantages for all

---

515 "California Consumer Privacy Act", https://oag.ca.gov/privacy/ccpa accessed 12 April 2023.

516 "Privacy Act Review Report", https://www.ag.gov.au/rights-and-protections/publications/privacy-act-review-report accessed 12 April 2023.

companies managing these challenges. Members must progress through a structured registration process where terms and conditions can be displayed and consents captured. Member data can be stored against an accessible profile to run reports as required. Loyalty systems can be configured to update consents and delete data on demand.

Key insights

- Loyalty programs can play a key role in the collection of member data.

- Consumers are becoming increasingly aware that loyalty programs are collecting personal information about them, and that their data has a tangible value. They appear to be more willing to share their data with preferred brands and companies, but with the expectation they will be rewarded for sharing or that the data will be used to personalise and enhance their experience.

- The rise of walled garden data and the death of cookies increases the argument for why a company should design, implement and operate a best-practice loyalty program. Those companies without a loyalty program may be forced to invest more in expensive promotional tools to support their digital marketing campaigns.

- Member personal data is collected directly by loyalty programs via the join process, digital interactions, transactions, surveys, apps, virtual home assistants, social media and household patterns.

- Data may also be collected indirectly via data brokers, data exchanges and database generators.

- Around the world, governments are restricting privacy regulations to increase consumer protections regarding their personal data, placing compliance burdens on loyalty program operators.

Suggested reading

- Van Rijmenam, M., 2013, 'A Short History Of Big Data, Datafloq, https://datafloq.com/read/big-data-history/239

- Cleary, Gillian, 2018, 'Mobile Privacy: What Do Your Apps Know About You?', Symantec Corporation, https://www.symantec.com/blogs/threat-intelligence/mobile-privacy-apps

- Molitorisz, Sacha, 2018, 'It's time for data brokers to emerge from the shadows', IT News, https://www.itnews.com.au/news/its-time-for-data-brokers-to-emerge-from-the-shadows-488450

REPORTING & ANALYTICS

'We are surrounded by data, but starved for insights.'

~ Jay Baer

Focus areas

This chapter will address the following questions:

- How should companies treat the data collected by their loyalty program?

- What are the many ways data analysts and scientists interrogate loyalty program data?

- What are the main reporting categories companies should create from their loyalty program data?

CHAPTER 13 FOCUSED on the multiple ways loyalty program operators collect member data, both directly and indirectly.

Today, there is more data available than ever, but not all companies are structured to make best use of it. This chapter focuses on the best-practice analysis of loyalty program data.

The amount of data collected by loyalty programs globally is best viewed through the lens of Big Data. The term Big Data was coined in 2005 by Roger

Mougalas,[517] and refers to a large set of data that is almost impossible to manage and process using traditional business intelligence tools.

In 2011, McKinsey Global Institute (MGI)[518] calculated that a retailer using Big Data could increase its operating margin by more than 60 per cent, while the US healthcare sector could create more than US$300 billion in value every year, of which two-thirds would be in the form of reducing US healthcare expenditure by about 8 per cent.

Four years later, a McKinsey & Company report[519] acknowledged that the level of impact MGI foresaw had proved difficult to realise. While certain companies such as Google and Apple had made data analytics the foundation of their enterprise, most companies had failed to unlock the full benefits that Big Data promised. They identified a range of reasons; management not perceiving enough immediate financial impact to justify additional investments; frontline managers lacking understanding and hesitating to employ insights; existing organisational processes unable to accommodate advancements in analytics and automation; and a lack of organisational adaptation required to take advantage of opportunities.

While companies are increasingly making the required investments and organisational adjustment to take advantage of Big Data, many companies still struggle.

This chapter details the ways in which collected data is prepared, analysed and structured into reporting. This enables critical insights to be made

---

517 Van Rijmenam, M., 2013, 'A Short History Of Big Data', Datafloq, https://datafloq.com/read/big-data-history/239, accessed 25 May 2020.

518 McKinsey Global Institute, 2011, 'Big data: The next frontier for innovation, competition, and productivity', https://www.mckinsey.com/business-functions/mckinsey-digital/our-insights/big-data-the-next-frontier-for-innovation, accessed 15 June 2020.

519 McKinsey & Company, 2015, 'Marketing & Sales: Big Data, Analytics, and the Future of Marketing & Sales', https://www.mckinsey.com/~/media/McKinsey/Business%20Functions/Marketing%20and%20Sales/Our%20Insights/EBook%20Big%20data%20analytics%20and%20the%20future%20of%20marketing%20sales/Big-Data-eBook.ashx, accessed 15 June 2020.

accessible across the business to support strategic decision-making, including opportunities to evolve the loyalty program and customer experience to drive deeper engagement.

In many companies, much of this work is completed by data analysts or scientists using coded scripts or sophisticated software. Some companies configure loyalty platforms or business intelligence tools (BI tools) to automatically generate reporting or provide easy access to bespoke reports.

Increasingly, companies are employing machine learning/AI platforms to manage this task, with the advantage that it is better at detecting and fixing anomalies, matching data to individuals, and processing larger data sets. While true AI is expensive, and therefore the domain of larger companies, the costs are rapidly reducing as the technology becomes more mainstream via platforms such as Open AI's GPT-4[520].

In the not-to-distant future, it is anticipated almost all analytical and reporting work will be primarily AI-generated.

Data preparation

Before commencing data analysis, it is critical to structure the data in a database or data lake in a clean and accurate set. This involves:

- **Merging:** combining data from the multiple direct and indirect sources to create a unified dataset. A range of unique identifiers may be used to match the data to an individual member, such as membership number, email address or mobile phone number.

- **Cleansing:** identifying and addressing data quality issues, such as missing values, duplicate records, inconsistencies in data formats and obvious errors (e.g., john.smith@gmial.con instead of john.smith@gmail.com).

- **Transformation:** converting raw data into a format suitable for analysis, which may include aggregating data, creating new variables, or normalising data to a common scale.

---

520 OpenAI, https://openai.com/gpt-4, accessed 17 July 2023.

Many companies struggle with the cleaning and structuring of their data. It can take significant resources to address a poorly structured database, but without this investment, any downstream analysis will risk being inaccurate, incomplete or even misleading.

Establishing business objectives

To provide guidance to a data analyst or scientist on the types of analytical insights they should be generating, it is important for the company to establish clear business objectives.

For a loyalty program, this will include measuring KPI's such as:

- Member acquisition and activity rates

- Spend (cross-sell, upsell, share of wallet, repeat purchase or visit behaviour, basket size)

- Retention

- Advocacy and sentiment

- Referrals

- Household clustering

- Lifetime value

The targets for these KPIs will typically be agreed as part of the commercial modelling developed pre-launch or via annual business planning, making it relatively easy to construct a comprehensive brief for the data analyst or scientist.

The business may also seek development of different segmentation and cohort models using the rich data set generated by the loyalty program. While many companies develop a single, broad segmentation model for their customer base, best-practice involves developing different segments dependent on the problem being solved.

Major frequent flyer program

A major frequent flyer program wanted to better understand core member characteristics that would determine their propensity to redeem points on different reward options, including domestic flights, international flights, upgrades or reward store products.

Rather than running a one-off piece of analysis, the data scientists created a new model that segmented members based on a range of characteristics that correlated with redemption preferences, such as average earn rate, total points balance, how they primarily earned (i.e., via flying or via spending with partners), demographics, status tier, and previous redemption behaviour (including reward type and the time of year redemptions were typically processed).

Evaluation of the model validated it was impressively accurate in determining likely redemption behaviour. This enabled the frequent flyer program to improve the relevance of communications and offers provided to segments, including stimulating redemptions on particular rewards or at specific times. This was useful in both managing deferred liability and optimising margin earned on points (covered further in Chapter 16).

Exploratory Data Analysis and Feature Engineering

Exploratory Data Analysis involves initial interrogation of the dataset to identify patterns, trends, and relationships between variables. This work helps the data analyst or scientist generate hypotheses to inform further analysis.

Techniques used can include:

- **Summary statistics:** calculating measures of central tendency and dispersion to describe the distribution of variables.

- **Data visualisation:** creating charts and graphs, such as histograms, bar charts, and scatter plots, to visually explore the data.

- **Correlation analysis:** identifying relationships between variables using correlation coefficients or cross-tabulations.

Feature engineering involves creating new variables or modifying existing ones to better represent the underlying patterns in the data.

This may include:

- **Creating interaction variables:** combining two or more variables to create a new variable that captures their combined effect.

- **Feature selection:** identifying the most relevant variables for the analysis based on their importance, correlation with the target variable, or other criteria.

Model Selection and Evaluation

Model Selection involves the data analyst or scientist selecting the appropriate statistical or machine learning models based on the analysis objectives and the nature of the data.

Some common models used in loyalty program analysis include:

- **Clustering algorithms:** this may include k-means where similar data points are clustered together to discover underlying patterns.

- **Classification algorithms:** this may involve logistic regression or decision trees, for predicting churn or member behaviour.

- **Recommender systems:** this may include collaborative filtering or content-based filtering, for personalised marketing.

The types of analysis a data analyst or scientist may use models for include:

- **Predictive analytics:** using machine learning/AI algorithms and statistical models to identify patterns in member data and predict future behaviour. Data scientists can use predictive analytics to identify the factors that drive member engagement and disengagement, such as the time of day, the type of reward offered, or the messaging used to communicate with members.

- **Segmentation:** grouping members based on specific characteristics, such as demographics, behaviour, or preferences. By analysing member data within different segments, data scientists can identify the unique needs and preferences of each group, which can inform loyalty program design and communication strategies. For example, a loyalty program may offer different rewards and promotions to members in different age groups.

- **A/B testing:** testing multiple versions of a loyalty program component, such as a reward or communication, on a subset of members to see which version performs better. By testing different components, data scientists can identify which elements of a loyalty program drive engagement and optimise these elements to improve overall program effectiveness. AI platforms have emerged which can test hundreds or even thousands of different versions simultaneously.

- **Sentiment analysis:** using natural language processing techniques to analyse member feedback, such as reviews or social media posts, to identify positive or negative sentiment. By analysing member sentiment, data scientists can identify areas where the loyalty program is performing well and areas where it needs improvement.

- **Churn risk:** determining the likelihood that a particular member may switch to a competitor brand or just stop using a product or service altogether. This insight enables a company to pro-actively manage a high-risk to improve overall retention rates.

- **Cohort analysis:** grouping members based on a specific characteristic, such as the main way they earn or their location. By comparing engagement levels across different cohorts, data scientists can identify trends and patterns that can inform loyalty program design and communication strategies.

- **Network analysis:** analysing the relationships and interactions between members within a loyalty program. By analysing these interactions, data scientists can identify the key influencers and advocates within the loyalty program and use this information to develop targeted communication and engagement strategies.

After selecting and training the models, the data analyst or scientist will evaluate the quality of their performance using various metrics, such as accuracy, precision, recall, or mean squared error. This helps identify the most suitable model for the analysis and ensures its validity.

This will also involve interpretation of results as a precursor to developing reporting to share with key stakeholders.

Major telecommunications company

A major telecommunications company utilised an advanced churn risk model to score customers based on their likelihood they would transfer their service to a competitor at the end of their contract period.

The model utilised a range of criteria including number of services in the account, call centre contacts made, type of mobile handset and plan, demographics, tenure length, and more.

High churn risk customers were targeted with benefits such as the offer of a free phone for re-signing for an additional 24-month contract, bonus loyalty points, or monthly fees waived for a period.

While this approach made commercial sense, it was privately viewed within the company as paradoxically anti-loyalty, as truly loyal customers were likely to have a lower churn risk score, and hence provided with little or no benefits.

This type of approach also persists across other industries including electricity, gas, insurance and financial services.

Reporting

A key output of data analysis is various reports that can help the business make informed decisions to drive acquisition, spend, retention and advocacy.

Some of the main reports best-practice companies generate using member data include:

- **Customer segmentation:** provides insights into the different groups of members that exist within a company's customer base. By analysing loyalty program data, companies can identify distinct member segments based on purchasing behaviour, demographic information, and preferences. This report enables companies to develop targeted marketing campaigns, personalised promotions, and tailored communication strategies to engage each member segment effectively.

- **Member Lifetime Value (MLV):** understanding the lifetime value of a member is crucial for companies to allocate resources efficiently and maximise profitability. A MLV report provides an estimate of the net profit a business can expect from a member throughout their relationship. This report considers factors such as customer acquisition costs, retention rates, and spending habits, enabling companies to prioritise high-value members and tailor marketing efforts accordingly.

- **Product affinity and cross-selling:** identifies associations between different products or product categories, revealing potential sales opportunities. By analysing loyalty program data, companies can uncover patterns in purchasing behaviour, such as products frequently bought together. This report can be used to optimise product placement, identify cross-selling and upselling opportunities, and design bundle promotions to drive increased sales and member satisfaction.

- **Member satisfaction and feedback:** assesses overall member sentiment towards a business, its products, and services. By analysing loyalty program data, including member feedback, purchase frequency, redemption rates, and customer support interactions, companies can identify trends and potential areas of concern. This report provides insights to fine-tune products, services, and marketing campaigns to improve member satisfaction and foster long-term loyalty.

- **Churn risk:** helps identify members at risk of defection and implement proactive measures to retain them. By leveraging loyalty program data and employing predictive analytics, companies can estimate the likelihood of a member churning. This report allows companies to design targeted promotions, personalised communications, and tailored loyalty initiatives to retain high-risk members and reduce churn rates.

- **Geographic and location-based**: for companies with multiple locations, this offers valuable insights into regional preferences and purchasing habits. By analysing loyalty program data, companies can identify location-specific trends and patterns, such as popular products or services in each region. This report enables companies to optimise store layouts, product offerings, and promotional activities based on regional trends, leading to increased member engagement and higher sales in each location.

- **Campaign performance:** evaluates the effectiveness of marketing campaigns, promotions, and initiatives targeted at loyalty program members. By analysing KPIs such as conversion rates, redemption rates, and revenue generated, companies can assess the success of their campaigns and identify areas for improvement. This report allows companies to optimise their marketing strategies to drive member engagement, loyalty, and sales.

- **Member behaviour and trend analysis:** provides insights into emerging trends, preferences, and patterns within a company's customer base. By analysing loyalty program data, companies can identify changes in purchasing behaviour, product preferences, and engagement over time. This report enables companies to stay ahead of market trends and adapt their products, services, and marketing strategies accordingly.

Fashion retailer

A fashion retail company decided to redesign their loyalty program. Whenever a member spent over a certain threshold, they would receive a dollar denomination voucher generated directly from the receipt printer, a popular feature of the program.

As part of the redesign project, the company conducted analysis of the behaviour exhibited by members when they earned a voucher. The analysis identified that nearly 50 per cent of members who received a voucher chose to redeem it by making an additional transaction. This represented incremental revenue for the company, a desirable outcome.

Enlightened by the insight, the company included in the redesign the ability to target members with a wider range of instant offers when they transacted to further boost the incremental transactions.

This included surprise and delight vouchers offering bonus points, percentage discounts and credit vouchers to stimulate more incremental transactions.

The data analyst or scientist will also generate reporting that specifically measures the performance of the loyalty program.

This may include:

- **Loyalty program registrations:** tracks the growth of the loyalty program, providing insights into new member registration rates and the overall size of the program. By monitoring the program's growth, companies can assess the effectiveness of their acquisition strategies and identify trends or patterns that impact enrolment. This report can also be used to measure the success of promotional campaigns aimed at attracting new members and identify potential areas for improvement.

- **Member activity and engagement:** evaluates the level of member involvement in the loyalty program. This report analyses key metrics such as the frequency of transactions, redemption rates, value earned, and the use of member-exclusive promotions or benefits. By understanding how members engage with the program, companies can identify the most effective initiatives and develop strategies to enhance member participation further.

- **Redemption rates:** a vital indicator of the success of a loyalty program, as it measures the extent to which members are utilising the rewards and benefits offered. A redemption rate report provides insights into the percentage of members redeeming rewards, the types of rewards redeemed, and the average time to redemption.

By analysing this data, companies can evaluate the attractiveness of their rewards offerings, identify trends in redemption behaviour, and optimise their reward structures to encourage greater member engagement.

- **Status tier progression and regression:** measures the movement of members up and down tiers over time to determine whether the base is increasing engagement. This report will also include member utilisation of the benefits provided within the tiers

- **Recency Frequency Monetary Value (RFM):** segments members based on when they last spent, how much they spend and how often they spend. Companies can use this report to develop strategies to massage members towards segments where they spend more, more often.

- **Retention:** measures the extent to which the program is successful in retaining its members. This report tracks member churn rates, or the percentage of members who leave the program over a specific period. By analysing loyalty program data, companies can identify factors that contribute to member attrition and implement targeted retention strategies to minimise churn.

- **Communications and interactions:** assesses the effectiveness of communication channels and touchpoints used to engage loyalty program members. By analysing data such as email open rates, click-through rates, and response rates to personalised offers, companies can determine the success of their communication efforts and identify areas for improvement. The report also helps in understanding which channels resonate most with members, allowing companies to optimise their communication strategies and drive further engagement.

- **ROI and financial performance:** a critical aspect of any loyalty program is its ROI and overall financial performance. This report measures the revenue generated from loyalty program members compared to non-members, the cost of running the program, and the net profit attributable to the program. By monitoring the program's financial performance, companies can ensure that their loyalty initiatives are delivering tangible value and driving member engagement.

- **Member satisfaction and feedback:** measures how members perceive the loyalty program and its offerings. By analysing member feedback, satisfaction scores, and overall sentiment, companies can identify potential areas of concern and address them proactively. This report allows companies to continuously refine their loyalty program, ensuring it remains relevant and engaging for its members.

A list of detailed analytical and reporting insights specifically relevant to loyalty programs is provided in the Appendix.

Loyalty & Reward Co client

One Loyalty & Reward Co client operates a chain of restaurants. Their loyalty program provides a range of attractive benefits to registered members who are required to pay an annual subscription free.

The company utilises an RFM model to segment the member base. Stimulation campaigns are then applied to drive different behaviours. Low value customers are rewarded for spending more, while infrequent customers are enticed with attractive bonus offers if they visit again. High-value, repeat visit members are recognised and rewarded to ensure they maintain their behaviour.

By providing tailored messages and offers based on tracked behaviour, the company optimises their campaign spend in their quest to grow incremental revenue.

Foster a Data-driven Culture

A successful reporting and analytics strategy requires a company culture that values and prioritises the use of data in decision-making. This includes fostering a culture of curiosity, experimentation, and continuous learning.

Companies should strive to encourage cross-functional collaboration and ensure that relevant stakeholders have access to the necessary data and tools to make informed decisions.

Additionally, providing ongoing training and development opportunities will help to build data literacy and analytics skills across the company.

Large electronics retailer

A large electronics retailer with over 250 locations successfully developed a data-driven culture using their loyalty program consumer data. Their loyalty program has over 2 million members and offers customers personalised discounts, exclusive deals and access to launch events.

The company faced increased competition from e-commerce giants and other large electronics retailers. They needed to better understand their customers' preferences and buying behaviours to increase customer loyalty, drive sales, and remain competitive in the market.

The company chose to strategically leverage its loyalty program data to gain insights and drive business decisions. They centralised and integrated data from multiple sources, such as their point-of-sale system, mobile app and e-commerce platform, to create a comprehensive view of their members' shopping habits and preferences.

The company established a dedicated data analytics team, which collaborated with other departments, such as marketing, store operations, and supply chain, to implement a range of data-driven strategies:

- **Personalised marketing campaigns**: by analysing member purchase histories, the data analytics team developed segments based on preferences and spending habits. The marketing department then created highly targeted and personalised campaigns, resulting in increased engagement and repeat purchase behaviour.

- **Offer management**: the company ran extensive test-and-learn trials of different offers to identify which were most likely to stimulate members to either make an incremental transaction or spend more when they shopped. The loyalty team used this to optimise their budget allocation to drive profitable growth in spend.

- **Inventory management:** the company used loyalty program data to identify popular products and predict demand trends. This allowed them to optimise inventory levels, reduce stockouts, and minimise excess stock, ultimately increasing profitability.

- **Store layout optimisation**: the company analysed customer movement data from their mobile app and in-store Wi-Fi to identify high-traffic areas within the stores. They used this information to optimise store layouts, strategically placing popular products to maximise sales.

- **Customer service enhancement**: by identifying common member pain points and preferences through the analysis of loyalty program data, the company improved the customer service experience. They introduced a more efficient returns process and expanded their selection of popular and trending gadgets. They used this as a key differentiator from major competitors such as Amazon, knowing the in-store experience was a critical engagement most members still desired.

- **Reporting enablement**: the company implemented Power BI and built a wide range of reports to provide easy access to data-led insights to key stakeholders across the company. They also organised data-use training workshops for staff to train them how to access and apply the insights to strategic decision-making.

As a result of their data-driven strategy, the company realised increases in customer retention, average transaction value, and customer satisfaction scores while reducing their overall inventory carrying costs.

Key insights

- Companies must invest in cleaning and properly structuring their data if they intend to generate useable insights and reporting.

- Interrogation of data is a scientific practice that requires a refined skillset. Increasingly, this will be the domain of AI.

- Data is only useful when it is accessible. Companies should strive to provide easy access to quality reporting across the business, while developing a data-driven culture to support intelligent decision-making.

Suggested reading

- Aluri et al, 2018, 'Using machine learning to cocreate value through dynamic customer engagement in a brand loyalty program', Journal of Hospitality & Tourism Research, Vol. 43, No. 1, January 2019, 78–100.

- Lee et al, 2019, 'Decision Tree: Customer churn analysis for a loyalty program using data mining algorithm', Soft Computing in Data Science. SCDS 2019. Communications in Computer and Information Science, vol 1100. Springer, Singapore.

- Kimura, M, 2022, 'Customer segment transition through the customer loyalty program', Asia Pacific Journal of Marketing and Logistics.

- Ross-Smith, Mark, 2015, 'How big data is changing the way you fly', https://www.linkedin.com/pulse/how-big-data-changing-way-you-fly-mark-ross-smith/.

- Nguyen, P., & Solomon, L., 2017, 'Consumer data and the digital economy – Emerging issues in data collection, use and sharing', Consumer Policy Research Centre, http://cprc.org.au/wp-content/uploads/Full_Data_Report_A4_FIN.pdf.

CHAPTER 15

LOYALTY MARKETING AND OMNICHANNEL PERSONALISATION

This chapter was co-written by **Stacey Lyons** (Loyalty Director, Loyalty & Reward Co)

'Yowza… so I said back to that – ever so eloquently – 'the seeds of churn are planted early, my friend'… and then I went on to explain that churn is not an end-of-lifecycle issue, it's a LIFECYCLE issue; meaning it can be caused during – and happen at – anytime in their customer lifecycle.'

- Lincoln Murphy, 2013[521]

Focus areas

This chapter will address the following questions:

- What is member lifecycle management?
- What are the elements of a basic member lifecycle management model?
- What approaches are taken for more complex lifecycle management models?

---

521 Murphy, L., 2013, 'The Seeds of Churn are Planted Early', Sixteen Ventures, https://sixteenventures.com/seeds-of-churn, accessed 18 February 2020.

- How can data drive personalisation across member communications, offers and experiences?

- How can loyalty support the delivery of an omnichannel personalisation strategy with a 1:1 focus?

- How can a test and learn optimisation approach be used to improve communications, offers and experiences?

A SIGNIFICANT ADVANTAGE loyalty programs provide to marketers is the ability to track the lifecycle engagement of an individual member. If a repeat customer transacts with a company but does not belong to their loyalty program, it is challenging to determine that multiple transactions were made by a single individual. If the same customer is a loyalty program member, marketers can efficiently track their engagement, build a comprehensive member profile, and use that profile to develop a personalised communications strategy. This increases the likelihood they will feel recognised, rewarded, valued and appreciated, and continue to transact with the company.

A Member Lifecycle Management (MLM) structure is the core segmentation strategy used to manage the communications which loyalty program members receive. Lifecycle models recognise where a member is within their lifecycle and provide them with relevant communications and offers with the aim to transition them to a more ideal lifestage where they are more profitable to the company and more likely to evolve into advocates. Lifecycle models can be basic or complex, both of which are reviewed within this chapter.

More relevant experiences are increasingly being sought after by consumers[522] with personalisation becoming increasingly important in driving engagement, profitability and competitive differentiation. A loyalty program can play a key role in supporting the growth of a company's omnichannel personalisation strategy by developing a first-party single view of customer approach which supports 1:1 communications, offers and experiences.

---

522 Deloitte, 2017, 'Customer loyalty: A relationship, not just a scheme', The Deloitte Consumer review, p9, https://www2.deloitte.com/au/en/pages/consumer-business/articles/consumer-review.html, accessed 3 January 2020.

Approaches to omnichannel personalisation and test and learn optimisation are reviewed later in this chapter.

Basic member lifecycle management model

A basic member lifecycle management approach focuses on six key areas, as demonstrated in Figure 18. The presented member lifecycle management model is relatively simple, however the experience of Loyalty & Reward Co suggests many companies struggle to execute even at this level.

The approach involves using analytics to segment the member base, allowing the program operator to manage each segment in a way which attempts to transition them to a more ideal lifecycle segment. For example, a member in the Retention phase may be targeted with specific offers to reduce the likelihood they will churn, and by doing so transition them back to the Growth phase.

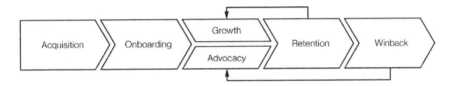

Figure 18: a basic member lifecycle management model.

Most models broadly follow a similar framework to the basic member lifecycle management model:

Acquisition

Acquiring new loyalty program members follows a similar conversion funnel pathway to product and service sales.

As discussed in Chapter 4, best-practice loyalty programs are simple to join.

Most loyalty programs require members to register by providing at a minimum their first name, surname, email address and a password, and to agree to standard terms and conditions and a privacy policy. Some loyalty programs may ask for more information in order to build a better profile of the member (e.g., mobile phone number, date of birth, postcode, gender, etc), while some may ask for less (e.g., just a mobile phone number).

Common ways in which members can join loyalty programs include:

- **In-store registration:** in many cases the member is provided with a plastic membership card, although digital cards which can be stored on mobile phones are becoming more prevalent. The member may be asked to fill in a paper form, with the details entered into a database at a later date, or a staff member may enter the details directly into a database as part of the check-out process. Alternatively, the member may be provided with a registration pack and directed to complete their registration online.

- **Online registration:** the new member accesses a web page to register for the loyalty program. This may be as a separate action or as part of an online shopping journey. The loyalty program may send the member a join pack in the mail containing a membership card and educational/promotional material, or they may be sent a link to a digital membership card.

- **App download:** the new member downloads an app and completes the registration process within the app. This will likely include them being asked to provide approval to receive notifications and track their location. They may also be asked to link a credit/debit card or bank account to their profile.

As discussed in Chapter 4, some loyalty programs provide only a single option for members to join, while others will present prospective members with a range of different channels and options in an attempt to increase the program's effectiveness in acquiring new members.

Apps are becoming increasingly prevalent as the main join channel, particularly in certain industries. An industry review by Loyalty & Reward Co identified that of the top 50 QSR's globally, 92 per cent offered a loyalty app.

Lastly, some loyalty programs provide join bonuses (46 per cent within the same top 50 QSR's examined) to entice the member to complete their registration, while also applying the endowed progress effect.

> ### Love Your Body™ Club
>
> The Body Shop have a global loyalty program called Love Your Body™ Club[523] available in 65 countries. Customers can join the Love Your Body™ Club simply by providing their first name, last name and email address in-store or online via web or app. Providing communication preferences, mobile phone number and date of birth are all optional and The Body Shop clearly explains how they will use each data point.
>
> If the member signs up in-store they are automatically registered as a club member and given a physical card. They already have an account set up for them and only need to create a password online using the same email address as their card.
>
> New members are immediately given 10% off their next purchase and can use the online account to update their preferences further, view their points balances and reward options.

Onboarding

The halo effect occurs when positive first impressions positively influence future judgments or ratings of unrelated factors.

Asch (1946)[524] conducted an experiment which identified that first impressions are more heavily weighted in forming an overall impression of a person than subsequent impressions. Subjects were read lists of adjectives about an individual. Half the subjects heard a list where the adjectives went from positive to negative, while the other half heard a list where the adjectives went from negative to positive. Asch determined that the order in which the adjectives

---

523 The Body Shop, https://www.thebodyshop.com/en-us/love-your-body-club, accessed 15 June 2023.

524 Asch, S. E., 1946, 'Forming impressions of personality', The Journal of Abnormal and Social Psychology, Vol 41, Iss 3, pp258–290.

were read influenced how the subject rated the individual, and that adjectives presented first had more influence on the rating than adjectives presented later. When positive traits were presented first, the participants rated the person more favourably and visa-versa. In other words, first impressions count.

Companies and loyalty program operators can harness the halo effect by developing excellent quality join and onboarding processes.

According to Murphy, 'The seeds of churn are planted early.' [525] This further stresses that the early days of a relationship with a new member are critical for educating them about the program and convincing them that they will be able to access value ongoing, thereby reducing the likelihood they will disengage immediately or over the longer term. Onboarding is one of the most critical strategies for increasing the lifetime value of members.

Best-practice program operators utilise sophisticated onboarding processes to educate and excite members about the program, encourage them to self-discover, start them on the pathway towards claiming their first reward, stimulate them to make a follow-up transaction earlier in the purchase cycle, and motivate them to share their positive experiences with family and friends.

Leading a new member towards claiming their first reward is critical for long-term engagement. For example, if a new member successfully registers, earns points for transacting, then redeems those points for a reward, they have worked through the earn and redeem cycle once, and hence understand how it works. Consequently, there will be an increased likelihood of further engagement with the program.

Onboarding approaches can incorporate a range of strategies to ensure they are sufficiently optimised and continue to evolve with changing consumer needs:

- **Optimised messaging**: the onboarding process is critical to ensure the new member feels adequately educated about the program and suitably rewarded for their early engagement. Best-practice program operators run focus groups and user testing with members to seek

---

525 Murphy, L., 2013, 'The Seeds of Churn are Planted Early', Sixteen Ventures, https://sixteenventures.com/seeds-of-churn, accessed 18 February 2020.

feedback on communication styles, thereby ensuring messaging is clear and understandable.

- **A/B testing**: optimisation of the onboarding process can be supported by A/B testing across communications frequency (how many communications), channels (eDM, DM, SMS, app, website and outbound call combinations), design, content, urgency (standard vs FOMO), and value (education vs offer).

- **Interactive walk-throughs**: for digital products, walk-throughs lead members through the product, introduce them to different elements, provide usage tips and help them establish their account to access value more quickly.

- **Preference centre**: establishing an approach to preference setting involves asking members to specify their product, communications, or interest-based preferences, encouraging them to share additional data. This enables program operators to tailor elements of the program with member desires to ensure they are provided with information genuinely relevant to them in a way that is palatable from the outset of their engagement. Preference centres have been shown to increase member engagement rates and reduce churn rates.

- **Dynamic communications**: a refined onboarding communications process will seamlessly transition the customer from Acquisition to Growth by acknowledging how they interact with each communication and adjusting accordingly using trigger and behavioural-based rules.

- **Progress trackers**: the early introduction of progress trackers can help communicate to the member that they are on the pathway to unlocking a reward, inspiring them to discover ways in which they can continue their progression.

- **Celebrations**: acknowledging that members have completed a key step can reinforce the behaviour and influence their motivation to continue engaging. This may be a pop-up, some bonus points, a badge or other low-cost reward.

Hungry Jacks

Hungry Jacks[526] have implemented a best-practice member onboarding experience which educates consumers, showcases value and stimulates desired behaviours (such as data sharing) across multiple channels. Each communication received by the authors across each channel is outlined below:

- App:
    - Pop-up request to 'Turn on Notifications'
    - 3x onboarding screens clearly outlining the three core benefits of the app; skip the queue, Shake and Win offers, exclusive app rewards (i.e., birthday offer)
    - Social sign in prompt
    - 'Get to know the app' landing screen which highlights how to navigate to the four key areas within the app
    - Personalisation front and centre of home screen: 'Hey <firstname>'
    - 'Turn on location services' pop-up prior to engaging in 'Shake and Win' game
- Push:
    - Personalised welcome message less than ten minutes after registration confirming the benefits of the app and stimulating data sharing: '<firstname>, welcome onboard! Shake and Win daily prizes and skip the queue, Plus complete your profile for a FREE Birthday Whopper'
    - 2 hours after registration, an additional exclusive offer received
- Email:
    - Personalised welcome message less than ten minutes after registration confirming the benefits of the app, Shake and

---

526 Hungry Jacks, https://www.hungryjacks.com.au/home, accessed 20 June 2023.

Win rules and stimulating data sharing (as per push) in greater detail

○ 2 hours after registration, an additional exclusive offer received

Growth

The primary ambition of a loyalty program is to generate deeper member engagement with the brand, leading to a greater share of wallet spend. The opportunities to stimulate incremental spend by members via well-designed loyalty programs are numerous.

Engaged members desire to earn more loyalty currency, so many programs promote bonus currency offers to stimulate member spend.

Within member benefits programs, members are motivated by discounts and value-adds. Therefore, the focus to grow engagement often revolves around highlighting the savings which members can access.

Status tier programs entice members to engage more to progress to higher tiers, and then encourage them to maintain their high engagement to continue to enjoy the benefits which come with their privileged status.

Best-practice loyalty programs deliver personalised communications to ensure members primarily receive offers which are relevant to them. They aim for a major proportion of their member base to be within the Growth segment to maximise program and company profitability.

Tesco Clubcard

While supermarket programs offer very low return on spend levels (generally 0.5 per cent of spend is returned in points), they successfully drive growth by running consistent bonus points campaigns (e.g., double and triple bonus points or fixed amount bonus points). This makes the customer feel they are being continuously well rewarded, despite the return only being increased to 1-1.5 per cent.

To capitalise on growth opportunities, Tesco[527] have leveraged the power of machine learning/AI technology to target their campaigns in an efficient and effective way, positively influencing purchase intervals and spend. The technology is used to automatically construct and send individualised communications with product promotions and specials to each member. They track member responses and evolve future communications to optimise engagement potential in an effort to continually keep members within the growth phase.

Opening up an increased number of compelling bonus points opportunities for members has also resulted in several news articles about Tesco being published which provide tips to readers on how they can boost their points balances, turning bloggers into program advocates and further supporting program growth.

Advocacy

Best-practice loyalty programs harness member advocacy to grow their program's brand awareness and perception, and to boost member acquisition and engagement.

According to Neilsen's global Trust in Advertising survey (2021),[528] 88 per cent of consumers said that they trusted recommendations from people they know above all other forms of marketing messaging.

A 2010 McKinsey study identified that word of mouth is the primary factor behind 20 to 50 per cent of all purchasing decisions. They defined word of mouth as either experiential (resulting from a consumer's direct experience with a product or service), consequential (when consumers directly exposed to traditional marketing campaigns pass on messages about them) or intentional (when marketers use celebrity endorsements to generate consumer discussion).

527 King, K., 2019, 'Using Artificial Intelligence in Marketing: How to Harness AI and Maintain the Competitive Edge', Kogan Page Ltd.

528 Neilsen, 2021, 'Global Trust in Advertising', https://www.nielsen.com/insights/2021/beyond-martech-building-trust-with-consumers-and-engaging-where-sentiment-is-high/ accessed 13 June 2023.

Loyalty programs can play a key role in all three areas, but particularly in experiential and consequential, by ensuring the product and service experience is exceptional and the marketing messaging is relevant and tailored.

Program operators can utilise a range of activities to stimulate advocacy:

- **Referral programs**: as detailed in Chapter 8, referral programs can be effective in incentivising and harnessing the member base to recruit new members.

- **Social media sharing**: programs can reward members with points, status credits or competition entries for following them, and sharing content on social media.

- **Recognition**: status tiers can harness social identity theory (as discussed in Chapter 5) by influencing the member to adopt their status within the program as part of their own self, motivating them to share their experience.

- **Reviews**: programs can invite satisfied and delighted members to write reviews which can be shared publicly.

- **Recommendations**: programs may reward existing members who provide recommendations which result in new business opportunities. This is especially true of B2B programs.

Dropbox

The Dropbox referral program resulted in exponential success with 3,900 per cent growth in a 15-month period.[529]

Since the Dropbox product offers storage space in the cloud, the referral program provides more storage space for referees. This perfectly structured reward means that referees are getting

---

529 Mengoulis, A., 2019, 'Dropbox grew 3900% with a simple referral program. Here's how!', Inside Viral Loops, https://viral-loops.com/blog/dropbox-grew-3900-simple-referral-program/, accessed 22 May 2020.

further benefits from the product enhancing their positive attitudes towards it.

Instead of 'Invite your friends', Dropbox framed the referral program as 'get more space' so referees are motivated to get something extra, taking advantage of the framing bias.

The invitation process is simple with the flexibility to invite contacts via Gmail, Facebook or copying a link, with referral statuses and rewards tracked and displayed to the member within their profile so they can see how much additional space they have earned (gamification).

Retention

Irrespective of how successful a loyalty program is, a percentage of the member base will at some stage show signs of disengagement. Best-practice loyalty programs monitor member engagement and detect members who are showing such signs. This may be via an identified lapse in transactions, a big 'cash-out' redemption event, a sudden increase in customer service enquiries, a reduction in account access, or even tracking showing engagement with competitors. These signs can often be a precursor to the member ceasing any involvement with the loyalty program altogether, enabling loyalty program operators to respond early with retention campaign activity.

A best-practice retention process involves two steps; firstly, developing a churn-risk score and secondly, developing automated retention campaigns triggered by high scores which indicate a risk that the member may churn.

Churn-risk score formulation is a machine learning/AI method which utilises data to indicate the likelihood that a member will churn within a predefined amount of time. A study by Kahn et al (2015)[530] used several terabytes of data from a large mobile phone network to build a model which they reported could predict whether a subscriber will churn with 89.4 per cent accuracy.

---

530 Khan, M. R., Manoj, J., Singh, A. & Blumenstock, J. E., 2015, 'Behavioral Modeling for Churn Prediction: Early Indicators and Accurate Predictors of Custom Defection and Loyalty', IEEE International Congress on Big Data, pp 677-680.

Developing a churn-risk score allows program operators to tailor communications to specific segments, measure member health and make strategic decisions to nudge member engagement. A churn-risk score can be automatically generated via a loyalty platform utilising a range of engagement metrics (e.g., frequency of engagement, recency of engagement, transaction patterns, changes in order type, seasonality or changes in points balance). If the churn-risk score increases past a certain threshold, automated trigger campaigns can target the member with an exclusive, tailored offer to arrest and reverse the decline.

As an example, a member may reduce their visit pattern over a three-month period, reduce their app usage and stop opening eDMs. These would all be obvious signs the member is reducing their engagement, but they may not be obvious to a busy marketing team managing millions of customers. A churn-risk score algorithm would calculate and identify the increase in the member's score, trigger an alert (the member now appears on a list as a potential churn risk) and automatically send the member a retention offer which is more valuable, and ideally more effective, than regular offers.

To offset the loss of a valuable member, the loyalty program operator will attempt to understand why the member is disengaging (e.g., ineffective campaigns, a service issue, strong competition) and rectify this if possible. Loyalty program operators may also try to tease out potential irritants which may trigger a disengagement event, implement analytics to track and identify affected members, and develop solid strategies to address the irritants. Examples of irritants include missing points, delayed flights, a poor service experience, a lack of available rewards or other issues where the member experience falls short of their expectations.

In that sense, a loyalty program team can expand their role into being advocates for a better customer experience across all areas of the business.

Qitaf

Saudi Telecom Qitaf rebuilt their loyalty program with the aim to deliver highly personalised and relevant engagement experiences in real-time.

Members can earn points when paying bills and buying products from Qitaf, but also earn across 170+ brand partners and 3,700 retail locations across Saudi Arabia. Earn transactions are processed instantly and customers receive notifications while shopping, detailing opportunities to earn more points.

In this tiered program, the primary goal is to reduce churn while upselling more products and services. Without revealing the exact data, the 2020 Loyalty Magazine Awards recognised that lower-tier members of the Qitaf program showed a material reduction in churn, while the higher tier members could access so many benefits that churn was almost at zero.

Customer lifetime value subsequently increased dramatically.[531]

Winback

Despite best efforts, a percentage of members will cease to engage with the program altogether.

One reason may be that they do not perceive they are accessing meaningful value. Another is they may not have attitudinal commitment to the brand. They may find interacting with the loyalty program to be too complicated and onerous. Or they may have changed their career path (e.g., different role) or life path (e.g., retirement) and no longer need to consume the product or service offered.

For example, frequent flyer programs often see complete disengagement from previously frequent travellers who no longer need to fly regularly, if at all. The airline can invest in incentivising the member to re-stimulate their

---

531 Ehredt, C., 'Innovators Break The Mould, At The 2020 Loyalty Magazine Awards', Currency Alliance, https://www.linkedin.com/pulse/innovators-break-mould-2020-loyalty-magazine-awards-charles-ehredt/, accessed 18 June 2020.

engagement, but it may not be successful if the member no longer has a demand for their product or services. Knowing why members have disengaged can help companies optimise usage of their retention and winback budget and will help maintain the health of the database.

Inevitably, a program will end up with a percentage of their member base who are completely inactive. Major coalition loyalty programs can have 30 to 60 per cent of their member base inactive. Even so, the opportunity still exists for the program to attempt to win a proportion of these members back using a variety of best-practice campaign approaches.

Kumar et al (2015)[532] ran a study which identified that the stronger the first-lifetime relationship with the firm, the more likely a customer was to accept a winback offer. One specific identifier was if the member had referred the company to family and friends in the past they were more likely to accept the offer. A service recovery experience which occurred when they were a customer was also positively associated with the likelihood of successful winback.

This research not only emphasises the key role loyalty programs can play when the member is a customer, but the value the program has provided even after the customer has churned.

One advantage a company has in trying to win back members is their data profile, as they can tailor communications and offers in a way that is not possible with non-members or potential new members.

The winback process generally starts with experimentation. Loyalty program operators may try a variety of different campaign approaches to determine which is most effective, with a strategy to stimulate a simple engagement from the member, then build on the successful response. Winback campaigns can be structured to run centrally and/or automatically from the loyalty platform. This may be a generic campaign to all target members on a monthly basis, or a tailored, targeted campaign run automatically utilising the dataset held against individual members.

---

532 Kumar, V., Bhagwat, Y. & Zhang, X., 2015, 'Regaining "Lost" Customers: The Predictive Power of First-Lifetime Behavior, the Reason for Defection, and the Nature of the Win-Back Offer', Journal of Marketing, Vol 79.

Audible

Audible[533] have a best-practice automated winback approach which consists of the following sequence (as observed by Loyalty & Reward Co):

- Three hours after unsubscribe: a list of personalised recommendations for audiobooks similar to those most recently enjoyed by the member (a subtle prompt to remind the member why they became a member in the first place).

- 60 days after unsubscribe: a 'get $8 off for 4 months' offer followed by a list of personalised recommendations (an incentive to nudge membership renewal with an offer that helps re-establish habitual membership rollover).

- 65 days after unsubscribe: a reminder to take advantage of the 'get $8 off for 4 months' offer, highlighting that the member will save 45 per cent off the normal price (a reinforcer).

- 90 days after unsubscribe: a new offer of 'come back for $2' together with a list of new benefits now available to the member since they last left (a more direct sell and more valuable offer with higher levels of instant gratification).

- 93 days after unsubscribe: a reminder to 'come back for $2' plus a 'free editors pick audiobook', together with a list of new benefits for being a member and personalised recommendations (a bonus benefit and harder sell).

- 102 days after unsubscribe: a 'hurry last days to come back for $2 plus a free editors pick audiobook' push, together with other popular book recommendations and personalised recommendations (creates urgency and generates FOMO).

- 104 days after unsubscribe: 'last chance to come back for $2 plus a free editors pick audiobook' push, together with other popular book recommendations and personalised recommendations (triggers loss aversion bias and FOMO).

---

533 Audible, https://www.audible.com, accessed 30 June 2020.

- 106 days after unsubscribe: 'come back and get $8 off for the first three months (the start of a new winback series with a different offer' based on member reactions to previous offers).

- 300 days after unsubscribe: 'come back and enjoy another free trial' (using the same mechanism which persuaded me to join the first time).

It is likely the sequence will continue to be adjusted and refined over time to further optimise the retention/winback approach.

More complex member lifecycle management models

More complex lifecycle management models typically involve developing granular member segments, which allows for better insight and communication approaches. For example:

- Members are segmented into Onboarding or Onboarded status.

- The Onboarding segment are categorised based on transactions made within a specified timeframe. This includes Retention (if they have only made a single transaction) or Winback (if they have not made any transactions), for which different engagement strategies can be triggered. If they make multiple transactions, they are reclassified as Onboarded.

- The Onboarded segment are categorised into tiers (e.g., Silver, Gold, Platinum) based on the total amount spent within a specified period. These tiers are generally covert, meaning the customer is unaware they have been segmented into a particular tier.

- The Onboarded tiers are further categorised based on the trajectory of total spend made within a specified timeframe. This includes Retention and Winback, as well as Growth (for increasing spend), Stable (for maintaining spend) and Reduced (for declining spend).

Variations of complex lifecycle models have also been developed. For example, Hu et al (2018)[534] proposed a two-part framework involving the development of a downward trend prediction process and the establishment of a methodology to identify the reasons why members may be in a downward trend. Their model identified at risk customers when they started to show a downward trend in engagement, often in an earlier stage of the customer lifecycle than the Retention phase. Their methodology utilised bad shopping experiences as inputs, which they then validate via A/B market testing. Their initial research demonstrated an 88.5 per cent incremental lift in spend.

Sawhney[535] developed an innovative lifecycle management approach titled CxDNA (customer experience DNA). The design involves two interwoven strands; Customer Action (the customer journey) and Organisational Action (the customer funnel management journey):

- **Customer Action**: focuses on optimising the Discover, Learn, Evaluate, Buy, Engage and Advocate stages of the member lifecycle.

- **Organisational Action**: focuses on Reach, Acquire, Convert, Develop, Retain and Bond stages.

By qualitatively and quantitatively detailing what each stage of the Customer Action strand looks like from a customer perspective, companies can clarify what information and content will be most useful for customers at each stage. Applying those insights across the Organisational Action strand will enable the company to identify the actions and processes needed to nurture customers across the lifecycle, ensuring the customer is at the centre of all actions taken.

The ultimate application of complex member lifecycle management involves machine learning/AI. As detailed in Chapter 11, such platforms can categorise members into a myriad of segments based on extensive transactional, demographic and psychographic information. Onboarding communications can be fully dynamic across multiple channels, automatically adjusting based

---

534 Hu, K., Li, Z.,Liu, Y., Cheng, L., Yang, Q. & Li, Y., 2018, 'A Framework in CRM Customer Lifecycle: Identify Downward Trend and Potential Issues Detection'.
535 Sawhney, M. S., 2019, 'It's Time to Radically Rethink the Customer Experience. Here's How to Get Started.', Kellogg Insight, Kellogg School Of Management at Northwestern University.

on how the member responds. Growth communications can be tailored specifically to the individual with the aim of delivering the right message to the right member at the right time, while reducing overall marketing spend. Retention and Winback communications can be triggered at the optimal time with the right offer to maximise impact at minimal cost.

If set-up and executed optimally, Machine learning/AI allows each individual member to be supported by their own tailored, multi-faceted lifecycle management strategy. This is a core technology foundation for the delivery of Digital EQ, the ability to anticipate and recognise customer sentiment and deliver a digitally enabled response which optimises the customer experience in real time, serving to build a deeper attitudinal commitment. [536]

Omnichannel personalisation

According to a McKinsey study, post Covid-19, personalisation is now a consumer expectation, making it a critical success factor for all companies. Research shows that 71 per cent of consumers expect personalisation, 76 per cent get frustrated when they do not receive it, 72 per cent expect to be recognised as individuals, 78 per cent are more likely to make repeat purchases from companies that personalise and 78 per cent and more likely to refer companies that personalise to families and friends.[537] Companies that personalise also grow at faster rates and generate more revenue[538] with some studies citing revenue increases of 5–15 per cent directly attributed to successful implementation of personalisation.

In today's digital world, another area which has gained significant attention is omnichannel personalisation. This involves the delivery of a seamless and personalised experience across any channel by which the member chooses to engage, delivering a cohesive and consistent member experience, irrespective of the touchpoint.

---

536 Savransky, M., 2020, 'The Power of Digital EQ', Loyalty & Reward Co, http://loyaltyrewardco.com/the-power-of-digital-eq/ accessed 13 June 2023.

537 McKinsey, Nov 2021, 'The value of getting personalization right – or wrong – is multiplying', accessed 11 April 2023.

538 McKinsey, Nov 2021, 'The value of getting personalization right – or wrong – is multiplying', accessed 11 April 2023.

By integrating customer data from various channels, program operators can identify patterns and trends, which can be used to optimise marketing strategies and deliver highly personalised content.

A growing body of evidence indicates that members who shop via multiple channels tend to spend more, shop more frequently and generate higher revenue for brands:

- Verhoef et al. (2015) found that multichannel customers spend more than single-channel customers, with each additional channel used leading to a higher purchase amount.[539]

- Deloitte (2020) published a study citing that omnichannel customers are more likely to make repeat purchases and have a 30 per cent higher lifetime value compared to single-channel shoppers.[540]

- Accenture (2018) concluded that 91 per cent of consumers are more likely to shop with brands that recognise, remember, and provide relevant offers and recommendations across channels.

- McKinsey & Company (2018) reported that omni-channel customers spend an average of 20-40 per cent more than single channel customers[541]

- Symphony RetailAI (2021) indicated that omni-channel customers shop more frequently and spend up to 20 per cent more than in-store only customers.[542]

---

539 Verhoef, P. C., Kannan, P. K., & Inman, J. J. (2015). From multi-channel retailing to omni-channel retailing: Introduction to the special issue on multi-channel retailing. Journal of Retailing, 91(2), 174-181, https://www.researchgate.net/publication/274404553_From_Multi-Channel_Retailing_to_Omni-Channel_Retailing, accessed 22 May 2023.

540 Deloitte. (2020). The omnichannel opportunity: Unlocking the power of the connected consumer, https://www2.deloitte.com/uk/en/pages/consumer-business/articles/unlocking-the-power-of-the-connected-consumer.html, accessed 22 May 2023.

541 McKinsey, 2018, 'Omnichannel Apparel Survey', accessed 22 May 2023.

542 Symphony RetailAI., 2021, analysis of Q1 2021 shopper data, https://www.globenewswire.com/fr/news-release/2021/06/23/2251987/0/en/

Therefore, to thrive in today's customer-centric market, brands must prioritise the delivery of seamless and personalised experiences across all touchpoints, harnessing the full potential of omnichannel personalisation to realise greater engagement, frequency and revenue from members.

A loyalty program can play a key role in driving a company's approach to omnichannel personalisation by incentivising and reinforcing the following:

1. Account creation and profile set-up

2. Data and preference sharing

3. Member identification across online and offline experiences (gaining a single view of customer)

This allows programs to drive omnichannel personalisation across communications, offers and experiences, each of which are discussed in detail below.

Personalisation of _communications_

The increasing availability of digitised data makes personalisation of marketing communications easier and more affordable to companies (Chung et al, 2009[543]; Wedel & Kannan, 2016[544]). Personalised marketing messages can provide consumers with reduced cognitive overload (Ansari & Mela, 2003[545])

Omnichannel-Grocery-Shoppers-Spend-Up-to-20-More.html, accessed 22 May 2023.

543 Chung, T. S., Rust, R. T., & Wedel, M. (2009). My Mobile Music: an adaptive personalization system for Digital Audio Players. Marketing Science, 28(1), 52–68, cited in Zhang, J., Liu-Thompkins., 2023, 'Personalized email marketing in loyalty programs: The role of multidimensional construal levels', Journal of the Academy of Marketing Science.

544 Wedel, M., & Kannan, P. K. (2016). Marketing analytics for data-rich environments. Journal of Marketing, 80(6), 97–121. https://doi.org/10.1509/jm.15.0413, cited in Zhang, J., Liu-Thompkins., 2023, 'Personalized email marketing in loyalty programs: The role of multidimensional construal levels', Journal of the Academy of Marketing Science.

545 Ansari, A., & Mela, C. F. (2003). E-customization. Journal of Marketing Research, 40(2), 131–145.

and a better preference match (Vesanen, 2007[546]). These in turn translate into higher customer satisfaction and loyalty (Rust & Chung, 2006[547]). When personalisation is done properly, the effectiveness of a marketing message can double that of non-personalised versions (Tucker, 2014).[548]

In the context of loyalty programs, personalised marketing communications play a crucial role for several reasons. Firstly, these communications contribute to the objective of fostering long-term relationships between customers and firms, ultimately enhancing customer loyalty (Kumar & Shah, 2004; Wagner et al., 2009[549]). By tailoring messages to individual customers, loyalty programs can directly show customers they know them, understand them and create meaning for them beyond the transaction, fostering long term mutually beneficial relationships.

Secondly, loyalty programs provide companies with a wealth of customer data, enabling them to design tailored and effective personalised messages. By leveraging all of the data held about an individual, messages can be crafted in a way that resonate with members on a personal level, increasing the likelihood of a positive response[550].

---

546 Vesanen, J. (2007). What is personalization? A conceptual framework. European Journal of Marketing, 41(5/6), 409–418, cited in Zhang, J., Liu-Thompkins., 2023, 'Personalized email marketing in loyalty programs: The role of multidimensional construal levels', Journal of the Academy of Marketing Science.

547 Rust, R. T., & Chung, T. S. (2006). Marketing models of service and relationships. Marketing Science, 25(6), 560–580, cited in Zhang, J., Liu-Thompkins., 2023, 'Personalized email marketing in loyalty programs: The role of multidimensional construal levels', Journal of the Academy of Marketing Science.

548 Zhang, J., Liu-Thompkins., 2023, 'Personalized email marketing in loyalty programs: The role of multidimensional construal levels', Journal of the Academy of Marketing Science.

549 Kumar, V., & Shah, D. (2004). Building and sustaining profitable customer loyalty for the 21st century. Journal of Retailing, 80(4), 317–329, cited in Zhang, J., Liu-Thompkins., 2023, 'Personalized email marketing in loyalty programs: The role of multidimensional construal levels', Journal of the Academy of Marketing Science.

550 Forbes, 2020, 50 Stats Showing The Power Of Personalization, https://www.forbes.com/sites/blakemorgan/2020/02/18/50-stats-showing-the-power-of-personalization/?sh=8b875972a942, accessed 23 May 2023.

Finally, personalisation within the loyalty program context can address the 'personalisation paradox', which refers to the challenge of increasing message effectiveness while simultaneously respecting consumer privacy concerns (Aguirre et al., 2015; Goldfarb & Tucker, 2012; Tucker, 2012).[551] Loyalty program members typically exhibit higher levels of trust in the company and are more willing to share personal information, allowing for more personalised communication (Awad & Krishnan, 2006; Stathopoulou & Balabanis, 2016).[552] By delivering personalised messages that are tailored to individual preferences and needs, loyalty programs can strike a balance between effective communication and respecting consumer privacy.

Zhang and Liu-Thompkins (2023) conducted research highlighting the importance of program operators considering both tier level and goal distance in designing personalised marketing communications within loyalty programs. The research examined the relative effectiveness of cognitive (rational messages) and affective appeals (emotional messages) within email communications through controlled experiments and a field study using email campaign data from an airline loyalty program. The study revealed that lower-tier consumers who are close to achieving their goals respond better to affective appeals, whereas the opposite is true for other consumers.[553]

---

551 Zhang, J., Liu-Thompkins., 2023, 'Personalized email marketing in loyalty programs: The role of multidimensional construal levels', Journal of the Academy of Marketing Science, https://link.springer.com/epdf/10.1007/s11747-023-00927-5?sharing_token=dF5nkIvbkdPxHRuAnCeHm_e4RwlQNchNByi7wbcMAY6EW-Pz5yxWxttUSwSDxZf_fzIf-FMhMUS7YyfAqrTgTTaRq_9X_bbDfEDeTT-gUToPiXoZziojr4ysMHOP3bULwxkZl-OqdETDM_fBM9KVTpz1kvwf4midZUI-ulfhnXaOtI, accessed 5 May 2023.

552 Aguirre, E., Mahr, D., Grewal, D., de Ruyter, K., & Wetzels, M. (2015). Unraveling the personalization paradox: The effect of information collection and trust-building strategies on online advertisement effectiveness. Journal of Retailing, 91(1), 34-49, https://www.sciencedirect.com/science/article/abs/pii/S0022435914000669, accessed 23 May 2023.

553 Zhang, J., Liu-Thompkins., 2023, 'Personalized email marketing in loyalty programs: The role of multidimensional construal levels', Journal of the Academy of Marketing Science, https://link.springer.com/epdf/10.1007/s11747-023-00927-5?sharing_token=dF5nkIvbkdPxHRuAnCeHm_e4RwlQNchNByi7wbcMAY6EW-Pz5yxWxttUSwSDxZf_fzIf-FMhMUS7YyfAqrTgTTaRq_9X_bbDfEDeTT-

Overall, personalised marketing communications in loyalty programs are crucial for building strong customer relationships, utilising customer data effectively, addressing the personalisation paradox, and driving more impactful marketing outcomes.

myWalgreens

myWalgreens[554] allow members to earn and redeem Walgreens Cash on all purchases via any channel they choose to shop i.e., in-store, on Walgreens.com or via the mobile app.

Customers can easily join and identify as members of the program via the website, app or at checkout using their email address or phone number, ZIP code and name.

Members automatically unlock special sale prices and personalised 'your weekly ad' deals on preferred products delivered via their preferred channel. Members can also complete personal health challenges, track their progress or sync a health device to earn additional Walgreens Cash.

Other member benefits include reduced wait time on drive-thru, curbside or in-store pickup. If delivery is the preferred option, members can access one-hour delivery with no order minimum.

Signing up for the myWalgreens credit card unlocks additional opportunities to earn rewards and extends the experience outside of Walgreens to things like doctor's visits, gym memberships, counselling services and more.

gUToPiXoZziojr4ysMHOP3bULwxkZl-OqdETDM_fBM9KVTpz1kvwf4midZUI-ulfhnXaOtl, accessed 5 May 2023.

554 myWalgreens, https://www.walgreens.com/topic/promotion/mywalgreens.jsp, accessed 15 June 2023.

Personalisation of _offers_

The Covid-19 pandemic hugely disrupted consumers' purchasing habits, leading them to try new sellers and brands while reevaluating the value they receive[555]. This unprecedented shift in consumer behaviour presented loyalty programs with a unique opportunity to reset their promotional strategies, making personalisation an imperative. As brands adapt to the changing landscape, academic research studies support the notion that delivering personalised, hyper targeted, 1:1 offers can yield substantial benefits.

Personalised offers are further enhanced by loyalty programs based on the purchase and browsing data they capture from all members. This gives companies a unique edge when it comes to cross-selling products by showing members products they may be interested in based on other members who have made similar purchases or who may have similar profiles. It also gives consumers the social proof that others are buying the same products or taking up the same offers.

Analysis by Boston Consulting Group (BCG) found that redirecting 25 per cent of mass promotion spending to personalised offers would increase ROI by 200 per cent, leading to a top-line growth opportunity of more than $70 billion annually.[556]

BCG say that in order to maximise value from the shift to personalised offers, retailers should follow three imperatives:

1. Integrate offers seamlessly into the experience
2. Use off-the shelf technology to automate offers (i.e., which can use dynamic templates connected to content management systems to generate offer variants at scale, then target, deploy, measure and optimise)

---

555 BCG., 2021, The $70 Billion Prize in Personalized Offers', https://www.bcg.com/publications/2021/personalized-offers-have-a-potential-70-billion-dollar-growth-opportunity, accessed 22 May 2023.

556 BCG., 2021, The $70 Billion Prize in Personalized Offers', https://www.bcg.com/publications/2021/personalized-offers-have-a-potential-70-billion-dollar-growth-opportunity, accessed 22 May 2023.

3. Operate using agile teams and a culture of controlled risk-taking to allow for rapid learnings[557]

In a study by McKinsey, when asked to rate the importance of receiving personalised content, 65 per cent of respondents reported that receiving targeted offers and promotions was either important, very important or extremely important.[558]

An additional study by Salesforce confirmed that consumers are 2.1x more likely to view personalised offers as important versus unimportant.[559]

In an era of rising cost of living pressures globally, de-standardising the promotional approach to offer consumers the right offer at the right time will be effective and appreciated. Leading programs such as Starbucks Rewards, Tesco Club and others who have redirected their investments to personalised offers are already seeing the benefits across categories.[560]

7-Eleven

7-Eleven have variations of their loyalty program in different global markets for example, 7Rewards in the US[561], My 7-Eleven in Australia[562] and CliQQ in the Philippines[563]. The program frameworks differ as well by earning points, digital stamps and coupons.

---

557 BCG., 2021, 'The $70 Billion Prize in Personalized Offers', https://www.bcg.com/publications/2021/personalized-offers-have-a-potential-70-billion-dollar-growth-opportunity, accessed 22 May 2023.

558 McKinsey, Nov 2021, 'The value of getting personalization right – or wrong – is multiplying', accessed 11 April 2023.

559 Salesforce, What Are Customer Expectations, and How Have They Changed?, https://www.salesforce.com/resources/articles/customer-expectations/?sfdc-redirect=369, accessed 23 May 2023.

560 Leading retailers who that have redirected their investments to personalised offers are now seeing the benefits across categories.

561 7Rewards US, https://www.7-eleven.com/7rewards, accessed 14 June 2023.

562 My 7-Eleven Australia, https://www.7eleven.com.au/my-7-eleven.html, accessed 14 June 2023.

563 CliQQ Philippines, https://www.cliqq.net/, accessed 14 June 2023.

What is consistent it the use of personalised offers and rewards to incentivise repeat visitation. The My 7-Eleven program in Australia does this particularly well. Members of the program provide basic demographic information when signing up via the app. Then for every 7 visits to a 7-Eleven members unlock a personalised reward to redeem in-store.

7-Eleven have set up a personalisation program[564] to tailor online and mobile experiences underpinned by the use of their customer data platform. This allows members to receive personalised offers that change daily. These range from discounts, two-for-one offers, combo offers and more. Personalised offers are further enhanced with geolocation, time and purchase behaviour data.

Personalisation of _experiences_

Today, a common foundation for experience lies in Pine and Gilmore's (1998)[565] experience economy, which pertains to the era of competitive advantage arising from the staging unique consumer experiences.

Brand interactions provide consumers a rich source of experience (Schmitt, 1999) and with the loyalty and marketing industries now inundated with technological advancements across machine learning/AI (i.e., Campbell et al., 2020) and Augmented Reality (i.e., Romano et al., 2020) and other alternatives detailed in Chapter 11, this provides program operators with an enhanced opportunity to facilitate more personalised brand experiences (Ramaseshan and Stein, 2014).[566]

---

564 My 7-Eleven Australia, https://www.7eleven.com.au/my-7-eleven.html, accessed 14 June 2023.

565 Pine, B. J., & Gilmore, J. H. (2011). The experience economy: Past, present, and future. Journal of the Academy of Marketing Science, 39(2), 286-306. DOI: 10.1007/s11747-010-0217-2.

566 Pallant, J. L., Karpen, I. O., & Sands, S. J. (2022). What drives consumers to customize products? The mediating role of brand experience, https://www.sciencedirect.com/science/article/abs/pii/S0969698921003398?dgcid=coauthor, accessed 23 May 2023.

With respect to loyalty program members, new research indicates 80 per cent of consumers are more likely to make a purchase when brands offer personalised experiences.[567] It is therefore critically important to provide personalised and relevant content which understands the intent around why a member visited and what they are interested in.[568]

Research has also found that the process of incorporating customisation across the member experience can increase consumer perception of symbolic value (Pallant et al., 2020[569]). Prior research has established an important reason consumers purchase specific brands is not only for their functional characteristics, but for the symbolic value they bring to the consumer (Kim and Sung, 2013; Sung et al., 2015[570]). This can be so strong that symbolic attributes of the brand often become the primary reason for purchase (Coelho et al., 2020[571]). As such, consumers invest in brands that allow them to build and express their self-concept, with personalisation and customisation across the journey an enabler.

---

567 Epsilon, 2018, New Epsilon research indicates 80% of consumers are more likely to make a purchase when brands offer personalized experiences, https://www.epsilon.com/us/about-us/pressroom/new-epsilon-research-indicates-80-of-consumers-are-more-likely-to-make-a-purchase-when-brands-offer-personalized-experiences, accessed 22 May 2023.

568 Wertz., 2023, Forbes, How Companies Can Balance Personalization And Privacy, https://www.forbes.com/sites/jiawertz/2023/01/31/how-companies-can-balance-personalization-and-privacy/?sh=4fe747ff2155, accessed 22 May 2023.

569 Pallant et al, 2020, Product customization: a profile of consumer demand, Journal of Retailing and Consumer Services, https://www.sciencedirect.com/science/article/abs/pii/S0969698919311609, accessed 18 July 2023.

570 Kim and Sung, 2013; Sung et al., 2015, cited in Pallant, J. L., Karpen, I. O., & Sands, S. J. (2022). What drives consumers to customize products? The mediating role of brand experience, https://www.sciencedirect.com/science/article/abs/pii/S0969698921003398?dgcid=coauthor, accessed 23 May 2023.

571 Coelho et al., 2020, cited in Pallant, J. L., Karpen, I. O., & Sands, S. J. (2022). What drives consumers to customize products? The mediating role of brand experience, https://www.sciencedirect.com/science/article/abs/pii/S0969698921003398?dgcid=coauthor, accessed 23 May 2023.

Nike

Nike's loyalty program is under the banner of Nike Membership. Nike have cleverly used their membership program to increase direct to consumer sales and build up their eCommerce channel. At the end of 2022, Nike posted digital growth of 34 per cent largely attributed to the membership program. Boasting 160 million active members the program is a best-practice example of personalised experiences.[572]

Nike members get access to shopping offers and discounts both online and in-store with Nike's CEO stating that 50 per cent of store demand comes from members. Members perks include free shipping, exclusive styles, invites to events and access to workouts. Members can also engage through a series of apps offered by Nike, including Nike Training Club, Nike Run Club and the SNKRS App.

The highly personalised digital experience across the Nike ecosystem makes it easy to purchase as well as share lifestyle and product preferences that Nike in turn use to inform new products, line planning and personalised member experiences.

Test and learn optimisation

A test and learn optimisation approach holds immense potential in improving the effectiveness of loyalty program communications, offers, and experiences. By employing an iterative testing and measurement process, companies can refine their strategies based on customer response and feedback, leading to enhanced customer engagement, satisfaction, and loyalty.

The test and learn optimisation process followed by Loyalty & Reward Co for clients involves:

- **Develop hypotheses:** identify areas within the loyalty program that can be improved, such as customer segmentation, promotional offers,

---

572 Backbock., S, 2022, The Current, 'Nike's membership program is the 'engine' of its DTC strategy', https://thecurrent.media/nike-membership-dtc, accessed 15 June 2023.

offer expiry dates, communication channels, or member experiences. Formulate hypotheses on how these aspects can be enhanced and establish specific metrics to measure the impact of proposed changes.

- **Design experiments:** design controlled experiments, such as A/B or multivariate tests, to compare the performance of different strategies, offers, expiry dates or communication tactics. Ensure that experiments are well-designed, with a representative sample size, appropriate control groups, and sufficient duration to obtain reliable results.

- **Execute tests:** launch the experiments concurrently and independently to minimise external factors' influence. Monitor the performance of each test group and collect data on defined metrics, such as open rates, click-through rates, conversion rates, or customer satisfaction scores.

- **Analyse results:** analyse the collected data to evaluate the effectiveness of each tested strategy, offer, or communication tactic. Use statistical methods to validate results, ensuring that observed differences between test groups are significant and not due to random chance.

- **Implement learnings:** based on the analysis, identify the most effective strategies and tactics that drive customer engagement, satisfaction, and loyalty. Implement the successful variations across the loyalty program's communications, offers, and experiences to optimise overall performance.

- **Continuous improvement:** continuously monitor loyalty program performance, leveraging customer feedback and data analysis to identify further areas for improvement. Foster a culture of ongoing experimentation and learning to ensure the loyalty program remains relevant, engaging, and effective in driving customer loyalty and retention.

Key insights

- A member lifecycle management model involves using analytics to segment a member database into lifecycle stages, allowing the program operator to manage members in a way which makes them feel recognised, rewarded, valued and appreciated, increasing the likelihood they will continue transacting with the company.

- A basic member lifecycle management model includes acquisition, onboarding, growth, advocacy, retention and winback stages, with each stage requiring different communications strategies.

- More complex lifecycle management models may involve developing granular member segments or trend prediction methodology which allows for better insight and more effective communications.

- The ultimate application of complex member lifecycle management involves machine learning/AI, which categorises members into a myriad of segments based on extensive transactional, demographic and psychographic information. This approach allows each individual member to be supported by their own tailored, multi-faceted lifecycle management strategy.

- A growing body of evidence indicates that members who shop via multiple channels tend to spend more, shop more frequently and generate higher revenue for brands.

- A loyalty program can play a key role in driving a company's approach to omnichannel personalisation across communications, offers and experiences.

- Consumers invest in brands that allow them to build and express their self-concept, with personalisation and customisation across the journey an enabler.

- An iterative test and learn optimisation approach holds immense potential in improving the effectiveness of loyalty program communications, offers, and experiences.

Suggested reading

- Murphy, Lincoln, 2013, 'The Seeds of Churn are Planted Early', Sixteen Ventures, https://sixteenventures.com/seeds-of-churn

- Mengoulis, A., 2019, 'Dropbox grew 3900% with a simple referral program. Here's how!', Inside Viral Loops, https://viral-loops.com/blog/dropbox-grew-3900-simple-referral-program/

- Kumar, V. & Bhagwat, Yashoda & Zhang, Xi., 2015, 'Regaining 'Lost' Customers: The Predictive Power of First-Lifetime Behavior, the Reason for Defection, and the Nature of the Win-Back Offer', Journal of Marketing, Vol 79.

- Hu, Kun & Li, Zhe & Liu, Ying & Cheng, Luyin & Yang, Qi & Li, Yan, 2018, 'A Framework in CRM Customer Lifecycle: Identify Downward Trend and Potential Issues Detection'.

- Mohanbir S. Sawhney, 2019, 'It's Time to Radically Rethink the Customer Experience. Here's How to Get Started', Kellogg Insight, Kellogg School Of Management at Northwestern University.

- McKinsey, Nov 2021, 'The value of getting personalization right – or wrong – is multiplying', accessed 11 April 2023

- Zhang, J., Liu-Thompkins., 2023, 'Personalized email marketing in loyalty programs: The role of multidimensional construal levels', Journal of the Academy of Marketing Science, https://link.springer.com/epdf/10.1007/s11747-023-00927-5?sharing_token=dF5nkIvbkdPxHRuAnCeHm_e4RwlQNchNByi7wbcMAY6EWPz5yxWxttUSwSDxZf_fzIf-FMhMUS7YyfAqrTgTTaRq_9X_bbDfEDeTTgUToPiXoZziojr4ysMHOP3bULwxkZl-OqdETDM_fBM9KVTpz1kvwf4midZUIulfhnXaOtl

- BCG., 2021, The $70 Billion Prize in Personalized Offers', https://www.bcg.com/publications/2021/personalized-offers-have-a-potential-70-billion-dollar-growth-opportunity

- Symphony RetailAI., 2021, analysis of Q1 2021 shopper data, https://www.globenewswire.com/fr/news-release/2021/06/23/2251987/0/en/Omnichannel-Grocery-Shoppers-Spend-Up-to-20-More.html

CHAPTER 16

COMMERCIAL BENEFITS
AND CONSIDERATIONS

This chapter was co-written by **Ryan De Boer** (CFO, Loyalty & Reward Co)

'The global loyalty program market is valued at $180 billion in 2022 (estimate). The market is forecasted to grow at a CAGR of 5–6 percent to $179–191 billion between 2022 and 2026 (forecast).'

- Loyalty Programs Market Intelligence report, Beroe Inc [573]

Focus areas

This chapter will address the following questions:

- How do loyalty programs generate value for companies?

- What accounting considerations are required when developing or managing a loyalty program, including the importance of fair value and how this is calculated?

- How do the commercial benefits of a loyalty currency differ compared to discounts or cashbacks?

- What is the typical investment required to launch and operate a loyalty program?

- How do you create a business case to support investment in loyalty?

---

573 Bereo Inc https://www.beroeinc.com/category-intelligence/loyalty-programs-market/ accessed 12 July 2023

LOYALTY PROGRAMS HAVE grown from merely rewards-based marketing tactics and cost centres to sophisticated data, marketing and customer engagement powerhouses. They are fundamental to a company's strategy, driving growth across all markets and most industries globally, and in some cases have become substantial profit centres.

The ways in which loyalty programs typically generate value for a business can be classified into five categories:

1. Behavioural changes
2. Cost savings and operating efficiencies
3. Strategic decision-making benefits
4. Third-party monetisation
5. Other monetisation opportunities

Each of these will be explored in turn:

1. Behavioural changes

As defined in Chapter 1, loyalty programs are desirable behaviour stimulation programs. There are multiple ways a company can influence member behaviours via a loyalty program to generate incremental acquisition, spend, retention and advocacy.

Depending on the company's core objectives, some of these areas may be more important than others. For example, within the telecommunications industry improving retention can be more important than spend stimulation as customers have already committed to a fixed spend each month. For supermarkets, spend stimulation can be more important as members may already be shopping habitually. Understanding the priority objectives is an important part of the design process as it should influence which program framework (or combination of frameworks) is adopted.

Incremental acquisition

Acquiring new customers generates incremental revenue but it can be expensive. Most companies associate two metrics related to acquisition:

- **ARPNC:** average revenue per new customer, or how much each new customer contributes to company revenue stream on average over a defined period of time.

- **CPA:** cost per acquisition, or the amount of money spent to acquire one new customer on average.

Loyalty programs are an excellent strategic tool to grow ARPNC while reducing CPA.

As detailed in Chapter 15, program operators attempt ARPNC growth by generating early engagement from the new customer via join bonuses, utilising sophisticated onboarding processes to educate and excite them about program benefits, supporting them to earn and claim their first reward early, stimulating them to make a follow-up transaction as soon as possible, and providing ongoing rewards and recognition.

Best-practice loyalty programs reward members with benefits that act as competitive differentiators which can stimulate acquisition. Non-customers may switch to the brand to take advantage of those desirable benefits. Unlike price discounts, which can be easy for competitors to replicate, unique loyalty benefits that appeal to a target audience can drive more sustained acquisitions, and even help to reduce CPA.

Loyalty programs which incorporate a referral feature, where members invite family and friends to join to earn a reward, are designed as a low CPA strategy.

Insights from the member database can be used for improved targeting to drive down CPA based on running look-a-like audience targeting.

If the company is part of a coalition program, they can work with the program operator to target non-customers with bonus points offers to attract new customers, ideally at a lower CPA that other channels. Bonus points offers can then be used to stimulate early repeat transaction behaviour to boost ARNPC.

Amazon Prime

Amazon Prime provides free delivery, free video streaming, exclusive early access to sales, and more. This allow Amazon to avoid having to solely compete on price or discounting to acquire new customers.

Rather than providing a percentage discount which would only benefit a single merchant, free delivery as a loyalty benefit helps multiple merchants selling via Amazon and is more valuable to customers as this is recurring value every time they shop.

Due to Amazon's scale, the delivery cost is lower for Amazon than what it would be if individual customers were required to pay it, therefore has a higher perceived value over cost. Furthermore, it is a cost that Amazon has greater control over rather than discounts, which would vary depending on what people buy.

The Prime streaming service is differentiated value that other online retailer cannot easily provide to their customers. There are very few companies globally that can match Amazon on their Prime program, making it a highly effective acquisition (and retention) tool.

Incremental spend

Influencing existing customers to spend more can be much more cost-effective than acquiring new customers.

Most companies associate two metrics related to spend:

- **ARPC**: average revenue per customer, or how much each customer contributes to the company revenue stream on average over a defined period of time. An alternative is Average Revenue Per User (ARPU).

- **AOV**: average order value, or the average transaction amount spent by members over time. This is calculated by dividing the total amount spend by the number of transactions made within the period.

- **SOW**: means share of wallet, which is the percentage of spend within a specific category that a customer spends with the company.

Loyalty programs are the ideal marketing strategy for growing ARPC, AOV and SOW, with operators focusing their tactical campaigns across key areas:

- **Frequency**: spend more often.

- **Basket size**: spend more each time they shop. This may be via -

    ◦ **Bulk-load:** buy more of a particular item.

    ◦ **Upsell:** spend on more expensive items.

    ◦ **Cross-sell:** spend in new categories.

- **Share of Wallet**: spend more with the brand and less with competitors.

- **Customer Lifetime Value (CLV)**: spend with the brand over a longer period of time.

Loyalty programs can generate exponential revenue growth when these elements combine. For example, a member who is influenced to spend more often on higher-value items and across different categories will be substantially more lucrative as a result.

Typically, loyal customers will have a higher AOV than non-loyal customers due to a greater willingness to buy and fewer barriers of resistance. This may be as a result of an established, trusted relationship with the brand or simply due to behavioural commitment. Loyalty program operators can build on this further by collecting data points about member spending patterns, match them to their unique profile, and target them with tactical campaigns.

Tactical campaigns may reward members for spending a certain number of times within a defined period, spending over a certain threshold in a single transaction, or buying particular products in a new category.

Campaign costs can be reduced by targeting specific members with an offer rather than providing it to all members. Further costs can be saved by requiring members to 'activate' the offer to access the benefit. Companies may also have the opportunity to push the cost of the bonus rewards onto a supplier.

By way of example, many supermarket programs require members to active bonus points offers. These may reward members with bonus points on selected items or for spending over a certain threshold. The offers are typically personalised to individual members or segments based on previous purchase history with the aim of incentivising them to spend more or buy specific products (with the bonus points funded by the supplier). To take advantage of the offer, members must click an 'activate' or 'boost' button in an email or in their account prior to transacting.

Incremental retention

Although it varies widely by industry, it can be anything from 5 to 25 times more expensive to acquire a customer than retain a customer. In addition, increasing customer retention rates by 5 per cent can increases profits by 25 per cent to 95 per cent.[574]

Most companies associate two metrics related to retention:

- **Churn**: the percentage of existing customers at the beginning of the year that remain customers at the end of the year.

- **CRC**: customer retention cost, or the average amount it costs to retain a customer at risk of churning. This is calculated by adding all incremental costs associated with retaining a customer divided by the active number of customers in the period.

Churn is typically reported as a percentage rather than the actual volume. Companies have an expectation that some of their customers will cease spending at some stage. In times of high growth, the amount of lost customers may also increase, however the relative proportion of lost customers as a function of existing customers is a more critical metric.

---

574 Gallo, A, 2014, 'The value of keeping the right customers', https://hbr. org/2014/10/the-value-of-keeping-the-right-customers accessed 14 July 2023

As stated by Murphy, 'The seeds of churn are planted early,'[575] therefore best-practice loyalty program operators invest in generating 'stickiness'. This is where the member either develops attitudinal commitment (where they choose to be loyal because of a positive brand preference) or calculative commitment (where they develop a sense of being locked into a service provider due to the economic costs of leaving) as discussed in Chapter 5.

Tactics employed to achieve stickiness include providing members with benefits that generate a sense of exclusivity and belonging, ensuring each touchpoint experience delivers convenience and delight, incorporating a risk to the member that stored value built up over time and via investment/effort can be taken away if engagement is not maintained (i.e., expiry), and threatening to remove highly-desired benefits if a certain level of spend is not periodically achieved (e.g., status tier demotion or regression).

Loyalty programs can also improve retention by delivering personalisation of communications, offers and experiences, as detailed in Chapter 15.

When calculating CRC, it is important to consider only the incremental costs associated to retaining or 'saving' a member. For example, incentives or benefits specifically given if a member chooses to renew or continue spending, rather than attributing all costs to serve members. This enables more effective comparison to CPA helping the business to make more informed decisions around whether to invest more in retaining existing or acquiring new members.

Incremental advocacy

Best-practice loyalty program operators strive to turn members into brand advocates and promoters. This can be measured in a variety of ways including Net Promoter Score (NPS).

Loyalty program operators can capitalise on advocacy by inviting members to provide reviews (sometimes incentivised), engaging positively with the brand's social media channels, or providing referral incentives.

---

575 Murphy, L., 2013, 'The Seeds of Churn are Planted Early', Sixteen Ventures, https://sixteenventures.com/seeds-of-churn, accessed 18 February 2020.

Companies may choose to over-invest in these members, particularly if they generate a high percentage of total company revenue. Specific budgets may be established to invest in building the relationship to grow share of wallet and ensure long-term retention.

2. Cost savings and operating efficiencies

In addition to generating incremental revenue, loyalty programs can also create cost savings and operating efficiencies.

Three areas where this can be achieved include improving marketing return on investment (ROI) and return on advertising spend (ROAS), margin retention and yield optimisation, and inventory management.

Improving marketing ROI/ROAS

Companies invest significantly in marketing efforts to generate incremental acquisition, spend, retention and advocacy. ROI and Return on Ad Spend (ROAS) are measures of campaign effectiveness based on the financial return relative to the costs.

As discussed in Chapter 15, loyalty programs enable brands to establish direct marketing channels with customers. This saves advertising budget by being able to run promotions and marketing directly rather than via external media. This also enables the company to provide communications, offers and experiences that are more relevant and tailored to individuals or member segments, making them more effective at a lower overall cost, ensuring a better campaign or program ROI.

By tying campaign responses to individual members, the company can more quickly discern how effective the campaign is, especially when running A/B testing or other analytical experiments.

Utilising tools that support look-a-like audiences can support optimisation of marketing and advertising spend by allowing companies to target promotions to non-customers with similar profiles to existing, engaged customers. This helps to optimise ROAS.

Margin retention and yield optimisation

One of the most common tactics used by companies to drive acquisition and spend is discounting. Whilst discounting can be effective, it creates a range of challenges.

An excellent article by Mark Ritson[576] detailed seven perils to be aware of when discounting:

1. **Negative signalling**: where the company indicates their products are worth less than they once thought.

2. **User disillusionment**: where existing customers who paid the non-discounted price (especially recent customers) feel upset.

3. **Questionable top-line impact**: where the revenue uplift from the campaign seems impressive, but the actual incremental margin benefits are low.

4. **Bullwhip effects on supply**: where the campaign pulls customers forward in the purchase cycle but does not generate new demand.

5. **Profit evisceration**: where the discounting significantly erodes the margin earned on sales.

6. **Starting a price war**: where competitors respond by also discounting, negating any benefit and eroding the profit margin of the entire industry.

7. **Commodifying brand equity**: where the brand image is damaged, a particular risk for premium brands.

A loyalty program offers a way to provide alternative value to a customer that is harder to replicate, while enabling more effective targeting of tactical promotions to protect margins. This supports a company to optimise marketing spend. Adjusting pricing through targeted offers based on a solid understanding of members is a sophisticated strategy to optimise yield.

---

576 Ritson, M, 2023, 'Tesla is about to experience the seven perils of discounting,' https://www.marketingweek.com/tesla-seven-perils-of-discounting/ accessed 14 July 2023

Where the loyalty program can provide efficient rewards (as detailed in Chapter 7), the margin retention compared to discounting can be significant. This approach is the foundational imperative which gave birth to the frequent flyer program. Airlines realised they had empty seats on flights, but they did not want to discount them as that would affect overall price perception. By providing members with miles, they invented a way to provide heavy discounts to their most valuable members while protecting their pricing strategies.

Improved inventory management

Managing inventory requires significant data to predict demand for a particular product at specific locations.

Loyalty programs play a critical role in collecting the data required for inventory analytics.

Through data science, companies can improve the accuracy of predicted demand, reduce shipping and holding costs, and avoid the risk of excess stock ordering.

3. Strategic decision-making benefits

As detailed in Chapter 14, best-practice loyalty program operators utilise data scientists and analysts to generate insights and reporting which can support strategic decision-making across the company.

From a financial perspective, these insights can identify and support opportunities to boost incremental revenue and reduce costs. Examples include:

- **Location and network decisions**: such as where to open other outlets in regions where similar target markets with unmet needs exist.

- **Customer Value Proposition evolution**: including optimising the product and service offering based on a better understanding of member needs to drive acquisition, spend, retention and advocacy.

- **Brand positioning refinement**: improving how a brand presents and promotes itself to better resonate with members, helping to drive acquisition, spend, retention and advocacy.

- **Value-chain extensions**: A value-chain is the various business activities and processes involved in creating a product or performing a service. Through a loyalty program the company may be able to perform more roles and therefore extend into more parts of the value-chain helping to unlock new revenue streams or save money. An example of this may be a company who previously outsourced all marketing, sales and business development services, however as a result of having a loyalty program and the ability to build their own database of customers, enables them to take control of their marketing and sales activities.

4. Third party commercialisation opportunities

Loyalty programs can create multiple opportunities to generate incremental revenue via third party relationships.

Opportunities include selling loyalty currency to coalition partners, selling marketing services and data analytics services, earning affiliate commissions, and providing reward fulfilment services.

Selling loyalty currency to coalition partners

As detailed in Chapter 1, coalition programs involve partnerships between multiple brands (a 'coalition' of partners), allowing members to earn across a wide range of participating companies.

Partner companies provide the coalition program operators' branded points/miles to their customers as a reward for transacting with them. The coalition partners pay the coalition program operator an agreed amount for the points/miles conferred on members, and in return the coalition program operator may promote the third-party partner to their member base.

Coalition loyalty program operators generate revenue by selling their loyalty currency (e.g., points or miles) to partners then making a margin when the currency is redeemed. Further revenue is generated when points expire (known and breakage) and via interest earned on deferred liability (cash set aside from currency sales by the program operator until the member redeems for a reward).

These concepts are explained in more detail later in this chapter.

Merchant-funded loyalty programs are a type of partner coalition often associated with credit cards, where the program operator is a financial institution, yet the benefits (generally cashback) are funded by the merchants. This enables the financial institution to deliver value to its members at little to no cost, with the merchants receiving marketing promotions targeted at members who have never shopped with them before (or only shopped rarely) supporting acquisition, or with spend thresholds driving spend stimulation.

Supplier-funded offers are widely used by grocery supermarkets where product brand owners fund the offers to members in the same was as merchants do above.

A valuable partner in many coalition programs are banks which often participate in coalition loyalty programs. Banks use the loyalty programs as a way to drive credit card acquisition. These 'co-branded cards' reward members with points or miles for spend. These are highly effective products as members earn wherever they spend regardless of whether the merchant is a partner or not, helping members accumulate points or miles faster.

By providing members with access to these cards, JetBlue aimed to improve member stickiness, as members would carry the brand around in their pocket while focusing on how to maximise their points earn. In addition, the growth in points earn would have helped boost Jet Blue's revenue for their loyalty program.

Some frequent flyer programs generate 50-60 per cent of total points or miles earn just from co-branded credit cards.

JetBlue

In 2016 JetBlue partnered with Barclays and Mastercard to launch four new co-branded credit cards:[577]

- **The JetBlue Card:** a basic entry level credit card where members earn up to 3 points per dollar spent on JetBlue purchases, 2 points at restaurants and grocery stores, and 1 point for all other purchases.

- **The JetBlue Plus Card:** a premium card charging $99 annual fee with points earn up to 6 points per dollar.

- **JetBlue Business Card:** similar to Plus card but with a slightly different earn rate for business spend.

- **Replacement Card:** The fourth card was not available to the public, but rather a replacement card to the previously issued JetBlue AMEX card.

Selling marketing services and data analytics services

Loyalty program operators which have developed sophisticated marketing and data analytics capabilities may also generate revenue from providing these capabilities as a service to third parties and partners (in the case of a coalition program). This may be by delivering valuable insights about members within a particular industry that are useful to others or helping to develop analytical models to predict behaviour for companies that do not have sufficient capabilities internally.

Promoting a partner offer to a large, engaged marketing database of members seeking additional points-earn opportunities can be very effective in generating incremental acquisition and spend, while also boosting currency earn.

Helping partners to collect, store, analyse, derive valuable customer, and generate business insights, along with providing the means to action these insights, is a valuable service.

---

577 Clements, N, 2106 'JetBlue Unveils Details Of New Credit Card With Barclaycard,: https://www.forbes.com/sites/nickclements/2016/03/10/jetblue-unveils-details-of-new-credit-card-with-barclaycard/?sh=347df3cf53e9 accessed 12 July 2023

Earning affiliate commissions

As detailed in Chapter 8, affiliate is a digital business model connecting thousands of advertiser and publisher businesses globally. The publisher business publicises the advertiser to their marketing database. The members click through to the advertiser's online store and transact. The advertiser pays a percentage of the total amount spent by the member to the publisher, known as affiliate marketing revenue. The publisher rewards the member with cashback or loyalty currency funded by the affiliate marketing revenue.

With the rise of card-linking and bank account-linking, affiliate models have extended in-store, rather than traditionally being online only.

An affiliate provides a loyalty program with an instant coalition of partners and pre-negotiated offers. The loyalty program operator in this instance is the publisher. The commission earned can be converted into a loyalty currency, account credit or cashback.

The loyalty program may choose to retain a percentage of the affiliate commission. For example, if the advertiser offers 10 per cent commission, the publisher may choose to retain 2 per cent and provide 8 per cent as points or miles, account credit or cashback to the member.

Reward fulfilment services

Similar to monetising data analytics and marketing capability established as a result of operating a loyalty program, an opportunity exists to leverage the infrastructure and capability established to operate rewards fulfilment operations for third parties.

This provides program operators a number of benefits including:

- **Increased purchase power**: additional volume can help the program operator negotiate better pricing for products sold through the rewards store, reduce postage and delivery fees, and gain access to brands and products they have previously been unable to secure due to low volumes or size of the company.

- **Improved economies of scale**: being able to spread the fulfilment costs, particularly the fixed overheads across a broader number of items, can help achieve greater economies of scale and reduce costs.

- **Additional revenue streams**: the ability to charge third parties for this service provides additional and diversified revenue streams that are not tied to underlying performance of the program operators own loyalty program.

5. Other monetisation opportunities

There are a range of other opportunities for loyalty programs to generate revenue:

Charging a membership fee or subscription model

Loyalty program operators may choose to charge membership fees to access certain loyalty benefits. Careful consideration should be made when deciding whether to introduce a paid element into the program as this can create a barrier to entry which could cost the business more in lost engagement than the incremental revenue earned from fees.

A subscription model is an option for loyalty program operators seeking to spread the cost of the benefits over a longer period.

Some operators implement 'freemium' models where the entry level tiers is free to join, but higher tiers require a fee.

Other fees and charges

Depending on the size and costs involved, a loyalty program may look to recover costs or look to profit from providing certain member services by charging a fee.

For example, they may charge partners for issuing paper statements, concierge support, points value protection, points top-up or transferring points.

Selling proprietary products/services

Having an engaged member base and a deep understanding of each member enables a loyalty program operator to establish and sell its own branded products. This could be co-branded financial services product like a credit card or debit card, or branded insurance products. It may be a product or service offering that appeals to the interests of the member base, such as a wine store or recreational club. It may even extend to providing the products it fulfils through its reward store for cash purchase, essentially becoming an online retailer.

Accounting considerations when developing or managing a loyalty program

Revenue recognition

There are a number of accounting considerations related to revenue recognition policies that are unique to the loyalty industry. For the purposes of illustration, the loyalty currency used in the illustrative examples will be points.

International Financial Reporting Standard 15 (IFRS15) was introduced on 1 January 2018 to replace the pre-existing standard for Customer Loyalty Programmes (IFRIC 13) among other revenue standards.[578] IFRS15 outlines the principles by which revenue is to be recognised in accordance with satisfying the performance obligations rather than the contract as a whole.

IFRS15 outlines that companies must estimate the future value of the loyalty currency (referred to in the standard as the 'transaction price'). Depending on the number of possible redemption options, IFRS15 outlines where there are more than two options which may vary in transaction price, the entity shall estimate an amount of variable consideration based on the expected value – being the sum of probability-weighted amounts in a range of possible consideration amounts.

This includes an estimation of breakage, the proportion of points that are

---

578 IFRS, 2023, "IFRS 15 Revenue from Contracts with Customers", https://www.ifrs.org/issued-standards/list-of-standards/ifrs-15-revenue-from-contracts-with-customers/ accessed 14 July 2023

expected to expire applied as a percentage to all new points issued. The net of these two values is what is regarded in practice as 'fair value'. For example, if the average value of a reward is $50 and 5,000 points are required for this reward then the future value of a point is 1 cent. Based on estimates (historical data, projected trends and planned program changes that may affect expiry) the loyalty program operator might calculate that breakage is expected to be 10 per cent (i.e., for every 10 points earned, 9 will be redeemed while 1 will expire). As a result, the fair value is adjusted to 1c per point x (1-10%) = 0.9 cents.

Calculating fair value enables the program operator to determine the amount of revenue to be set aside for the future, known as 'deferred revenue liability'. Only when points are redeemed is this revenue able to be recognised as 'redemption revenue'. At this point, the actual cost of fulfilling the reward will be determined, known as 'redemption cost'. The net difference between redemption revenue and redemption cost is referred to as 'redemption margin'.

When selling points to coalition partners at a value above fair value in order to earn a margin, the program operator must consider two components to the performance obligation. The primary obligation is to the member, where the points value will eventually be redeemed for a reward in the future. The secondary obligation is to the partner, being the margin component earned. This component of revenue relates to promotion and management of the program and has no future contract beyond that of the member obligation. As a result, the loyalty program can recognise this portion of revenue upfront on issuance of the points (known as 'marketing revenue').

The following summarise the various stages of recognising revenue associated with a coalition program using points.

Step 1: Points issuance

Calculated as:

Billings – Fair Value = Marketing Revenue (recognised on income statement in the period the points are issued to members)

Where:

- Billings = the amount charged to partners for purchase of the points

- Fair Value = revenue amount that needs to be deferred until points are redeemed, calculated as the points issued x fair value amount per point

Journal entries:

DR   Cash (billings amount)

                 CR Deferred Revenue Liability (fair value amount)

                 CR Marketing Revenue (difference between billing and deferred revenue)

Step 2: Points Redemption

Calculated as:

Redemption Revenue – Redemption Costs = Redemption Margin (recognised on the income statement in the period the points are redeemed by member)

Where:

- Redemption Revenue = total points redeemed x Fair Value per point

- Redemption Costs = the actual costs to fulfil the reward (e.g., a $20 gift card with a 10 per cent discount from the supplier would be $18).

Journal entries:

DR   Deferred Revenue Liability

                 CR Redemption Revenue

DR   Redemption Costs (actual cost of reward fulfilment)

                 CR Cash (actual cost of reward fulfilment)

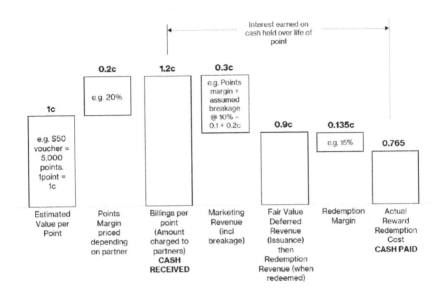

*Figure 19: Economics and revenue flows of a point
under a loyalty points currency approach*

Points issued on internal activities

A coalition loyalty program may also need to agree on an internal rate that the program will charge within its own company for the purposes of determining deferred liability.

For example, for a grocery retailer where a member purchases some groceries and earns points, a notional amount of revenue will need to be deferred to cover the future cost of points. Depending on how the loyalty program is setup, in the event the loyalty program is a separate business unit operating its own profit and loss, the business may agree to set an internal transfer price to which points are purchased by the company from the program. The internal transfer pricing rate agreed between the sales department and the loyalty program is usually set at no margin (or a low margin to help cover program operating costs).

Changes to fair value estimates and determining the value of a point

Annually, as part of preparing financial statements, the loyalty program operator should re-evaluate the fair value estimate. This includes calculating the 'value of a point' and estimated breakage.

The accounting standard does not specify exactly how this should be done, but rather enables the program operator to use a 'best estimate' approach, which is subjective. One strategy involves analysing historical data for the past 12 months to determine the weighted average points value based on points redeemed, then making an adjustment for known or planned changes (e.g., pricing changes expected in the next 12-months).

It is important to distinguish between reward value and cost when calculating the fair value. While reward cost is used to calculate the redemption cost amount, reward value is used to calculate fair value.

'Value' can also be subjective. If fair value is lower, less deferred liability is required and more marketing revenue can be recognised upfront. In that sense, it is an advantage for the program operator to use the lowest reward value to calculate fair value (e.g., for an airline this could be lowest fare of the day during a 12-month period).

Breakage is also re-estimated on an annual basis. For complex programs, actuaries are often engaged to assist in calculating assumed breakage as it is a complicated calculation.

Where there is a material change to the fair value estimate, a program operator may choose to recognise it as a 'one-off adjustment'. For example, a program holds 1 billion points across member accounts and had deferred liabilities at 0.9 cents per point based on their fair value calculation, with a deferred liability of $9m. As part of an annual re-estimation, due to higher that forecast breakage, the fair value is recalculated to 0.8 cents per point, meaning the deferred liability requirement reduces to $8m. The program operator may choose to retain the $9m (knowing breakage may reduce in future years) or decide to recognise $1m in incremental revenue, with zero redemption costs.

The decision to leave as-is and not recognise the one-off estimate change is not possible if the liability is short of the required provision. For example, if the fair value was recalculated to 0.95 cents per point, then $500,000 would need to be added to the deferred liability (reduced from revenue) as a one-off adjustment.

> **Nectar**
>
> Nectar 360 Limited reported a one-off reduced breakage adjustment of £35m in the 2021 financial year leading to a Loss Before Income Tax of £26m. This was based on the company reducing their breakage estimation by 0.76 per cent.[579]

Commercial benefits of a loyalty currency versus discounts / cashback

An important factor in optimising the value provided for loyalty program engagement is the mechanism for rewarding members. Chapter 8 details the wide range of loyalty program frameworks available to program operators which include various value-transfer options.

From a commercial perspective, it is important consider some unique benefits which loyalty currencies provide versus discounts or credits/cashback. For illustrative purposes, we will refer to points in the below examples:

- **Ability to influence the perception of value:** as detailed in Chapter 6, loyalty programs utilise the representativeness heuristic to make the value provided seem larger than it is. Unlike discounts which are transparent and easily replicated by competitors, points provide the company with the ability to increase the perceived value of the reward, thus increasing desired behaviour outcomes at no change in cost. For example, some airlines offer members the ability to redeem their points for a limited number of business or first-class upgrades.

---

579 Nectar 30 Limited, Mar 2022, 'Annual report and financial statements,' https://www.about.sainsburys.co.uk/~/media/Files/S/Sainsburys/documents/corporate-governance/s172/Accounts%20FY21_22/Nectar%20360%20Limited%20Accounts%20FY21_22.pdf accessed 9 July 2023

Dividing the dollar value of the flight or upgrade by the points required results in a high redemption value per point (e.g., 10c per point). With this value per point in mind, when offering the ability to earn 2 or 3 points per $1 spent, this equates to 20-30 cents per $1, which is the equivalent to an attractive 20-30 per cent discount. Assuming most members will redeem their points on less valuable rewards, the actual cost of the points is likely to be much lower (most airlines cost per point is 1c or less). Therefore, it costs the business 2-3 per cent (being 1c per point times 2-3 points per $1 issued) but has a perceived value of 20-30 per cent.

- **Ability to set the price of the points charged to partners:** in addition to driving greater member behaviour changes, increasing the perceived value of points also helps to increase the price charged to partners (billings). For example, per Figure 19 billings per point is charged based on the value per point to members plus a margin. A higher value per point should increase the company's ability to charge more to its partner network. In reality, this requires negotiations with each individual partner, however it provides the company with significant leverage to achieve a higher billings rate.

- **Price and brand protection:** as detailed earlier, discounts and cashback often risk diluting value perception. Utilising points enables the ability for companies to provide deep discounts without impacting value perception, while simultaneously creating a highly desirable reward.

- **Unique competitive advantage**: unlike discounts, which every business can provide, a best-practice points-based loyalty program can be more difficult to replicate, providing competitive advantage and protecting against further pricing dilution.

- **Striving behaviour**: much like having a savings goal, the psychology behind accumulating value to use for a larger reward supports the concept of 'striving'. Striving behaviour results in members more actively engaging and likely to behave in a certain way so that they can reach their goal. Contrast this with discounts or cashback which the value is immediate – it is not tied to a longer-term goal and is therefore unlikely to drive the behaviour as effectively as a points proposition.

- **Breakage**: unlike discounts, which is a cost to the business at the time the transaction occurs, points can expire resulting in zero cost to the business.

- **Working capital benefits**: program operators can exploit the timeframe between when a point is issued and when the point is redeemed to access working capital. The cash from the partner is collected upfront while the cost for the reward is paid only upon successful redemption. This results in a significant working capital saving, especially for larger coalition programs where the average time between earn and redeem can be in excess of 2 years.

- **Redemption margin**: unlike discounts or cashback where the reward is fixed to the percentage provided, points are converted into a reward at the time of redemption. The redemption options often include a mix of gift cards, consumer products or experiences. These rewards are sourced from suppliers which offer margin discounts which can increase with volume. As the total points value from the member base grows, this entire amount can be used to incentivise suppliers to offer greater pricing to increase attractiveness of their rewards, providing even more opportunity for bigger margins.

- **Gamification**: unlike discounts and cashback, points can be used to stimulate non-transactional behaviours in a cost-effective way. This may include rewarding members with small amounts of points for completing surveys, engaging with social media channels, filling in profile information, providing reviews, checking in at stores or a myriad of other behaviours.

Costs associated with, and investment required to, support an effective loyalty program

Investment in a loyalty program is generally separated into design, implementation and ongoing operations.

Costs will vary considerably across these two aspects depending on a number of factors:

- **Situational factors**: whether the program is completely new, or enhancements to an existing program are being made.

- **Program complexity**: whether the program involves multiple engagement touchpoints and incorporates a range of mechanisms, tactics and channels to drive desirable behaviours.

- **Internal capability**: whether required capability to launch and support the program can be leveraged by the existing business as opposed to that which will need to be acquired (internally developed or acquired through others (licensed) (i.e., does the business have project managers, marketers, an established data analytics capability, digital product development and IT capability, etc?).

- **Purpose/target**: whether the program aims to drive broad market awareness of its existence or only be promoted to the existing customer base. This will influence the marketing budget if broader awareness is required.

- **Rewards available**: whether rewards and benefits are able to be provided using internal assets versus rewards and benefits which will need to be purchased from external third parties. The amount of value the company is willing to be provided to members for target behaviours. The opportunity to access efficient rewards.

- **Capability development strategy**: whether the company plans to build internal capability or outsource the development and operations (or aspects thereof) via a license to third party providers.

- **Partnership/co-funded marketing opportunities**: whether any external partners will benefit from the program either directly or indirectly. If so, whether these can be leveraged to contribute to the investment of the program or offset ongoing costs.

- **Technical complexity**: How complex the IT solution across the program operator's company is, and all other partners and suppliers that need to connect into the program. The effort required to establish API connections and data flows.

- **Implementation approach**: whether the company intend to launch everything at once, in phases, or incrementally over a longer-term roadmap. Often a new loyalty program will be launched in stages with the company initially focused on launching the MVP (minimum viable product). This is the least number of features which will still be considered valuable by members. From here, the company will continue to enhance the program and release more features.

Design and implementation costs

The following costs are typically encountered when designing, then launching or relaunching, a loyalty program:

- **Program strategy and design/redesign**: market research, loyalty specialists' expertise, data analytics, stakeholder interviews, design workshops, commercial modelling, technical documentation (use cases, process flows, business and technical requirements), platform vendor sourcing, development of member lifecycle management strategy and more.

- **Project management**: project plan development and team/stakeholder/vendor management.

- **Platform**: integration, configuration and development, covering building components of the solution, integrating with existing platforms, front-end design, data flows and database setup, operational data file setup, reward fulfilment setup and testing.

- **Reward sourcing**: internally and/or from third-party partners and suppliers.

- **Marketing**: launch campaign.

- **Training**: loyalty team and front-line staff.

- **Legal**: development of program terms and conditions and partner contract negotiations.

Design and implementation costs are typically capitalised and amortised/depreciated over 5+ years.

Operational costs

Once launched, the costs of running the program will vary depending on the size and complexity of the program. Costs can be broken into the following categories:

- **Rewards and benefits**: typically, the largest program cost, with program operators that have access to efficient rewards enjoying a significant advantage. Benefits provided to members (e.g., status tier benefits) should be accounted for as part of the loyalty costs and not disguised or hidden in other cost centres.

- **Marketing**: in addition to owned and paid channels, lifecycle management requires ongoing optimisation and evolution using data analytics. Personalised communications, offers and experiences require investment in ensuring relevant data is used to inform models which feed into the loyalty and marketing platforms.

- **Technology platforms**: covering loyalty platform, marketing engine, CDP, CRM, data base/lake, business intelligence tools and other systems to run the program with as much automation as possible.

- **Data analytics**: data scientists and analysts who utilise analytics tools to generate insights and reporting. Business Intelligence (BI) reporting tools are also required to track key program metrics ongoing.

- **Customer service**: a dedicated resource or team to assist with member queries and issue resolution. Often these roles are incorporated into existing support teams, with self-service tools on websites such as FAQs or webchat helping to reduce costs.

- **Strategy and ongoing program design refinements**: internal or external resources focused on the ongoing evolution of the program utilising data insights, test and learn experimentation, industry trends and design creativity.

Business case modelling for loyalty programs

As investment in a loyalty program is a long-term strategy that should be expected to provide benefits to the business over many years. A Net Present Value (NPV) approach is often taken to determine whether investment in a new loyalty program or enhancements to an existing program is worthwhile. Under the NPV approach new cashflows generated for each year are converted into an equivalent present-day value. This is to reflect that $1 earned in 10 years' time is not the same value as $1 earned in the current year, as inflation reduces the value of money over time.

Simply put, NPV equals today's value of the expected cash flows minus today's value of invested cash.

To calculate this, a business case model is typically used to estimate revenues and costs which form the basis of cash inflows (typically revenues) and cash outflows (typically costs). The invested cash is the equivalent to the implementation costs discussed above.

To convert future years cashflows into today's value (known as 'present value') a business will apply a discount rate. This discount rate is often the percentage return the company would normally achieve if it was to invest this money in an alternate initiative.

Development of a loyalty program business case should focus on establishing clear profitability drivers aligned with the core strategic objectives from which assumptions can be derived.

Where possible, historical data analysis combined with market research should be used to validate assumptions. Sensitivity analysis can be used to identify the more important drivers along with value ranges the business case may deliver under different assumption scenarios.

When determining the potential value that may be generated, incremental analysis is recommended whereby a baseline profitability/cashflow scenario (assumes no loyalty program or program remains 'as-is') is compared to a new scenario which includes a new or redesigned program. The new scenario should include incremental acquisition, spend, retention, marketing cost savings, and other sources of value mentioned in this chapter. Comparing the profitability/cashflow of these two scenarios can reflect a reasonably accurate estimation of the potential value generated by the program. The net incremental cashflows are used to calculate the NPV.

Once launched, loyalty programs can take time to build an engaged member base, therefore a minimum period of 3 years is recommended for the model, including a monthly build-up of membership and activity rates.

Cost should be structured into upfront investment costs (which are often amortised over the life of the program (or at least 5 years), and ongoing costs. Ongoing costs should be broken down into the categories outlined in the section above.

Careful consideration should be factored into calculating reward costs. Elements such as actual value versus perceived/member value should be used, and breakage needs to be factored in where loyalty currency or other stored-value models are part of the proposition.

The timing of costs should also be carefully factored. For instance, if using a loyalty currency where value is accumulated over time, then the cost should be modelled in the year it is expected, otherwise this will negatively impact the NPV.

Measuring program value and uplift

Once the loyalty program is launched and live, attributing value to it can sometimes be challenging due to program activities often being entrenched in broader company activities. There are a variety of techniques which can be used to assist in determining the financial impacts of the program. The combination of a few or all of these methodologies will help in determining loyalty program incremental revenue and cost savings.

Target and control group methodology

Target and control group methodology is a form of analysis that compares the behaviour change in groups of people that are exposed to an activity (known as the target) versus other people who are not exposed (the control group). The difference in spend across these two groups can be assumed to be the uplift caused by the activity.

Control groups are typically much smaller than the target group but need to be large enough to be statistically significant for the analysis to be reliable. It is important for those within the control group to have similar characteristics to those within the target groups to minimise any variants outside of the program or campaign itself.

To illustrate, a company that is about to launch a new loyalty program has 1 million existing customers. These are broken into the following groups/segments:

A. 200,000 highly engaged
B. 300,000 moderately engaged
C. 500,000 not engaged

All 1 million customers are eligible to join the program. The company chooses to create control groups comprised of 2,000 from Group A, 3,000 from Group B and 5,000 from Group C. This ensures that when comparing the change in spend from Target Group A, they can be compared against a control group with similar characteristics (Control Group A) rather than a mix of A, B and C.

Once the program has been launched, the company can measure the incremental revenue uplift. This can be expressed by the following formula:

Value uplift = (Ta - Ca) x A + (Tb – Cb) X B + (Tc – Cc) X C - IC

Where:

Ta is the average contribution margin of Target Group A customer

Ca is the average contribution margin of Control Group A customer

A is the total customers in Group A

Tb is the average contribution margin of Target Group B customer

Cb is the average contribution margin of Control Group B customer

B is the total customers in Group B

Tc is the average contribution margin of Target Group C customer

Cc is the average contribution margin of Control Group C customer

C is the total customers in Group C

IC is the implementation cost

IC or Implementation Cost may include marketing, project or any other costs associated with implementing the program or campaign. Consideration should be given to the anticipated benefit period. For example, the costs associated with the launch of a full-scale loyalty program which is likely to drive benefits for years should be considered over a multi-year period compared to a shorter-term marketing campaign that may run for a few weeks or months.

Target and control group methodology provides a good indication as to the likely uplift however it does have some limitations. Running this analysis over long periods of time is problematic as circumstances change and other influences are at risk of impacting the results. In addition, customers included in control groups are excluded from program participation or campaign activity. While control groups are small, it still represents a group of customers that may not be realising their full engagement potential.

That being said, this methodology can be used to accurately measure improvements in acquisition, spend, retention and advocacy, making it a useful tool for proving the program's ability to generate incremental revenue.

Pre-post behavioural analysis (regression modelling)

This analysis compares changes in spend and other relevant activity before and after an event. For example, an event could be an existing customer joining the loyalty program, allowing their transaction data to be compared 12-months prior and post the join date.

Analysis at an individual member level can be assessed and compared with other members via statistical regression models to determine whether there is a correlated uplift in behaviour caused by the activity.

This type of analysis is often helpful to run before and after redemption events to validate if redeeming for a reward drives an uplift in engagement with the brand.

This analysis can also be used to test for purchase frequency, AOV and other non-financial metrics.

Where possible, factors such as general pricing increases, changes in product mix and other external factors should be accounted for in the analysis.

A limitation of this approach is the need to be able to identify individuals for the entire measurement period (pre and post). For online purchases, an email address is often held prior to loyalty program implementation so this can be used to associate sales. This approach is more challenging if the majority of transactions were processed in a retail store.

Customer Lifetime Value

Customer Lifetime Value is a predictive measure used to estimate the total net profit of a customer over their entire relationship with the company. This calculates all revenues generated less all costs associated with acquiring, servicing and retaining the customer.

CLV is an important metric as it helps a company to understand how much it can invest in a customer to ensure they remain profitable over the long-term.

Given the role of a loyalty program is to generate incremental spend and retention, CLV is a powerful metric to measure the program's effectiveness.

For example, if the CLV measure indicates members are three times more valuable over their lifetime than non-members, a company can calculate how much investment to make in converting more non-members into members.

There are a number of ways CLV can be calculated depending on the data available and insights observed about a customer base.

A simple CLV calculation assumes average purchase value and frequency remains the same over the period a member remains active. However, in practice prices and margins change, as does member behaviour. If a loyalty program is effective, it could be assumed that the purchase value, frequency and margin would increase year on year along with retention rates. As such, the calculation can be broken down into years with assumptions changing and the total value summed to determine the CLV.

Simple CLV Calculation = CLV = (((Average Transactions per year * Average Contribution Margin per Transaction) – Retention and Servicing Costs per annum) * Average Customer Lifespan in years) – Acquisition Costs

> Where:
>
> Average Contribution Margin per Transaction = (Total Revenue per annum – Costs of Goods Sold or Costs of Sales) / Total Transactions in year
>
> Average customer Lifespan (yrs) = (1 / (1-retention rate %))
>
> Retention rate: % of customers at the beginning of the year that remained customers at the end of the year (e.g., if the company has 1,000 customers at the beginning of the year and only 800 remain at the end of the year, then the retention rate is 80 per cent).

Given CLV involves valuing cash flows in future years, the value calculated can be discounted to be even more reflective of actual value.

Key insights

- Loyalty programs have evolved from marketing cost centres to valuable business units driving valuable long term profit outcomes for companies in almost all categories globally.

- There are a number of ways loyalty programs deliver value for companies including driving profitability from behavioural changes, cost savings and operating efficiencies, improving strategic decision-making, as well as unlocking 3rd party and other monetisation opportunities.

- The commercial benefits of a loyalty currency versus offering members discounts or cashback incentives is an important consideration as part of the program design with much greater value and control of program profitability able to be achieved via a currency.

- There are a number of important accounting concepts for finance teams within companies operating a loyalty program to understand.

- Loyalty program costs will vary depending on the complexity of the program, capability within the business and a range of other factors. Launching with an MVP, then building on this foundation can be an effective strategy to reduce investment risk.

- There are a range of ways uplift from a loyalty program can be measured, however it is not an exact science and accurate attribution relies heavily on available data and sophisticated data modelling.

Suggested reading

- Ritson, M, 2023, 'Tesla is about to experience the seven perils of discounting,' https://www.marketingweek.com/tesla-seven-perils-of-discounting

- Gallo, A, 2014, 'The value of keeping the right customers', https://hbr.org/2014/10/the-value-of-keeping-the-right-customers

- IFRS, 2023, "IFRS 15 Revenue from Contracts with Customers", https://www.ifrs.org/issued-standards/list-of-standards/ifrs-15-revenue-from-contracts-with-customers

CHAPTER 17

LEGAL

This chapter was reviewed by **Lincoln Hunter**, Principal and Founder, Loyalty Legal.

'I agree to the Terms and Conditions and to the collection and processing of my personal data by Beam Suntory Group as data controller, for the main purpose of membership to Laphroaig's Global Community, receiving newsletters and event updates in line with the Privacy Policy and Cookie Policy.'

- Friends of Laphroaig loyalty program join process.

Focus areas

This chapter will briefly address the following questions:

- What are the main regulatory regimes that may apply to operating a loyalty program? (Noting the context outlined below and that each jurisdiction has different laws and may address issues differently).

- What are some of the key legal considerations a loyalty program operator should address in the program agreement for members?

- What are some of the key legal considerations a loyalty program operator should address in a coalition merchant participation agreement?

Note on context / Introduction

Writing a chapter on regulatory considerations for loyalty programs with a global context is challenging because laws and regulations are jurisdiction specific. This means that any item included in this chapter may or may not apply to loyalty programs in a particular jurisdiction, and the chapter of necessity contains generalities and not specifics.

It also means that:

- The chapter gives a brief snapshot only of just some of the key sorts of regulatory regimes and legal issues that loyalty programs typically face, without specifically referring to particular laws or jurisdictions;

- The reader cannot rely on the content of this chapter as relevant or applicable to any particular loyalty program or jurisdiction;

- This chapter is not legal advice, and appropriate legal professionals should be consulted for specific advice relevant to the jurisdiction/s in which the program is operating;

- The information provided in this chapter is general only, is not exhaustive, is highly abbreviated and may not apply to all jurisdictions and there will certainly be other regulatory and legal issues that program operators will need to consider, address and comply with in designing and operating their loyalty program, wherever it is located or offered; and

- How (and if) the principles outlined in this chapter apply to any particular loyalty program or jurisdiction will depend on the specific applicable laws.

This chapter focusses primarily on larger proprietary and coalition loyalty programs for consumers who are individuals and less on other loyalty programs such as B2B programs. Although much of the laws and regulation referred to will equally apply to business programs, there can often be a different focus for B2B arrangements.

This chapter also does not address laws, regulations or codes applying to financial reporting, financial management, valuation or accounting for loyalty programs.

Most of the laws and regulations referenced in this chapter relate to the conduct of business in the relevant jurisdictions generally. Most advanced jurisdictions have a wide range of laws relating to doing business in that jurisdiction which loyalty programs like any other business are required to comply with. This chapter attempts to provide a brief outline of those laws and regulations likely to be of particular relevance to the operational activities of a loyalty program, but there will no doubt be others.

Note also that the authors have not conducted a comprehensive survey of all regulatory regimes throughout the world. Instead, the general propositions set out in this chapter are based on general principles applied in Australia (the author's home country) and the author's basic understanding and expectations of other similar jurisdictions in June 2023.

For the purposes of this chapter, a jurisdiction is defined as 'the territory over which legal authority is exercised'. This may be a single state, a single country or multiple countries. In the context of loyalty programs, this could refer to any territory in which the program operates or is available to members. Hence, a loyalty program may need to adhere to the laws of a single jurisdiction or multiple jurisdictions.

Regulatory Regimes

Generally, consumer loyalty program operators (and consumer focussed companies generally) can expect that most advanced jurisdictions will seek to protect consumers from adverse or unfair trading practices by companies (and by doing so also seek to address the imbalance of power when large companies trade with individuals, as is often the case with loyalty programs), by way of a variety of laws and regulations which are often typically grouped into the following bundles:

- Consumer protection

- Privacy and data protection

- Competition laws

- Financial products and financial services regulation

Given the nature of consumer loyalty programs, this chapter is focussed on these laws and regulations. Some of the key elements of each of these bundles that are often applied by law makers are set out, noting the context above and that there can be significant variations in how these are construed and applied across different jurisdictions (and that some of these elements may not apply at all in a given jurisdiction). In addition, certain jurisdictions may have other regimes in addition to these, which also need to be considered.

Penalties for non-compliance with these sorts of regulations can often be significant and so loyalty program operators would do well to ensure that they understand and comply with their obligations in all relevant markets / jurisdictions.

Consumer protection

Typical elements of consumer protection regulation include some form of prohibition of certain activities, such as misleading or deceptive conduct, unfair trading practices (such as making false or misleading representations in advertising) and unconscionable conduct, rules for addressing unfair terms in consumer contracts, and statutory implied product and service warranties. Some common features of these are described briefly below.

Misleading or deceptive conduct

Generally, a prohibition of misleading or deceptive conduct (which may also extend to a prohibition of conduct that is likely to mislead or deceive) is usually a broad baseline provision that applies across most areas of doing business, and typically it does not matter if there is an intention to mislead or not.

This sort of regulation could address many wide and varied business practices, such as misleading advertising (and the extent to which small print can be used to clarify advertising headlines and other content), offers of 'free' items to customers, the use of puffery or hyperbole in advertising, and comparative advertising. It could also apply to statements about how member data is collected, used or shared.

In a loyalty program context, the most obvious area (though by no means the only area) that this sort of a regulation may apply is in the advertising and marketing of offers and benefits to program members. For example, using the word 'free' to describe benefits provided to loyalty program members may be misleading when considered against the activities that a member is usually required to perform to earn points or the data the member is required to provide – consumer protection laws (especially 'truth in advertising' regimes) are often directly relevant here.

Loyalty program operators should ensure that every area of their business (including their advertising and marketing to members, and that of participants who advertise through the program) complies with regulations applicable in the jurisdictions in which they operate.

Unfair trading practices

In the context of consumer protection, law makers may seek to prohibit or regulate certain adverse or unfair trading practices, such as companies making false or misleading representations about goods or services. If so, it will often not matter if there is an intention to mislead or not, as the test is typically an objective one (e.g., are the representations incorrect or likely to mislead?).

In practice, depending on the relevant activity, there can be overlap between misleading or deceptive conduct prohibitions and prohibitions on false or misleading representations, as well as other principles of consumer protection. As a result, more than one regulation could apply to a particular statement or representation. Within these regulations, most of the basics for regulation of advertising and marketing in the applicable jurisdiction will be found (which may then be augmented by additional specific industry regulations etc).

Such regulations can extend to requiring companies to monitor what is said about them on social channels and review pages (e.g., by customers) and to correct or modify such posts if they are or could be misleading, deceptive or false.

Other unfair trading practices regulations of relevance to loyalty programs may include rules around promoting all-inclusive pricing and component pricing, offering rebates, gifts, prizes or other 'free' items in connection with the supply of goods or services, making 'premium' claims in relation to goods or services (e.g., descriptions that infer that a product has a particular premium quality over generic substitutes, such as nutritional claims, environmental or organic claims and country or place of origin claims), and 'bait and switch' advertising.

Although compliance with these regulations will typically apply to most companies in the relevant jurisdiction, given the nature of loyalty programs, program operators will need a full understanding of these sorts of regimes specific to their jurisdiction/s (if applicable) and how they apply to program operations, as well as members, merchant participants and other stakeholders.

Unconscionable conduct

At the more extreme level, law makers may also legislate that companies must not engage in unconscionable conduct in connection with the supply or acquisition of goods or services (or similar activities).

In this context, we are referring to unconscionable conduct as conduct which is more than simply unfair – it will usually need to be against good conscience as judged against the norms of society (or some other prescribed test in the applicable jurisdiction) and may also need to be harsh and/or oppressive.

For the most part, loyalty programs should have little trouble in complying with these sorts of requirements (given that they usually apply to reasonably extreme activities) – but, for example, a sudden large devaluation of points redemption values or introducing a short points expiry period where one did not previously apply (in each case without reasonable notice or compensation) could arguably give rise to unconscionable conduct allegations.

Unfair contract terms

In the context of consumer protection, law makers may also seek to prohibit or regulate unfair contract terms in certain consumer contracts. In connection with these sorts of regulations, a contract term determined to be unfair could be voided or prohibited, or some other remedy applied. Some jurisdictions also allow unjust or unconscionable contracts to be voided but these are likely at the more extreme end of unjust contracts and regulation, so we have not included this detail here, other than to mention that such rights may be available in some jurisdictions.

It is likely that each jurisdiction that imposes unfair contract terms regulations will apply its own definition of what is unfair and what contracts are covered by the regulations. Typically, they are aimed at contracts where consumers do not get the opportunity to negotiate the terms (or accept or reject particular terms), such as a standard form contract that has been prepared by a trading business and presented to a consumer on a 'take it or leave it' basis. Similarly, an unfair term might include a clause that causes a significant imbalance in the parties' rights and obligations and would cause significant detriment to the consumer if it were applied (particularly where there is no reasonable business need for the clause).

In most circumstances, it would be expected that loyalty program consumer or member-facing terms and conditions may be subject to these sorts of regulations (if applicable) given the nature of loyalty program contracts with members. If so, the loyalty program operator will need to ensure that the program and the program terms and conditions will not be impacted by any applicable unfair contract terms regime (to ensure the terms are enforceable and to avoid the remedy imposed by law or claims by members). This may also extend to the privacy policies of the program (depending on how they are presented to members), particularly if they are part of the standard form member contract or comprise a separate one.

In some jurisdictions, unfair contract terms regulation may extend beyond consumer contracts to small business or other contracts (which may then be relevant to B2B loyalty programs). Loyalty program operators may also need to consider any such laws.

Statutory product and service warranties

Some jurisdictions may also have laws which apply a basic set of product and service warranties (or guarantees) to certain goods and services acquired by consumers (or other purchasers), as part of or in addition to basic product safety regulations (we have not outlined in detail here wider product safety regulations – though they may also be relevant and there is some overlap - instead we have focussed on regimes which apply warranties as part of the sale or supply of goods and services).

If so, these statutory warranties are typically designed to give consumers a basic, guaranteed level of protection for the goods and services they buy (e.g., that the goods are of an acceptable quality and match the advertised description, etc). While companies may also offer extra product warranties (e.g., voluntary or extended warranties) in relation to their goods or services, the statutory warranties will typically apply regardless of any other warranties offered by a seller or manufacturer of goods or services. And typically, the statutory warranties cannot be contracted out of, or avoided, by using a 'drop ship' model.

If the statutory warranties are not complied with, consumers can typically take action to obtain a remedy from the supplier or, in some cases, the manufacturer or importer. The remedies are generally a repair, replacement, refund or having a service performed again (but may also include compensation in certain circumstances).

Statutory warranties such as this are likely to be relevant to loyalty programs primarily in connection with the supply of rewards. If applicable, loyalty program operators should address this risk in relation to the supply of rewards and also in their arrangements with the original product/service supplier/manufacturer.

Loyalty program operators should also be careful not to mislead members about their rights under relevant statutory warranties (e.g., referring members to the original supplier for defective goods and indicating that the program is not liable for defects, etc) as that could itself breach other consumer protection regulations.

Other rules may also apply to extra product warranties (e.g., voluntary or extended warranties) provided by a supplier or manufacturer.

Privacy and Data protection

These days, the collection, use and disclosure of personal data, and the sending of electronic marketing messages, are regulated in most advanced jurisdictions. Note that 'personal data' is also referred to as 'personal information' or 'personally identifiable information' (or similar) depending on the jurisdiction and each jurisdiction often applies a slightly different definition of the same concept. So, in this chapter 'personal data' is used to refer generally to the relevant personal data/information that is the subject of relevant privacy laws in the relevant jurisdiction.

At their core, loyalty programs are essentially a marketing, promotional and data capture tool for companies, with data captured directly by the program via multiple member touchpoints, as well as indirectly, as detailed in Chapter 13. As such, privacy and data protection laws are particularly relevant and it is expected that compliance with privacy, data protection, member consent and marketing related regulations will be part of the 'DNA' and the corporate culture of program operations in order to safeguard the significant data assets of the loyalty program and comply with applicable regulatory obligations.

Privacy regulations and loyalty programs

As a first step, loyalty programs will need to ensure that the program terms and conditions and privacy policy reflect applicable regulations, and all required consents are obtained from members in the applicable jurisdiction. Further, the internal policies and procedures applied by the loyalty program (e.g., marketing preferences and member profile records) will need to comply with and enact these requirements.

While there is significant variation between various jurisdictions in the content and approach adopted by privacy laws and regulations, it is expected that at a minimum loyalty programs (where regulated under the applicable regulations) will typically need to comply with the following sorts of requirements when handling personal data (these requirements are loosely based on

Australian laws and, although requirements in other jurisdictions may be more or less onerous than these, it is expected that most advanced jurisdictions will apply privacy requirements along these lines or which canvas these sorts of issues as a baseline):

- To maintain and make available a privacy policy about the program's management of member personal data, including how personal data is collected, held and disclosed.

- To collect personal data only where reasonably necessary for one or more of the program's legitimate functions or activities, and directly from the member to whom it relates (unless impracticable or consent or an exception applies).

- To notify a member, at or before the time of collection, or shortly thereafter, of the particulars of collection and provide the member with access to the program's privacy policy.

- Not to use or disclose member personal data for a purpose other than that for which it was collected, unless the member consents, the member would reasonably expect their personal data to be used for the other purpose, or an exception applies.

- Not to use personal data for direct marketing purposes unless the member reasonably expects it, or consents to it, and prescribed 'opt out' processes are in place but have not been actioned.

- Before personal data is disclosed to an overseas recipient, to comply with certain prescribed requirements and/or assume liability for the overseas recipient's handling of the personal data.

- To take reasonable steps to ensure the personal data that the program collects, uses or discloses is accurate, up to date and complete.

- To take reasonable steps to protect the personal data that the program holds from misuse, interference and loss, and from unauthorised access, modification or disclosure.

- To take reasonable steps to destroy or de-identify personal data that the program no longer needs, unless otherwise required to retain it by law.

- To provide a member, upon request, with access to their personal data and other relevant data unless a prescribed exception applies.

Although as mentioned most jurisdictions with privacy laws will apply similar themes, many jurisdictions will implement variations on those themes and some may apply additional rights and obligations (e.g., refer to the variations between Australian privacy laws, the EU General Data Protection Regulation 2016/679 (GDPR)[580] and the California Consumer Privacy Act of 2018 (CCPA)). Additional elements may include (to name just a few) express rights for individuals over their personal data, civil remedies for individuals for serious breaches of their privacy, an obligation on regulated entities to ensure their collection, disclosure and use of personal data is fair and/or reasonable in the circumstances (in addition to it being appropriately authorised such as by consent), and/or a right for individuals to be 'forgotten' (and their personal data to be deleted or de-identified). Early advice on the scope of privacy and data laws that apply to specific loyalty programs is highly recommended.

Data breaches

Generally, privacy regulations will also require program operators (that are regulated entities) to notify members and the regulator about certain 'data breaches'.

A relevant data breach for a loyalty program (that is a regulated entity) would typically include an event where there is unauthorised access to, or unauthorised disclosure of, or a loss of, personal data that a program holds which is likely to result in serious harm (or another prescribed harm level) to one or more members, and the program operator has not been able to prevent the likely risk of serious harm with remedial action. This definition is likely to be different in each jurisdiction so program operators will need to refer to their privacy advisers.

---

580 GDPR https://gdpr-info.eu/ accessed 11 June 2023

Cybercrime and cybersecurity legislation also remain a core focus of governments in most advanced jurisdictions (often developing in response to the latest cyber hack affecting the applicable jurisdiction) and will usually apply to loyalty programs and the data held by them.

Risk and mitigation strategies associated with data breaches and cybercrime are covered in Chapter 18.

Direct marketing, targeting and spam regulation

Many jurisdictions have also implemented restrictions on direct marketing, targeting of marketing or spam which typically apply to commercial/electronic marketing messages that a company sends or causes to be sent (but can also extend to hard copy and other forms of marketing).

If so, in the case of commercial electronic messages sent by a loyalty program, the program operator will generally be required to comply with a variety of requirements which typically include the following:

- **Consent**: the message must be sent with the member's consent.

- **Identification**: the message must contain accurate information about the loyalty program that authorised the sending of the message.

- **Unsubscribe**: the message must contain a functional 'unsubscribe' facility to allow the member to opt out of future marketing.

Personalisation - the drift toward further regulation arising from the focus on personalisation

As detailed in Chapter 15, personalisation of communications, offers and experiences is a core feature of best-practice loyalty programs. This can often include using personal data and/or de-identified data and profiling members based on that data.

But this drive toward personalisation brings with it added attention from regulators, for example with regard to transparency (ensuring that members are aware that the program operates this way), discrimination or differentiation (where people may unfairly miss out on or be targeted with particular offers) and even with regard to providing financial services to members (where personalised offers may extend into the realm of providing financial advice). Personalisation, targeting and profiling, using personal data or de-identified data, are increasingly the focus of regulators.

Foreign regulations

Whatever jurisdiction a loyalty program operates from, in addition to complying with local regulations in that jurisdiction, the operator may also need to comply with personal data and data protection regulations in foreign jurisdictions. This can depend on factors such as where else they are located and/or operate, where the program is offered, where their data processing activities take place, where their members or data subjects reside, and the applicable laws.

For example, the EU GDPR is the primary source of personal data regulation in the EU. Companies are generally required to comply with this regime if they have an establishment in the EU (regardless of whether they process personal data in the EU). They are also required to comply if they do not have an establishment in the EU, but offer goods and services in the EU, or monitor the behaviour of individuals in the EU.

It is important for loyalty program operators to obtain specific legal advice in all jurisdictions in which the program operates or which could apply to the program.

Competition laws

Although ordinarily the conduct of a loyalty program should not give rise to any particular concerns regarding anti-competitive conduct per se (other than in relation to the regulations outlined earlier in this chapter), there are circumstances under which a particular jurisdiction's competition law regulations may need to be considered in relation to loyalty programs, particularly for large coalition programs. This may include where coalition programs operate in concentrated markets, where competing loyalty programs wish to coordinate activities (e.g., under a points transfer agreement) or where independent operators wish to, or are required to, collectively bargain with a loyalty program.

This chapter does not intend to provide a detailed outline of competition laws. Instead, it seeks only to briefly mention some of the noteworthy elements of those laws that may have particular application to coalition loyalty programs. Competition laws are typically aimed at prohibiting or limiting certain practices that may prevent or unfairly inhibit competition in a relevant market, they typically apply broadly and generally across all industries and participants in a relevant market, and therefore will require compliance by loyalty programs and other companies which operate in the applicable jurisdiction. Further advice is required on all of these items. Competition laws may include the following common regulations and other regulations aimed at ensuring fair trade within relevant markets.

Restrictive trade practices/Anti-competitive conduct

Most advanced jurisdictions will have a variety of regulations in place aimed at prohibiting or regulating anti-competitive conduct by companies. The key elements of such regulations may prohibit activities such as:

- Anti-competitive agreements, contracts, understandings or practices.

- General cartel conduct or collusion (including price fixing and collective boycotts).

- Exclusive dealing.

- Resale price maintenance.

- Misuse of market power.

Depending on local laws, this conduct may only be unlawful if it results in the substantial lessening of competition (or some other prescribed level of adverse impact) in a relevant market and sometimes the conduct can be exempted by a regulator if a relevant public benefit can be established.

Specific to loyalty programs, Chapter 3 provided the example of SAS EuroBonus in Norway, where the operation of their frequent flyer program was deemed sufficiently anti-competitive for the program to be curtailed, demonstrating the power of competition regulators in some jurisdictions.

Exclusive dealing - Third line forcing

In Australia, a form of exclusive dealing known as 'third line forcing' occurs when the supply of goods or services is made on the condition that the purchaser buys goods or services from a particular third-party, or supply is refused because the purchaser will not agree to do so or has not acquired certain goods/services from a third-party. This activity (in Australia) is generally prohibited if the activity has or is likely to have a substantial lessening of competition in a relevant market. Variations of this law may apply in other jurisdictions.

In any jurisdiction that applies these sorts of regulations, loyalty program operators and merchant participants should consider these third line forcing laws (typically in relation to program benefits offered to customers of merchant participants) to ensure they either do not apply (and no third line force arises) or that no adverse impact on competition (to the prescribed level) arises in the relevant markets.

Exclusive dealing - Exclusivity

Another form of exclusive dealing conduct could potentially arise (depending on local laws) where the supply of goods or services, or the supply of goods or services at a discount, is conditional upon the buyer not acquiring, or limiting the acquisition of, goods or services from a competitor of the supplier. Again, depending on local laws this conduct may only be unlawful if it results in substantial lessening of competition (or some other prescribed adverse impact) in a relevant market.

Typically, coalition loyalty programs will require 'exclusivity' from any third-party merchant participant in the program, and merchant participants will require category exclusivity, as part of the negotiations for the participation agreement.

Loyalty program operators should consider any applicable exclusive dealing laws (if any) to ensure they either do not apply or that no adverse impact on competition (to the prescribed level) arises in their relevant market.

Financial products and financial services regulation

Similar to the consumer protection regulations outlined in this chapter, generally advanced jurisdictions will seek to regulate offering, marketing, dealing in and issuing financial products and financial services to protect consumers from adverse or unfair trading practices by companies (and by doing so also seek to address the imbalance of information and knowledge that applies to financial products and financial services).

If so, some of the key financial products/services and related regulatory issues that may arise in relation to a loyalty program are summarised below. Again, not all of these may apply in all jurisdictions (and where they do apply, they may be implemented and construed quite differently) and there may be other issues specific to certain jurisdictions.

Financial products regulation and the program itself

As a general definition, a financial product is often referred to as a facility through which, or through the acquisition of which, a person makes a financial investment, manages a financial risk, or makes non-cash payments. A non-cash payment facility allows payments to be made otherwise than by physical delivery of fiat currency (in the form of notes and coins).

It could be argued that a currency-based loyalty program itself or the stored value facility offered under it may be considered a non-cash payment facility or financial product and could therefore be regulated as a financial product in jurisdictions that apply such laws. If so, the loyalty program provider may require a financial services licence and/or be required to comply with regulations applicable to providing financial products/services in the jurisdiction in which the program operates (if such laws apply in that jurisdiction).

Similarly, some anti-money laundering style regulations extend to stored value products which may allow money laundering or terrorism financing by way of non-cash value transfers or cryptocurrencies for example. Depending on how these laws are framed they may apply to loyalty programs, especially cash-based programs where members can 'cash out'.

It is possible that where these sorts of regulations apply, the law makers or the regulator will exempt certain loyalty programs from certain of the regulatory requirements on certain prescribed conditions (as is the case in Australia). On the other hand, loyalty programs owned and operated by financial institutions may be more likely to be regulated as the institution is likely already a financial services licensee and the programs are more likely to be, be part of or offer financial products and services.

Financial services regulation and operating a program

Even if the loyalty program itself is not considered a non-cash payment facility or financial product under local legislation, financial services regulations may still be relevant.

Typically, these days large coalition loyalty programs have banking and financial services earn participants. In this situation, a variety of related financial services regulations may apply, depending on the exact nature of the services that are being provided by or through the loyalty program (and naturally the applicable regulations in the jurisdiction).

A loyalty program operator may be deemed to be providing a financial service where it provides advice regarding a financial product or deals in a financial product, which may require the program operator to hold a financial services licence. This may include providing advice regarding financial products (such as banking products, mortgages and general insurance) issued by third-party participants to the program members. Other restrictions and obligations may also apply, such as requirements to implement a formal dispute resolution process to address complaints by customers.

These or similar laws may also apply to advice and/or distribution services provided in relation to credit cards (and other payment cards and consumer finance). Given that some loyalty programs allow points earn on credit card acquisition and use (e.g., airline frequent flyer programs and bank programs), these laws may be relevant, if applicable. Further, other related regulations focussed on associated industry payments in respect of credit cards (like interchange paid between acquiring and issuing banks and merchant service fees) often directly impact the card issuer offers and the loyalty programs in relation to these cards.

Finally, general use 'gift cards' (commonly offered as redemption items or benefits through loyalty programs), are also often subject to regulation, usually to ensure that gift card consumer customers are able to use their gift card as expected and as represented. Regulations will often include requirements that gift cards are issued with a minimum expiry period, clearly disclose the expiry date (if one is applied) and are not subject to fees imposed after issue of the card (which dilute the gift card value), although in some jurisdictions gift cards provided through loyalty programs may be exempt from these requirements. Obviously, each jurisdiction's regulation of gift cards may be different.

The loyalty program operator will need to consult its financial services advisors in relation to these sorts of regulations to ensure compliance, and obtain specific legal advice, in all jurisdictions in which the program operates.

Key legal considerations for key loyalty program agreements

Generally, the types of agreements and documents that a loyalty program operator will typically provide to members include program terms and conditions (i.e., the membership terms or rules), privacy policies, cookie policies, data collection statements and website terms of use (as well as all other marketing and service communications etc). These documents will generally form part of the contract between the program operator and the member.

The operator will also likely need merchant participation agreements, as well as third-party supplier agreements (e.g., for the loyalty program operating platform, data services, analytics, marketing agencies, communications, mailing and CRM services, call centres, reward suppliers and other operational requirements etc).

The loyalty program operator will need appropriate legal advice (in all applicable jurisdictions) on all of these documents. This section focusses on some key items only for the program terms and conditions (the key element of the contract with the members) and a basic merchant participant participation agreement.

A valid contract with members

A critical, but often overlooked aspect, of running a loyalty program is the importance of ensuring that a valid contract is in place with members. This requires ensuring that all of the elements of a contract are present and that the mechanics of offer and acceptance are adequate to confirm those elements on the applicable terms. However it is done, the loyalty program operator needs to ensure that under the laws applicable to the jurisdiction/s in which it operates, a valid and binding contract is entered into by the member and the program, so the terms of the program (and data consents, etc) can be enforced.

Among many other terms and conditions, loyalty programs typically need to ensure that the following key program terms are set out clearly and accepted by the member:

- When points will expire and how members will be made aware of this. The expiry of points is usually an important issue for consumers and regulators, as well as for loyalty program operators who require the flexibility to expire points in order to manage liabilities and incentivise valuable customers. Accordingly, this is a contentious issue on which it is likely loyalty program operators will need legal advice in applicable jurisdictions.

- In a small number of jurisdictions (such as Ontario and Quebec, Canada), points expiry rules have been the subject of specific regulation. In 2018, the Government of Ontario legislated a ban on loyalty and reward points expiry as part of a series of consumer-side protections, allowing consumers to request that companies reimburse them for improperly expired points. [581] These consumer protection laws do not come into play if the loyalty program operator decides to close a member's account due to reasonable grounds of inactivity or fraud.

- The conditions on which discount and value-add offers from third-party merchant participants can be accessed.

---

581 Chharbra, S., 2018, 'Ontario's reward points expiry ban is now in effect,' https://mobilesyrup.com/2018/01/01/ontarios-reward-points-expiry-ban-now-effect/, Mobile Syrup, accessed 19 April 2023.

- The precise terms on which the member agrees that his/her personal data can be collected, used and disclosed by the program.

- Marketing communication permissions.

- The ability of the loyalty program operator to change the value proposition and terms unilaterally – again, this is usually an important issue for consumers and regulators and it is also critical to ensure that the program operator can change the terms to reflect market practice and to ensure the operator's liability is manageable, under an agreement that usually has an open ended term.

- Earn rates and redemption rates for loyalty currency transactions.

- Circumstances in which the program may be terminated, and the member can terminate his/her membership, or his/her membership can be terminated by the program operator.

- Other benefits and restrictions, as applicable.

- What happens at the end? The account termination process (and any runoff period for ongoing reward redemption) and any terms which apply post termination.

Many of these terms may be affected by the regulatory issues outlined in this chapter , as well as the need to make the program attractive and rewarding for the members. For example, in 2019, Quebec introduced laws that specifically regulate unilateral amendments to the member loyalty program agreement by the loyalty program operator including in relation to the member value proposition (other jurisdictions may rely on general laws like the unfair contract terms regulations outlined in this chapter).

Including privacy policies, cookie policies and data collection statements as part of the contract between the program operator and the member requires careful consideration too – achieving transparency by incorporating these documents in the member contract could in turn place restrictions on making changes to those documents.

Participation agreements – merchant participants

The terms on which third-party merchants participate in a coalition program or member benefits program are typically set out in a 'program participation agreement'. These agreements and their terms are critical, as they often generate third-party revenue earned by the program and provide for offers to be made available to members. They also give rise to important costs and administration issues.

Many of the terms included in such an agreement may be affected by the regulatory issues outlined in this chapter, as well as the commercial objectives of the parties, and the need to make the program attractive and rewarding for the members.

Some of the key issues include:

- **Commercial terms and offers:** this may cover themes including points or discount offers to members, services to be provided by each party, fees to be paid by the merchant participant, the details of, and payments applicable to, any redemption opportunity, payment terms, liability, etc.

- **Data and data use rights**: the data received by the loyalty program from merchant participants and the loyalty program's ability to use that data, is one of the primary drivers of value for the loyalty program. Accordingly, the provisions for data exchanges and each party's data use rights are therefore critical.

- **Exclusivity:** an undertaking that the merchant participates exclusively in the relevant loyalty program is often critical for the loyalty program to manage risk and differentiate itself from other offerings in a market. Equally, and arguably more so, merchant participants often require category exclusivity within the program for similar reasons, and to avoid exposing customers to competitor offers. The bifurcated nature of the customer relationship, together with the regulatory requirements and the genuine interest each party has in relation to their customer relationships, ensures that this issue is often the most hotly contested during negotiation of participation agreements. Legal advice should be obtained in each applicable jurisdiction on this issue and the commercial consequences.

- **What happens at the end?** it is important to include arrangements that should apply at and after the end of participation. This is important because at the end of a lengthy participation arrangement each party can often hold details of the members/customers of the other party, which can then be exposed to offers from that other party's competitors after the participation agreement ends.

Other comments / issues

Although the following issues are not dealt with in this chapter, note:

- A loyalty program operator (especially when designing a loyalty program) should ensure that it obtains thorough and detailed tax advice in relation to potential treatment for tax purposes of loyalty currency issued as part of the program (in respect of members, merchant participants and the loyalty program operator) and in all applicable jurisdictions. This advice may impact directly on the value of the program to those stakeholders and may need to be reflected in the member terms.

- There will be many other laws and regulatory issues (and industry codes and guidelines, etc) to be considered in addition to those mentioned in the chapter (generally applicable to doing business in a relevant jurisdiction and otherwise in relation to the program or the underlying business). For example, most advanced jurisdictions have introduced corrupt practices (e.g. anti-bribery) legislation and modern slavery legislation which must be complied with by entities governed by them (including loyalty programs like any other business). Early legal advice should be obtained on all potential issues.

Key insights

- Appropriate legal professionals should be consulted for specific loyalty program legal guidance relevant to the jurisdiction/s in which the program is operating.

- The main regulatory regimes that a loyalty program operator will typically need to comply with when designing and operating a loyalty program include consumer protection regulations, privacy and data protection laws, competition laws, and financial products and financial services regulations. Not all of these regimes and the typical elements of them outlined in this chapter will apply in all jurisdictions, and certain jurisdictions may apply other regimes in addition to these.

- The following good practice principles should help loyalty programs comply with the key day to day regulatory requirements outlined in this chapter:

  ○ present terms, conditions and privacy policies in a way that members can readily understand.

  ○ avoid making unilateral changes to terms and conditions in a way that may be unfair to members.

  ○ ensure that marketing and promotional material is clear and complies with applicable 'truth in advertising' obligations.

  ○ collect, use and disclose member data in ways that comply with applicable laws and also align with members' preferences. This could include providing members with full transparency regarding and control over the sharing of their data (especially with unknown third parties), and the ability to opt out of targeted advertising.

- Generally, the types of agreements and documents that a loyalty program operator should provide to members include program terms and conditions, privacy policies, cookie policies, data collection statements and website terms of use.

- The loyalty program operator needs to ensure that under the laws applicable in the jurisdiction/s in which it operates, a valid and binding contract is entered into by the member with the program owner/operator, so the terms of the program can be enforced.

- Program participation agreements for third-party merchant participants in coalition programs and member benefits programs are critical, as they often generate third-party revenue for the program and provide for some of the offers made available to members.

CHAPTER 18

SECURITY AND FRAUD RISKS, AND MITIGATIONS

This chapter was co-written by **Michael Smith**, Co-Founder, Loyalty Security Association.

'A lock does no more than keep an honest man, honest.'

- Robin Hobb, Assassin's Quest, 1997[582]

Focus areas

This chapter will address the following questions:

- What is loyalty fraud?
- What are the different types of security and fraud issues which can affect loyalty programs?
- How can security and fraud risks to loyalty programs be mitigated?
- What are some remediation tactics for when loyalty fraud occurs?

---

582 Hobb, R., 1997, 'Assassin's Quest, accessed via https://kirbyidau. com/2016/12/28/a-lock-does-no-more-than-keep-an-honest-man-honest/, 3 April 2023.

SECURITY BREACHES AND fraudulent activity are extensive in loyalty programs, and there has been a much greater focus on this area in recent years. With an estimated US$320 billion[583] of value sitting in points accounts around the globe, and many loyalty program operators not taking necessary steps to properly address security risks, account hacks and fraud continue to be perpetrated. Whilst no company willingly reports the exact amount of money lost to security and fraud each year, the value is immense. One study has shown that 61 per cent of IT executives estimated that recovering compromised accounts cost their company more than US$100,000[584].

Loyalty fraud is defined as where deception is used to intentionally secure unfair financial, personal or third-party gains from loyalty programs.

Balancing the customer experience (i.e., easy join, earn, and redemption) with proper security and fraud prevention processes and associated security and fraud management costs is challenging. However, understanding potential risks helps to identify issues early so they can be addressed quickly. In addition, understanding the technology available to automate security and fraud checks is also helpful.

One of the main risk exposures for many loyalty programs is a lack of Know Your Customer (KYC) protocols. Unlike financial institutions, where KYC is usually a legal requirement, many companies allow members to join their loyalty program by entering unverified credentials (or easily verified

---

583 Statistic is taken from this article: https://medium.com/@simoncheong/gatcoin-is-blockchains-answer-to-loyalty-programs-d0193c2f4cef. Exact calculation of the value of unredeemed miles/points is hard to get at as many programs do not publish publicly available information. Consultant estimates give a figure in excess of US$220 billion. Other market research estimates of the size of the 'global market for loyalty programs' (which is not defined in terms of outstanding value of points) are also north of US$200 billion (from this article: https://www.prnewswire.com/news-releases/loyalty-programs-market-to-reach-201-billion-by-2022-according-to-beroe-inc300794907.html). It is safe to say that the amount is an enormous number.
584 Arkose Labs., 2021, 'The True Cost of ATOs – Are your customer accounts safe?', accessed via https://www.arkoselabs.com/wp-content/uploads/Arkose-Labs-Invasion-of-Privacy-How-Safe-is-Your-Account.pdf, 3 April 2023.

fraudulent credentials such as a fake email address). This makes instances of fraud more possible as potential fraudsters can enter any details they wish.

Best-practice program operators utilise anti-fraud companies or technology solutions to verify everything from the age of an email address to its validity as part of an automated background check. They also execute two-factor authentication (2FA) on the email address and/or mobile number as part of the registration process. 2FA requires members to provide an additional piece of information as part of the authentication process. This may be something they know (e.g., a PIN or a secret question), something they have (e.g., a unique code sent to their mobile, or a security token) or something they are (e.g., a fingerprint or voice scan). This makes it more difficult for fraudsters to access accounts, and if they do, to complete transactions.

Building loyalty fraud into the overall business model as a line item in the P&L can help; both in terms of the old adage of 'what gets measured, gets done' but also because it forces the business to work out how to gather the data from the loyalty platform to calculate the amount of potential exposure.

This chapter focuses on loyalty-specific security and fraud issues and suggests mitigation approaches for each.

There is a much greater focus on account takeover in this 2nd edition of the book as there has been significant recent activity in the space.

In addition, remediation tactics for companies to follow to best manage data breaches when they do occur is a new addition at the end of this chapter.

Mass data breaches and account take-overs

Risk

Loyalty programs are attractive targets for database hacks, with enormous amounts of valuable member personal data held within systems which may lack appropriate security protections. The rise of social media platforms like Telegram has also led to conferences being organised by hackers around how to exploit programs and commit fraud.

As a result, staying ahead of hackers and protecting the program from mass data breaches and account takeovers is becoming more difficult and more critical than ever before.

Hackers may use phishing, malware and other techniques (e.g., brute force using common passwords) to capture member password details to access accounts. The FBI recently released a warning to consumers alerting them to the risks associated with using public USB charging ports usually found in shopping centres, airports and hotels, noting that hackers can infect such devices with malware and steal their data.[585]

Once accounts have been accessed, hackers may attempt to financially benefit from the hack. This may include:

1. **Fraudulent transactions**: financial information such as credit card details could be accessed via the hacked account and used to conduct fraudulent payments.

2. **Selling member data**: hackers may attempt to sell member data on the internet (i.e., for identity theft) rather than use it themselves. In recent years, there has been an increase in personal data for sale on the dark web. An article by Quartz[586] indicated a stolen identity can sell for an average of US$20, with a range from less than US$1 to about US$450.

3. **Ransom payment:** hackers may lock out the owner of the database and demand a ransom for control to be provided back to them.

---

585 Oladipo, 2023, The Guardian, 'FBI warns consumers of malware threat to phones from public charging stations', https://www.theguardian.com/technology/2023/apr/11/public-charging-stations-malware-phones-fbi, accessed 16 May 2023.

586 Collins, K., 2015, 'Here's what your stolen identity goes for on the internet's black market', Quartz, https://qz.com/460482/heres-what-your-stolen-identity-goes-for-on-the-internets-black-market/, accessed 9 June 2020.

4. **Credentials stuffing:** where the hacked username and password is used to access the member's account on other sites. The approach preys on the tendency for consumers to use the same credentials across multiple websites.

5. **Peeking:** fraudsters may access, or 'peek into', a members account to determine the loyalty currency value within the account and sell the compromised account on the dark web to other hackers with the skills to be able to cash out the value from the account.

6. **Cashing out:** fraudsters may buy compromised accounts on the dark web and cash out. This requires a very different set of skills to picking which is often why these actions are conducted by different people.

Hackers may sell member data on the internet rather than using it themselves. In recent years, there has been an increase in personal data for sale on the dark web. An article by Quartz[587] indicated a stolen identity can sell for an average of US$20, with a range from less than US$1 to about US$450.

Mitigation

Member data should be encrypted 'in motion' (active data traveling between devices, either through private networks or over a public or untrusted network) and 'at rest' (inactive data stored physically in any digital format in persistent storage). While many companies apply encryption in motion, fewer apply encryption at rest. Both are important, because if a hacker manages to intercept data during transit or access the database directly, the encrypted data cannot be used, ensuring the member is adequately protected.

Companies should conduct regular monitoring of online marketplaces that are buying/selling points. In addition, they should check all sections of the web (especially the dark web) to identify if their program data is for sale. Companies such as Amazon have started actively scanning member email addresses for

---

587   Collins, K. 'Here's what your stolen identity goes for on the internet's black market,' July 2015 https://qz.com/460482/heres-what-your-stolen-identity-goes-for-on-the-internets-black-market/ accessed 9th June 2020

known data breaches on other platforms and then recommending to their customers to change their passwords to prevent credentials stuffing attacks.

Ensuring members and staff are required to create complex and unique passwords (i.e., at least 8 characters and using a combination of letters, numbers and symbols), and having checks in place to recognise common passwords is an important measure in preventing account takeovers. A number of recent case studies globally highlight the prevalence of a lack of credentials policies, including:

- **Air India:** where an IT employee left and was able to hack the IT system, administer user rights to himself and other accomplices, allowing them to bypass KYC, and access the loyalty currency in member accounts.[588]

- **British Airways**: where customer service helpfully suggested a work-around to members who could not log-in to their accounts after the introduction of a complex password system, recommending the use of Pineapple3 as a password instead of their own 'because that works'.[589]

- **IHG Rewards**: where the system password was set as 'Qwerty1234' (as detailed in the case study below). [590]

IHG Rewards

IHG Rewards was hacked using password 'Qwerty1234' which took the entire IT system down for two days.

---

588 NDTV, 'Techie Held For Hacking Air India Frequent flyer Accounts', https://www.ndtv.com/delhi-news/techie-held-for-hacking-air-india-frequent-flyers-accounts-1432648#:~:text=New%20Delhi%3A%20A%2023%2Dyear,arrested%20from%20Jaipur%20on%20Friday, accessed 16 May 2023.

589 Smith, M., contributor to Loyalty Programs: The Complete Guide, a recount of his own experience.

590 Ollila, J., 2022, Loyalty Lobby, 'IHG Was Hacked Using Password "QWERTY1234"', accessed via https://loyaltylobby.com/2022/09/17/ihg-was-hacked-using-password-qwerty1234/, 3 April 2023.

The hacker group from Vietnam called TeaPea said the following:

'TeaPea say they gained access to IHG's internal IT network by tricking an employee into downloading a malicious piece of software through a booby-trapped email attachment.

The criminals then say they accessed the most sensitive parts of IHG's computer system after finding login details for the company's internal password vault.

'The username and password to the vault was available to all employees, so 200,000 staff could see. And the password was extremely weak,' they told the BBC.

Surprisingly, the password was Qwerty1234, which regularly appears on lists of most commonly used passwords worldwide'.[591]

An instance of an account take-over can sometimes be identified by monitoring for unusual activity. For example, a password change can often be the sign of an account take-over, particularly if it is preceded by a redemption. Automated reporting can help quickly identify these instances by generating alerts to monitoring teams. It is therefore important to ensure there is not a complete disconnect between loyalty program managers and those monitoring security and fraud practices such as IT teams. It is also recommended to protect any profile changes by requiring password authentication as part of the process.

There are numerous tools in the marketplace provided by companies that provide real time monitoring of the signs that an account has been taken over and is compromised. There are also many emerging tech companies which provide end-to-end fraud prevention software solutions to automate security and fraud checks and defect against cybercriminals and bots. In addition, best-practice loyalty platforms globally have invested in their security and fraud capabilities as this has now become a high priority for their customers. This is an important feature to focus on when selecting a loyalty platform vendor.

---

591 Ollila, J., 2022, Loyalty Lobby, 'IHG Was Hacked Using Password "QWERTY1234"', accessed via https://loyaltylobby.com/2022/09/17/ihg-was-hacked-using-password-qwerty1234/, 3 April 2023.

A free tool launched by the Dutch police called 'No More Leaks'[592] is aimed at preventing the misuse of login credentials by enabling the police to share encrypted data with accredited private partners. The police allow participating parties (such as accredited loyalty program operators) to check their database of half a billion compromised accounts to see whether information from the program is there and has been compromised so preventative action can be taken.

The ability for a hacker to fraudulently redeem a member's accumulated loyalty currency and rewards can be reduced and/or blocked by implementing 2FA, as it requires the member to authenticate in a way a hacker may not be able to fulfil. One limitation of this approach is it requires an additional step in the redemption process, which may frustrate members, particularly if they themselves cannot complete the 2FA step (e.g., 'I forgot what my favourite holiday destination is'). It is important to note that relying on secure sign on via Captcha tools (where members are required to 'pick all boxes that have traffic lights', a process that can take time and reduce conversion rates[593]) is not always secure due to the existence of human 'fraud farms' where real people are paid to bypass this security measure on behalf of hackers. If available, using biometrics (i.e., fingerprints, speech and facial recognition on smartphones) is a preferred sign-on method to combat this.

If a fraudulent redemption does take place, sending a message to the member's email and phone (e.g., 'We hope you enjoy your new toaster') can act as an alert to the member so they can escalate to customer service and have the incident investigated.

Technology can also play a key role in helping to detect fraudulent redemptions. A recent example includes an airline cancelling a fraudulent redemption because their systems detected that the member was on a flight with the airline that had no available Wi-Fi during the time of the redemption.

Part of the reason bank accounts are hacked less than loyalty accounts

592 Politie, No More Leaks, https://www.politie.nl/onderwerpen/no-more-leaks.html, accessed 30 May 2023.

593 Kahn, R., 2021, Anura, 'CAPTCHA and reCAPTCHA: How Fraudsters Bypass It', accessed via https://www.anura.io/blog/captcha-and-recaptcha-how-fraudsters-bypass-it, 3 April, 2023.

(beyond KYC and better password requirements) is that customers understand that cash is real value. Programs may be able to better engage members to take account security more seriously by communicating that there is real value in the account which needs to be protected.

Hilton Honors

After a 2014 hack of the Hilton Honors program, members reported receiving emails for unauthorised reward redemptions and noticed their points balances were significantly depleted.[594]

One member's account was used to pay for six hotel stays at Hilton properties; the corporate credit card associated with the account was then used to buy more reward points for the hacker. Many of the points drained from accounts later appeared for sale online at a fraction of their value. For instance, one vendor sold 240,000 points for US$3.50, another sold off 883,000 points for US$20 worth of Bitcoin; others traded stolen points for US$100 gift cards.

An investigation later identified the points were stolen in a mass brute force attack from multiple hackers permitted by weak security protocols. One user on a forum released a simple code alleged to have been used to breach accounts protected only with a four-digit PIN on the Hilton site.

One positive note for Hilton was that the redemption emails alerted many members to escalate the incident with customer service as soon as it occurred.

Following the attacks, Hilton introduced a more robust sign-in process (including more complex passwords and CAPTCHA codes) as a measure to avoid a recurrence of such breaches.

---

594 Pauli, D., 2014, 'Hackers plunder Hilton "HHonors" rewards points, go on shopping spree', The Register, https://www.theregister.co.uk/2014/11/05/hilton_honor_cards_breached/, accessed 20 May 2020.

Misappropriated paper join forms

Risk

Despite living in a digital age, some loyalty programs still require members to fill in a paper form to join. These forms are stored, and at a later stage a staff member is required to manually enter the details into the member database to create the account.

With the forms containing member personal details, fraudsters could gain access to the discarded forms and use them for identity theft and other detrimental activities.

Mitigation

Companies should avoid a join process which requires a member to fill in a paper form. Starting the registration process, then providing the member with a code to complete it online is a safer process, and ensures the member still earns for the specific transaction.

If this is unavoidable, the company should implement a monitoring process which ensures the forms are tracked at all times, and destroyed once the details have been inputted into the member database.

Compromised third-party system links

Risk

Many loyalty platforms communicate with other third-party systems. This includes payment systems such as Point of Sale (POS) and points redemption portals. Each link represents a risk, with an opportunity for a hacker to access the loyalty platform and database if appropriate security protocols are not established.

Mitigation

Periodic audits of system interconnectivity should be conducted to identify weak links. Penetration testing ('pen' testing or ethical hacking) should be conducted to identify security vulnerabilities that a hacker could exploit.

British Airways

In 2018, cyber-criminals stole payment card details from an estimated 500,000 British Airways passengers who bought flights on the www.ba.com website or through the British Airways app, or made transactions involving Avios – their loyalty program currency.[595]

Investigations revealed the hack in part involved customers being diverted to a fraudulent website, through which their details were harvested, including account customer information, payment cards and travel booking details.

It was identified the security of personal data was compromised due to an outdated IT system. British Airways were fined £183.4m for the breach, which does not account for other costs such as reimbursing affected customers, apology advertisement spend, and the damage to the brand's reputation.

British Airways took action to appeal the fine. On 16 October 2020, the Information Commissioners Office (ICO) issued British Airways with the final penalty notice of £20m, an almost 90 per cent reduction of the original fine. It is understood that a majority of the reduction (approx. £150 million) was due to the ICO placing less blame on BA than it originally had upon conclusion of their full investigation into the events which led to the attack; another £6 million was discounted based on BA's response, and a further £4 million to reflect the effects that Covid-19 had on the airline[596].

595 Cellan-Jones, R., 2019, 'British Airways faces record £183m fine for data breach, BBC, https://www.bbc.com/news/business-48905907, accessed 20 May 2020.

596 Hickman, T., Timmons, J., 2020, White & Case, 'UK ICO fines BA £20m for data breach', https://www.whitecase.com/insight-alert/

Airline IT provider

SITA provides IT services for 400 airlines across the industry, including passenger travel planning and booking, airport operations and security, baggage, aircraft connectivity and in-flight cabin and cockpit operations.

Hackers were able to access the back-end computer system of the SITA Passenger Service System for up to a month before the hack was uncovered, compromising the data from Star Alliance and OneWorld members with Singapore Airlines, New Zealand Air, Lufthansa, Malaysia Airlines, Cathay Pacific, Finnair and Japan Airlines among those affected.

The frequent flyer data breached was contained to passenger names, frequent flyer numbers and program status with members of these programs contacted and urged to change their account passwords 'out of an abundance of caution'.[597]

This highlights the importance of avoiding the sharing of customer PII, payment information or passwords with third parties.

Join bonus fraud

Risk

A fraudster may join the program multiple times using fake personal details to access join bonuses.

Mitigation

This is primarily an issue when the join bonus is overly generous and/or the program allows for points to be transferred. It is recommended to keep the join bonus relatively low (i.e., start members on the journey to a redemption) and,

---

uk-ico-fines-ba-ps20m-data-breach, accessed 3 April 2023.

597 ABC News, 2021, 'Airline IT provider hacked, Star Alliance and OneWorld frequent flyer data breached', https://www.abc.net.au/news/2021-03-06/airline-it-provider-hacked-frequent-flyer-data-breached-sita/13223300, accessed 15 June 2023.

in some cases, avoid allowing members the ability to transfer or pool points altogether.

Limiting one membership to one mobile phone or mobile phone number can reduce the risk further by making it more difficult and expensive for a fraudster to take advantage of the join bonus.

Earn fraud and promotion exploitation

Risk

This occurs at a rule level where individuals identify ways to exploit the program to earn an enormous amount of value in a short time frame. This may be due to known risks or risks which are not obvious to the program operator.

Promotions, such as bonus points campaigns, can act to stimulate member engagement, but they may also provide opportunities for exploitation. Promotions sometimes inadvertently contain loopholes which can allow members to access value in excess of what was planned. In the social media age, these can be shared very quickly with other members, causing an exponential expansion of the impact.

A group may use a single loyalty card for multiple transactions, pooling all the points into one account.

Interestingly, the activity they engage in to exploit the opportunity may be perfectly legal, as per The Pudding Guy case study below.

Mitigation

Reporting should be implemented which generates alerts if a single account earns a large number of points, or engages in multiple transactions in a specified period. The identified accounts can then be isolated and frozen pending further investigation.

Program and/or promotion terms and conditions should be constructed in a way which weighs them in favour of the program operator to allow sufficient control in the event an issue is identified.

Social media monitoring should be conducted to identify exploitation of promotions that have spread to the mainstream. Rapid identification can help close the promotion down, thereby curtailing the damage.

Healthy Choice and The Pudding Guy

In 1999, David Phillips, a civil engineer from California, earned 1.2 million airline miles by taking advantage of a Healthy Choice promotion by purchasing large volumes of puddings.[598]

The promotion rewarded participants with up to 1,000 travel miles for the airline of their choice for every 10 product codes they collected.

Recognising the potential, Phillips shopped around for the cheapest products he could find, eventually discovering single pudding cups selling at 25 cents.

Purchasing more than 12,000 cups of pudding, he earned 1.2 million miles for just US$3,140, also earning him the nickname 'The Pudding Guy'.

Phillips donated the puddings to The Salvation Army, allowing him to claim US$815 in tax deductions.

Starbucks Rewards

Starbucks Rewards ran a promotion which provided members with a free item on their birthday or after accumulating 12 stars.

One member took advantage by using their free beverage to create the most expensive Starbucks drink ever.[599] It included 60 espresso

598 Herreria, C. R., 2016, 'Carla, Meet David Phillips, The Guy Who Earned 1.2 Million Airline Miles With Chocolate Pudding', HuffPost, https://www.huffpost.com/entry/david-philipps-pudding-guy-travel-deals_n_577c9397e4b0a629c1ab35a7, accessed 20 May 2020.

599 Northrup, L., 2014, 'New Starbucks Free Drink Record Set With $54 Sexagintuple Vanilla Bean Mocha Frappuccino', Consumerist, https://consumerist.com/2014/05/27/

shots, protein powder and syrups in a giant Slurpee cup totalling US$54.75, all for free.

Restrictions were quickly implemented into the program terms and conditions to prevent other members from replicating the behaviour.

Points transfer/pooling fraud

Risk

The ability to transfer points from one account to another provides opportunities for fraudsters to increase their ability to remain undetected, as it allows them to keep fraudulent earn events small and infrequent, but on a vast scale. Points can then be consolidated into a smaller number of accounts for easy redemption, or even sale. This can lead to vast amounts of fraudulent accounts (often created automatically via bots) which skews reporting.

Frequent flyer and hotel programs often contend with travel agents creating member accounts for travellers without the traveller's knowledge. After the travel is completed, the travel agent transfers all points earned to a single account for their own usage.

eBay and other consumer commerce sites have been used to sell bundles of points or miles, despite this being expressly prohibited by the terms and conditions of the program.

Mitigation

The most effective mitigation is to deny members the ability to transfer or pool points altogether as part of the design of the program.

If a decision is made to progress with transfers or pooling, then monitoring systems for bot detection and/or where a significant number of accounts are opened either with the same or a similar email address should be implemented,

---

new-starbucks-free-drink-record-set-with-54-sexagintuple-vanilla-bean-mocha-frap-puccino/, accessed 21 May 2020.

with clear escalation pathways. For example, fraudsters may have emailaddress1@, emailaddress2@, emailaddress3@ and so forth.

Placing limits on transfer activity can minimise the impacts of fraudulent behaviour. This may include only being able to transfer a minimum/maximum number of points at one time, having limits on the number of transfers which can be processed each year, restricting transfer to family members only, or charging a transaction fee.

An example of this is the Lufthansa Miles & More frequent flyer program which provides a 'Transfer Miles' service allowing members the option to transfer and receive points from another Miles & More member for a transaction fee, with a maximum transfer of 50,000 miles per calendar year.[600]

The Travel Agent

A former travel agent was charged for stealing nearly 3.7 million airline miles from high-end clients, and then using them to buy flight tickets for herself and her family.[601]

The travel agent frequently denied her clients access to their airline miles or misled clients into believing that the airlines had imposed restrictions on generating loyalty bonuses.

In truth, the airline miles were misappropriated for the travel agent's own benefit. Some 135 flights for herself and her family worth more than US$109,000 were booked before the fraud was discovered.

Policies allowing clients to purchase tickets for other clients and convert frequent flyer miles to other accounts had enabled the travel agent to do the unlawful deed for years.

---

600 Lufthansa, 'Help & Contact', Lufthansa Airlines, https://www.miles-and-more.com/row/en/general-information/help-and-contact.html, accessed 21 May 2020.
601 Airlines IATA, 2019, 'Fraud prevention: Strengthening the defences', International Air Transport Association (IATA), https://www.airlines.iata.org/analysis/fraud-prevention-strengthening-the-defences, accessed 21 May 2023.

Though the ability to transfer or pool points is a beneficial feature when used appropriately, without any mitigation or monitoring strategy in place, the potential risks for fraudulent transfers are evident and can go unnoticed. In this case, it was discrepancies in the frequent flyer account of one of the company's top clients which revealed the fraudulent behaviour.

World of Hyatt

Hyatt allows points transfers between any account but only allows this once every 30 days.

'A single member may only participate in a points combining transaction (transferring or receiving points) once every 30 days.'[602]

This clause, along with the tedious and manual points combining request form which needs to be submitted, would significantly minimise fraud risks associated with points pooling.

Retro claims fraud

Risk

If the method by which a member can make a retrospective (or retro) claim (e.g., post-purchase entering codes from receipts) does not have appropriate controls, fraudsters may make multiple claims, thereby earning large amounts of points. This will create a secondary issue of increased workload for customer service in processing the claims.

Mitigation

It is recommended to not support retro claims.

If retro claims are introduced, it is recommended to limit claims to a small number per account to minimise fraud exposure and to place time restrictions

---

602 Hyatt, 'World of Hyatt – Purchase, Share & Gift Points', https://world.hyatt.com/content/gp/en/rewards/purchase-share-gift.html, accessed 29 May 2020.

on when a claim can be made (most airline programs limit the time claim to six months, while with QSR's this is much shorter).

Referral program fraud

Risk

If the loyalty program is designed to reward members when they successfully invite a new member to join the program, fraudsters can utilise bots to generate multiple new accounts, thereby earning large amounts of bonus points. The program will be filled with fake member accounts, skewing program analytics.

Mitigation

This issue can be resolved if the new member must make at least one transaction for the referral bonus to be released.

Referral tracking reporting can be used to identify accounts which show an unusually large amount of referral activations, with alerts triggered to inform the program operator to investigate.

Limiting the number of referrals an individual member can be rewarded for will help to reduce the magnitude of the risk.

Status matching fraud

Risk

Major loyalty programs which support status tiers sometimes run status matching campaigns. This allows high-status members of other programs to access the same status level without having to earn it via traditional channels such as flights and/or spend.

Depending on the verification processes, it can be possible for fraudsters to create counterfeit membership cards which show they are a high status (e.g., Platinum). They will then receive Platinum with the program. This will then allow them to take advantage of other programs conducting status matching, although this time with a genuine card.

The Covid-19 pandemic saw airlines unable to fly, and many airlines leaned heavily on their loyalty programs for survival. This included frequent flyer programs extending members status expiry periods. With a resurgence in travel in 2023, a rise in status match promotions ensued. More status matching promotions have led to a rise in status matching fraud.

Mitigation

Status matching campaigns should require the member to present more than just a card (or image of a card). They should also be asked to provide evidence of their transaction activity with the program which earned them the status tier. For example, this may be their loyalty program transaction history which proves the accumulation of status credits.

Some airlines have begun collaborating with competitors to verify the status of members seeking status matches as a method to reduce incidences of fraud.

Once the status tier matching has been processed, additional rules can be implemented to further reduce the risk to the program. For example, a member who has received frequent flyer status matching may be required to take two flights within three months or their tier status will be lost.

United Airlines

US airlines have begun collaborating to reduce fraud associated with status matching.[603]

One instance involved a member being denied a status match from United Airlines after they were informed their current competitor status was not earned.

---

603 Leff, G., 2018, 'United Shares Member Info With Other Airlines to Combat Status Match Fraud', https://viewfromthewing.com/united-shares-member-info-with-other-airlines-to-combat-status-match-fraud/, accessed 21 May 2020.

The member had a promotional status generated from an earlier status match. United contacted the competitor airline to research the status, and denied the match on the ground their current status was not earned.

Of note, United's status match campaign at the time did not say anything about limitations regarding promotional versus earned.

Redemption fraud

Risk

One example of redemption fraud involves 'double-dipping'. This is where members attempt to conduct a redemption simultaneously via two different channels in an attempt to spend the points twice. For example, a member may attempt to redeem points via a call centre while redeeming online at the same time.

Fraudsters may also attempt to double-dip on single-use digital vouchers. This involves taking a screenshot of the voucher barcode and sharing with friends. The group may then attempt to use the vouchers at the same time via different Point of Sale systems.

Punch cards can be counterfeited, allowing fraudsters to make multiple reward claims without spending with the retailer. This may involve using a fake stamp or creating an entirely fake card.

Another example involves members spending on products to earn points, then redeeming the points on rewards, only to return the products for a refund. The loyalty program wears the cost of the reward, while the business gains no benefit from the transaction.

If the program allows gifting of vouchers, fraudsters may be provided with the opportunity to exploit time zones. For example, one time zone may not have the fraud team actively monitoring suspicious activity, allowing fraudsters to redeem for a voucher which is then sent to another time zone to be spent.

Lastly, a member may make a legitimate redemption, such as redeeming a reward night from a hotel program, and sell the redeemed night to a third party, operating outside of the program rules.

Mitigation

IT systems should be sufficiently sophisticated to block duplicate redemptions from occurring. If they do occur, the system should trigger an instant alert to enable the reward delivery to be blocked. A short delay in reward delivery may be required to support this process. This is particularly important for redemptions involving digital downloads and for higher value and/or near cash rewards (e.g., gift cards or items like flat screen TVs). From a design perspective, this can be challenging in circumstances where the member base has an expectation of instant gratification, and therefore a balance may be required.

Apps can be configured such that they block the ability for the phone to take a screenshot of the digital voucher barcode. This does not prevent a photo to be taken with another phone, however systems should be high-tech enough to block duplicate redemptions without affecting voucher processing times.

Physical punch cards should only be used for low-value rewards. Redeemed punch cards should be inspected for evidence of fraud. Staff should be trained to be on alert for customers making multiple redemptions. Ideally, the program should be transferred from a physical card into a digital card.

The loyalty platform should be configured to deduct points from member accounts in the event of a refund. This can be challenging for coalition programs but is still possible if the program operator is committed. Delays in points being credited to member accounts can help reduce refund fraud. For example, frequent flyer programs can have delays of up to 60 days in points being credited to member accounts, making it more difficult for fraudsters to commit refund fraud.

Systems can be configured so that if the IP address/geolocation where the voucher is created is presented in a different location, it can be blocked.

New rules to limit the third-party sale of redemption nights are being applied by programs, with checks in place to validate the identity of the end-user of the redeemed reward.

Subway Sub Club

In 2005, Subway's Sub Club loyalty program rewarded members with free meals every time they filled a punch/stamp card with stamps.[604]

Advances in computer and laser printer technology allowed fraudsters to make counterfeit punch cards that were indistinguishable from the real cards. They also sold Subway stamps on eBay.

Instances of fraudulent staff redemptions were also reported where staff would collect stamps on behalf of customers who did not ask for them, use them to complete stamp cards for themselves, and cash them out when a customer was paying cash for their order. This involved ringing the order up as a reward (i.e., freebie), pocketing the cash payment from the customer for themselves, then placing their completed stamp card in the till to ensure the till was balanced[605].

The program experienced such extensive levels of fraudulent claims that the program had to be closed down.

It has since been relaunched as the Subway MyWay program after taking new technological advances into consideration.

Today's program runs on apps and unique QR codes, making it much more challenging for fraudsters to exploit.

Refund fraud

Risk

Refund fraud may occur when customers steal the goods instead of purchasing them, then return them for a refund.

604 Ogles, J., 2005, 'Fraud Sinks Subway's Sub Club', Wired, https://www.wired.com/2005/09/fraud-sinks-subways-sub-club/, accessed 21 May 2020.

605 Reddit user, 2021, https://www.reddit.com/r/AskReddit/comments/o1hasb/serious_employers_whats_the_most_insane_complaint/?sort=top, accessed 3 April 2023.

Alternatively, refund fraud may occur when members of a program identify loopholes which allow them to earn rewards for a purchase, which they subsequently redeem, before returning the goods for a refund. In this case, the rewards would be unable to be reversed when the refund is processed since they have been redeemed prior.

Mitigation

Companies and programs should ensure that customers are unable to return items unless they can provide proof-of-purchase. Storing all member purchases against a member's profile, including digital receipts, ensures that honest members which have genuinely lost their proof-of-purchase can always receive a refund in line with the refund policy.

In the case of ensuring the rules of the loyalty program protect against refund fraud, there are a number of ways this can be managed. The first is issuing rewards in a 'pending' status when an order is placed, then moving them to 'available' status, where they are available to be redeemed once the refund period has passed. Another method is to delay the issuance of rewards completely until after a cooling off period (i.e., after 30 days, or after a member has taken the flight, or stayed at the hotel). Lastly, the member may receive a loyalty currency such as points when they purchase, but the points are restricted from being redeemed until after a certain period.

UK Shoplifter

A UK shoplifter has recently been convicted of stealing goods from UK high street retailers over a thousand times between 2015-2019, and returning them for £500K in refunds she was not entitled to.

The shoplifter would find loopholes in the returns policies of various retailers, and travel around the country committing refund fraud. Between 2015-2017, she received £60,787.09 in refunds from Boots despite having only spent £5,172.73. She also received £42,853.65 in refunds from Debenhams despite having only spent have £3,681.33 during a four-year period, and she received £33,131.61 in refunds from John Lewis stores including Milton

---

Keynes, Newbury and Reading, having only spent £5,290.36 between the same period.[606]

If the shoplifter were required to provide a receipt, or provide her membership details to access digital receipts stored within her account, the UK retailers targeted would not have been exposed. This method protects companies from fraud, whilst also protecting and benefiting members with insurance against honest mistakes associated with receipt loss.

First party fraud

Risk

Loyalty programs may be affected by fraud conducted with the complicit acknowledgement of the account holder. For example, they may process a redemption, but then call the call centre acting as a customer claiming the points have been taken without their knowledge or consent.

A variation is where the member's family or friends manage to access their account and process redemptions without their knowledge or consent.

Mitigation

Reporting systems (same IP address used, geolocation identifiers, etc.) can help identify some of these instances, and then they can be addressed as customer service issues. Some loyalty programs, where they have strong grounds to suspect fraud, will suspend the member.

Reporting to monitor for significant abuse is best practice. This includes training call centre staff to write notes detailing the claim, which can be referred to later if the member makes a similar claim. It also includes reporting which details claim activity to support fraud monitoring processes.

---

606 Waites, D., 2023, 'Fraud made £500k by returning stolen goods to John Lewis and Boots, The Reading Chronicle, https://www.readingchronicle.co.uk/news/23391884.fraud-made-500k-returning-stolen-goods-john-lewis-boots/, accessed 16 May 2021.

The program terms and conditions should ensure the operator has the right to freeze or suspend an account if the correct sign-in details have been used but the account shows signs of suspicious activity. The program should also be covered for member reimbursement claims if a redemption event has taken place.

Staff fraud

Risk

Encouraging frontline staff to participate in a loyalty program can be beneficial because it can help to educate them about the benefits, leading them to promote it to customers. However, it can also lead to fraud issues.

For example, frontline staff may choose to scan their own loyalty card when processing a transaction if the customer is not a member, thereby collecting the points. They may process false transactions to generate points earn. Staff may also use multiple accounts to minimise the risk of detection. Staff fraud events may be as simple as the staff member providing a friend with several stamps on a stamp card (instead of one).

With direct access to the loyalty platform, customer service staff can be a major source of fraudulent behaviour. This includes providing bonus points to accounts (their own or family/friends), providing points refunds on vouchers (even though the voucher has been used), secretly creating new promotions with large bonus points offers for their own use, promoting family and friends to high status tiers, and asking the member for their password (so they can later hack the member's account). Call centre staff are also in a position to collect sensitive information such as credit card details and account passwords/pins which they can use to place fraudulent transactions elsewhere or even conduct identity theft.

Some programs provide staff with incentives to sign new members. This can lead to a situation where customers are registered without them being aware.

Lastly, IT staff have the technical ability to execute fraud (such as accessing member accounts and redeeming their rewards) as well as the technical ability to remove traces of their fraud quickly.

Mitigation

Earn monitoring reporting can be used to identify most instances of this type of activity, as it will identify accounts which show consistent earn behaviour throughout the day, a contrast to most member earn activity. If the staff member is using multiple accounts, it may be harder to detect. Limiting one membership to one mobile phone or phone number can reduce the risk further.

An investigation should be conducted to ascertain whether staff can override systems to award extra points to an account by entering false information into the POS.

Some companies ban their own employees from participating in their loyalty program, which may be a consideration for some companies who deem the risk to be too high.

Monitoring and reporting of individual customer service staff is important to identify the amount of points they are crediting to accounts. Any points credited to an account should be supported by notes from the agent justifying the action.

Any accounts which have repeat credits should also be identified as part of the monitoring process. If required, the accounts should be blocked. The ability to do this should be clearly detailed in the terms and conditions.

In instances where members complain that their account has been compromised, any call centre engagement should be included as part of the investigation to determine whether a call centre agent may be involved.

It is also best practice for all calls to be recorded for quality and assurance purposes. This allows for the call log to be accessed to better understand how a call centre agent may have committed fraud and how many members may have been impacted.

To reduce the incentive for staff to sign new members without the customer being aware, a condition should be implemented whereby the member needs to transact within a specified time period for the staff member to be awarded their bonus.

Mandatory security and background checks should be conducted on all staff prior to being onboarded into the business. For staff leaving the business, offboarding processes and protocols should exist to ensure access to all systems and networks is terminated as quickly as possible.

The Airline Agent

One airline employee accumulated loyalty points from thousands of passengers.[607]

The agent put in accurate passenger details, but then used his member details instead of the passengers, which allowed him to accumulate approximately 2.6 million air miles before anyone noticed.

The agent was only caught when a victim customer went into their account to use miles to buy a trip, checked their balance and discovered there was nothing there.

When the customer brought this to the attention of the parent company, an investigation ensued, and the agent's fraud was discovered. This led to him being sent to prison.

Staff account take-over

Risk

An event even more serious than member account take-over is staff or customer service account take-over. This can provide the fraudster with the ability to credit large amounts of points to multiple accounts, and redeem those points

---

607 Hofmann, S., 2019, 'How to Stop Fraud in Loyalty Programs', Fraud Conference News, https://www.fraudconferencenews.com/home/2019/2/25/how-to-stop-fraud-in-loyalty-programs, accessed 21 May 2020.

for cash-equivalent rewards (such as gift cards) in sizeable volumes, causing considerable financial damage to the company.

Cases of staff account take-over can be exacerbated in circumstances where the compromised account has administrator or high-level security-related rights and privileges, potentially providing fraudsters access to extremely sensitive and valuable data.

Mitigation

Sufficient controls should be established to reduce the likelihood of incidence, such as enforced regular password changes, best-practice password formats, staff training on security protocols and 2FA for login.

Damage minimisation steps can also be introduced, such as a limit on the amount of points which can be credited to an account, and a limit on the number of points credits an agent can process in a set time period.

Marriott

In September 2018, Marriott became aware of a potential security breach after an internal security tool flagged an unusual database query to the Starwood guest reservation database.[608]

After engaging with security experts, it was discovered that information on up to 500m guests was compromised. For 327m of these guests, this information included a combination of personal details, travel and reservation transactions, and communication preferences. For several million members, compromised details included passport numbers, payment card numbers and expiration dates.

Investigators uncovered the database query was made by a user with administrator privileges, but revealed the person to whom the

---

608 Mitchell, V., 2019, 'Marriott creates new loyalty program following hacking scandal', CMO, https://www.cmo.com.au/article/656393/marriott-creates-new-loyalty-program-following-hacking-scandal/, accessed 21 May 2020.

account was assigned was not the one who made the query; the hacker had executed a staff account take-over.

Clues pointed to a combination of tools, including Remote Access Trojans, to capture user login details. However, the complexity of the breach was greater. It was revealed that unauthorised access had occurred to the Starwood network as early as 2014, and when Marriott acquired Starwood in 2016, they inherited thousands of new hotels and adopted an old reservation system unknowingly infected with malware and compromised by hackers.

Marriott unveiled a new customer loyalty program brand, Marriott Bonvoy, the next year and brought together its three legacy loyalty brands under the one banner, presumably discarding antiquated systems in the process.

In February of 2020, Marriott suffered a second breach after a hacker used login credentials of two employees from one of its franchise properties to access customer information from Marriott Bonvoy's backend system.[609]

This time, the hacker had direct access to the loyalty data of 5.2 million hotel guests, including personal data, loyalty account information like points balances, partnerships and affiliations (linked airline programs), and preferences (such as room and language preferences).

Remediation strategies

Whilst the program can be underpinned with technology that helps prevent, detect and mitigate fraud risks, and the program can be designed in a way which best mitigates fraud risks, fraudulent activity may still occur.

This section is designed to address remediation strategies a company can take to manage both large and small security breaches as quickly and effectively as possible.

---

609 Barrett, B., 2020, 'Hack Brief: Marriot Got Hacked. Yes, Again.', Wired, https://www.wired.com/story/marriott-hacked-yes-again-2020/, accessed 21 May 2020.

Large security breaches and cyber security hacks

Steps include:

1. **Incident response planning:** before a breach occurs, it is crucial to have a well-defined incident response plan in place. This plan outlines roles and responsibilities, communication channels, and steps to be taken during and after a breach.

2. **Identify and isolate the breach:** once the breach is detected, the first step is to identify the affected systems, applications, or networks. Isolating the compromised systems from the rest of the network helps contain the breach and prevent further damage.

3. **Engage a response team:** assemble a cross-functional team comprising of IT security professionals, legal advisors, public relations experts, and internal stakeholders. This team will be responsible for coordinating and executing the response plan.

4. **Conduct analysis:** conduct a thorough forensic analysis of the breach, usually by a specialised cybersecurity firm. This involves identifying the attack vectors, determining the extent of the compromise, and gathering evidence for potential legal action.

5. **Notify law enforcement and regulators:** as often required by law, promptly report the breach to the appropriate law enforcement agencies and regulatory bodies. They will provide guidance and may initiate investigations.

6. **Notify affected members:** it is crucial to inform affected members about the breach as soon as possible. Develop a clear and concise notification message, explaining what happened, what data was compromised, and the steps they should take to protect themselves.

7. **Provide support and assistance:** offer support and resources to affected members, such as credit monitoring services or assistance in resetting passwords. Establish a dedicated helpline or email address to handle member inquiries and concerns.

8. **Enhance security measures:** review and strengthen security controls to prevent similar breaches in the future. This may include implementing multi-factor authentication, encryption, intrusion detection systems, and employee security awareness training.

9. **Collaborate with media:** develop a media communication plan to address public perception and minimise reputational damage. Prepare key messages, designate a spokesperson, and proactively engage with media outlets to ensure accurate reporting.

10. **Engage external communication experts:** if necessary, enlist the help of external communication experts to navigate the complexities of communicating with the media, public, and stakeholders. Their expertise can assist in managing the messaging and mitigating reputational risks.

11. **Evaluate legal and regulatory obligations:** work closely with legal advisors to understand any potential legal obligations arising from the breach. This includes complying with data breach notification laws, contractual obligations, and any associated financial or legal liabilities.

12. **Conduct post-incident review:** after the initial response, conduct a comprehensive review of the incident response process to identify any weaknesses or areas for improvement. Update the incident response plan accordingly to enhance preparedness for future incidents.

Small and contained security breaches affecting a minimal number of individual member account(s)

Steps include:

1. **Identify and verify the breach:** confirm the occurrence of the breach and affected account(s)

2. **Gather evidence:** collect relevant data and evidence related to the breach, such as transaction logs, access records, and other information that can assist in determining the nature and extent of the breach.

3. **Isolate and secure the account:** freeze or lock the affected account to prevent further unauthorised access and mitigate potential damage.

4. **Determine the type of fraud:** investigate the breach to identify the specific type of fraud or unauthorised activity that has taken place.

5. **Assess impact and losses:** evaluate the impact and potential losses resulting from the breach, both for the member and the loyalty program operator.

6. **Review terms and conditions:** examine the loyalty program's terms and conditions to ensure they contain provisions that protect the program and its interests in cases of security breaches, fraud, or unauthorised account activity. This step helps establish a legal framework for response and potential liability management. For example, the program may not be liable for member data breaches that occur as a result of the member creating a bad password or logging into their account using public Wi-Fi or public charging stations.

7. **Notify the member:** inform the affected member about the breach, the actions taken to secure their account, and any relevant terms and conditions that apply to their situation.

8. **Assist the member:** provide support and guidance to the member in recovering their account, reporting fraudulent activity, and addressing any potential consequences. Ensure that the terms and conditions provide clarity on the member's rights and responsibilities during this process.

9. **Internal reporting and investigation:** document the breach, response actions, and investigation process for internal reporting purposes. This documentation can assist in assessing the effectiveness of the terms and conditions and identifying any areas for improvement.

10. **Review security measures:** evaluate the existing security measures and controls in place, including any mentioned in the terms and conditions. Identify any necessary enhancements to prevent future breaches and protect the program and its members.

11. **Staff awareness and training**: conduct internal training sessions to educate staff members about security best practices, compliance with the terms and conditions, and their role in protecting the loyalty program.

12. **Monitor for further activity:** continuously monitor the affected account and associated systems for any potential reoccurrence or related fraudulent actions, even after securing the account.

Key insights

- Loyalty fraud is defined as where deception is used to intentionally secure unfair financial, personal or third-party gains from loyalty programs. Understanding potential risks helps to identify issues early so they can be addressed quickly.

- Different types of security and fraud issues which affect loyalty programs include mass data breaches and account take-overs, misappropriated paper join forms, compromised third-party systems and system links, join bonus fraud, earn fraud and promotion exploitation, points transfer/pooling fraud, retro claims fraud, referral program fraud, status matching fraud, refund fraud, redemption fraud, friendly fraud, staff fraud and staff account take-over.

- Each security and fraud challenge has at least one mitigation approach, meaning program operators that are proactively managing risk can significantly reduce their exposure to fraudsters, while simultaneously increasing their response time if a security breach or fraudulent act is detected.

- Technology serves as a valuable asset in the detection and mitigation of fraud; however, it operates within a dynamic landscape where adversaries continuously adapt their tactics, necessitating constant vigilance and adaptability in response.

- If a large or small data breach occurs, a loyalty program operator should have a clear remediation strategy to manage systems, member communications, media and regulators and staff to identify and isolate the breach, resolve the indecent and protect against future incidents.

Suggested reading

- Pauli, Darren, 2014, 'Hackers plunder Hilton 'HHonors' rewards points, go on shopping spree', The Register, https://www.theregister.co.uk/2014/11/05/hilton_honor_cards_breached/, accessed 20 May 2020.

- Hauser, C., 2020, 'EasyJet Says Cyberattack Stole Data of 9 Million Customers', New York Times, https://www.nytimes.com/2020/05/19/business/easyjet-hacked.html, accessed 15 June 2020.

- Zhong, R., 2018, 'Cathay Pacific Data Breach Exposes 9.4 Million Passengers,' New York Times, https://www.nytimes.com/2018/10/25/business/cathay-pacific-hack.html, accessed 15 June 2020.

- Cellan-Jones, Rory, 2019, 'British Airways faces record £183m fine for data breach , BBC, https://www.bbc.com/news/business-48905907, accessed 20 May 2020.

- Herreria Russo, 2016, 'Carla, Meet David Phillips, The Guy Who Earned 1.2 Million Airline Miles With Chocolate Pudding', HuffPost, https://www.huffpost.com/entry/david-philipps-pudding-guy-travel-deals_n_577c9397e4b0a629c1ab35a7, accessed 20 May 2020.

- Northrup Laura, 2014, 'New Starbucks Free Drink Record Set With $54 Sexagintuple Vanilla Bean Mocha Frappuccino', Consumerist, https://consumerist.com/2014/05/27/

new-starbucks-free-drink-record-set-with-54-sexagintuple-vanilla-bean-mocha-frappuccino/, accessed 21 May 2020.

- Ogles, Jacob, 2005, 'Fraud Sinks Subway's Sub Club', Wired, https://www.wired.com/2005/09/fraud-sinks-subways-sub-club/, accessed 21 May 2020.

- Barrett, Brian, 2020, 'Hack Brief: Marriot Got Hacked. Yes, Again.', Wired, https://www.wired.com/story/marriott-hacked-yes-again-2020/, accessed 21 May 2020.

- https://viewfromthewing.com/ihg-crack-fraud-china-careful-gifting-award-nights/, accessed 16 May 2023.

CHAPTER 19

LOYALTY OPERATIONS

This chapter was co-written by **Max Savransky** (ex-COO, Loyalty & Reward Co)

'The first rule of any technology used in a business is that automation applied to an efficient operation will magnify the efficiency. The second is that automation applied to an inefficient operation will magnify the inefficiency.'

- Bill Gates

Focus areas

This chapter will address the following questions:

- Should loyalty operations be maintained internally or outsourced?
- What is involved in running the operations of a loyalty program?
- What teams, roles and responsibilities are required to operate a loyalty program?

THE OPERATION OF a best-practice loyalty program may involve managing a member database engaging in multi-transaction value accumulation and extensive redemption choices, a large-scale member benefits program that requires partnership sourcing, a card-linked cashback program or many other variations.

As established in Chapter 8, there are many different types of program designs. Most loyalty programs layer horizontally across the company, which means that multiple divisions must support the operational execution to achieve desired objectives.

Data analytics support marketing communications and offers, sophisticated accounting rules manage program liabilities, and technology platforms utilise automated capability to optimise lifecycle management. Call centre operations ensure adequate member support is provided, while third-party partners are assisted by commercial teams, and all aspects of the program operations are subject to legal review to minimise litigation exposure and protect consumer rights.

The complexity of the operation requires a team of experienced and educated professionals to ensure it can run smoothly and profitably. Teams may range in size from one or two people (supported by a wider organisation) to several hundred.

This chapter details the requirements for running the operations of a loyalty program. All programs are different, therefore some of the areas discussed may not be relevant, or the teams may fulfil roles which are variations to the functions detailed.

Insource or outsource

The loyalty industry is highly lucrative. Billions of dollars of points and miles are earned and redeemed each year, while hundreds of millions of dollars is invested in technology to power programs, and significant marketing budgets are devoted to promoting the program benefits.

A company can choose to insource the entire operation (including building their own technology platform), or they can opt to outsource some or all of the operations to third party service providers.

Outsourcing appears to be increasingly prevalent. *MarketsandMarkets* forecasts the global loyalty management market size to grow from US$7.6 billion in 2020 to US$15.5 billion by 2025, at a Compound Annual Growth Rate (CAGR) of 15.3 per cent during the forecast period.[610]

---

610 Loyalty Management Market by Component (Solutions and Services),

With outsourcing becoming increasingly prevalent, it is worth exploring the advantages and challenges of outsourcing loyalty operations.

Outsourcing advantages

- **Access to expertise**: companies can gain access to expertise from experienced loyalty professionals, with the potential to drive program operational efficiencies and strategic evolution. Good quality loyalty professionals with extensive experience operating across a variety of programs and industries can be difficult to find and costly to hire internally.

- **Independent perspective**: external agencies can apply a fresh, informed perspective to recommend improvements to an existing program, identifying issues which internal management may either be blind to, or not have the appetite to address.

- **Quality existing solutions**: as detailed in Chapter 11, technology platforms are becoming increasingly sophisticated and more affordable, making the idea of building an internal solution less attractive.

- **Time efficiencies**: external agencies can support launching a new program faster by utilising their knowledge and experience to reduce time wastage. Loyalty platforms can introduce significant automation into daily processes. Reward aggregators can deliver hundreds, thousands or even millions of reward options with no need for the program operator to hold stock.

- **Sophisticated marketing ability**: loyalty agencies may be able to execute marketing campaigns with a level of sophistication which is not possible or viable for the company, delivering personalisation, promotional budget optimisation, and all other associated benefits.

Organization Size (Large Enterprises and SMEs), Deployment Type, Operator (B2B and B2C), Application (Web and Mobile), Vertical, and Region - Global Forecast to 2025, June 2020 https://www.marketsandmarkets.com/Market-Reports/loyalty-management-market-172873907.html accessed 18 August 2020.

Outsourcing challenges

- **Cost**: the services provided by the agency may come at a higher cost than if the company executed internally.

- **Consistent service**: the company may not receive the consistent level of service expected and required, as the agency may have too many other clients (all with competing priorities) and insufficient resources.

- **Knowledge gap**: there may be a continuous knowledge gap between internal teams and outsource agencies which results in the company being too heavily reliant on the skills of the agency to run day-to-day operations. This may impede the company's ability to directly resolve issues and enquiries which arise.

- **Security and fraud risks**: outsource operations can require member personal data to be held in third-party systems, as well as a need for direct access to member data via third-party staff members.

Outsourcing options

Typically, at least some of the operations associated with larger loyalty programs tend to be outsourced. Within this environment, many service providers have evolved to help companies with the design, implementation and/or operation of their program.

In Chapter 11, four types of loyalty technology solution providers were detailed (full-service loyalty solutions, partial service loyalty solutions, off-the-shelf loyalty solutions and niche loyalty solutions) which can all support loyalty program operations to some extent.

In addition to this are loyalty consultancies, such as Loyalty & Reward Co, which can offer a mix of different services and solutions. These consultancies and agencies specialise in strategically designing and implementing loyalty programs, but also support post-launch operations and future roadmap evolution. This allows a company to access experienced loyalty professionals as required whilst maintaining the desired level of flexibility and control over loyalty program operations and future strategy.

Operational areas

This section details the role played by different areas of a company or outsource consultancy which are likely to be involved in the day-to-day running of a loyalty program.

Strategy

The ambition of a Strategy team is to design, refine and optimise the loyalty program to achieve longer-term company objectives.

The responsibilities of the Strategy team include:

- **Strategic planning**: development of an overall strategic program roadmap supported by analytics (program performance, member segmentation, market research insights, front-line staff interviews, competitor approaches, loyalty trends, loyalty psychology, relevant heuristics and biases, technology advancements, commercial modelling, loyalty fraud risk analysis, legal guidance, program testing and other data points) and lifecycle frameworks. Liaise with senior leaders to translate the strategy into business function plans and work streams.

- **Insights capture**: work with Analytics and Marketing to develop the capability to capture, interrogate, understand and apply data-based insights, with a core focus on identifying critical moments that drive delight and build loyalty.

- **Trend monitoring**: proactively identify relevant loyalty trends and translate the future opportunities these trends may unlock for the program.

- **Partner needs**: work with Partner Management to identify opportunities to harness the full potential of the program to support partner customer engagement strategies and company growth.

- **Program benefits**: develop new, or revise existing, program benefits, experiential rewards and the functionality required to increase the program's competitiveness in relevant markets for different segments.

- **Terms and conditions management**: as required, facilitate strategic changes to the program terms and conditions to ensure the program remains on track to deliver to long-term objectives.

The team may also be involved in the wider strategic development of the company, with broader objectives provided at a senior level needing to be incorporated into the more detailed objectives of the loyalty program.

Unless there are highly experienced loyalty professionals within the organisation, a company may consider outsourcing this function. Loyalty strategy and design is very specialised with new and innovative approaches, technology, trends, data analytics methods and reward options constantly emerging.

Marketing

A best-practice loyalty program Marketing team will strive to execute communications across multiple channels to deliver hyper-personalised offers targeting the right member with the right message through the right channel at the right time.

The responsibilities of the Marketing team include:

- **Strategic planning**: development of a marketing communications strategic roadmap supported by analytics (program performance and benchmarking, member segmentation, market research insights, competitor approaches and other data points) and lifecycle frameworks.

- **Marketing execution**: implementation of planned and short-term tactical campaigns designed to achieve the core program objectives by delivering to the strategic roadmap. Communication of past and planned campaign activity to relevant areas of the business to facilitate learnings, member support and enquiries.

- **Campaign tracking**: evaluation of campaign performance and optimisation of subsequent campaigns to increasingly drive member engagement.

- **Agency management**: collaboration with external marketing agencies (as required) by providing strategy, direction and input towards the development of required campaigns that are aligned with the program's brand positioning.

- **Budget management**: development of a detailed plan for management and utilisation of the marketing budget to maximise return on investment.

The team may also be involved in formal projects focused on development of the program, including redesigning, rebranding, strategic formulation and implementation of new technology approaches, changes to the terms and conditions of the program, and other enhancements.

This function is best held within the company. If the program is large, it may be a dedicated loyalty marketing team embedded within the company. For a smaller program, it may sit with the Marketing team of the wider company.

With the rise of machine learning/AI, some larger programs are outsourcing their marketing operations to specialised AI companies, which could herald a future trend if the operational costs make it a cost-effective option and the results clearly deliver better outcomes. There are data security and control risks associated with this approach as detailed in Chapter 18.

Operations

In the same way that a superior quality product or service experience can play a critical role in building customer loyalty, a quality loyalty program member experience is imperative in maintaining longer-term engagement. The ambition of a best-practice Operations team is to strive to enable an outstanding member experience across all member touchpoints.

The responsibilities of the Operations team include:

- **Member experience improvements**: identification of opportunities to add incremental value to the member experience across multiple touchpoints, then championing and engineering initiatives to facilitate the additions.

- **Irritant resolution**: identification of key member irritants across multiple touchpoints, then championing and engineering neutralisation of the irritants.

- **Operational efficiency development**: review, recommend and implement new methods and procedures to increase the efficiency and effectiveness of daily operations.

- **Reward range management**: procuring reward products or reward suppliers, managing the range, facilitating fulfilment, and acting as an escalation path for order issues.

- **Procurement**: support the procurement of products and services for the operational running of the program via approved vendor-engagement processes.

- **Vendor management**: management of relationships with vendors and virtual teams, including vendor onboarding, system integration support and contract compliance.

- **System configuration**: support the configuration of systems as required to execute on agreed changes.

- **Testing**: design and execution of user acceptance and system integration testing processes for system development and configuration changes.

- **Training**: lead the development and facilitate the implementation of training across front-line staff and other teams (as required) for system and process enhancements, and terms and conditions changes.

Due to the extensive variability in loyalty program designs and company sizes, the Operations team roles may vary widely from what is detailed.

This is a function which can be fully or partially outsourced to access operational or cost efficiencies. For example, the program operator may outsource the rewards range management, but choose to maintain the system configuration function within the program.

Partner management

It is important that the Partner Management team are supported with the right tools to help facilitate partner sourcing and negotiations. This may include professionally crafted presentations, other partner case studies, clear-language contracts, and commercial model templates (to help the partner model the benefits of participating in the program).

Specific to points-based programs, the Partner Management team should recognise that individuals outside the loyalty industry may not be aware how programs work, therefore providing a basic education on their structure may be a useful first step.

The responsibilities of the Partner Management team include:

- **Partner strategy**: development and evolution of a partner strategy to identify gaps and growth opportunities for specific companies, categories and industries supported by analytics (local market review, market research, member segmentation, loyalty trends, competitor approaches and other data points) and financial imperatives. Identification of opportunities and innovative strategies to grow the membership base via partnerships.

- **Partner sourcing**: identification and negotiation of new commercial relationships across target categories and industries that deliver to the strategy (e.g., new points earn partners or new offer-provision partners).

- **Partner management**: development and maintenance of positive relationships with program partners. Identification of partner needs and aspirations, and development of initiatives to support their success. Management of any operational or customer issues. Owner of any contractual, program terms and conditions and proposition elements that influence members and operational delivery.

- **Internal collaboration**: work collaboratively with the program team to drive and achieve outcomes focused on partnership delivery and business growth. This may include Marketing (to ensure appropriate promotion of partners to the member base), Finance and Legal (to support contract negotiations and target setting) and Operations (to set-up new partners in the loyalty platform).

- **Financial management**: ownership of partner financial targets and team budgets.

Similar to operations team responsibilities, the Partner Management team scope may vary depending on the type of program design. The size of the company and the program framework chosen will dictate the partner management approach for the program.

A coalition points-based program or an affiliate model will require a business development team to acquire new coalition partners, negotiate contracts and manage relationships, a function which tends to reside within the program.

For a member benefits program which focuses more on growing a network of third-party partners that can provide discounts and offers, fully or partially outsourcing to aggregators can deliver some cost-efficiencies.

For a smaller retail company program, Partner Management responsibilities may be minimal and be able to be handled by the existing Marketing department.

Analytics

The primary aim of the Analytics team is to understand members and provide insights to engage them effectively across all touch points, thereby translating raw data into commercial action and success. There are many types of analytics, including descriptive, diagnostic, predictive and prescriptive, and each have a role to play in a best-practice loyalty program operation. The team may be supported by a separate team of data scientists.

The responsibilities of the Analytics team include:

- **Strategic planning**: creation and implementation of a member insights strategy to support the achievement of program objectives. Development of data-driven loyalty strategies to maximise customer lifetime value. Identification of trends in member behaviour over time.

- **Data-led forecasting**: estimation of the impact of different strategic scenarios using robust analytical/financial models.

- **Capability expansion**: coordination of technology and process initiatives to further improve the program's ability to understand and engage members.

- **Member segmentation**: development and evolution of member segments based on profiles, preferences, purchase behaviours and the specific elements of member behaviour the program is attempting to influence.

- **Campaign optimisation**: utilisation of analytics and testing methodologies to optimise member targeting and future marketing campaign performance in conjunction with the Marketing team.

- **Insights reporting**: development and production of periodic reporting (daily, weekly, monthly, annually) to support the company in understanding member behaviour and responses to products, services, marketing campaigns, offers and changes in the external environment.

As loyalty programs become more focused on delivering to the needs of members, personalisation of communications and offers will continue to increase in importance. This will place greater focus on the Analytics team and analytical systems, with a recognition they play a critical role.

Large programs tend to have sizeable teams of data scientists and analysts which play a critical role in driving member engagement. Analytics functions can be costly, making it harder for smaller programs to perform effectively in this area. Loyalty platforms can play a role here by providing the program operator with a well-structured data and reporting dashboard enabling easy access to essential member insights. This may be supplemented by a small amount of additional analytics support from the platform provider's team.

Technology

The core focus areas of the Technology team include overseeing technology operations, and evaluating and prioritising them according to established business requirements and goals. The technology department also devises and establishes IT policies and systems to support the implementation, operation and evolution of program strategies.

The responsibilities of the Technology team include:

- **Strategic planning**: analysing the business requirements of all teams to determine their technology needs. Optimising the use of existing systems to deliver to the needs. Identifying and recommending new or upgraded technology solutions when existing systems are inadequate, with a primary focus on automation and configuration capability.

- **Technology operations**: monitoring the use of technology systems and software to ensure functionality, efficiency and interoperability. Ensuring strategic capacity planning. Coordinating IT activities to ensure data availability and network services with as little downtime as necessary. Managing the IT help desk.

- **Policy formulation**: formulation and establishment of IT policies and processes to support the implementation of team strategies.

- **Security management**: identification and elimination of security vulnerabilities.

- **System procurement**: identification and purchase of efficient and cost-effective loyalty systems and software.

- **Vendor management**: building relationships with platform vendors and creating cost-efficient contracts.

- **Budget management**: control budget and report on expenditure.

The future loyalty landscape will include a mix of the technology 'haves' and 'have-nots'. The 'haves' will succeed by utilising loyalty platforms and technology innovations to enable the program operators to deliver omnichannel personalisation. The 'have-nots' may struggle because their ability to innovate will be continually stifled by legacy platforms which are inflexible and expensive to maintain and enhance.

While some companies have built their own loyalty platform solution, this is becoming increasingly rare due to the global availability of high-quality, low-cost technology.

Customer service

The role of the Customer Service team is to provide appropriate member support across multiple channels, utilising profile data to personalise the experience as much as possible.

The responsibilities of the Customer Service team include:

- **Strategic planning**: analysing the strategic vision of the program to determine future member support needs. Auditing and identifying system and process needs, and working with IT to identify and recommend new technology solutions when existing systems are inadequate.

- **Contact centre operations**: managing the running of the contact centre, including effective resource planning, reporting analysis, and development of customer service procedures, policies, and standards to exceed agreed service metrics. Ensuring team compliance to all legislation, policies and procedures, and codes of conduct.

- **Irritant resolution**: identification of key member irritants across multiple touchpoints. Resolution of those irritant directly, or via escalation to Operations and other teams.

- **Member experience improvements**: identification of opportunities to add incremental value to the member experience across contact centre touchpoints, then escalation to Operations, Technology, and other teams to own and resolve.

- **Training**: hiring and training of new contact centre agents. Training of agents on new product and service launches, terms and conditions changes, marketing campaigns and other events which may generate contact centre inquiries.

- **Budget management**: control budget and report on expenditure.

Contact centres are increasingly using a range of technologies to provide members with the option to choose how they connect. This includes AI-powered chatbots, apps, social media channels and voice-recognition. Status tier programs may choose to prioritise higher tier members, such that they are moved to the front of the queue during high-volume periods.

The function can just as easily be insourced or outsourced, with the trend to outsourcing continuing globally. Some status tier programs maintain a small team to provide premium tier members with priority service, while other members are directed to an offshore contact centre for support. Some full-service and partial service agencies provide the Customer Service support function as part of their overall product offering.

Finance

The Finance team leads the finance and accounting function, including overseeing statutory reporting, budgeting and forecasting, revenue deferrals and points liability management, compliance, treasury and taxation. Such a team is specifically relevant for large points-based programs which generate sizeable profits from sizeable member bases.

The responsibilities of the Finance team include:

- **Strategic planning support**: working closely with the Strategy team to model the financial impacts of future strategy roadmap scenarios and provide funding approval. Analysing the financial climate and market trends to assist senior executives in creating strategic plans for the future.

- **Finance operations**: directing financial planning and strategy. Overseeing accounts payable, accounts receivable, tax, treasury, payroll, financial and management accounting functions. Reviewing team budgets.

- **Financial reporting**: managing the financial reporting for the program. This includes monthly financial reporting, budgeting and forecasting, multi-year financial plans, and all statutory financial reporting.

- **Risk management**: assessing, managing, and minimising risk, including ensuring that all the program's financial practices are in line with statutory regulations and legislation.

- **Breakage management**: auditing, tracking and managing breakage. Providing recommendations to the Strategy team to adjust terms and conditions to support management of breakage within a pre-defined range.

- **Supplier relationship management**: contract auditing and actuarial services to conduct financial monitoring and modelling. Create and maintain relationships with service providers and contractors, including banking institutions and accountants.

Smaller programs and non-points-based programs can usually access support from the wider company's Finance team, rather than requiring a dedicated loyalty team.

This function tends to be insourced, although auditing may be outsourced.

Security and fraud

The Security and Fraud team is involved in oversight and management of all facets of loyalty program security and fraud. This includes ensuring all teams are equipped with the support, knowledge, and solutions required to identify and mitigate any risks.

The responsibilities of the Security and Fraud team include:

- **Strategic development**: investigate best-practice processes and tools required for an effective strategy to appropriately detect and mitigate security risks and safeguard the company and program. Ensure preparation and readiness for external and internal threats, and act quickly and decisively when threats and attacks are identified.

- **Security and fraud operations**: manage day-to-day security and fraud monitoring, reporting and advising teams of potential risks, including security breaches of other companies which may cause risks for the program's members. Maintain appropriate structure, processes and documentation at all times. Conduct audits and deliver professional reports in situations of investigation with the appropriate facts and findings. Provide feedback to further develop and improve security and fraud management processes and mitigation strategies.

- **Relationship management**: build strong and trusted relationships across all teams to improve detection performance and mitigate risk. Support teams in implementing and maintaining security monitoring processes and policies, and where necessary, provide further guidance in reporting, incident responses and investigations to limit exposure and liability.

- **Training**: provide regular training across the company to educate teams about risks and risk detection, as appropriate.

Large programs with appropriate security and risk technology and processes may only require a single team member to mitigate risks effectively. Smaller programs may merge this team into the role of another individual or outsource it to the technology platform provider. Platforms are increasingly building security and fraud detection software and reporting into their platforms to assist in this area.

Legal

The Legal team focuses on the legal and commercial issues that need to be addressed as part of the establishment and operation of a loyalty program. In most countries, the laws applicable to loyalty programs and wider member engagement approaches are a disparate bundle of regulations that can create compliance challenges for program operators. Legal expertise in this area is important to ensure the program operations do not unnecessarily expose the company to risks.

The responsibilities of the Legal team include:

- **Strategic planning**: legal review of the strategic plans of teams to ensure compliance. Developing a forward view of regulatory changes which may create future impacts on the program operations (e.g., GDPR).

- **Marketing review**: legal review of advertising and marketing campaigns to ensure due disclosure and compliance with competition and consumer laws. Audit of data capture processes to ensure compliance with privacy regulations.

- **Promotion risk mitigation**: implementation of appropriate terms and conditions to protect the program and company from financial and brand damage in the event a promotion is unexpectedly exploited by members.

- **Partner and supplier contracts**: formulation and review of partner and supplier contracts to support the partner sourcing and product/service procurement processes.

- **Legal representation**: representing the program in instances where legal action has been taken by members, partners, suppliers, government bodies or other parties, or where legal action is being taken by the program against other parties.

- **Training**: assisting in the development of policies, procedures and training for staff on relevant legal issues.

Similar to the Finance team, a large and complex loyalty program may require a dedicated Legal team, while a smaller program may utilise the general counsel of the wider company.

Even larger programs with a dedicated Legal team may from time to time outsource work to a legal firm specialising in loyalty regulations.

Key insights

- The complexity of loyalty program operations requires a team of experienced and educated professionals to ensure it can run smoothly and profitably.

- Loyalty program operations involve teams and/or roles and/or responsibilities which touch many different areas of the business including Strategy, Marketing, Operations, Partner Management, Analytics, Technology, Customer Service, Finance, Security and Fraud, and Legal. The size of the company and the program will influence whether dedicated teams and/or roles are required to manage the program operations, or whether the responsibilities may fall under a broader, existing role within the company.

- A program operator may choose to maintain all the operations within the company, outsource some or outsource all. Outsourcing is becoming increasingly prevalent, however loyalty program operators need to consider both the advantages and challenges of this approach.

THE FUTURE OF LOYALTY

'The best way to predict the future is to create it.'

- Abraham Lincoln

BEST-PRACTICE LOYALTY PROGRAM operators utilise a complex combination of design principles, loyalty psychology and behavioural biases, desirable rewards, appropriate design frameworks, games and gamification, technology, analytics and personalisation, lifecycle management, security and fraud protections, and efficient operations to drive industry-leading member engagement.

There appears to be sufficient academic research and empirical evidence to suggest that loyalty programs, when designed and executed correctly, can work to generate increased acquisition, spend, retention, advocacy and brand affinity. For this reason, they will continue to attract large amounts of investment and innovation globally which will work to increase their impact and cost-effectiveness.

What does the future for loyalty hold? The conclusion of *Loyalty Programs: The Complete Guide* reviews a collection of innovative developments and emerging challenges which are forecast by Loyalty & Reward Co to have a material impact on the future of loyalty program design and execution.

Data, machine learning/AI and personalisation

This topic has been covered extensively throughout the book. Improvements in data collection methods and the application of machine learning/AI technology will allow more loyalty programs to deliver personalisation of communications, experiences, and offers at scale. This will eventually manifest in Digital EQ; the ability to anticipate and recognise customer sentiment and deliver a digitally enabled response which optimises the customer experience in real time, serving to build a deeper attitudinal commitment.

Personalisation will not just be limited to digital interactions but will extend into retail outlets via in-store strategies and phone communications via chatbots. Some retailers will provide the opportunity for members to choose whether they are identified or remain anonymous, while others (such as supermarkets and major retailers) will insist on identification as part of their overall shopping experience.

Machine learning/AI will extend further into contact centre operations, utilising extensive personal data profiles to service member needs, with more complex issues handed over to agents. This will reduce reliance on staff (thereby saving on costs) while allowing for 24-hour service support.

Data challenges

With personalised member experiences powered by data, the capture, analysis, use, and monetisation of member personal data by loyalty programs will become increasingly topical. This will be led by consumers, who will demand better controls over their data, including the right to insist it is deleted from program databases, and government bodies, which will legislate more data protections as a counter to the growing dominance of tech giants.

At the same time, digital marketing will suffer the loss of cookies, disrupting current digital targeting and remarketing practices. In parallel, the rise of walled garden data will force digital marketing costs higher.

These developments will increase demand for the capture of zero-party and first-party data. Loyalty programs will be harnessed to play a lead role in the capture of this data and the management of member consent to use the data.

This demand will, in turn, stimulate genuine innovation in the loyalty industry, with the added benefit that the importance placed on the member will increase.

Loyalty programs as a product and services brand

With the growth in importance of zero-party and first-party data, the value of the engaged member databases controlled by large loyalty programs will grow. This will enable the loyalty program to harness their brand by developing a range of products and services which they can promote directly to their member base.

This approach will gain traction as co-branded credit card usage diminishes. Many central banks around the world are working to reduce transaction fees payable by merchants, making it harder for banks to fund bonus points. This excludes the USA where such a move is deemed unlikely.

For a loyalty program, expanding their offering with bespoke clubs, or branded products and services (such as insurance) will help to grow revenues, or at least offset their decline, while growing attitudinal commitment.

Legal trends

It is challenging to predict the approach so many different jurisdictions around the world will take to adjusting regulatory frameworks. That said, loyalty program operators should consider certain trends which point towards a general tightening of consumer protections. Changes to consumer protections will likely impact program disclosures, communications and operations in the jurisdiction/s in which the program operates.

One area is the collection, use and sharing of data. This includes expanding member personal data definitions (e.g., to include technical data such as IP addresses, device identifiers, location data and other online identifiers), separating out consents for data collection and use (e.g., such as third-party sharing) and seamless deletion of data on the request of a member. The EU led the way with GDPR, followed by California. A number of US states, the Australian government and other countries are all progressing with their own changes.

Part of this movement involves regulators increasing pressure on loyalty program operators to ensure terms and conditions and privacy policies are concise, transparent, intelligible, easily accessible, and written in clear and plain language.

Governments are also focusing on other regulator overhauls impacting fair and reasonable tests for processing personal data, unfair contract term regulations, location tracking and surveillance, and cryptocurrency or digital currency regulation.

With major hacks of loyalty program data bases continuing globally, loyalty program operators should expect that cybercrime and cyber security legislation reform will continue, with more onus on the operator to take proactive preventative actions, implement proper alert monitoring, and respond quickly when breaches are detected.

Penalties for breaches of regulations are growing larger, increasing the financial risk (and brand perception risk) for loyalty program operators.

Another area to monitor is financial licenses. As large coalition loyalty programs continue to grow, regulators may consider reversing the exemptions enjoyed by loyalty programs. Most laws applicable to financial products (or non-cash payment facilities) do not currently impact loyalty programs, but this could change. In the future, loyalty programs may be treated as financial products and accordingly will be subject to financial product licensing and other conditions.

Governments around the world may continue to push for credit charge interchange fee reforms, which will make it harder for banks to fund bonus points associated with credit cards. This will impact bank programs but will have a far greater impact on frequent flyer programs which rely on such earn for a sizeable proportion of their revenue.

If operating a loyalty program, seeking sound legal advice for the jurisdiction/s in which the program operates is recommended to ensure the team running the program understands how to ensure member rights are protected at all times.

Ever-evolving member expectations

As discussed in Chapter 1, companies such as Netflix, Amazon, Uber and Spotify have redefined what it means to be a service business with a new manifesto;[611] know me, respond quickly, be where I want to be, tell me what you stand for, speak to my pains and passions, give me value for my privacy and reward me for loyalty.

As more companies replicate the customer experience practices of these market-leaders, consumer expectations defined by the new manifesto will be reinforced, increasing the likelihood they will demand the same experience from other brands. If their expectations are not met, brands risk rapid rejection and vocal disapproval.

The clearest example of this is the expectation of personalisation. Post Covid-19, numerous studies have shown it is now an expectation. Companies that do not move towards the delivery of omnichannel personalisation will be left behind.

The big opportunity for brands is to develop a culture focused on customer experience optimisation and evolution. For some companies, this may start with hiring a customer experience (UX) expert in a senior role in the business to help them commence their journey. Given the accelerating global trends of digital transformation and adoption, the expectations for innovative customer experiences will continue to grow.

Games and gamification

Gamification approaches and techniques will continue to improve, and loyalty platform development will make it easier for program operators to execute campaigns which persuade members to engage in specific behaviours.

While gamification will deliver a significant amount of value, the bigger emerging trend is games. Members of loyalty programs can expect increasing

---

611 Sawhney, M., n.d., 'Applications of AI in Marketing and Customer Experience Management; Identify use cases in Marketing, Sales and Customer Service - Course 5', accessed 23rd May 2020.

innovation in this area, particularly for programs which centre around an app. As the trend gathers momentum, more sophisticated white-label platforms will emerge, supporting the ability for loyalty programs to launch rich gaming experiences at low cost.

Convenience

Gary Vaynerchuk stated that convenience is king. 'In a marketplace of distraction, the company's (sic), products and services that can save you TIME, are going to win. That is why Amazon is a market leader. That is why Prime Now wins. They have simplified the process of buying and selling. They have saved you enormous amounts of time.'[612]

Vaynerchuk also mentions Google Now, Siri, text messages, emojis, spellcheck and abbreviations as convenience-generating. In particular, he focuses on machine learning/AI as important technology that can save users time by learning and automating processes which would have taken much longer.

There are genuine commercial benefits from focusing on convenience. A US Department of Commerce report[613] identified that stores and offerings focused on convenience have been responsible for an estimated 67 per cent of retail growth. A National Retail Federation report[614] found that 90 per cent of consumers surveyed said they were more likely to choose a retailer based on convenience.

A Deloitte report[615] argued that Covid-19 has accelerated the trend towards

612 Vaynerchuk, G., 2017, 'What start-ups really sell', https://www.garyvaynerchuk.com/startups-really-sell/, accessed 24 June 2020.

613 US Department of Commerce, 'Monthly Retail Trade', https://www.census.gov/retail/index.html, accessed 3 April 2020.

614 National Retail Federation, 2020, 'Consumer View Winter 2020', https://nrf.com/research/consumer-view-winter-2020 accessed 24 June 2020.

615 Lobaugh, K. M., Stephens, B. &Reynolds, C., 2020, 'The future is coming... but still one day at a time', Deloitte Insights, https://www2.deloitte.com/us/en/insights/industry/retail-distribution/retail-and-consumer-products-predictions.html?id=us:2el:3pr:4di6513:5awa:6di:MMDDYY:&pkid=1006899#endnote-sup-4, accessed 24 June 2020.

consumer desire for convenience, 'with more than 50 per cent of consumers spending more on convenience to get what they need, with 'convenience' increasingly being defined by contactless shopping, on-demand fulfilment, and inventory availability. As such, there has been a surge in mobile payment usage, delivery app downloads, and buy-online-pick-up-in-store (BOPIS) adoption.'

Loyalty programs have a clear role to play in the manifestation of convenience. Utilising customer data, marketing channels, machine learning/AI and other opportunities, loyalty program designers and operators will increasingly seek innovative ways to increase the convenience for members in engaging with their brand.

Generation Touch Free

In 2013, Josh Elman coined the term *Generation Touch*,[616] referring to Millennials who grew up tech and device savvy and with the expectation that everything will work by touch.

Covid-19 will completely reset this expectation, with most consumers set to develop an expectation that everything will work *touch free*.

Loyalty programs will play a key role in delivering to the expectations of *Generation Touch Free*. This will include utilising data, technology and psychology to build rich augmented reality experiences (such as virtual try-ons), touch free payment solutions, and a variety of technological innovations which personalise the remote or stay-at-home experience. Any innovation which removes the need for members to touch something that other people have touched will be rapidly embraced.

Payments and convergence

Banks, card schemes and major coalition programs are all investing heavily in converging loyalty and payments. Many start-ups are emerging globally with sophisticated white-label platforms which can enable solutions, allowing

---

616 Elman, J., Sept 2013, 'Generation Touch Will Redraw Consumer Tech', TechCrunch, https://techcrunch.com/2013/09/29/generation-touch-will-redraw-consumer-tech/, accessed 20 July 2020.

a member to link a credit card or bank account to a program which instantly rewards them when they spend, digital receipt software that also delivers bonus offers, app integrations that allow members to spend points and miles anywhere, and loyalty programs that run through smart payment terminals.

This extends into payment apps which are merging multiple loyalty programs into their offering, allowing them to access valuable member personal data, as well as global players that now offer payments capabilities.

Social media is rushing into this space to ensure they do not miss the opportunity. WhatsApp users can now send and receive money by way of its messaging app, using Facebook Pay, the payments service WhatsApp owner Facebook launched in 2019.[617]

With so much investment in this area, and significant potential in delivering a seamless, instantly rewarding experience, the convergence of loyalty and payments will continue to be a mega trend over the next decade.

Security and fraud incidents

With loyalty program operators globally continuing to under-invest in mitigation strategies, one unfortunate trend which is likely to continue is security breaches and fraudulent behaviour. This may be as small as a fraudster exploiting a birthday reward offer to receive it every day, or as big as a database hack accessing the personal data of hundreds of millions of members.

Since the launch of the 1st edition of *Loyalty Programs: The Complete Guide* there have been a staggering number of major hacks around the world where loyalty program data has been accessed.

The continuing global proliferation (and digitalisation) of loyalty programs will require loyalty program operators to keep pace with rising loyalty fraud, and related risks and preventative solutions.

---

617 Singh, M. & Lunden, I., 2020, 'WhatsApp finally launches payments, starting in Brazil', https://techcrunch.com/2020/06/15/whatsapp-finally-launches-payments-starting-in-brazil/?guccounter=1, accessed 24 June 2020.

The rise of B2B programs

B2B industries have typically been laggards in the loyalty industry, both in implementing programs and in embracing innovative design. As detailed in Chapter 10, B2B programs contain some natural advantages over consumer programs, but also some unique challenges.

As more companies launch attractive programs for their business customers, and the body of knowledge expands regarding what constitutes an effective program, B2B loyalty is already gaining momentum as a significant trend.

Outsourcing

Loyalty technology outsourcing is set to continue for programs both large and small. The industry has evolved sufficiently such that highly sophisticated platforms can be accessed at a low cost, and far cheaper than a company could build internally.

Other outsourcing options, including strategic design and evolution, automated marketing, reward supply, data analytics, and call centre operations will also continue to grow.

Web3 and blockchain

Web3 and blockchain technology will continue to evolve, mature and become more seamlessly integrated into online and digital platforms, with a greater consideration for the day-to-day user experience. More people will be using these technologies without evening knowing it. Greater legal certainty across financial and policy regulators will provide confidence for companies and consumers.

With the growth of general adoption and more practical use cases, the loyalty industry will see more companies embrace Web3 as one component of their overall loyalty program strategies. This will lead to unexpected collaborations between companies, and the development of new participatory ecosystems where members are active contributors to the creation and exchange of value. More brands will give community members and hyper-passionate customers (their omni-advocates) the opportunity to be involved in the creative process, making these members feel a genuine stickiness to the brand.

*

A well-designed loyalty program can work to successfully drive engagement between a brand and members, building deeper attitudinal commitment which manifests in a range of valuable benefits.

Generating sustained, meaningful engagement with members requires a deep understanding of member behaviour and expectations to effectively respond to their needs at each stage of their journey. Loyalty psychology, technology, design frameworks, commercial models, legal requirements, security and fraud risks, and future trends all need to be considered and incorporated for the program to operate as best practice.

The overarching goal of this book has been to provide the definitive guide for loyalty program theory and practice. Future editions will build on this foundation as Loyalty & Reward Co and contributors continue their research and practice in the loyalty industry. Any feedback on this 2nd edition is welcome and encouraged.

With an incredible history, loyalty programs are more critical than ever and clearly have a bright future.

KEY LOYALTY PROGRAM METRICS FOR PROGRAM OPERATORS

Member base

Overall

Total members

Total active members (typically measured by activity over a time period)

Total net member growth/decline (typically measured against a previous time period)

Total net member tier movement (for programs that have status tiers)

Total net member segment movement (for programs that have well defined segments)

New

Total new joins

Total new joins by channel

Website

Web App

Native App

Social media

In-store

Kiosk (or any other stand-alone piece of technology located in-store)

Affiliate partner

Total new joins by segment

CPA (cost per acquisition)

Reactivated

Total reactivated members (typically measured as a % against total inactive)

Churn

Total actual churned members (lost members, based on inactivity or deregistration from program)

Total predicted churn (over a pre-determined time frame)

Churns core rating of existing members

For program operators that value benchmarking analysis, an interesting addition is to measure member activity rates against those of programs within the same industry to see how they compare.

For example, a program operator within supermarkets might find that average activity rates for program members is 60 per cent (vs overall members).

This benchmarking analysis will quickly identify whether a program operator is sitting above or below industry averages, and if any action needs to be taken.

Member marketing and communications

Total opt-ins by channel

Email

SMS

App

Total unsubscribes (typically measured as a % against the overall opt-in base)

Email open rate

Email click through rate

Social media followers (split by platform)

Member activity

Onboarding effectiveness

Average time period from joining for new member to transact:

Same day (% of members vs total new joins)

Within the first week (% of members vs total new joins)

Within the first month (% of members vs total new joins)

Average per new member:

Spend per transaction

Frequency of transactions

Overall

% of members transacting in-store (vs non-members)

% of members transacting online (vs non-members)

Average transaction value (typically measured against a previous time period)

Average purchase frequency (typically measured against a previous time period)

Average spend per visit (in-store, online, app, etc.)

Total vouchers / credits earned (over a particular time period)

Total vouchers / credits redeemed (over a particular time period)

Total vouchers / credits expired (over a particular time period)

% of available benefits used by members (provides an indication of how benefits are resonating with members)

Benefits unused by members (this identifies unused benefits, which a lifecycle strategy might highlight to the member to demonstrate value)

Average number of referrals by member

Referral effectiveness (% of referrals that result in the desired action)

For points programs

<u>Earn</u>

Programs operators should also measure points earned by type, because these will indicate whether the members are receptive to marketing offers.

Total base points earned

Total bonus points earned

Total non-transactional points earned (these might be for filling in surveys or engaging on social media)

Point earn by channel/partner

<u>Redeem</u>

Total amount of points redeemed

Total $ value of points redeemed

% of points redeemed, split by category (e.g., gift cards, merchandise, etc.)

% of members with a redeemable balance (e.g., minimum required for the lowest price reward)

<u>Expiry</u>

% of actual breakage

$ of actual breakage

% of forecasted breakage (typically measured against a previous time period)

$ of forecasted breakage (typically measured against a previous time period)

If the forecasted breakage is increasing, it is worthwhile to measure this against the net member base movement. If the latter is showing decline, then this is a good indicator of member disengagement and steps will need to be taken to rectify it.

For tier programs

Total members within each tier (as a % of total members)

Summary of upward member tier movement (and associated insights related to transaction activity, engagement, etc)

Summary of downward member tier movement (and associated insights related to transaction activity, engagement, etc)

Cost of member benefit provision (and points earn, where applicable) per tier

Analysis of cost per tier vs budget

For member benefits programs

% of members engaging with any benefit (vs those that do not engage at all)

Frequency of member engagement with any benefit

% of members engaging with more than one benefit

Most popular member benefit categories

Most popular member benefit products and/or services

Impact of benefit engagement on member lifetime value

Impact of benefit engagement on member churn

For cashback / affiliate / card-linked programs

Total cashback / affiliate revenue earned (over a particular time period)

Top merchants cashback / affiliate revenue earned at (over a particular time period)

Top online merchants browsed but not transacted at (over a particular time period)

Preferred card used

Average basket size (in-store vs online)

For games / gamification programs

Total games played (over a particular time period)

Total game time (over a particular time period)

Average game time (by game vs overall)

Impact to member engagement post gameplay (transactions or other engagement metric)

Impact to ROI (vs comparable time period without gameplay)

Operational areas

Finance

Annual revenue generated from customer

Annual general costs of acquiring, serving and retaining the customer

Total points earned per annum

Total points redeemed per annum

Billings per point

Cost per point forecast

Cost per point actual

Annual interest earned on individual's points revenue deferred

Breakage (total points expired)

Program costs of acquiring, serving and retaining the customer

Total cost of earned currency

Total cost of redemptions

% of overall revenue contributed by members (typically measured against a previous time period)

% of revenue contributed by members by channel (typically measured against a previous time period)

Sales incrementality (member vs non-member)

Member Lifetime Value by identified segments (typically measured against a previous time period)

Recency, Frequency, Monetary Value movement by segment (typically measured against a previous time period and look for upwards movements)

Marketing and Analytics

Member engagement by lifecycle stage (join, onboarding, growth, retention, winback)

Member engagement by lifecycle (overlaid by persona)

Churn risk score (by segment and persona)

Test and learn analysis (campaign based)

A/B test analysis (campaign based)

Member communications by channel (eDM, push, SMS, web, social, digital, etc)

Engagement by channel

Revenues by channel

Cost per channel

% of total budget used per channel

ROI by channel

Member benchmarking analysis (by program and/or industry)

Machine learning and/or AI models and their success in driving sales / incrementality

Call Centre

% of member enquiries (vs non-member enquiries)

% of escalated member queries (vs resolved within the first call)

Irritant summary (by category and # of queries)

Points earned (by member)

Total points awarded manually (by member)

Points redeemed (by member)

Points expired (by member)

Technology

Total members in database

% of active members in database (vs total members)

Cost per active member (total program revenue divided by total active members)

% of technology costs vs overall program costs

Security and Fraud

Member accounts that have earned points more than once per day

Member accounts that show an earning pattern that's significantly different to previous earn history

Member accounts with a higher than usual propensity to avail of bonus earn campaigns

Member accounts that have transferred points more than once per day

Member accounts that show a transfer pattern that's significantly different to previous transfer history

Member accounts that have redeemed points more than once per day

Member accounts that show a redemption pattern that's significantly different to previous redemption history

Member accounts that have credits applied against them more than once in a week/month

Member accounts that have credits applied against them more than what is typical over the life of an account

Member accounts that have credits applied against them over and above the permissible amount

Member accounts with higher than usual refund activity

Member accounts with no notes against the profile, even though there is a record of call centre contact

Member accounts with higher than usual password resetting activity

Member accounts with higher than usual referral activity

Creation of a large portion of member accounts within a very short timeframe

Creation of member accounts with very similar emails

List of accounts that have been frozen due to suspicious activity

Staff members accessing member accounts out of standard office hours

Staff members accessing member accounts more frequently than usual

Total fraudulent earn transactions (vs overall member transactions)

% of fraudulent earn transactions by channel

Total fraudulent redeem transactions (vs overall member transactions)

% of fraudulent redeem transactions by channel

% of fraudulent transactions (vs overall member transactions)

Operations / Partner Management

% of new earn partners (over a particular time period)

% of members earning with partner (vs overall member base)

Average member transaction amount with partner (vs other partners)

Average member frequency of transaction with partner (vs other partners)

% of new redeem partners (over a particular time period)

INDEX - COMPANY & BRAND

7

A

B

C

D

E

F

G

L

M

N

S

T

Z

Made in the USA
Middletown, DE
22 March 2024

51530213R00323